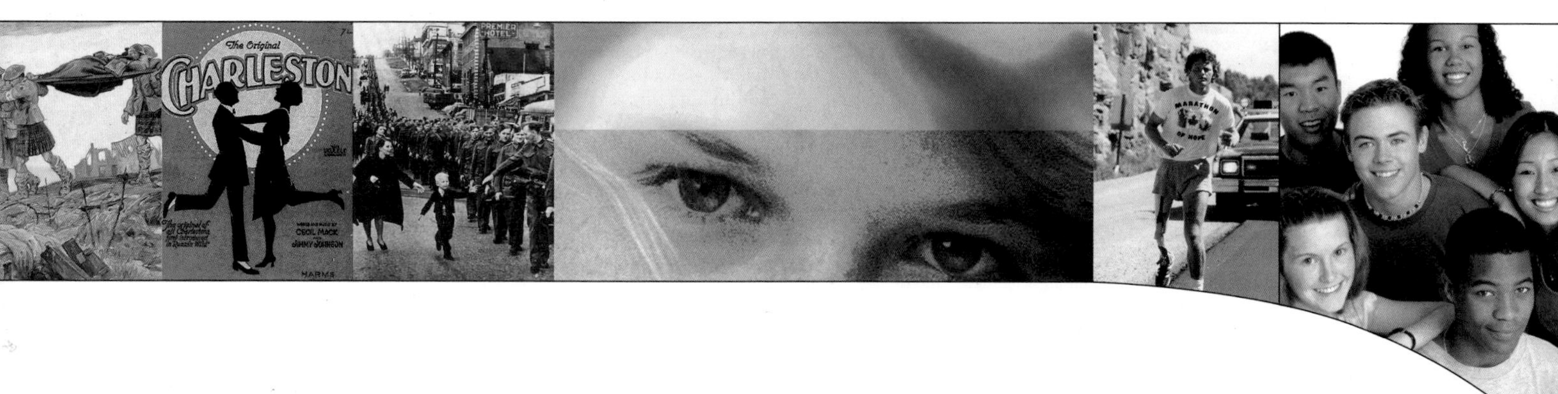

Experience History

Canada Since World War I

Dennis DesRivieres
Colin M. Bain

OXFORD
UNIVERSITY PRESS
70 Wynford Drive, Don Mills, Ontario M3C 1J9
www.oup.com/ca

Oxford University Press is a department of the University of Oxford. It furthers the University's objective of excellence in research, scholarship, and education by publishing worldwide in

Oxford New York
Auckland Cape Town Dar es Salaam Hong Kong Karachi
Kuala Lumpur Madrid Melbourne Mexico City Nairobi
New Delhi Shanghai Taipei Toronto

With offices in
Argentina Austria Brazil Chile Czech Republic France Greece
Guatemala Hungary Italy Japan Poland Portugal Singapore
South Korea Switzerland Thailand Turkey Ukraine Vietnam

Oxford is a registered trade mark of Oxford University Press in the UK and in certain other countries

Published in Canada
by Oxford University Press

ISBN-13: 978-0-19-542430-0
ISBN-10: 0-19-542430-1

The moral rights of the author have been asserted

Database right Oxford University Press (maker)

First published 2006

2 3 4 – 09 08 07 06

Printed in Canada

Publisher: Janice Schoening
Managing editor: Monica Schwalbe
Developmental editors: Chelsea Donaldson, Kathy Evans, Rena Sutton
Copy editor: Karen Alliston
Photo and permissions researcher: Patricia Buckley
Production editor: Arlene Miller
Text and cover design: VISU*TronX*
Formatting and art: VISU*TronX*

ACKNOWLEDGEMENTS

Experience History is the story of the Canadian people since 1914. It is a story that could not have been told without the help of so many people who shared either their expertise or their experiences with us.

Thanks to MaryLynne Meschino and Janice Schoening who got the project underway, and to Managing Editor Monica Schwalbe, who spent many hours coordinating the work. (New production editor Arlene Miller came to her assistance just in time.) We appreciate the energy of our skilled team of developmental editors: Chelsea Donaldson, Kathy Evans, and Rena Sutton. They patiently repackaged our manuscript to fit the attractive design. In this, they were aided by good advice from reviewers, and by the professional skills of Patricia Buckley, Karen Alliston, and VISU*TronX*.

Many other people have contributed to this book in important ways, for which we thank you.

- Darcy Hiltz, Archivist, Guelph Public Library; Lisa Singer, Outreach and Partnership Development Officer, Archives of Ontario; Sarah Fontaine, Archivist and Information and Privacy Analyst, Archives of Ontario.
- Robert (Bob) DesRivieres and Shirley DesRivieres (née Tripp) for use of their comments about bygone days.
- All of the people who appear in the Career Profiles or who comment upon changes in Canadian society since 1914. Their names and photographs appear in the book.

As authors, we have applied many years of classroom experience to help students meet provincial history curriculum standards. We hope that students will actively join in learning with *Experience History*. In this, we take full responsibility for the content and activities of this textbook.

Dennis DesRivieres
Colin M. Bain

Cover images: *Stretcher Bearer Party* by Cyril Henry Barraud/CN#8021/CWM; Granger; LAC/C-38723; CP Picture Archive; © Jon Feingersh/CORBIS/MAGMA

Contents

Features

History Skills

History Games

Profiles

Career Profiles

Performance Tasks

EXPERIENCE HISTORY WEBSITE

When you see this icon on pages in this book, go to the Experience History online resource centre at www.oup.com/ca/education/companion and click on the cover. You can also go to the site directly at www.oup.com/ca/education/companion/experiencehistory.

Introduction

Welcome to *Experience History*! What's the importance of learning about the past? The fact is, knowing the way things were helps us understand the way things are. History can also provide clues about what might happen in the future. For example, imagine that your family has just moved to a different province or territory. When you find a new doctor, he or she would want to know your medical history. If you applied for a part-time job, you would have to give your employment history.

What you have done in the past gives clues to understanding what kind of a person you are now. In the same way, we can understand people better if we know something about their past. It's the same with nations.

In this course, you are going to learn about Canada's history from 1914 to approximately 2000. The purpose is to help you better understand Canada today. For example: Why is Canada not a great world military power? Why is it one of the most multicultural nations in the world? Why do over 80 percent of our exports go to one country (the U.S.)? The answers to questions like these are to be found in our history.

▲ You will find photos like these across the top of the pages in each unit of your textbook. What can they tell you about different time periods in Canada's history?

People and Their Stories

Look at the people in the picture above. This crowd is filled with the people who make history. They are affected by the events and personalities of the time period in which they live. They know history from experience, and many of them have left behind stories of their times in diaries, letters, and even interviews. From them, we can get a real sense of what it must have been like to live in times past. Their stories are an important part of Canada's story.

Reading or hearing people's stories is one of the best ways to learn history. That's what you will be doing in this textbook. It is called *Experience History* because it will give you a real sense of the past by presenting the stories of people who lived it. Their stories may be funny or sad, suspenseful or dramatic, but they all are true. We think that you will enjoy reading them.

▲ Do you recognize this Canadian hero? Why do Canadians remember him so well?

Using Your Textbook

Information about history comes in many different forms. In *Experience History* you'll find it in photographs and diagrams, maps and graphs, selections from diaries and letters, and much more. You will also use a number of special features designed to increase your interest and improve your learning.

- Learn about some of the people who have made a difference in Canadian history through the *Profiles* features. These are short biographies of important Canadians and their accomplishments.
- Each unit also includes a *Career Profile*. These are based on interviews with Canadians who use their knowledge of history in their jobs. These short profiles may give you some ideas to set you on the path to your own history-related career.
- Learn by experience as you play *History Games*. These games appear in each unit and allow you to have some fun as you learn about Canada's past.
- Check your progress with the *Checkpoint* and *Wrap It Up* activities. The *Checkpoint* questions appear throughout each chapter, while the *Wrap It Up* activities focus on the chapter as a whole.
- *Literacy Hints* provides tips and strategies that will help you, not only in this course, but in any course that requires you to read, view, and interpret information.

- *Living Language* notes fill you in on how our language developed by looking at the origin and use of words and phrases related to a particular period in history.
- *Did You Know?* features are full of interesting anecdotes, trivia, and details about the events and people covered in the text.
- Most chapters have a special *History Skill* feature to show you how to research, interpret, and report on history topics. You'll find the first one, on the Inquiry Process, on the next page. Refer back to this skill often as you work through the research activities in the text. Other skill features will help you to refine your skill at each stage of the inquiry process.
- Finally, the *Experience History Website* icon identifies topics for which you will find links to more information on the online resource centre.

Your textbook also has a few useful tools at the back:

- a *Glossary* for definitions of important words. These words are highlighted in **bold print** in the text and are defined both in the glossary and in the text where they first occur.
- an *Index* to help you find information quickly

Take some time to look through your textbook. Find some interesting examples of people's stories, and look for all the special features designed to help you do well in history.

History Skill: Using the Inquiry Method

When you study history you find answers to questions about the past. As you look for information to answer these questions, you are doing an "inquiry." An inquiry has three main parts: research (Steps 1, 2, and 3), interpretation (Step 4), and communication (Step 5).

Step 1

Write out a question to identify what you want to find out. Here are four different types of questions historians ask:

- ***factual:*** What were the facts?
  Example: What are some examples of Canada's role as peacekeepers?
- ***causal:*** What were the causes?
  Example: What were the causes of World War II?
- ***comparative:*** How does it compare?
  Example: How does American influence on Canada today compare with its influence in 1914?
- ***speculative:*** What might happen or have happened?
  Example: The margin photograph has a good example of a speculative question.

▲ What do Canada's actions in the past suggest about its response to human tragedies in the future?

More questions may come up as you are researching, but always keep your overall question in mind.

Step 2

To look for answers to your questions, start with the easiest and most general resources, and work toward the more detailed or specialized ones.

Here are some tips:

- For quick, general information, try an encyclopedia or almanac (in print or online).
- For general information, use historical sources such as *The Dictionary of Canadian Biography* or *The Oxford Companion to Canadian History*.
- For more detailed information, check history textbooks.
- When you know the basic details about your topic, use the *Internet*.

Other sources include:

- magazines and newspapers
- vertical files (information collected and filed by library staff)
- media such as recordings, CDs, films, slides, and videos
- brochures/booklets (from museums, historic sites, government offices, historical societies)
- people (for interviews and first-person accounts)

Step 3

Record and organize your information. Use notes and graphic organizers such as charts, timelines, webs, and maps. Be sure to document your sources.

Step 4

Interpret and evaluate your information. Interpreting means deciding whether it is useful and accurate, making connections between different ideas, and drawing conclusions based on what you have found out.

Step 5

Communicate your findings to others. For example, you can give an oral or written report, prepare a display, write a news article, or create a visual.

Practise It!

1. What was the *most important* cause of World War I? Start by reading pages 7 to 9 of this textbook to find some basic information. Take notes on what you learned.
2. Now consult one other source—an encyclopedia or almanac, a history book, or an Internet site—and add at least three facts or pieces of information to your notes. Highlight these additional facts with a highlighter.
3. Compare your notes with those of a partner. Add his or her information to your notes and highlight them in a different colour.
4. Go through your notes and cross out any pieces of information that do not relate directly to the question.
5. Draw a conclusion based on what you have read. Give reasons for your conclusion.

To use the historical inquiry method . . .

- ✓ decide on your question
- ✓ consult a variety of sources
- ✓ record and organize the information
- ✓ interpret the information and draw conclusions
- ✓ communicate your findings

UNIT 1 Emerging Identity, 1914-1920

Your Predictions Please # 1

Study the three photographs, which show features of Canadians' lives between 1914 and 1920. Consider the clues for each one. Then make some predictions about what you think you'll discover in this unit.

Clue 1 What emotions do you think his face shows?
Clue 2 How practical and effective do you think his fighting clothes are?
Clue 3 From what you can see, what are his living conditions like? Where might he be?

clue

◀ Private Antoine Minnewasque, Ojibwa First Nation, a volunteer for war duty in the Canadian army, around 1915.

Prediction 1
Based on the clues, what do you think you'll learn about soldiers and war in this unit?

Clue 4 Note what the women are wearing. What does this tell you about their group?
Clue 5 What work might these women do during a war?
Clue 6 Are there some women not included in this group? Why?

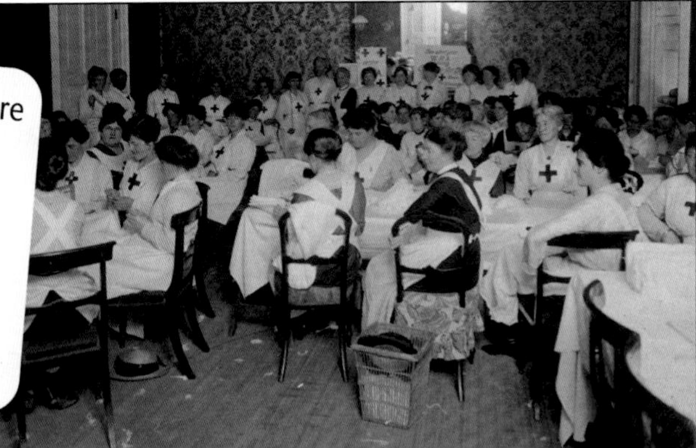

▲ Women's Patriotic Association workers at Newfoundland's Government House, around 1914.

Prediction 2
Based on the clues, what do you think you'll learn about how World War I affected the lives of Canadian women?

Clue 7 At the end of a war, what has to be agreed upon?

Clue 8 What does the photo tell you about Canada's role among other nations?

Clue 9 If a group of world leaders assembled today, how would they differ from this group?

Prediction 3

Based on the clues, what do you think you'll learn about how World War I affected Canada's role in the world?

▲The Paris Peace Conference in session, 1919. Canadian Prime Minister Sir Robert Borden is seated on the right, second seat from the end of the table.

In this unit you will explore . . .

- some forces and events that have influenced Canada's policies and identity
- Canada's participation in World War I
- changes in Canada's international status
- the impact of the war on Canadian society
- understanding primary and secondary sources
- interpreting visuals

Experience History

An important part of people's experiences in history is the way they feel as events take place. For example, the things that happen to you during one day might make you happy, sad, angry, or afraid. People in the past were no different. Thoughts and emotions are part of experiences in history.

Choose one of the people shown in these pictures. Put yourself in his or her place and imagine what the person is thinking or feeling at that moment. Use what you see in the picture to help make your ideas more realistic. Record your ideas about the experience as a diary or journal entry.

Unit 1 Performance Task

At the end of this unit you'll use what you've learned to **create a multimedia display about World War I.**

Chapter 1

Canada in World War I

Private Fraser's War

Donald Fraser didn't like the look of it. He had seen a lot more war with the Canadian Expeditionary Force than the new officer had, and Fraser sensed danger. The 6th Brigade Machine Gun Company was leading pack horses in single file, bringing supplies to the nearby front line. Private Fraser's horse was slung with eight gasoline cans filled with drinking water for the men. The Passchendaele (pronounced *passion*-dale) area of Belgium had been fought over for the past three years. Now it was a sea of mud filled with huge shell craters. There were no trees or any other shelter along the dangerous road.

Just ahead, enemy shells started falling in quick one-two-three-four bursts. Fraser knew the brigade should stop, but the officer ordered them on. Moments later the next series came, four bursts followed by a deafening explosion that threw Fraser and his horse into the ditch. Mud

Literacy Hint

What does this true account about Private Fraser help you feel and understand about the war? Make a prediction about what happens to him.

▲ **Figure 1-1** *Canadian Gunners in the Mud (at Passchendaele)* (1917) by A.T.J. Bastien. What words come to mind when you look at this painting?

and water choked him. Blood soaked his uniform, and his face stung like needles from the shrapnel. Fraser couldn't move—his dead horse was sprawled across his legs.

With great effort he squirmed free, and looked around to see that several other men and horses had been killed. More shells fell, so close that he could hardly breathe. After his heroism in so many battles, would he die carrying water on a supply march?

Checkpoint ✓

1. Discuss what mistake the new officer made. Why didn't Fraser just follow his instincts and the knowledge he had gained from his own war experience?
2. From what you've read and seen so far, how does this war differ from modern warfare? Compare the dangers of fighting in each one.

Key Learnings

In this chapter, you will explore

- the influence of Great Britain and Europe on Canadian policies
- the causes of World War I and how Canada became involved
- Canada's military contributions in World War I
- the technological innovations that have changed war
- how individuals contributed to a growing Canadian identity during the war

Words to Know

nationalism
imperialism
alliance systems
no-man's land
storm troops
U-boat
unrestricted submarine warfare
merchant marine
convoy
naval blockade
armistice
primary source
secondary source

For links to general sites about World War I

The Great War

The Great War, later known as the First World War or World War I, was fought mostly in Europe, between August 1914 and November 1918. It was a world war, because there were sea battles in the Atlantic and Pacific Oceans, as well as conflicts in Africa and the Middle East. The war was terribly destructive—historians estimate that over 10 million lives were lost.

Donald Fraser was one of the lucky ones to survive a particularly grim battle of the Great War. He was carried off to a nearby field hospital, where he woke up a day later. Here is part of his journal entry about that day:

November 5, 1917

Later, I awakened in a tent in a dim light where about thirty fellows lay on stretchers moaning and groaning. A bag containing the shrapnel taken out of my shoulder was pinned to my clothes, while the left arm was wreathed in bandages. The other [was] wrapped the same way, but in addition, strapped to my body. At this stage I was very dazed and sore and if I felt strong after I was hit, I felt the opposite now. . . .

In the morning a Red Cross train was at hand and in a short time the carriages were filled. Two nurses came into my carriage and sat about ten feet away on the opposite side. I could tell by the way they looked at me every now and then that they expected me to peg out.

As the train slowly sped away and I realized that my fighting days had passed forever, I silently said farewell to the line that had been my home for the last two years and two months.

Reginald H. Roy, ed., *The Journal of Private Fraser: 1914–1918, Canadian Expeditionary Force* (Victoria: Sono Nis Press, 1985), pp. 315–316

peg out: a slang term that meant to faint or pass out

Literacy Hint

This is an example of material quoted from another source. Here are some ways to tell:

- a sentence in the regular text introduces it
- square brackets mean that someone has made a change or added something to the text
- a series of dots (called an ellipsis) means that part of the original text has been deleted
- it is usually in a different font or format than the regular text

When you're reading, you need to keep track of who is "speaking."

Donald Fraser's injuries affected him for the rest of his life. He had little strength in his arm and was left with limited energy. But he considered himself lucky, claiming that he "lasted longer than 90 percent of those who went over with me."

Some 61 000 Canadians were dead or missing by the end of the Great War, and more than 150 000 others suffered terrible damage to body and mind. In military terms, Canada had more than 210 000 war casualties—a terrible toll. Newfoundland, which was not part of Canada at that time, sent almost 5000 soldiers. Over 1200 of these men were killed. As well, almost 3300 Newfoundlanders joined the Canadian forces and served with them.

Canadian troops are especially remembered for their part in battles at Ypres, the Somme, Vimy Ridge, and Passchendaele. Since Fraser fought in them all, much of this chapter is about Private Fraser's war.

Checkpoint ✓

3. Think of other accounts you've heard or read that were about people who served in war or peacekeeping missions. Or, think of news coverage you have seen about war or armed conflict. What were those accounts of military service like?
4. Based on the information in these pages, describe your first impressions of this war. Jot down your ideas or make some sketches in a mind map formed around "The Great War." You can add to this graphic organizer as you learn more about the war.

Causes of the Great War

Today, most of the countries of Europe cooperate as members of the European Union. But a century ago, they had not yet learned the lessons of two horrible world wars that took 70 million lives. Instead, Britain, Germany, Russia, France, Austria-Hungary, and Italy struggled constantly for power and wealth. They were in conflict along their borders and in the lands they held in distant corners of the world. The tension and hostility gave rise to four main causes or situations that historians usually use to explain why this war occurred.

Nationalism

A century ago, Europeans felt great pride in their own nations—a feeling called **nationalism**. Citizens were expected to be devoted and loyal to their own nation.

Private Fraser was born in Scotland in 1882 and immigrated to Canada when he was 21 years old. Although he lived in Canada, he had a deep connection and loyalty to Scotland and Britain. When the Great War broke out in Europe, a feeling of loyalty to Britain swept across Canada and other nations with ties to Britain, such as Australia, India, New Zealand, Newfoundland, and South Africa. Fraser, who had been working as a bank clerk in Vancouver, enlisted in the first few months of the war. He felt that Britain's war was his own.

Imperialism

Each nation put itself first and competed jealously with the other European powers. For example, Britain, France, Belgium, and Germany all sent explorers and soldiers to claim colonies in Africa, Asia, and the Pacific. This policy of extending a country's rule over other countries or territories is called **imperialism**. The colonies were used to enhance the prestige of the "mother country." They were also a cheap supply of resources and food. Relations among nations were full of distrust, disagreement, and military threats as European countries carved up the face of the globe in the late 19th century.

Literacy Hint

Words that appear in bold (darker type) are important words to remember. When thinking about nationalism, remember that a nation can be a country (a political state or territory) and it can be a group of people who share a common cultural identity (heritage, language, history, etc.).

The Arms Race

A century ago there was no United Nations to help settle disputes between countries. Instead, European nations kept armies ready in case they wanted to settle things by force. As tensions grew, nations built up their military power.

Otto von Bismarck, first chancellor of the German Empire, was behind Germany's development of the largest and most modern army in Europe. But Britain had a special military advantage—for three centuries the British Navy had ruled the seas. In 1906 they built HMS *Dreadnought*, the first in a series of big, armoured ships with huge guns. Germany challenged Britain by building its own fleet of battleships and submarines. Meanwhile, the Austro-Hungarian army had developed big-bore artillery guns that could fire shells several kilometres on land. The arms race was on.

▲ **Figure 1-2** British battleship HMS *Dreadnought*. The name means "fear nothing." Why might that be an appropriate name for this ship?

Alliance Systems

As tensions mounted in Europe, rival countries started looking for friends—called allies—that they could count on for military help. Step by step, two **alliance systems** developed, each with three powerful members. Germany, Austria-Hungary, and Italy formed the Triple

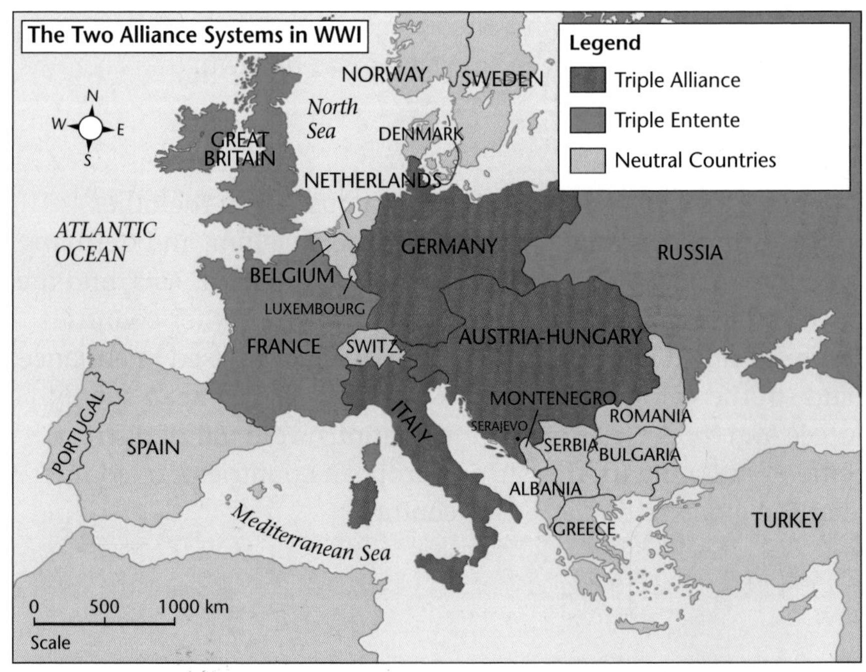

Figure 1-3 The two alliance systems. Which alliance do you think had the better strategic locations for war? Why? ▶

Alliance (or the Allies) in the centre of Europe. Arranged around them was the Triple Entente, consisting of Britain, France, and Russia. These alliances were dangerous, because any conflict between two rival powers could quickly draw four more countries into the fight.

Checkpoint ✓

5. Make a summary chart of the four main causes of the war, including one example or event related to each.

Cause of the Great War	Example/Event
1.	
2.	
3.	
4.	

6. If a war started between two countries in Europe, how would it spread to involve the other powers? Why would it be a world war?

The First Shots Fired

The June 28, 1914, parade was turning into a disaster. The future king and queen of Austria-Hungary, Archduke Franz Ferdinand and his wife, Sophia Chotek, were visiting Sarajevo. Sarajevo was a little Bosnian city in the southern corner of the empire. The Archduke and Sophia were travelling the unguarded route in an open car, and seemed unaware of the presence of the Black Hand terrorist group. This group was made up of Serbian nationalists who were strongly opposed to Austro-Hungarian rule.

Suddenly, a terrorist tossed a homemade bomb into the car. Ferdinand threw it out, accidentally blowing up the car behind them and injuring the passengers and some spectators. The parade route was quickly changed. There was great confusion as Ferdinand's driver turned the wrong way down a narrow street. As the cars slowed to turn around, a young man broke forward and fired two shots.

Black Hand terrorist Gavrilo Princip killed both royals. Those were the shots that soon led to the Great War. Later, in prison, he claimed that if he had known his actions would trigger a world war, he would have turned the gun on himself instead.

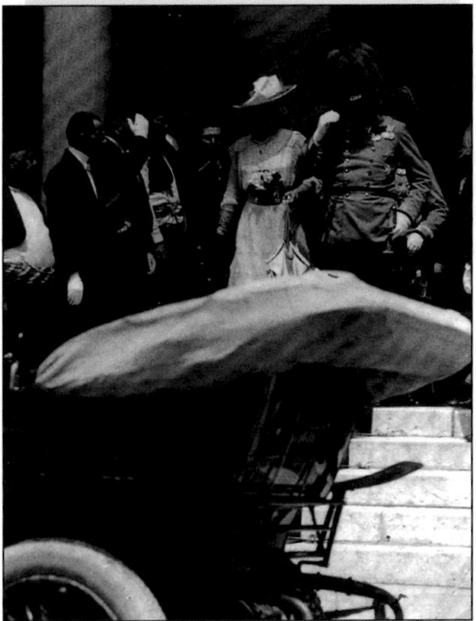

▲ **Figure 1-4** Archduke Franz Ferdinand and his wife, Sophia Chotek, on the day of their assassination. Could an assassination like this happen in the world today?

From Assassination to World War

Did Gavrilo Princip really cause World War I? Traditionally, historians have believed that because of the many background causes, little could have been done to prevent war. For years, nationalism, imperialism, the arms race, and the alliance systems had been piling up like dry wood for a bonfire. The assassination of Archduke Ferdinand was the spark that set Europe on fire. European rivals were moving toward war almost on their own, but Princip struck the match.

TIMELINE: The Outbreak of War

- **July 28, 1914** Austria-Hungary blames Serbia for the murders of the royals and declares war on Serbia.
- **July 28– July 31, 1914** Russia, Britain, France, and Germany all get ready for war.
- **August 1, 1914** Germany declares war on Russia.
- **August 3, 1914** Germany begins a surprise attack on Paris through neutral Belgium. The plan was to conquer France and then rush the German army east by railroad to crush Russia.
- **August 4, 1914** Britain joins the fight, and the two allies, France and Britain, stop the Germans just short of Paris.

Checkpoint ✓

7. Did Gavrilo Princip work alone? Reread carefully, looking for evidence.
8. How responsible was Gavrilo Princip for causing the war? Discuss the question, using information from what you have just read.

Canada Enters the War

When Britain declared war, Canada was also automatically at war because it was part of the British Empire. Canada did not yet have control over its own foreign affairs.

Sam Hughes was Canada's Minister of Militia and Defence when Britain declared war on Germany on August 4, 1914. Canada immediately pledged to support Britain with 25 000 troops, even though it had only 3000 regular soldiers at the time. It was Hughes's job to mobilize the country for war, and he was eager to get started.

◀ **Figure 1-5** The training camp at Valcartier, Quebec. How does this camp compare with Canadian armed forces barracks today?

Hughes sprang into action. He rushed hundreds of telegrams to militia colonels, ordering them to recruit healthy single men and send them to Valcartier, Quebec, for training. The training camp didn't even exist at that point, and there weren't enough uniforms and weapons. But Hughes got contractors and manufacturers on board, and by September 4, there were 32 000 volunteers at Valcartier.

After a month of very basic training, the Canadian Expeditionary Force (CEF) sailed to Britain along with the Newfoundland Regiment. They spent the winter there preparing for combat. Then, in the spring of 1915, they landed in Belgium and France. While these raw troops were still in Britain, a second group of recruits, including Donald Fraser, was already taking basic training in Canada.

By mid-1915, more than 100 000 men and women from Canada and Newfoundland had volunteered. Women were not eligible to fight, but joined the Army Medical Corps as nurses and ambulance drivers.

Aboriginal men volunteered at twice the national rate, with some reserves sending most of their eligible males. One of the best-known Aboriginal volunteers was Tom Longboat (Cogwagee), an Onondagan from the Six Nations Reserve near Brantford, Ontario. Before the war, he won many long-distance races and competed in the 1908 Olympics. With his speed and endurance, Longboat served as a dispatch runner, carrying messages through the dangers of the battlefront.

▲ **Figure 1-6** Sam Hughes was a determined and energetic military leader. He was criticized, however, for his treatment of French Canadians and for supplying troops with faulty equipment. Based on the photograph, what impression do you have of this man?

Did You Know?

Sam Hughes persuaded Ottawa to equip the soldiers with the Canadian-made Ross rifle. The rifle was great for target shooting and hunting, but it proved too long and heavy in actual battle action. The Ross rifle jammed easily and often seized up when fired rapidly. However, the Ross rifle remained the soldiers' "official" weapon until mid-1916.

▲ **Figure 1-7** What techniques did these recruiting posters use to get Canadians to enlist?

Figure 1-8 Black volunteers were eager to serve their country, but racist attitudes restricted them to an all-Black construction battalion. How would you feel if you volunteered to fight for your country and were told you weren't really wanted?

At first, it was easy to get plenty of volunteers for the Canadian Expeditionary Force. Reasons include the following:

- Canada's large, loyal British population wanted to fight for Britain.
- Recruiting posters appealed to feelings of heroism and obligation.
- For the unemployed, army life gave wages and three meals a day.
- People thought the war would be over quickly.

In reality, however, the Great War was so terrible that, as it dragged on, recruiting became very difficult.

Checkpoint ✓

9. Use the recruiting posters from page 11 to list three important characteristics of an effective poster. How do these posters appeal to feelings of heroism and patriotism? Which of the posters would have had the greatest effect on you?
10. Design an effective poster, either to recruit for the Canadian armed forces today or to remember the sacrifices of Canadian soldiers in past wars.

LIVING LANGUAGE

"Over the top" means that something is outrageous or excessive. The expression was first used in World War I. Soldiers would "go over the top" of the trenches to attack the enemy—a very dangerous move.

War in the Trenches

At the beginning of the war, British Field Marshal John French claimed that the troops would be "home by Christmas." They were not. Instead, across Belgium and northern France, British and French troops faced the German army in ditches, or trenches, only a few hundred metres apart. In this war soldiers had to live underground in mud and water, because the human body was no match for the new weapons that had been developed. Machine guns, hand grenades, exploding shells, and long-range artillery guns forced soldiers into constant hiding.

Never had there been such a stalemate—a situation in which no side is winning. There were millions of casualties in the trenches, and only the severely wounded spent Christmas 1914 back home.

Trench warfare was dangerous and dirty. The area between the opposing trench lines was often criss-crossed by barbed-wire fences to prevent surprise attacks. Officers frequently ordered soldiers to charge across this narrow zone, nicknamed **no-man's land**. Skilled snipers were ready to pick off anyone who showed his head above the parapet.

Death and injury could come in other ways, too. Soldiers ate and tried to sleep in these muddy ditches. Life was made even more miserable by the rats and lice that thrived in the filth.

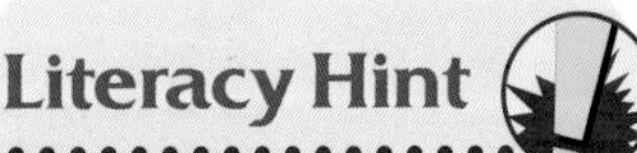

Literacy Hint

As you read, try to picture what you are reading about. This is called "visualizing." Visualizing helps you understand the text by "seeing" it in your own mind.

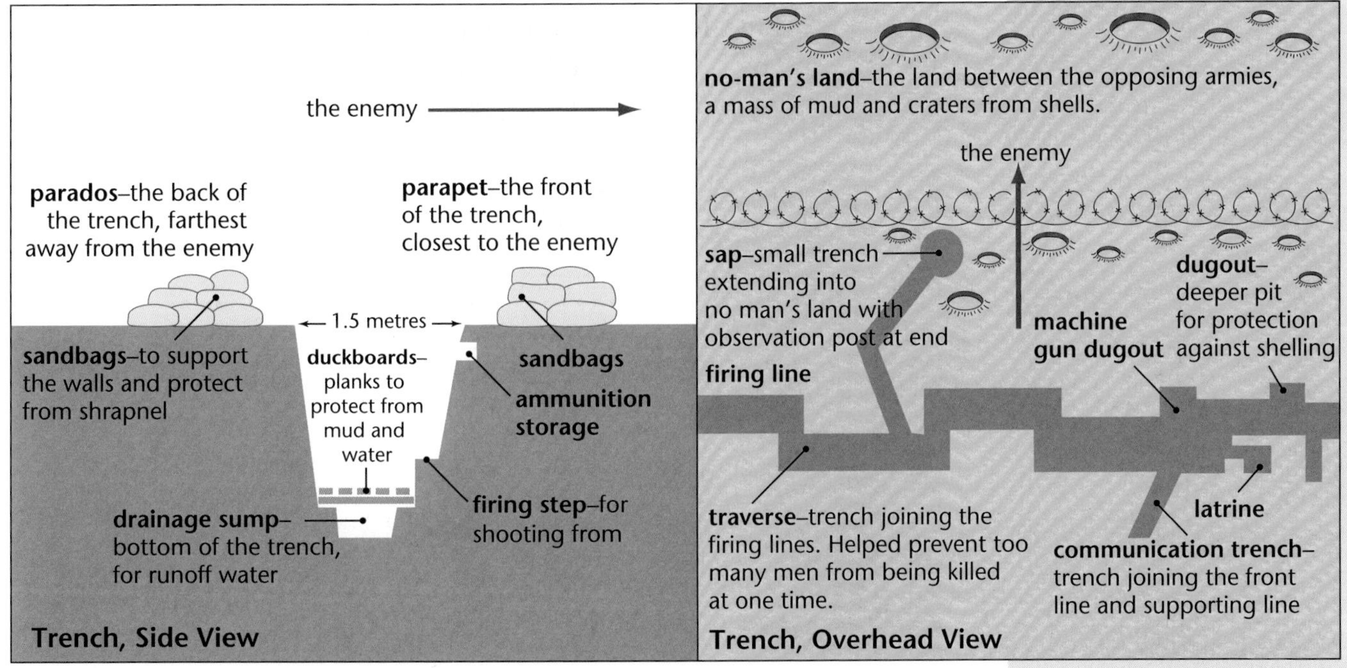

▲ **Figure 1-9** Trench warfare. See also the diagram that appears in the "Battle on the Western Front" game on page 28. Based on these diagrams, how do you think this kind of warfare could lead to a stalemate?

For links to sites about trench warfare

Checkpoint ✓

11. a) Why was most of this war fought from trenches?
    b) Study the diagrams of the trench. Then make your own sketch, with labels and explanations of the parts.

Important Battles of the Great War

The Great War came to be seen by the Allies as a moral crusade of good against evil. There was never much thought of peace negotiation, except by some small anti-war groups. As the bitter fight continued, the Canadian army developed a reputation as being tough and reliable. More and more, Britain came to rely on Canadian troops for major attacks or to try to win ground where other Allies had failed. Four battles stand out in Canada's history.

Did You Know?

After Ypres, both sides used either chlorine gas or mustard gas as weapons. Later in the war, a German corporal named Adolf Hitler would be hospitalized for weeks after an Allied poison gas attack.

Second Battle of Ypres, April 1915

Most troops didn't know what it was. But the strange yellow-green fog was spreading fast, and headed toward their trench. Within seconds they were clutching their throats. Mouths wide open, they couldn't breathe! Eyes and throats burned, but breath would not come. Some fell to the ground where the air was cleaner, and survived. Others never had a chance. The German army had violated the conventions of warfare by using poisonous chlorine gas in an effort to break the Allied line at Ypres (pronounced "*ee*-pre"), Belgium.

For links to sites about Ypres and other important battles

▲ **Figure 1-10** *The Second Battle of Ypres* (1917) by Jack Richard. From this painting, identify four general characteristics of trench warfare.

Ypres was Canada's first major battle of the war. While thousands of other Allied troops in the battle either died or ran, Canadians distinguished themselves by their bravery. Although 2000 Canadians were killed at Ypres, the survivors stood their ground, gasping through handkerchiefs soaked with their own urine (the ammonia helped lessen the effects of the gas). Canada's section of the battle line never broke as the German troops charged. However, 4000 Canadian soldiers were badly injured, and many of the survivors suffered permanently damaged lungs. Private Fraser got his first experience of war at Ypres. He arrived in September 1915, several months after the deadly gas attacks.

EXPERIENCE HISTORY WEBSITE

For links to sites about the Somme, Beaumont Hamel, and Newfoundland's role in World War I

The Somme, 1916

July 1, Canada Day, is also Memorial Day in Newfoundland and Labrador. On that day in France, in 1916, the Newfoundland Regiment fought a deadly battle at Beaumont Hamel. The Regiment was almost wiped out.

Beaumont Hamel

Beaumont Hamel was the opening of the Somme campaign. Allied commanders had ordered a major offensive in the Somme River district of northern France. British commanders ordered the regiment to charge forward into German machine-gun fire in broad daylight. The men paid heavily for their loyalty, with the regiment destroyed in just 30 minutes. Of the almost 800 Newfoundland soldiers and officers in that charge, only 68 answered roll call the next morning. Over 300 died, and more than 350 were injured or missing.

Day after day, British General Douglas Haig ordered more hopeless charges to break the enemy line so that his cavalry (troops on horses) could rush through. He did not stop until six months later when only a few kilometres of land had been captured. The cost: over half a million Allied soldiers were dead or wounded.

▲ **Figure 1-11** Soldiers of D Company, First Newfoundland Regiment, ready to sail overseas on March 20, 1915. Based on this photograph, what might these men have been thinking and feeling about their future?

The Battle Continues

Canadian troops were not sent into the Somme until later that summer. Although they knew of the recent bloodshed, Private Fraser and the 6th Brigade Machine Gun Company marched to their duty. Any soldier who refused to go could be shot for desertion or "cowardice" after a quick military hearing. This happened to 265 Britons and 23 Canadians during the Great War.

At the Somme, Fraser spotted a tank; it was the first time this new weapon was used in battle. He described it as "a gigantic toad" and "a weird, ungainly monster." But it helped lead the troops across no-man's land, in the worst fighting Fraser had faced. His diary confirms why there were 24 000 Canadian dead or wounded at the Somme.

LIVING LANGUAGE

"Shell-shocked" originally meant that soldiers, as well as towns or locations, had been hit by shells (explosive projectiles or bombs). During the war, it came to mean the psychological damage that fighting caused.

September 15, 1916
The air was seething with shells. Immediately above, the atmosphere was cracking with a myriad of machine-gun bullets. . . . Bullets from the enemy rifles were whistling and swishing around my ears in hundreds, [so] that to this day I cannot understand how anyone could have crossed that inferno alive. . .

The Journal of Private Fraser, pp. 204–205

▲ **Figure 1-12** Tanks, built by the British, were used for the first time in the Battle of the Somme. How would they have changed trench warfare?

Checkpoint ✓

12. Why is the Second Battle of Ypres an important part of Canada's history?

13. Discuss how you, as Allied commander, might have planned advances after Beaumont Hamel.

14. Soldiers were punished or even executed for cowardice, which means they refused, out of fear, to fight. Use examples from Fraser's diary to suggest reasons for cowardice. Then develop reasons for and against executing a soldier for cowardice. Explain your own views on the topic.

Vimy Ridge, April 1917

Near the top of a long ridge in northern France stands a majestic Canadian monument. It honours our dead heroes and commemorates four days that historians see as a turning point in Canadian history.

◀ **Figure 1-13** The Canadian War Memorial that stands at Vimy today. Describe what a war veteran might feel when visiting a memorial site such as this.

Vimy Ridge was a strategic location that neither the French nor the British troops could capture and hold in two years of fighting. That was before the Canadian troops were called in. Between April 9 and 12, 1917, they made the biggest Allied advance since the war began.

The German army had really dug in at Vimy. They held three parallel lines of trenches along the ridge, protected by machine guns and big artillery placements. The key to Canadian victory would be detailed planning. A few weeks before, all the soldiers were taken for practice at a mock battlefield. Private Fraser wrote, "This rehearsal gave us a very good idea of the distance we had to travel, and when the actual test came I had absolutely no difficulty in making for my objective."

But it wasn't easy. Canada had more than 10 000 casualties at Vimy, and Fraser came within seconds of losing his life to poison gas.

April 9, 1917

I was on the point of climbing out of the trench when a shell with a dull pop burst on the parapet almost in my face. My breathing stopped at once. With open mouth I could neither breathe in nor out. Breathing was paralysed. It was a peculiar sensation. In a flash I knew it was a gas shell and it completely fouled the air. In a fraction of a second . . . I had my respirator on and was breathing freely. . . .

The Journal of Private Fraser, p. 263

Did You Know?

The Canadian army mastered the "creeping barrage" technique and used it at Vimy Ridge. Artillery gunners would lob shells toward enemy lines in a "barrage" of gunfire. Then, Canadian troops would slowly "creep" forward behind this screen. Minutes later, the gunners would angle their shots a little higher so that the shells would fly a bit farther. This allowed the infantry to creep forward again.

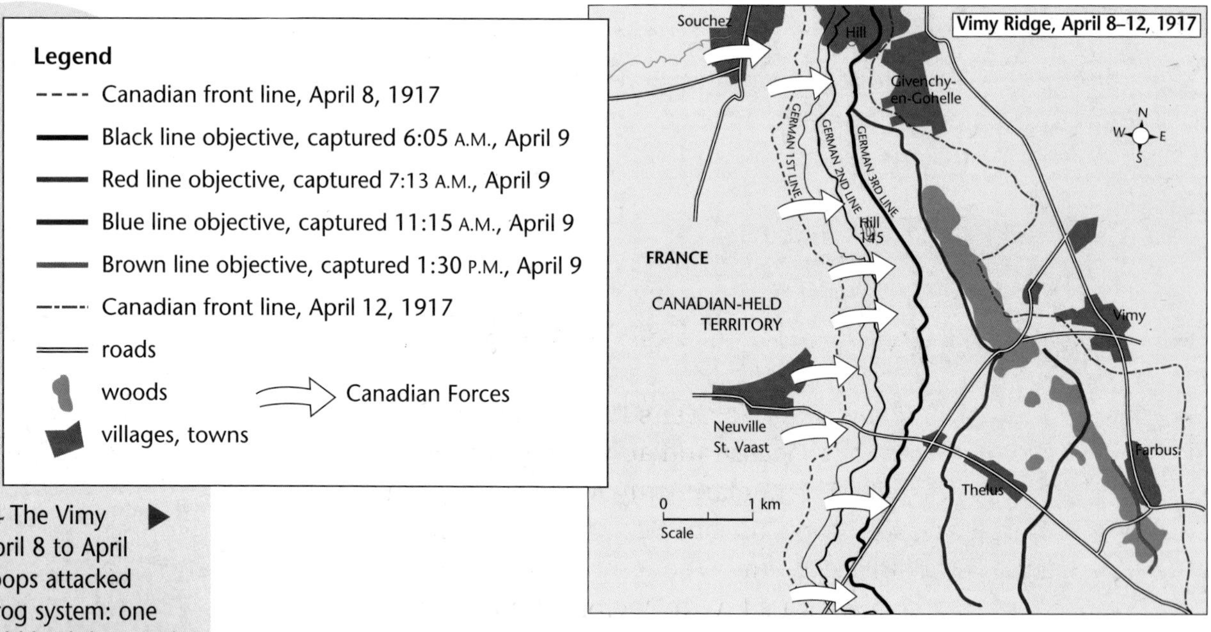

Vimy Ridge, April 8–12, 1917

Legend
---- Canadian front line, April 8, 1917
Black line objective, captured 6:05 A.M., April 9
Red line objective, captured 7:13 A.M., April 9
Blue line objective, captured 11:15 A.M., April 9
Brown line objective, captured 1:30 P.M., April 9
-·-·- Canadian front line, April 12, 1917
roads
woods
villages, towns
Canadian Forces

Figure 1-14 The Vimy battlefield, April 8 to April 12, 1917. Troops attacked using a leapfrog system: one battalion would lead the attack to a certain point and then be quickly replaced by another. It was like playing a hockey game with different attacking lines so that each line gets a rest. Use the diagram to trace with your finger how the "creeping barrage" technique worked.

Passchendaele, November 1917

For months British General Haig had tried unsuccessfully to take Passchendaele Ridge in Belgium. Then he passed the job over to Canadian General Arthur Currie and his reliable **storm troops**.

Heavy bombardment and rains had turned the landscape to mush. Currie warned Haig that these conditions would result in many casualties, but Haig was insistent. Many horses and soldiers actually drowned in flooded trenches and shell craters. Canadians took the low ridge and the nearby village in two weeks of hard fighting. However, they suffered almost 16 000 dead or wounded, including Private Fraser. He was alive, but his war was over (see page 6).

Passchendaele marked the first battle in which Canadian troops were led by their own general instead of a British one. Afterwards, General Currie reported to Canadian Prime Minister Borden his disgust with the battle conditions. Both men felt that the victory was not worth the human cost. The next time he met British Prime Minister David Lloyd George, Borden angrily shook him and threatened that any repeat of Passchendaele would mean that no more Canadian troops would be sent to Europe.

This attitude was very different from Canada's eager support of Britain in 1914. Canada had matured in the four major battles at Ypres, the Somme, Vimy Ridge, and Passchendaele.

Checkpoint ✓

15. How did each of the following techniques help Canada win at Vimy Ridge?
    a) the leapfrog system b) battlefield practice
    c) the creeping barrage
16. Imagine that you are reporting on the great victory at Vimy Ridge. Use the map on page 18 to describe the Canadian advance from April 9 to 12.

Canadian Women in the Great War

In 1997 a girl dressed as a nurse for her school Remembrance Day service. She read from her great-grand aunt's thick and yellowed World War I diary. Its author, Canadian Army Medical Corps nurse Lieutenant Clare Gass, was born in Nova Scotia in 1889. She was among the first Canadian army nurses sent overseas and was stationed on the coast of France. She worked with Doctor John McCrae, who became famous for writing the remembrance poem "In Flanders Fields" after the Second Battle of Ypres. Clare's first patients came from that battle. She was shocked and saddened by what she saw, but remained on duty for the rest of the war. Here is part of her diary.

▲ **Figure 1-15** Lieutenant Clare Gass.

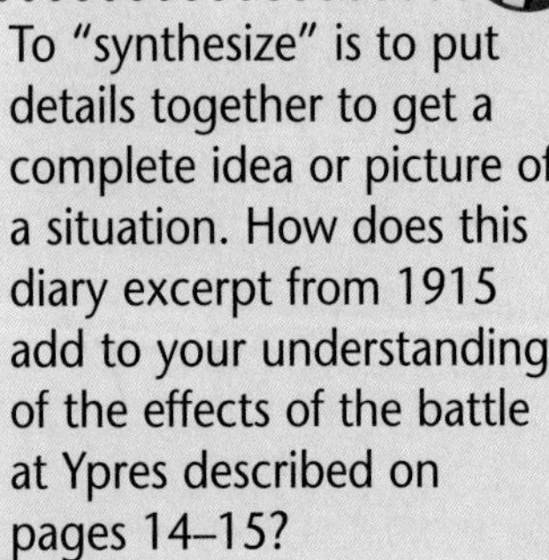

June 7, 1915
Some of these new patients have dreadful dreadful wounds. One young boy with part of his face shot away, both arms gone & great wounds in both legs. Surely Death were merciful. Many head [injury] cases which are heartbreaking. . . . These are the horrors of war, but they are too horrible. Can it be God's will or only man's devilishness.

Susan Mann, ed., *The War Diary of Clare Gass, 1915–1918* (Montreal and Kingston: McGill-Queen's University Press, 2000)

Literacy Hint

To "synthesize" is to put details together to get a complete idea or picture of a situation. How does this diary excerpt from 1915 add to your understanding of the effects of the battle at Ypres described on pages 14–15?

Two thousand women from Canada and Newfoundland served overseas as army nurses in the Great War, and hundreds more drove the ambulances to and from the field hospitals.

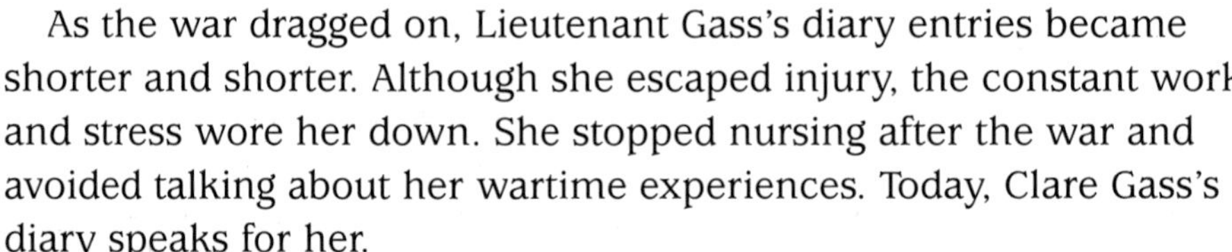

As the war dragged on, Lieutenant Gass's diary entries became shorter and shorter. Although she escaped injury, the constant work and stress wore her down. She stopped nursing after the war and avoided talking about her wartime experiences. Today, Clare Gass's diary speaks for her.

▲ **Figure 1-16** Canadian Army Medical Corps nurses at work. What challenges would these women have faced?

Checkpoint ✓

17. a) What are some words from the diary entry that show how upsetting the war was to Clare Gass?
b) What lasting effect did the war experience seem to have on her?
c) What would you say to Clare Gass if you had met her either in a war hospital or afterwards in Canada?

18. Find the words to the poem "In Flanders Fields" by John McCrae. Discuss with others both the meaning and the feeling of this poem.

The War in the Air

Sometimes the "Circus" came to the men in the trenches. Allied troops used this term to describe a group of brightly coloured enemy airplanes manoeuvring overhead. Baron Manfred von Richthofen, known as "the Red Baron," was the first to paint his plane. Later, other German pilots and squadrons copied the idea. Flyers like the Red Baron and Canada's Billy Bishop became real-life heroes in their home countries. Here is how Bishop's biographer described Bishop's heroic image:

> **"It was a barbarous, filthy war...Amid this mechanized slaughter of literally millions of men emerged Bishop, the lone warrior flying above the clouds in a little open cockpit biplane with scarf flapping rakishly in the wind. For all appearances he was the modern knight in shining armour—a rugged individualist who took on swarms of opponents and always triumphed."**

Dan McCaffery, *Billy Bishop: Canadian Hero*, James Lorimer: Toronto, 1988, p. 1-11

Right after the Battle of Vimy Ridge, Private Fraser saw von Richthofen's Circus outgunning the Allied pilots in machine-gun battles in the sky, called dogfights. Fraser wrote the following:

April 15, 1917
Knowing by the colour of the planes who they were, made it much more interesting. Our planes all looked alike and were drab in comparison. The Circus planes were a riot of colour, one would be pink with a green nose, another black with yellow wings, a further one with a blue body and orange tail. Their best known men seemed to have red as the basic colour. . . . [von] Richtofen's, the daddy of them all, was a glaring blood red.

The Journal of Private Fraser, p. 272

A year later the Red Baron's luck ran out as he was shot down by Canadian pilot Roy Brown.

Flying was very exciting, but it was also extremely dangerous. Half of the top aces (listed in Figure 1-18) were killed in action. Airplanes had only recently been invented. These flimsy machines had light wooden frames covered by tent canvas. Their gasoline engines would often stall during sharp turns or dives, and enemy bullets easily set these warbirds aflame. Worst of all, the parachute had not been invented yet.

The airplanes' main purpose was to photograph enemy positions and observe troop movements. Faster planes were designed to protect or to attack these low-flying observers. As a result, aerial fighting often took place directly above the trenches.

▲**Figure 1-17** Aerial combat of World War I. What are some differences between air combat then and now?

Figure 1-18 ▶ The Top Aces: Pilots with More than 50 Victories.

Pilot and Country	Victories*
Manfred von Richthofen** (Ger.)	80
René Fonck (Fra.)	75
Edward Mannock** (Ire.)	73
Billy Bishop (**Can.**)	72
Raymond Collishaw (**Can.**)	62
Ernst Udet (Ger.)	62
James McCudden** (Brit.)	57
Georges Guynemer** (Fra.)	56
Donald Maclaren (**Can.**)	54
Erich Löwenhardt** (Ger.)	54
Werner Voss** (Ger.)	53
William Barker (**Can.**)	51

* "Victories" means grounding the enemy plane
** Killed in action

In 1917, flight training centres were set up in Ontario. And since Canada had no military flying service until 1924, more than 20 000 Canadians joined Britain's Royal Flying Corps or the Royal Naval Air Service. By the end of the war, 40 percent of the pilots flying for Britain were Canadians. The success of these pilots—including Billy Bishop, Raymond Collishaw, Donald Maclaren, and William Barker—was a great source of pride for Canadians, and contributed to a growing sense of national identity.

Checkpoint ✓

19. a) Suggest reasons why the pilots were public heroes, admired and envied even by soldiers.
b) What do you think the life of a Great War pilot might really have been like? Use some evidence from what you have just read.

20. Draw and label a bar graph for the Top Aces. Use colours or symbols to identify a) German pilots b) Canadian pilots c) other Allied pilots

For links to sites about the war at sea and in the air

The War at Sea

On June 27, 1918, a German **U-boat** (submarine, from the German *unterseeboot*) torpedoed the clearly marked hospital ship *Llandovery Castle* off the Irish coast. All 14 Canadian army nurses and most of the 244 men aboard perished. Worst of all, the survivors reported that they had been machine-gunned in their lifeboats. Canadians were outraged by the news. The German navy claimed that the ship was really carrying munitions from Halifax to England.

Nurse Clare Gass had already seen and heard too much in this long, terrible war. Her diary entry for July 6, 1918, was very short:

> News of the sinking of our Hospital Ship Lan-dovery Castle reached us today. All the Sisters are lost.

The War Diary of Clare Gass, 1915–1918, p. 197

Literacy Hint

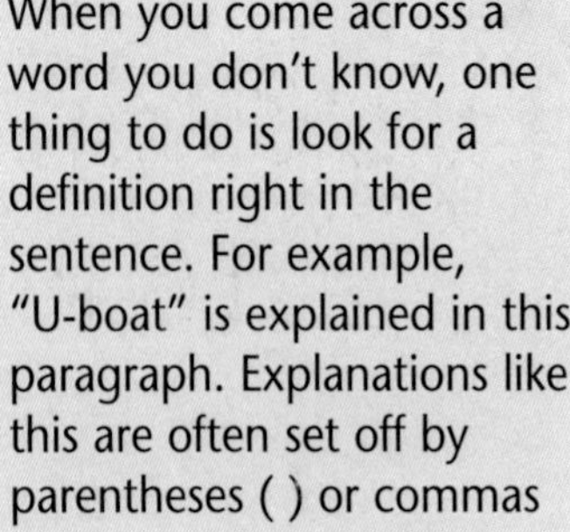

When you come across a word you don't know, one thing to do is look for a definition right in the sentence. For example, "U-boat" is explained in this paragraph. Explanations like this are often set off by parentheses ( ) or commas (,) or are introduced by a dash (—) or a colon (:).

Before 1914, both Britain and Germany had built up their navies. Germany had invested heavily in U-boats, which were smaller and much less costly to build than battleships. In January 1917, Germany declared **unrestricted submarine warfare**, meaning that any Allied or neutral ship approaching Britain would be sunk without warning. The aim was to stop food imports and weapons from reaching Britain. More than a thousand ships were torpedoed by U-boats, including the *Llandovery Castle* and many ships of Canada's **merchant marine**.

To protect themselves from German submarines, Allied boats began to cross the Atlantic in a **convoy**, which meant that a group of supply ships travelled together under the protection of an escort, such as a Canadian navy battle cruiser or a specially disguised ship called a Q-ship. (The reason behind this name is unknown.) These innocent-looking supply ships actually had a navy crew, hidden guns, and depth charges to blow U-boats out of the water.

Meanwhile, Britain used its battleships to enforce a **naval blockade**. This blockade prevented any trading ships from entering German-controlled ports. Basic food shortages soon developed in Germany, making it impossible to feed either the army or the civilians.

LiViNG LANGUAGE

A "Q-ship" was a military decoy—something that distracts the enemy or lures them into danger. The word "decoy" is thought to be from the Dutch *ende-kooy*, meaning "the duck cage." Hunters used food to lure ducks into an area of water where netting would then trap them.

◀ **Figure 1-19** *Canada's Answer* (1918) by Norman Wilkinson. What is the purpose of the ship in the middle of the painting?

Checkpoint ✓

21. How successful were the following?
   a) Germany's policy of unrestricted submarine warfare
   b) Britain's naval blockade

22. Based on what you have read, discuss which of the armed forces (army, navy, or air force) you would have preferred to be in, and why. Would your answer change if you were to enlist in today's forces? Why?

The End of the War

In 1917 the balance of war tipped in favour of the Allies. This came as a result of major changes that happened on both the Western Front and the Eastern Front.

In this chapter, you've been learning about the Western Front in Belgium and France, because that's where most Canadians and Newfoundlanders served. But Germany and Austria-Hungary had been battling Russia along the Eastern Front for almost three years. The Russian people were hungry and tired of the war. In 1917, Communist revolutionaries led an uprising in which the ruler, Czar Nicholas, was overthrown. They then surrendered to Germany, to pull Russia out of the war. This ended the battle on the Eastern Front.

At about the same time, German U-boats sank some American merchant ships under the German policy of unrestricted submarine warfare. This led an angered United States to declare war on Germany. To counteract this, Germany quickly moved all troops from the Eastern Front and launched a major offensive in the west. The aim was to win the war before any American troops could land.

Clare Gass anxiously recorded the news of the German advance:

> *March 24, 1918*
> **The war news today is very discouraging. Peronne & St Quintan have been captured by the Germans and 25,000 prisoners & 400 guns have been taken. The Germans seem to be making a desperate effort all along the line. Long distance shelling of towns that have escaped for months has begun in every sector.**

The War Diary of Clare Gass, 1915–1918, pp. 190–191

The Germans were stopped just before Paris. The Allies—led by fresh American soldiers and the reliable Canadians—launched their own offensive to end the long war.

For links to sites about the end of the war

The Hundred Days

As the front line moved back and forth, Prime Minister Borden thought the war might last until 1920, but the military had different ideas. During what came to be known as the "Hundred Days," in the late summer and fall of 1918, General Arthur Currie led the Canadian army to a stunning string of victories. The gains were great, but the cost was high: 48 000 Canadian casualties, including 9000 dead.

Allied troops smashed through German defences and captured a wide band of territory across Belgium and France. Entire battalions of hungry and tired German soldiers surrendered as Canada defeated one-quarter of their army. By November, the Allies had pushed the Germans back almost to Germany, and they officially surrendered.

The Last Shot Fired

The **armistice**, the agreement to end the fighting, had been arranged for 11:00 A.M. on November 11, 1918. Canadian soldiers were being careful as they marched into Mons, in Belgium. Their footsteps echoed on the bridge leading into the town. Silently, a sniper levelled his rifle and waited. At 10:55 a single bullet ripped into Private George Price's chest. Five minutes later he died, the last Canadian killed in the Great War.

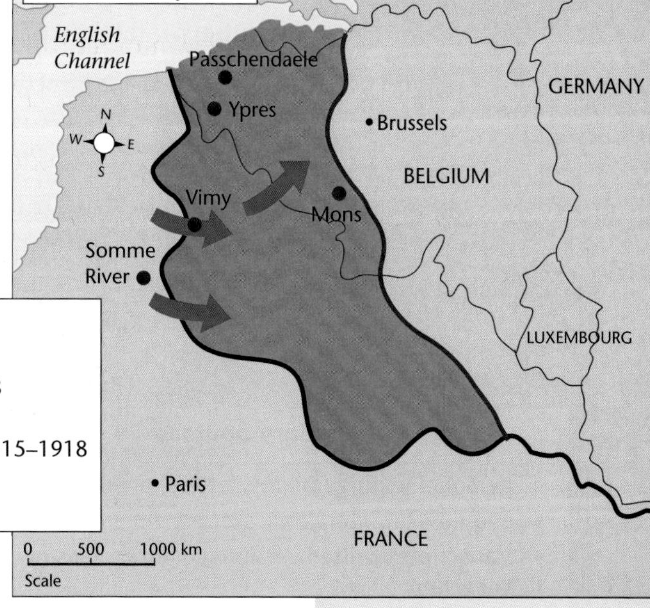

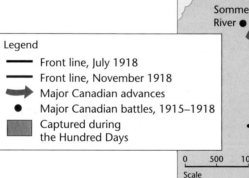

Figure 1-20 1918: The Hundred Days. What does the shading indicate on this map? What do the two different front lines show?

Checkpoint ✓

23. Explain how Russia and the United States affected German strategy in the last year of the war.

24. What do you think might have happened if the United States hadn't declared war on Germany in 1917? Would Germany still have been defeated? Explain.

25. Besides relief, what other emotions must people have felt after the war was over? What would you have felt?

History Skill: Understanding Primary and Secondary Sources

Doing historical research means looking at many different sources of information. Any material that's from the time being studied is called a **primary source**. It is "first-hand," or original, material. A later description by someone who didn't live through the experience is called a **secondary source**. It is "second-hand" material.

Primary Sources

Real-life stories can help us see things from another person's viewpoint. They help us better understand the people and the times. Primary documents make historical events seem more real.

Secondary Sources

Secondary sources can offer facts and data—accurate information that can't be argued. Other types of secondary sources offer people's interpretations of subjects or events. They offer analyses and opinions.

Note

Some materials can be either primary or secondary. For example, a photograph of a battle in World War I is a primary source, but a reference book that contains photographs and descriptive text about the war is a secondary source.

Step 1

To identify the material as a primary or secondary source:

- Look for information that appears with the material, such as an author, source or credit line, date, caption, introduction—anything that explains where it's from, and from what year.

Primary Sources	Secondary Sources
• personal writing (diaries, letters, poems, journals) • people—for interviews, stories, e-mail • transcripts (written versions) of interviews or speeches • material such as government documents, treaties, contracts, posters, advertisements, sheet music, maps, magazines and newspapers, comic books • recorded songs, interviews, speeches • visual material such as drawings, paintings, carvings, sculptures, photographs, original films, videotapes of performances, television shows • artifacts such as souvenirs, tools, antiques	• reference material (encyclopedias, atlases, guide books, fact books, dictionaries) • books, usually non-fiction • magazines and newspapers • CD-ROMs • some websites • videotapes, audiotapes, films, television shows

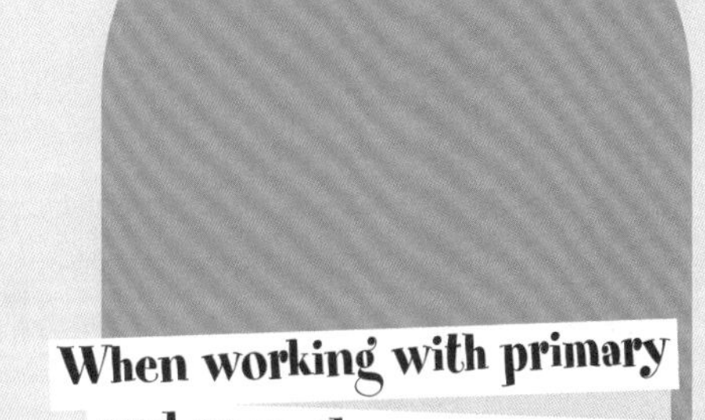

- Use clues to help you identify the source material. Within a book:
  - look for quotation marks or special designs for primary sources
  - look for a credit line that explains where it comes from
  - primary-source writing is often written in the first person, so it has words like "I," "my," and "we"
  - primary-source writing often has words that are from a different time, or slang such as "'em" instead of "them," or a conversational tone, such as "Well, then I just told her . . ."
- Visuals that are primary-source material often have an old look.

Step 2

Consider how the source of the material might affect its value and its meaning for you. For example, ask yourself:

- Who created this? How does that affect the meaning for me?
- Why was the material created? How does that affect its meaning?
- What information can this material give me?
- Should I find other sources to help me see other viewpoints?

When working with primary and secondary sources . . .

- ✓ Look for direct information stating where and when the material is from.
- ✓ Look for clues about where and when it's from. (Does the artifact look old? In a book, does the text look different from the rest of the book? Is it written in the first person?)
- ✓ Consider how the source of the material affects its meaning for you.

Practise It!

1. Decide whether each of the following is a primary source or a secondary source:
   - a Hollywood movie about the Vietnam War
   - a menu from the *Titanic*
   - a transcript of a story told by a First Nations elder
   - a documentary about Canadian Red Cross workers
   - a book of essays about World War II
   - a book of diary entries about World War II
   - a comic book from the 1940s
2. Skim through this book to find examples of primary sources. What clues suggest to you that they are primary sources?

History Game:

GERMAN TRENCHES

	1 HILL 10	2	3	4	5 FIELD HOSPITAL	6
SUPPORT TRENCH	8	9	10	12	15 COMMAND POST BUNKER	16
FRONT LINE	18	20	24	25	30	36

OBSERVATION POST

NO-MAN'S LAND

OBSERVATION POST

36	30	25	24	20	18
16	15	12	10	9	8
6	5	4 FIELD HOSPITAL	3 COMMAND POST BUNKER	2	1 HILL 20

CANADIAN TRENCHES

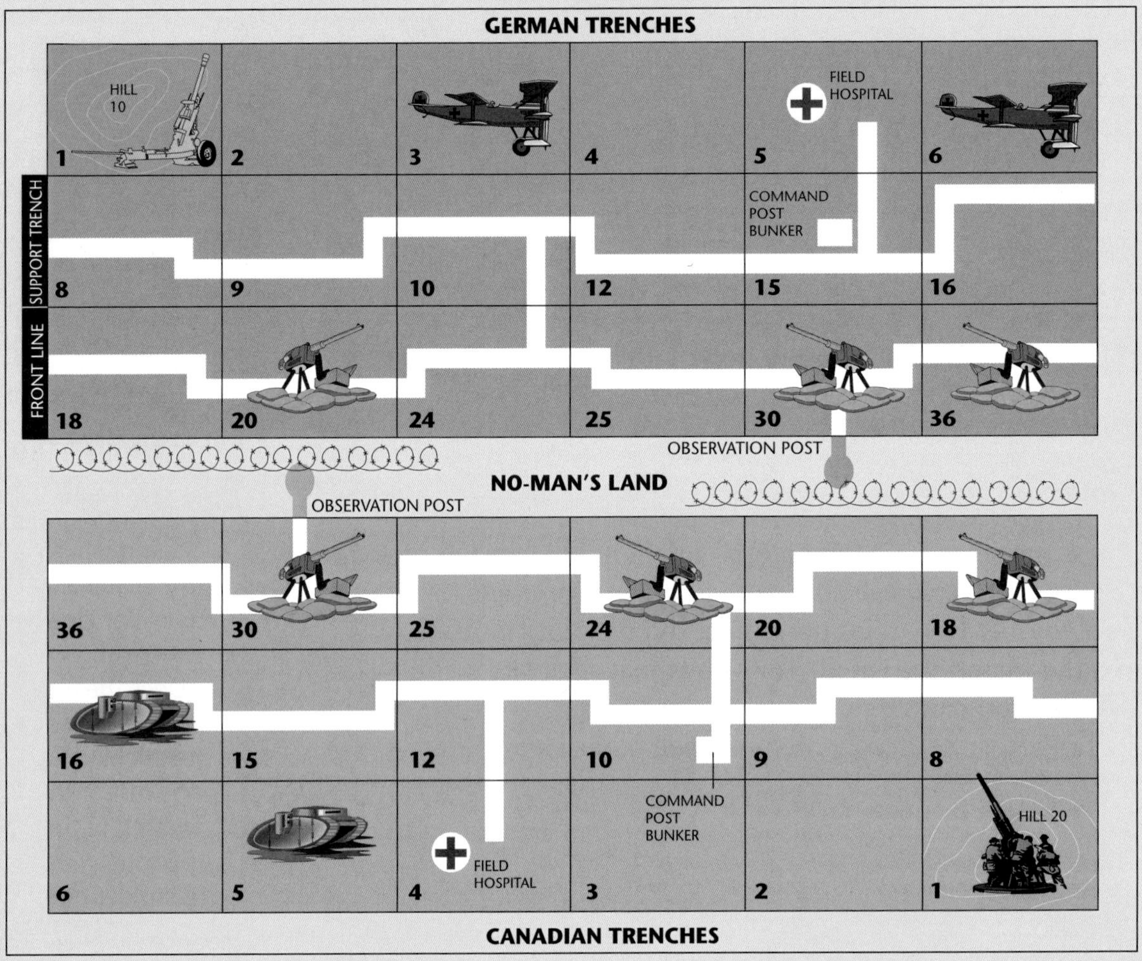

Required to Play:
- game board
- pair of dice
- score sheet, pencil

Purposes:
- To become more familiar with the typical World War I battlefront plan
- To practise multiplication

Objective: To win the game by taking all the six strategic squares on your opponent's side of the game board (a bit like the game Battleship). You do this by landing a shell from your big artillery gun on selected numbered squares.

How to Play:
1. Choose a side. Either two or four people can play at one game board.
2. Take turns by rolling the dice and multiplying the two numbers on the dice. For example, if you roll a 5 and a 6, multiply 5 x 6, which equals 30.
3. Find that numbered square on your opponent's side of the game board. For example, square 30 would take out one of your opponent's machine guns.
4. Record the square number and the weapon or command bunker taken.
5. When you score a hit, you also get an extra turn.
6. Note: When you roll two 1's you eliminate the enemy's big artillery piece and win the battle because the opponent can no longer fire at your positions.
7. Continue playing further rounds until your teacher indicates that time is up.

Follow-Up:
1. Examine the game board. How is it similar to some of the characteristics of the Great War?
2. What is your opinion of games that are about war? Why are they popular? How might they be harmful? How might they be helpful?

Some called it "the war to end all wars." People thought that somehow this war would settle all the tensions between the leading powers of Europe. Today we know how wrong they were. In this chapter, you have learned about:

- Nationalism, imperialism, the arms race, and alliance systems helped cause the war.
- New technologies such as airplanes, machine guns, and grenades changed the way war was fought.
- Canadians played a key role in most of the major battles of the war, including the Somme, Vimy Ridge, Ypres, and Passchendaele.
- Women served in the war as army nurses and ambulance drivers.

This was a total war, one that involved far more than the Canadian armed forces overseas. In the next chapter, you'll learn about the crucial parts played in the Great War by both the government and citizens on the home front.

causes of the Great War

role of Canadians

type of warfare & technologies

Wrap It Up

Understand It

1. Describe the main causes of the Great War, using symbolic illustrations for each.
2. Make a chart comparing modern warfare with the Great War. Be sure to include both similarities and differences.
3. Summarize Canada's main battles in the Great War by completing a chart like the one below.

Think About It

4. What was settled by the Great War? To what extent could this war have been prevented from ever happening? Write a dialogue between Donald Fraser and Clare Gass in which they discuss these questions.

Communicate It

5. Carry out research on one aspect of World War I technology, either on land, sea, or in the air. Then build a model or prepare an illustrated display.

Apply It

6. Design another game based on the Great War (recall the one on page 28). It can be about the war on land, sea, or in the air. Sometimes it helps to start by thinking about other simple games you've played using dice, cards, or a computer.

	Ypres	Somme	Vimy Ridge	Passchendaele
Date				
Location				
Description of Battle				
Role of Canadians				
Number of Casualties				

Chapter 2
On the Home Front

If You Were in Charge

War is a difficult time in a country's history. Suppose that you were a government official at the time of World War I, the Great War. How would you answer each of these questions? Choose either Yes, No, or Unsure.

In a time of war, should the government be able to...

1. Force able-bodied men to join the armed forces?
2. Put citizens born in the enemy country into work camps?
3. Introduce new taxes to pay for war supplies and weapons?
4. Reduce school hours so that boys can help work on farms?
5. Have control over what's printed in newspapers?
6. Use propaganda (one-sided information) to support its views?
7. Reduce or limit citizens' personal freedoms?
8. Limit the amount of food people could have at home?
9. Bar some groups from the armed forces because of their ethnic origin?
10. Give military manufacturing contracts to friends of officials?

As you read this chapter, compare your survey answers with what the Canadian government actually did in the war years.

Literacy Hint

A good way to begin a chapter is to skim it, which means to quickly read some of the parts. Read the headings, the words in bold, and the first sentences of paragraphs. When you see what the chapter is about, you can better understand your purpose for reading it.

Checkpoint ✓

1. Compare your answers with those of other students. Discuss how and why government powers differ between peacetime and wartime.
2. If Canada went to war tomorrow, which government powers on this list do you think would be introduced? Which of these powers do you oppose? Why?

Key Learnings

In this chapter, you will explore

- the ways in which the War Measures Act affected Canada
- Canadians' war effort at home and some of the effects of World War I on Canada
- contributions of religious communities (Hutterites, Doukhobours, Mennonites)
- conscription and how it divided English Canada and Quebec
- the labour movement and the Winnipeg General Strike

Words to Know

War Measures Act
munitions
enemy aliens
internment camps
conscientious objectors
pacifists
conscription
coalition government
Wartime Elections Act
reparations
Bolsheviks
general strike

Total Commitment: The War at Home

By the spring of 1918 Private Donald Fraser's war wounds were healing well, and he sailed for home. Lieutenant Clare Gass didn't get back to Canada until more than a year later, recrossing the Atlantic several times on troop ships before her long war service was over. Both of these Canadians gave their total commitment to winning the war. The same was expected of citizens on the home front.

Government Actions to Support the War

Ethel Chadwick was a fairly well off young woman living in Ottawa when the Great War began. Like Private Fraser and Lieutenant Gass, she kept a detailed diary. But her notes were a personal record of the home front, filled with her opinions and her social activities. In August 1914, Ethel's social connections got her a seat in the public galleries as a special "War Parliament" was underway in Ottawa. There, she heard the War Measures Act introduced.

The **War Measures Act** gave strong powers to the prime minister and Cabinet and limited the freedoms of civilians. It said that in a state of emergency (the war), Prime Minister Robert Borden and his government ministers could

Figure 2-1 Ethel Chadwick (right) on a cottage vacation, summer of 1914. This photo was taken a few days before Canada declared war on Germany. How can you tell that Ethel Chadwick was better off than many Canadians in 1914? How might this shape her observations and opinions?

legally make laws without having to debate them and pass them through Parliament. The War Measures Act also allowed officials to arrest and imprison people without charging them with any offence. Furthermore, people born in enemy countries could be deported without trial.

The Great War cost Canada about a million dollars a day. Prime Minister Borden knew that large amounts of money, food, and weapons were needed, so he used the War Measures Act to ensure that Canadian citizens participated in the war effort. For example, in 1917, a "temporary" income tax of 3 percent was applied to people with a certain level of income. Here are other ways the government directed the war on the home front:

- The government issued War Savings Stamps and Victory Bonds with good interest rates. People could buy the stamps and bonds, with the money going toward the war effort, and then cash them in after the war.
- The government formed the Canada Food Board to direct food production and consumption. People were asked to ration (limit to a fixed amount) their food so that there would be more to send to the troops overseas. The board set fines for hoarding food.

Literacy Hint

Bulleted lists like this organize information so that you can find the facts quickly. They are often introduced by a sentence that explains what the list is for.

Did You Know

Daylight Savings Time (in which the clocks "spring forward" and "fall back" one hour) began during World War I to save energy and use the light of the sun. Germany was the first to enact it, followed by Britain, much of Europe, Canada, and the U.S.

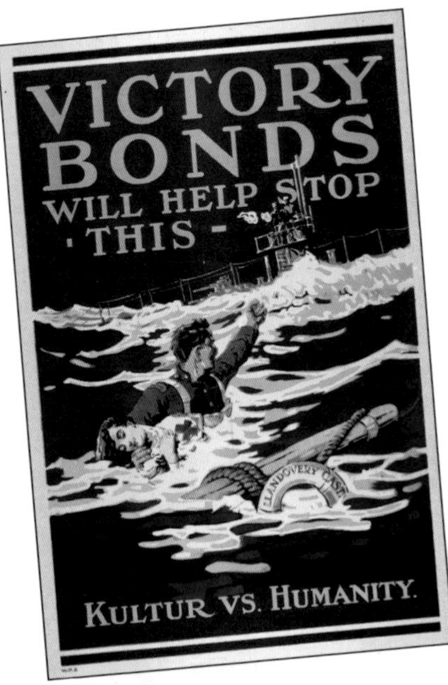

▲ **Figure 2-2** What has just happened in this picture? How does it relate to buying bonds at home?

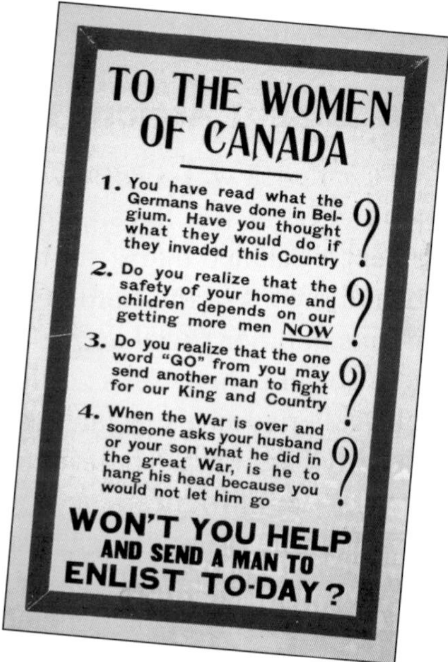

▲ **Figure 2-3** What emotions does this poster play on?

- The government took more control over newspapers, and used them for propaganda (messages sent out to the public to promote a cause). It could also stop papers from printing stories it didn't want the public to read. That practice is called censorship.
- The government used propaganda and advertising to get citizens to support the war. Posters and famous spokespeople such as ace pilot Billy Bishop were used.
- The government issued large contracts to manufacturers through the Imperial Munitions Board. They were to produce weapons, ammunition, and war materials for the Allies.

▲ **Figure 2-4** The Soldiers of the Soil program gave boys reduced school hours to help with farm work. Why do you think they had a uniform for these boys?

Checkpoint ✓

3. Review the bulleted list. Choose the two most important ways the government directed the war on the home front. Explain your choices.
4. a) Do you think the War Measures Act gave the prime minister and Cabinet too much power? Explain your opinion.
   b) What additional powers, if any, would you need if you were governing Canada during a state of emergency today?

Did You Know?

Canadian factories produced 60 million shells, about one-third of the total used by British forces in the last three years of the war.

Women on the Home Front

No one was more affected by the war than those who fought on the front lines. But the war had a major impact on all Canadians. The next few pages focus on the immense effect the war had on the lives of women.

The Wives and Families of Soldiers

The Great War was a difficult time for the wives and families of soldiers. The Canadian government did pay a monthly "separation allowance" of $20 to each family, regardless of the number of children. This amount was later increased to $25. However, the separation allowance was seldom enough to pay for even the essential food, shelter, and clothing.

Soon, community-based charities were formed to help military families who were short of money. These charities included the Canadian Patriotic Fund and, in Newfoundland, the Women's Patriotic Fund. Educated, middle-class women played leading roles in these organizations. They had the time to devote to the cause. They set up local groups and raised millions of dollars. They also visited homes to see that families had enough (and to check whether the money was being used wisely).

Figure 2-5 Across Canada, the government allowance was not enough for a military family to live on. Did money from the Patriotic Fund make up the difference? Where in Canada did military families go short of money?

Average Living Costs per Family Compared to Military Benefits, 1915

Region of Canada	Monthly Cost of Living (wife and children)	Government Separation Allowance	Canadian Patriotic Fund
Atlantic	$37.59	$20.00	$13.34
Quebec	$37.00	$20.00	$16.30
Ontario	$37.92	$20.00	$17.22
Prairies	$47.09	$20.00	$22.29
British Columbia	$53.45	$20.00	$19.79

Source: Desmond Morton, *Fight or Pay: Soldiers' Families in the Great War* (Vancouver: UBC Press, 2004, Table A5), p. 245.

Many working-class women, however, still had to rely on relatives for additional help, or they had to find other ways to raise a little extra money. Many military wives resented the "Nosy Parkers" from the Patriotic Fund. One British Columbia woman complained (anonymously) about having to account to them for every penny she spent:

> No decent-minded woman likes to think of having to take charity and that's what we are made to feel it is very often. Our men are working 24 hours a day, 7 days a week. Are we not entitled to a comfortable living when they are doing this? . . . And while they are fighting for their own homes, they are also doing it for the other fellow who has not gone. And this includes the committee of the Patriotic Fund.

Desmond Morton, *Fight or Pay: Soldiers' Families in the Great War* (Vancouver: UBC Press, 2004), pp. 187–188. Original letter in *British Columbia Federationist,* March 30, 1917, p. 5.

◀ **Figure 2-6** A political cartoon from the time, called "Christmas, 1917." This type of drawing is called a "split image." How does that technique work in this cartoon?

Wartime profiteering was another source of frustration and anger for many Canadians on the home front. Businesspeople like bacon producer Sir Joseph Flavelle made huge profits when prices for basic goods spiralled upward during the war. Today we know that prices for many goods in Canada increased partly because of shortages. But in 1917, many fingers were pointed at "greedy" businessmen.

For links to sites about life on the home front

Checkpoint ✓

5. To what extent do you agree or disagree with the following?
   a) the military wife's opinion that her family deserved a comfortable living
   b) her attitude toward the people from the Canadian Patriotic Fund
6. Draw a split-image cartoon about an injustice you feel strongly about today.

Women Support the War

For links to sites about women's roles during the war

Earlier, you met Ethel Chadwick. Like many Canadian women, she became very active in wartime volunteering and fundraising. She spent two mornings a week as a volunteer with the Red Cross, either making bed clothing or rolling bandages. Another two afternoons were for selling baking and crafts to buy tobacco and treats for the soldiers. And, there was a day spent visiting soldiers' families to see that the Patriotic Fund had supplied groceries and coal, if needed. Plenty of spare time was spent knitting socks for the troops. Many groups of women and older girls, called "Farmerettes," volunteered to work on farms. Every citizen was expected to do his or her part.

Canadian Women and the Great War

- 1000 worked for the Royal Air Force in Canada
- 2000 served as nurses in the Canadian Expeditionary Force
- 5000 handled administrative jobs in Canada's civil service
- 30 000 worked in the munitions industry in Canada
- 500 000 were employed, mainly in jobs left open by soldiers

(Note that numbers are approximate.)

Source: "Work force by occupation and sex, census years 1891–1961" in F.H. Leacy and M.C. Urquhart, eds., *Historical Statistics of Canada*, 2nd ed. (Ottawa: Statistics Canada, 1983).

▲ **Figure 2-7** Members of "The Coloured Women's Club of Montreal" and Red Cross workers were active on the home front. How was their work important to the war effort?

Women in Industry

Government contracts put manufacturers to work producing war goods. There was a huge increase in the production of **munitions**, meaning military equipment, weapons, and ammunition. By 1917, 600 factories across Canada were producing all types of munitions.

These industries were not without scandal. Early in the war, Sam Hughes gave some of these manufacturing contracts to his friends. Unfortunately, the quality of the goods was sometimes poor, such as boots that fell apart in the rain and shells that exploded inside artillery pieces.

Finally, Prime Minister Borden had enough and took control by setting up the Imperial Munitions Board. Soon, Canada was producing two million dollars' worth of quality-controlled munitions daily. Hughes was eventually dismissed.

As the war dragged on, women began working in the munitions industry. Their wages were often lower than what the men whom they replaced had earned. And it was always assumed that these women would step aside when the soldiers returned home. But without their efforts, Canada could not have delivered the food and supplies needed. Years later, one upper-middle-class woman spoke about her Great War days filling shell casings at a munitions plant in Toronto.

> There was everybody, every single class. . . . In finding they were just the same as we were, just hadn't had the chances we had for education, we began to realize that we were all sisters under the skin. . . . Another thing too; there's nothing that draws people together more than mutual trouble. The war went so much against us so often that we felt, "the boys are doing that for us, what are we doing for them?"

Sandra Gwyn, *Tapestry of War: A Private View of Canadians in the Great War* (Toronto: Harper-Collins, 1992), p. 443

Figure 2-8 *Women Making Shells* (1919) by Henrietta Mabel May. What might have happened if women hadn't done these jobs? How might the change in women's roles during the war have changed women's opinions of themselves?

Profile: Nellie McClung and Votes for Women

With all the support that women gave to the war effort, it seems strange that they weren't even allowed to vote. Nellie McClung, a leader in promoting political rights for Canadian women, helped change all that.

McClung was born in Ontario in 1873 and moved with her family to a farm near Brandon, Manitoba, when she was seven. She became a teacher, but had to quit when she married—in those days, married women were not allowed to teach.

She began a writing career and also became involved in the Women's Christian Temperance Union (WCTU), a group that helped battle the effects of alcohol abuse on family life. Much of her political fighting was on behalf of less fortunate women—those who were poor, overworked, underpaid, and forgotten by society.

Early in the 20th century, women were not allowed to vote. But women in some countries were taking part in the suffragist movement ("suffrage" means the right to vote). McClung was a leading suffragist, and, in 1916 the province of Manitoba was the first to grant women the right to vote. Only White British women had this right, however. That year, McClung wrote, "Women are going to form a chain, a greater sisterhood than the world has ever known."

By May 1918, women in Canada were granted the right to vote in federal elections. Women of colour and Aboriginal men and women did not recieve this right until much later. Women's work during the war helped prove McClung and the suffragists' point that women deserved equal opportunities to men.

TIMELINE: When Canadian Women First Voted

1916	1917	1918	1919	1922	1925	1940	1949	1960
Man. Sask. Alberta	Ontario B.C.	Nova Scotia Federal elections	New Brunswick	P.E.I.	Nfld.	Quebec	Nfld. Aboriginal men and women	Other Aboriginal men and women

Checkpoint ✓

7. Make a chart with two headings: "Traditional Roles" and "Non-Traditional Roles" to record Canadian women's roles during the war. List three examples for each.
8. It was assumed that women would let men take over the jobs the women had been doing during the war. How would you have felt if you were a woman in this position? How would you feel as a man?
9. a) Explain how the Great War led to many women getting the right to vote.
   b) Use the timeline to prove the link between the war and women voting.

History Skill: Interpreting Visuals

You can get a lot of historical information from cartoons, posters, paintings, and photographs. Follow these five steps.

Step 1

Identify the subject or topic. Look for clues not only in the visual itself, but in the caption. In this case, the poster heading and the image reveal that the subject of the poster is food hoarding during WWI.

Step 2

Decide what point the artist is making. For example, the point of this poster is to convince people not to store food.

◀ **Figure 2-9** A wartime poster.

Step 3

Find specific information in the visual that supports the main point. You might point to the words "Are You Breaking the Law?" as well as images such as the list of fines on the wall, the police officer's shadow, and the worried looks on the people's faces.

Step 4

Finally, think about what the image tells you about the historical period or event. This poster, for example, gives a clear idea that the government took hoarding seriously, and shows how patriotism is used in wartime.

Practise It!

1. Skim through the chapter and the one before it to find
   a) a poster
   b) a photograph
   c) cartoon
   d) a painting
   Practice using the steps listed here to interpret these visuals.
2. Compare the four visuals you examined. Which one did you find most informative? Why?

Note

If you are looking at a photograph in a secondary source, such as a textbook, you will need to consider why the author of the textbook has included the image. What did he or she want you to notice?

To interpret visual sources . . .

Ask the following questions:

- ✓ What is the topic?
- ✓ What is the main point?
- ✓ What specific information supports the main point?
- ✓ What does the image reveal about this historical period or event?

Conflicts and Crises at Home

While everyone's attention was focused mainly on the war overseas, Canada still faced some major problems at home, some of them related closely to the war.

"Enemy Aliens"

The people most affected by the government's strong powers under the War Measures Act were those considered to be "**enemy aliens**" in Canada. In 1914, this meant anyone born in Germany, Austria-Hungary, or Turkey. These people were under suspicion of being allied with the enemy because of their place of birth. They were issued identity cards that had to be signed by police each month to track their whereabouts.

As the war went on, public and government suspicion of these people grew. Failing to report monthly, travelling without permission, or simply being out of work could lead to imprisonment. In all, almost 8600 men (and about 200 of their wives and children) were confined to **internment camps**.

There were 24 of these camps set up across Canada to imprison anyone who was thought to be a security threat. Living conditions were usually very rough, and the discipline strict. Six men were shot while trying to escape from the camps, while another three committed suicide. Nick Olynyk, held at the Castle Mountain camp in Alberta, wrote to his wife about some of the problems of camp life:

> **As you know yourself there are men running away from here every day because the conditions here are very poor, so that we cannot go on much longer, we are not getting enough to eat. We are as hungry as dogs. They are sending us to work, as they don't believe us, and we are very weak.**

Cited in Lubomyr Luciuk, *In Fear of the Barbed Wire Fence* (Kingston: Kashtan Press, 2001), p. 86

For links to sites about internment camps in Canada

Literacy Hint

Use context to guess a word's meaning. When there's a word you don't know, reread the sentence or read ahead to see if you can guess the meaning. For example, if you don't know the word "internment," you can guess its meaning from the next sentence: "to imprison anyone who was thought to be a security threat."

◄ **Figure 2-10** Castle Mountain internment camp, Alberta. What would the barbed-wire fence symbolize to the people inside?

More than 5000 of those interned were of Ukrainian descent, even though their homeland was only a distant part of the crumbling Austro-Hungarian Empire. The Ukrainians had no loyalty to that empire, and had come to Canada for land and freedom. In fact, many hoped that Austria-Hungary would lose the war so that Ukraine could gain independence.

Did You Know?

Leon Trotsky, a leader of the Russian Revolution, spent time in an internment camp in Nova Scotia. In 1917, Canadian authorities found him on a ship in Halifax. Since Canada and Russia were allies, he was arrested on suspicion of plotting against the Russian government.

Checkpoint ✓

10. In your own words, discuss the terms "enemy aliens" and "internment camps." Give examples to show that many of the enemy aliens weren't treated fairly. Do you think the camps were a good idea or not? Why?
11. If a war broke out tomorrow, do you think Canada would target enemy aliens or not? What would your attitude be toward fellow citizens who were born in the country we were at war with?

Conscientious Objectors and Pacifists

Some cultural and religious groups had come to Canada, partly to avoid military service in their home countries. They were **conscientious objectors**, people who absolutely refuse to fight in wars as a matter of personal conscience. Such views are often, but not always, associated with particular religious beliefs.

In Canada during the Great War, religious communities of Mennonites, Hutterites, Quakers, and Doukhobors were all classed as conscientious objectors. These groups had formed large, close-knit farming communities, especially in western Canada and Southern Ontario. Their communities helped Canada indirectly by supplying much-needed food for the home front and Europe.

Other Canadians (including Sam Hughes's niece) were **pacifists**. They preferred peaceful negotiations rather than war to settle differences. They were a small minority among Canadians during the war and, like the conscientious objectors, often paid a heavy price for their beliefs. For example, a Winnipeg social worker, Reverend J.S. Woodsworth, spoke out against the Great War and forced enlistment. As a result, he was fired from his government social research position. In 1921 Woodsworth was elected to Parliament. As you will read in Chapter 5, he later became the founder of what is now the New Democratic Party (NDP).

Did You Know?

For every Mennonite who didn't have to enlist, Ontario Mennonites donated $100 for relief (but not for the war itself). Today, the Central Mennonite Relief Committee continues to raise large amounts of money for people around the world affected by wars and natural disasters.

Figure 2-1 1 Children playing at a Hutterite colony near Lethbridge, Alberta, 1915. Conscientious objectors like the Hutterites were exempted from military service by the Canadian government. They were, however, criticized by the public for refusing to enlist. Do you think the government was right to exempt them?

Checkpoint ✓

12. List similarities and differences between a conscientious objector and a pacifist. Were conscientious objectors and pacifists treated fairly during the war? Give examples for each group.
13. The law recognizes the right of people who are pacifists or conscientious objectors to be free from military service. Should these Canadians serve in some other way?

Literacy Hint

Take notes. While you're reading, keep a pen and either strips of scrap paper or sticky notes handy. If you read something you don't understand, make a note on the paper. Place it in the book and come back to it later to see if you've learned the answer. If not, ask your teacher about it or do some further reading.

The Conscription Crisis

In 1917, Prime Minister Robert Borden returned from London, England, shaken by the news. He had learned that his Allies expected the war to last until 1920—another three years. But Borden had already met his pledge that Canada would supply 500 000 troops to the war. Canada had only 8 million people in 1917. One in 16 was already in uniform, all of them volunteers. Most of the eligible men of Ontario, Western Canada, and the Atlantic region had already volunteered.

But, like most British Canadians, Borden was determined to support the King and the Empire. There must be more Canadian troops.

The prime minister decided he must get more recruits by using **conscription**, which means that military service was required by law. The Military Service Act was passed in the summer of 1917, making military service compulsory for men between the ages of 20 and 45. Newfoundland's government passed its own Military Service Act almost a year later, in May 1918. Borden called on Canadians to support the decision in the upcoming December election. Re-election of his government would prove that the public supported conscription.

Casualties and Enlistments in 1917

Month	Casualties	Enlistments
Jan.	4 396	9 194
Feb.	1 250	6 809
Mar.	6 161	6 640
Apr.	13 477	5 530
May	13 457	6 407
June	7 931	6 348
July	7 906	3 882
Aug.	13 232	3 117
Sept.	10 990	3 588
Oct.	5 929	4 884
Nov.	30 741	4 019
Dec.	7 476	3 921
Totals	**122 946**	**64 339**

Figure 2-12 How do the figures for the first three months differ from those of other months? What effects did battles at Vimy Ridge (April) and Passchendaele (November) have on these figures? Given these figures, why was Prime Minister Borden so worried? ▶

The Conscription Election of 1917

The December 1917 election divided people more than any other national election in Canadian history. To many, a vote against conscription seemed disloyal, almost treasonous.

Conscription

French Canada generally did not enlist in large numbers or support conscription because

- many people had lived in Quebec for generations and had few ties to either Britain or France
- Quebec was largely rural; fewer farmers volunteered all across Canada
- many French Canadians married early and had large families who needed support
- the army had no French-speaking brigades at first, and few French-speaking officers

Liberal leader Sir Wilfrid Laurier refused to support the Military Service Act because

- he knew that Quebec opposed conscription.
- throughout his long political career, Laurier had worked hard to unite French and English Canadians, not divide them.

Farmers and labour unionists were slow to enlist because

- they believed food and materials they produced at home were essential to the war effort.

Prime Minister Robert Borden (Conservative) asked Laurier to form a **coalition government**, a temporary alliance. When that didn't work, he took steps to win the election:

- he split Laurier's party by offering its English politicians key posts if they joined a Union Government
- he passed the **Wartime Elections Act**, taking the right to vote away from conscientious objectors and the so-called "enemy aliens." Meanwhile, it gave the vote to women who were connected to the military.

Conscientious objectors and pacifists could not support the Military Service Act because

- they opposed war as a matter of conscience

Tensions were already high between the French and English in Canada. Just before the war, some provincial politicians were busy eliminating French language instruction from schools. Popular French-Canadian politician Henri Bourassa, a Liberal, angrily reminded English Canadians of this fact in an open letter about the war:

> The backward . . . policy of the rulers of Ontario and Manitoba gives us additional argument against the intervention of Canada in the European conflict. To speak of fighting for the preservation of the French civilization in Europe while endeavouring to destroy it in [North] America appears to be an absurd piece of inconsistency.

Sandra Gwyn, *Tapestry of War*, 1992, p. 327, quoting from Bourassa's original letter published in the pamphlet "Canadian Nationalism and the War," 1916

endeavouring: trying

The bitter Conscription Election split Canada. Sir Wilfrid Laurier's Liberals won very few seats outside Quebec, while Borden's Union Government of Conservatives and English-Canadian Liberals swept most of English-speaking Canada. In the end, conscription was hardly worth the trouble it caused. Very few of the men called for service actually got into the war.

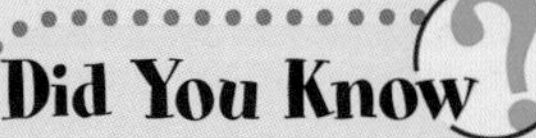

Under the Military Service Act of 1917 . . .

- 400 000 were given draft notices
- 300 000 were granted exemptions (for family situation, health, age, etc.)
- 100 000 were forced to join the military
- 25 000 went overseas

(Numbers are approximate.)

Checkpoint ✓

14. Complete the following summary chart:

Politician	Title and Political Party	For or Against Conscription?	Reasons for Their Views
1. Robert Borden			
2. Wilfrid Laurier			
3. Henri Bourassa			

15. Read again about how Borden made sure he would win the election. Do you think this strategy was fair? What are some political tactics used in elections today?

16. How do you think you would have voted in the 1917 election? Why?

The Halifax Explosion

During the war, many trans-Atlantic convoys started their voyage from Halifax, Nova Scotia. On December 6, 1917, a horrific tragedy happened: two ships collided in the narrowest part of the busy Halifax harbour. A French ship, the *Mont Blanc*, which was holding about 3000 tonnes of explosives for the war, was struck by a Norwegian ship, *Imo*. That ship was carrying supplies to Belgium. Fire broke out on the *Mont Blanc*, and it was completely blown apart. More than 1600 people were killed and 9000 were injured as large areas of Halifax were completely flattened.

Did You Know?

The Halifax Explosion was the biggest human-made blast before the atomic bomb. The shock was felt more than 400 km away, and windows were broken 80 km outside the city. The explosion caused a huge wave in the harbour that tossed ships inland like toys.

Alive After 26 Hours

Imagine searching for your family in the collapsed ruins of a city.

Private Benjamin Henneberry had returned from the war in Europe to the Halifax Explosion, and five of his children were missing. The next day, rescuers dug a dirty and burned child from the ruins of his apartment block, and Henneberry rushed her to hospital. A few days later, a hospital visitor recognized the child as her missing niece and then saw the name tag on the little girl's cot. "That is not a Henneberry child. That is a Liggins!" she cried. Little Annie Liggins had lived in the same apartment building as the Henneberry family. Her mother and brother had died in the explosion, while her father was fighting in France.

(Adapted from Janet F. Kitz, *Shattered City: The Halifax Explosion and the Road to Recovery*, [Halifax: Nimbus Publishing, 1989], pp. 75–76.)

Figure 2-13 The day after the Halifax Explosion. Today, when we see newspaper and TV images of destruction such as this, what are some different reactions? How do you think you would feel if you saw it first-hand? ▼

Checkpoint ✓

17. Imagine that you are a news reporter or photographer on the scene in Halifax in 1917. Based on what you just read, either write a news headline and a 150-word story or draw a picture with a caption.
18. Recall a recent tragedy you saw reported on the news. Make a word web to describe the "5WH" of the event and your feelings about it.

Did You Know?

After the war, many Aboriginal veterans returned to their previous means of livelihood, but unemployment was high. This created great hardship because Aboriginal veterans did not receive the same assistance as other returned soldiers under the Pension Act of 1919.

More Troubles After the Great War

The Great War finally ended on November 11, 1918. Canadians believed that four years of sacrifice and loss were finally over. They hoped that the troubles of the Great War might all disappear at once, but serious problems were still to come in the months ahead. Many returning soldiers faced high prices and either low wages or unemployment. Many women who had been employed were expected to give up their jobs to the returning men. Labour unrest, issues of prejudice, and an epidemic—Canadians faced all these problems after the war.

The Treaty of Versailles

The world needed lasting peace. The important negotiations were held in Versailles, France, not far from Paris, in 1919. They were led by British Prime Minister David Lloyd George and presidents Georges Clemenceau of France and Woodrow Wilson of the United States. Canada and some other former British colonies successfully argued their right to participate and sign the treaty themselves. There were two Canadian representatives, including Prime Minister Borden, in the negotiations at Versailles. Despite the heroic war efforts of its people, Newfoundland was not permitted to join other former colonies at the talks.

After the negotiations were completed, Borden again showed the world Canada's growing independence. He insisted that the Canadian Parliament must debate and approve the treaty before King George could sign it for the British Empire.

▲ **Figure 2-14** *Armistice Day* (1919) by George Reid. What mood or feeling is shown by this painting?

▲ **Figure 2-15** Sir Edward Morris, prime minister of Newfoundland, had participated in the Imperial War Cabinet. However, the island was not allowed to join in the Paris Peace talks. Why were Newfoundlanders bitter about this?

For links to sites about the Armistice and the Treaty of Versailles

Reactions to the Treaty of Versailles

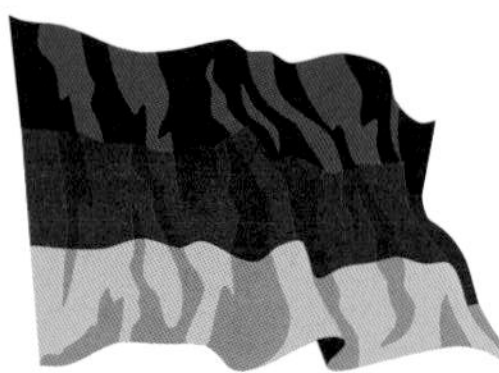

German *representatives were shocked by the treaty, and at first refused to sign it. But an Allied threat to resume the war, and the threat of keeping a naval blockade on all materials entering Germany, soon changed their minds.*

Canadian *Prime Minister Robert Borden admitted that the Treaty of Versailles was harsh, but he believed that it should be harsh.* ***Britain's*** *general view was the same.*

American *President Woodrow Wilson argued for a policy of forgiveness toward the defeated nations. But the Americans had joined the war only in its late stages, which weakened his position.*

French *negotiators wanted to be sure that Germany would never again be a threat—most of the fighting and destruction had taken place in France. The French negotiators wanted a tougher treaty than they got.*

Some Terms of the Treaty of Versailles

- The western corner of Germany, called the Rhineland, was to be occupied by Allied troops for 10 years.
- Germany's army and navy were strictly reduced, and no air force was permitted.
- Germany had to sign a War Guilt Clause, admitting that they caused the war.
- Germany had to pay **reparations**, or damages, of about $30 billion to the Allies.

- New boundaries would shrink Germany and break up Austria-Hungary.
- A League of Nations was to be formed to help keep world peace.

Ferdinand Foch, the French General-in-Chief of the Allied Armies, was unhappy with the Treaty. He said, "This is not a peace treaty; it is an armistice of 20 years." He was to be proven right. Adolf Hitler started World War II just 20 years and one month later.

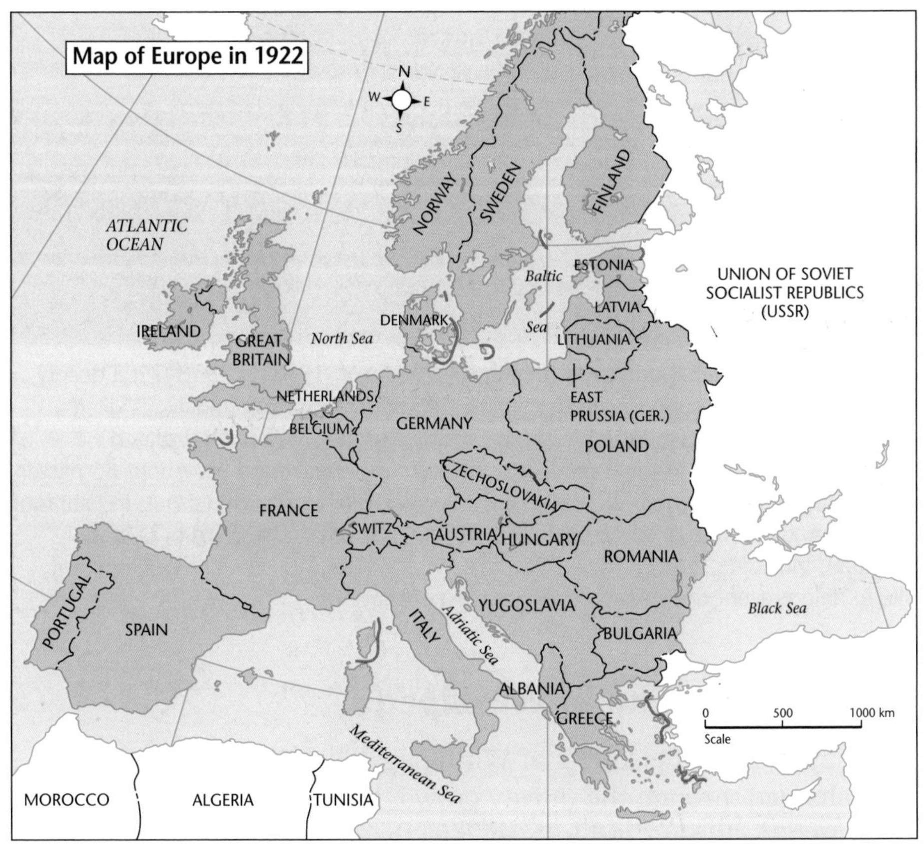

◀ **Figure 2-16** Europe in 1922, after the Treaty of Versailles. Compare these boundaries with those shown on the map on page 8.

Checkpoint ✓

19. How did the peace talks and treaty show Canada's growing independence? What effects do you think they would have on Newfoundland's future? Why do you think Borden insisted on Canada's involvement?

20. Select two terms from the Treaty that you think would have made the German delegates refuse to sign. Explain your choices.

21. Should a defeated enemy be forgiven or punished? In your opinion, who had the most justified view of the Treaty: Wilson, Borden, or Foch?

The Spanish Flu

▲ **Figure 2-17** Okak Moravian settlement, Labrador, c. 1918. In 1918–19, a deadly influenza called the Spanish Flu hit the world. Carried by returning soldiers, it killed at least 20 million people, 50 000 of them in Canada and Newfoundland. Isolated Aboriginal communities in the Canadian north were especially hard-hit. About 85 percent of the population of northern Alberta's Beaver Indian Reserve was wiped out. In Labrador, a supply ship unknowingly spread the disease, and more than one-third of Labrador's population, including most of the Okak, died. What efforts can Canada's government make to help prevent the spread of such diseases today?

Did You Know?

The Stanley Cup series has been cancelled only twice—in 2005 due to salary disputes and in 1919 as a result of the flu epidemic. The epidemic forced cancellation of the finals after the Montreal Canadiens and the Seattle Metropolitans had each won two games. No winner was ever declared.

Literacy Hint

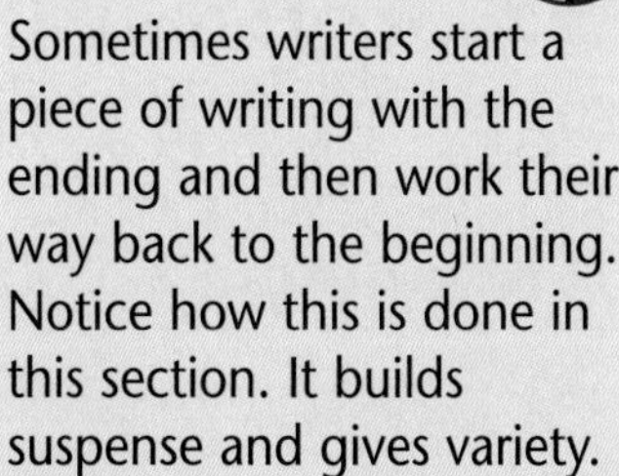

Sometimes writers start a piece of writing with the ending and then work their way back to the beginning. Notice how this is done in this section. It builds suspense and gives variety.

The General Strike in Winnipeg

A man lay dead in the streets of Winnipeg, killed as the Mounted Police charged through the unruly crowd. Labour leaders called it murder, while citizens' groups saw it as the price of defying authority. Either way, this violence marked the end of the 1919 Winnipeg General Strike.

Workers and war veterans wanted a better life. Union organizers in western Canada decided that One Big Union would be a powerful way to press for better wages and working conditions. Some thought it was the work of the **Bolsheviks**, Russian revolutionaries whose ideas, many people felt, must have come to Canada with immigrants. Prejudice against people from Central and Eastern Europe was strong

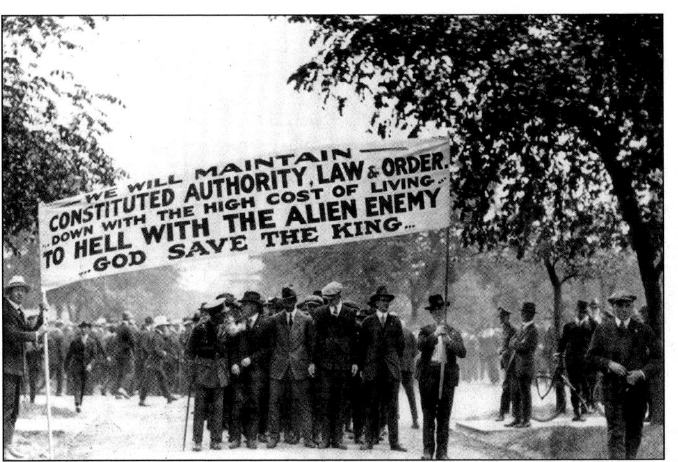

◀ **Figure 2-18** This banner, carried by the Great War Veterans Association during the Winnipeg strike, drew much public support. It also reflects their prejudice. How did the banner aim for public support?

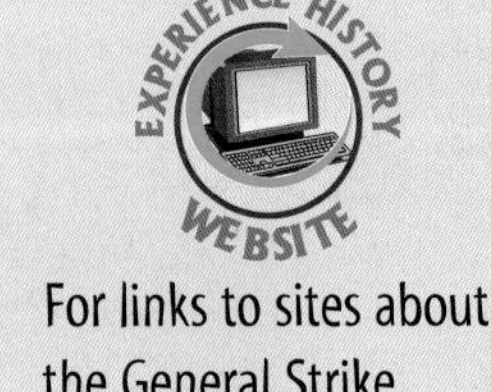

For links to sites about the General Strike

after the Great War. Many English Canadians felt that no returning soldier should be out of work because of these "undesirables."

In May 1919, workers at three big metal factories in Winnipeg went on strike for better wages. They called for other workers to join them in a **general strike**, meaning a strike by almost all workers. In just a few days, 30 000 Winnipeg workers had walked out, and sympathy strikes took place across Canada.

Alarmed business leaders formed the Committee of One Thousand in opposition. The mayor of Winnipeg banned all parades and urged the federal government to arrest the strike organizers. Almost all of them turned out to be British-born, quite a surprise to those who thought that "enemy aliens" were leading the strike.

On June 21 angry strikers filled downtown streets to protest the arrest of the leaders. They even turned over a city streetcar operating in defiance of the strike. That's when the mayor ordered the Mounties to break up the crowd on what became known as "Bloody Saturday." It was a huge setback for the labour movement in Canada.

Checkpoint ✓

22. a) Discuss how each of the following was responsible for "Bloody Saturday" in Winnipeg: fears of Bolshevism; business leaders and the city mayor; the federal government and its Mounties; the strikers.

b) Which of the above factors do you consider most responsible for the bloodshed? Explain.

23. Recall recent strikes in Canada. What is your view of strikes?

Career Profile

Dan McCaffery, Journalist

Name:
Dan McCaffery
Job Title:
Journalist

What I like about my work:

“Every day is different. When you go to work you have no idea what you'll be doing. I've interviewed high school football players one day and the prime minister of Canada the next.”

Dan McCaffery is a career journalist with a southwestern Ontario newspaper. He knows that time is everything with his job. “When the editor says there's a 10 A.M. deadline for a story, that's it. Anything later won't make the day's paper.” And nobody wants to read yesterday's news.

In high school Dan liked history and English a lot more than math and science. This led to a diploma in journalism at Lambton College in Sarnia, Ontario. After graduation he landed a reporter's job with a small local newspaper. Then, a few years later, he moved to a larger paper, his current employer. Dan remembers some career highlights:

- *Favourite interview*: Muhammad Ali, former world heavyweight boxing champion. McCaffery likes the sport and has written a book about Tommy Burns, a Canadian who held the same championship more than a century ago.
- *Favourite feature assignment*: Three months spent crafting a series of historic news stories to mark the newspaper's 150th anniversary in 2003.
- *Favourite award*: Western Ontario newspaper Award in 1995 for his coverage of the Ipperwash land dispute in the region.

McCaffery's keen interest in history led him to a writing hobby that's similar to his day job. He has researched and written eight popular books. Most are focused on aviation history, stories about airplanes and pilots. He really enjoys the detective work needed to dig up little-known facts and details about his subject. His bestseller, *Billy Bishop: Canadian Hero* (see page 20), took years to research, using Bishop's personal letters, military records, and interviews with aging World War I pilots. But McCaffery's most recent book is his personal favourite. *Dad's War* recounts his late father's World War II experiences in the Royal Canadian Air Force.

1. If you were a journalist, whom would you most like to interview, and why?
2. What skills do you think you'd need to be a journalist?
3. If you could write a history book about any subject, what subject would you choose?

Chapter Summary

The Great War had several different effects on Canadians at home. When Donald Fraser and Clare Gass came home, it was to a changed country. In this chapter you learned about the Great War:

- The government used the War Measures Act and various programs to commit citizens to the war effort.
- Women's roles and family life were greatly affected by the war.
- There were problems at home, such as the Conscription Crisis, internment camps, poor French-English relations, and the Halifax Explosion.
- There was labour strife after the wear as returning soldiers sought jobs held by women and immigrant labourers.
- Canada had become more independent from Britain and more respected by the rest of the world.

In the next unit, you'll see that Canada went through many further economic and social changes in the two decades that followed the Great War.

War Measures Act

women's roles & family life

effect on Canadians at home

Wrap It Up

Understand It

1. Create a chart with the headings "Before the War" and "After the War" and use it to show the social changes that Canada went through as a result of the Great War.

Think About It

2. How successful was the War Measures Act in World War I? Explain your judgment of the Act by identifying the benefits and the problems of giving such great powers to the prime minister and Cabinet during the war. Create a T-chart or draw a weigh scale with "Benefits" on one side and "Problems" on the other.

Communicate It

3. Write and audio-record a speech that might have been made to armed forces personnel on their return home to Canada, outlining all the changes and events that took place while they were away.
4. Make a video documentary in which you interview women about their lives, new roles, and getting the vote during World War I.

Apply It

5. How does the Canadian government assist the spouses (wives or husbands) of armed forces personnel when they're overseas? How does this compare with the support provided in the Great War? Write a brief report.

Performance Task

Review Your Predictions

At the beginning of this unit you made predictions based on three photos. Refer back to your predictions. How accurate were they? Make a list of three key things that you learned about each of the main topics in the unit.

Create a Multimedia Display About WWI

In this unit you learned about the sacrifices made by Canadians in World War I. Now it's time to put your new knowledge to work by creating a display commemorating Canada's participation in the war.

Step 1

Review the History Skills from this unit:

- Chapter 1: Understanding Primary and Secondary Sources (pages 26–27)
- Chapter 2: Interpreting Visuals (page 39)

You'll be using the skills in the following activity.

Step 2

Review the Inquiry Method on page xii. Use these steps to guide your research in Step 3.

Step 3

Design a multimedia exhibit about World War I that incorporates both primary and secondary sources related to the war. Use at least three different media (e.g. print, audio, visuals, images, scale models) in your display.

You should include at least one of each of the following visuals, along with a caption interpreting its meaning and historical significance:

- a poster
- a painting
- a photograph
- a political cartoon

To complete your exhibit, choose from the following suggestions or think of your own:

- Write poems in honour of World War I veterans.
- Collect poems written by other people about the war.
- Design a monument to commemorate some aspect of the war or a particular battle.
- Create a scale model or diagram of a key battle in which Canadians took part.
- Play songs about the war or that were sung during the war.
- Role-play and videotape an interview with a vet or a monologue about his or her experiences.
- Find letters written by soldiers or by those on the home front during World War I.
- Play recordings of veterans' experiences in the war.
- Interview relatives to find out what role members of your family played in the war.
- Make a timeline showing major events in the war and Canada's role in them.

Note

You could also look through the activities you completed for Chapters 1 and 2 to get ideas for your exhibit.

Step 4

Arrange to present your display to other students in your school.

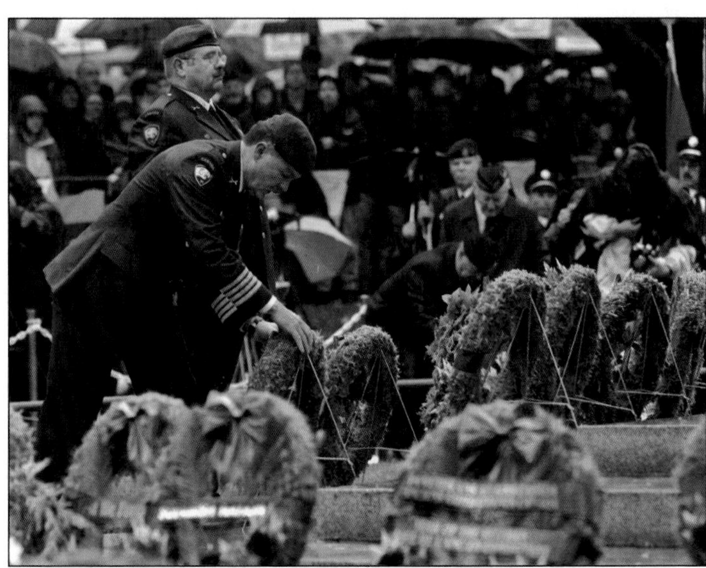

UNIT 2

Growing Independence, 1920-1939

Your Predictions Please # 2

Study the three photographs. They show some features of Canadians' lives between 1920 and 1939. Consider the clues for each one. Then make some predictions about what you think you'll discover in this unit.

Clue 1 How are the band members dressed?
Clue 2 What can you tell about the club they're playing in?
Clue 3 What mood or atmosphere does the photograph suggest?

clue

▲ The Elks Jazz Band, Manitoba, around 1925.

Prediction 1
Based on these clues, what do you think you'll learn about popular culture in Canada in the 1920s?

Clue 4 How well off is this family? How can you tell?
Clue 5 What emotions are expressed on their faces?
Clue 6 Why might this Saskatchewan family have left their province?

clue

▲ Saskatchewan farm family, Edmonton, about 1935.

Prediction 2
Based on the clues, what do you think you'll learn about economic life in the 1930s in this unit?

Clue 7 What do you think the passengers on the ship are looking at?

Clue 8 What emotions do you think they're feeling?

Clue 9 What reasons do you think Canada and other countries gave for not accepting these refugees?

Prediction 3

Based on these clues, what do you think you'll learn about Canada's reaction to international events before World War II in this unit?

◀ Jewish refugees from Germany, on board the SS *St Louis*. After the ship was denied permission to land in Canada and elsewhere, it returned to Europe, where many passengers died in concentration camps.

In this unit you will explore . . .

- how some technological developments affected Canadians after World War I
- how changing economic conditions and patterns affected Canadians
- Canada's international status after World War I
- how Canada reacted to events in Europe leading up to World War II
- how to interpret visual information
- how to use graphic organizers to organize historical information

Experience History

People live with others in a family, among friends, or in a community. Those around you may be either witnesses to, or directly involved in, the things that happen to you. Often complete strangers observe your situation, and sometimes may even respond to it. The same thing is common in history: others can play a part in a person's experiences, and the historian offers observations on events.

Choose one of the three photographs and imagine that you're right there as an observer. You see and hear everything that's going on at that very moment. Use your imagination to identify sensations suggested by the photo—especially what you'd hear, smell, see, and touch. Record your ideas about this experience in chart form.

Unit 2 Performance Task

At the end of this unit you'll use what you've learned to **present a radio broadcast from the 1920s or 1930s.**

Chapter 3

The Twenties: Growth and Change

Canadian Inventors Match-Up

What do you think is the greatest Canadian invention? Perhaps you think it's the Canadarm—the robotic arm developed by a Canadian company for use on the International Space Station. But that isn't the only invention Canadians can take pride in.

Not all inventions are recent. The 1920s was a particularly creative decade for Canada. See if you can match the following Canadian inventors with their inventions. Some of the answers are provided in this chapter. Your teacher will provide the others.

Inventor	Invention
William Stephenson (his invention is the forerunner of the fax machine)	a) quick-frozen foods
Frederick Classens (dentists used his invention)	b) insulin
Frederick Banting and Charles Best (their discovery saved millions of lives)	c) electronic organ
Wallace Turnbull (he allowed us to reach new heights)	d) Pablum baby food
Arthur Sicard (he modelled his invention on the rotating blades in farm machinery)	e) variable-pitch propeller
Ted Rogers Sr. (he helped Canadians tune into the world)	f) portable X-ray machine
Frank Morse Robb (his invention copied sound waves electronically)	g) snowmobile
Archie Huntsman (you could say he is the father of TV dinners!)	h) wire-photo transmitter
T.G. Drake, Alan Brown, and Frederick Tisdall (they gave us all a good start in life)	i) snow-blower
J.A. Bombardier (he made winter more fun)	j) alternating-current radio

Words to Know

Red Ensign
King–Byng crisis
Balfour Report
Statute of Westminster
push factors
pull factors
urbanization
consumerism
Persons Case
flapper
Temperance movement
prohibition

For links to sites about inventors and their inventions

Key Learnings

In this chapter, you will explore

- Canadians' growing independence from Britain after World War I
- the factors which encouraged (or discouraged) people from immigrating to Canada in the 1920s
- how urbanization changed people's lives
- the significance of the Persons Case to women's rights
- how American culture influenced Canadians after World War I
- some Canadian inventions from the 1920s and 30s

Did You Know

Mackenzie King was one of the most colourful of Canada's prime ministers. King's diaries reveal that the prime minister sometimes consulted spirits from the past. At times, he even turned to his dead dog Pat for advice!

Canada and the World

On New Year's Eve, 1919, many Canadians must have felt relieved that a new decade was about to begin. The previous one had been filled with troubles: the Great War, the Halifax Explosion, the Spanish Flu, and a wave of strikes that started in Winnipeg. People hoped the 1920s would bring a fresh start.

For many Canadians, the 1920s did in fact bring happier times. As the economy "roared," old social rules gave way to a new sense of freedom, and Canada forged a new relationship for itself with the rest of the world. The timeline on the following page shows several incidents that helped shape this new relationship.

Figure 3-1 The 1920s began with some fresh political faces. After Wilfrid Laurier died in 1919, William Lyon Mackenzie King (shown here) became the Liberal leader. The following year, Prime Minister Robert Borden retired, and Arthur Meighen took his place for the Conservatives. Meighen lost to King and the Liberals in the 1921 election.

▲ **Figure 3-2** Canada's flags. The Union Jack (top) was Canada's official flag until 1924, when it was replaced by the Red Ensign (middle). The Maple Leaf (bottom) did not become our official flag until 1965. How do the designs on these flags reflect Canada's growing independence from Britain?

Literacy Hint

Sometimes you can guess the meaning of a word by looking at how it's used in context. See if you can find another word in the 1931 timeline entry that means the same thing as "statute."

TIMELINE: Canada Forges a New Attitude

1919 Canada becomes one of the original members of the League of Nations, formed as part of the Treaty of Versailles to prevent further wars and encourage international cooperation.

1922 Canada's new prime minister, William Lyon Mackenzie King, refuses to support Britain in a conflict with Turkey. He makes it clear that he wants a more independent foreign policy, and that Canada will no longer automatically stand alongside Britain.

1923 Canadian officials negotiate and sign the Halibut Treaty with the United States on their own. King refuses to allow British officials to participate.

1924 Parliament approves the use of a new flag. The Canadian **Red Ensign** replaces Britain's Union Jack on government buildings outside Canada.

1926 Lord Byng, the Governor General appointed by Britain, refuses to allow Prime Minister Mackenzie King to call an election when the government begins to fall. Instead, he appoints Conservative leader Arthur Meighen as prime minister. Some see this move as British interference in Canadian affairs. Meighen's government lasts only days, and Canadians vote King and the Liberals back in. The incident becomes known as the **King–Byng crisis**.

1926 King attends a conference in London, England, to discuss a report submitted by Lord Balfour, a former British prime minister. The **Balfour Report** recommends that Britain recognize the independence of former British colonies such as Canada, Australia, and New Zealand.

1931 The statements of the Balfour Report become law in Britain in the **Statute of Westminster**. The law establishes complete legal equality between the parliaments of Britain and Canada. This is the closest that Canada has ever come to declaring its independence.

Checkpoint ✓

1. Compare the flags in Canada's history. What do they have in common? How do they differ? Find out what is represented by the colours and symbols on each flag.
2. Choose three events from the timeline that you think were most important in moving Canada toward independence. Justify your choices.

Profile: Tom Thomson and the Group of Seven

Around the same time that Mackenzie King began demanding a more independent role for Canada, Canadian artists began to reflect Canada's newfound identity through their art. One of these artists was Tom Thomson.

In 1912, Thomson visited Algonquin Park in Ontario for the first time. This wild, secluded area would become a kind of spiritual home for him. In the years that followed he visited it many times, sometimes spending months in the bush. He soon became an expert canoeist.

Tom Thomson was not a trained artist, but he loved to draw and paint. He began trying to capture the landscape on canvas. He used bold brush strokes and vivid colours to express not only what he saw, but how it made him feel.

▲ **Figure 3-3** *The West Wind* (1917). Tom Thomson had a great influence on Canadian art. Why do you think he and the Group of Seven thought painting the wilderness would reflect a sense of Canada's identity?

Thomson worked for a commercial art company in Toronto. His boss, J.E.H. MacDonald, was struck by Thomson's original style, and encouraged him to keep painting. Thomson, for his part, inspired MacDonald and his friends to see Canada's wilderness in a new light. Some of these artists organized their own painting trips to Algonquin and elsewhere. They began to talk about creating a uniquely Canadian style of painting—one that would do justice to the raw beauty of the Canadian landscape.

Then, in 1917, Tom Thomson's career came to a sudden and dramatic end. On one of his trips to Algonquin Park, he disappeared. His body was later found in Canoe Lake. The cause of his death has never been determined.

Three years after Thomson's death, some of his friends, including MacDonald, held an art show together. They called themselves The Group of Seven. The show got mixed reactions—one traditional art critic said that their colourful paintings reminded him of the contents of a "drunkard's stomach"! But over time, the Group of Seven has come to be recognized as the first truly Canadian school of art.

The Group of Seven

- Frank Carmichael
- Lawren Harris
- A.Y. Jackson
- Franz Johnson
- Arthur Lismer
- J.E.H. MacDonald
- Frederick Varley

The Labrador Boundary Dispute

As you have seen, Canada was growing more independent. Sometimes, however, the government still turned to Britain for help. In the 1920s, Canada and Newfoundland disagreed about the boundary of Labrador. Both parties were separate members of the British Empire at this time, so they asked the Privy Council of Britain to decide the case.

Newfoundland traced its claim to Labrador back to 1763. Canada did not dispute the claim, but argued that it applied only to a narrow strip of land along the Atlantic coast, where fishing boats traditionally landed. The rest of Labrador, it claimed, belonged to Quebec.

In 1927, the Privy Council rejected Canada's claim. The judges put Labrador's boundary far inland, along the height of land that divided rivers flowing to the Atlantic from those going to Hudson Bay. Quebec disagreed with the decision, but had no choice but to accept it.

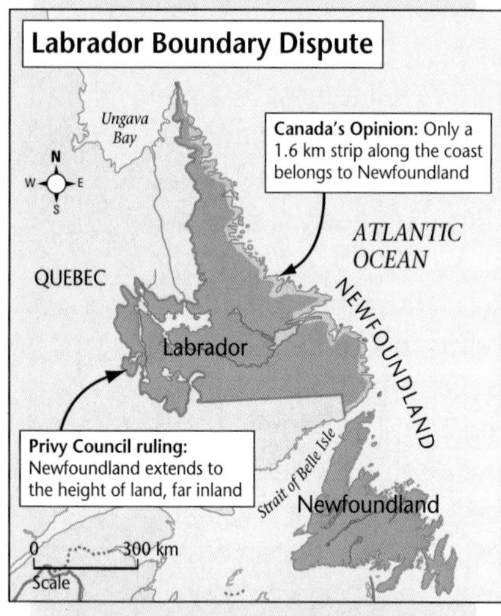

▲ **Figure 3-4** Changes in the boundary of Labrador, 1927. Why was Quebec not happy with the 1927 Labrador boundary decision?

Immigration to Canada

As Magne Stortroen looked out the window of the train chugging through the northern Ontario landscape, he must have felt a great sense of adventure. It was 1923, and the 20-year-old had left his home in Norway with his friend Karl to find work in Canada.

Back home, the countries of Europe were still struggling to recover from the war. Magne and Karl were among many young people in Europe who were eager to start a new life somewhere else. At that time, Canada must have been a very inviting choice. It had not been directly affected by the war, its economy was booming, and there were

Year	Number of Immigrants	Year	Number of Immigrants
1920	128 824	1925	84 907
1921	91 728	1926	135 982
1922	64 224	1927	158 886
1923	113 729	1928	166 783
1924	124 164	1929	164 993

Source: F.H. Leacy and M.C. Urquhart, eds., *Historical Statistics of Canada*, 2nd ed. (Ottawa: Statistics Canada, 1983).

▲ **Figure 3-5** Immigration to Canada, 1920 to 1929. More than a million people immigrated to Canada during the 1920s, most of them from Britain, other European countries, and the U.S. Why do you think Canada has so often encouraged immigration?

lots of jobs, especially in the mining and lumbering industries along Canada's northern frontier.

After landing at Quebec City, Magne and Karl made their way by train to a logging camp in Timmins. Even for two eager young men who were used to working hard, cutting lumber was backbreaking work. For two days, Magne and Karl used hand saws to cut and trim two-metre-long logs. They were paid four cents per log. By the time they had prepared 378 logs, they were already tired of the lumbering life. But at least they would receive about $7.50 each for two days work, a decent wage in 1923. Or so they thought. Magne explains what happened:

> The next morning we packed our bags right after breakfast and when the men had gone into the bush, we went to see the clerk. He told us that the scalers had counted our logs and there were nine less than we had said, but he had to go with the scalers' report. Well, we were not about to show him he was wrong, not for a five-mile [8-km] walk and thirty-six cents, so Karl told him to keep the logs. After he had deducted our meals, shirt and pants, and rent for the tools, he handed us each a cheque. Karl's was for fifteen cents, and mine was for ten cents.

Bill McNeil, *Voice of the Pioneer*, Vol. II (Toronto: Macmillan, 1984), pp. 31–32

scaler: someone who measures logs to estimate the volume of lumber

◀ **Figure 3-6** Men working at a logging camp in Northern Ontario in the 1920s. What details in the photo indicate that this was a tough way to earn a living?

Did You Know?

Of the 8 787 949 people living in Canada in 1921, less than 1 percent claimed Asia or the Caribbean as their birthplace. By comparison, 17 percent of Canadian residents at that time were born in Europe (including Britain).

Canada's Immigration Policy

Magne may have had no trouble getting into the country, but others did. Government ads encouraged White migrants from Britain, some parts of Europe, and the United States to come to Canada. At the same time, racist policies made it almost impossible for people of colour to immigrate in the early 20th century.

For example, the same year Magne came to Canada (1923), the government passed the Chinese Exclusion Act. It banned virtually all new Chinese immigration to Canada, including wives or family members of Chinese Canadians. A 1928 law limited Japanese immigration to just 150 people a year.

Figure 3-7 Factors affecting immigration. Conditions that push people to move—such as war, poverty, and lack of jobs—are called **push factors.** **Pull factors** explain why immigrants choose a particular country. Government policy also affects immigration, either by welcoming migrants or by discouraging them from coming. How do each of these factors apply in the case of Magne Stortroen?

Checkpoint ✓

3. Write a letter that Magne might have sent to his friends back home in Norway about his first experiences in his new country.
4. Use an atlas to make a simple sketch map of Magne and Karl's route from Norway to Quebec City to Timmins. With the map scale, calculate the approximate straight-line distance they travelled. How might this distance make the decision to immigrate harder?
5. Draw and label a line graph of the number table in Figure 3-5. Choose two different colours to shade the first and second halves of the 1920s. Which half of the 1920s, the first or second, brought more immigrants to Canada?
6. Today, Canadian society is much more multicultural than it was in the 1920s. List three arguments you could use to convince immigration officials in the 1920s that a multicultural society has benefited Canada.

An Urban Way of Life

Magne Stortroen came to this country at a time when another kind of migration was beginning to make a noticeable difference in Canada. As steam- and gasoline-powered farm machinery slowly replaced much of the human labour required on farms, less work was available in rural areas. Young people had to move to towns and cities to find jobs. Between 1871 and 1931, Canada's population gradually shifted from being mostly rural to being mostly urban. This process of **urbanization** changed people's lives profoundly, especially in the fields of education, employment, leisure, and **consumerism**.

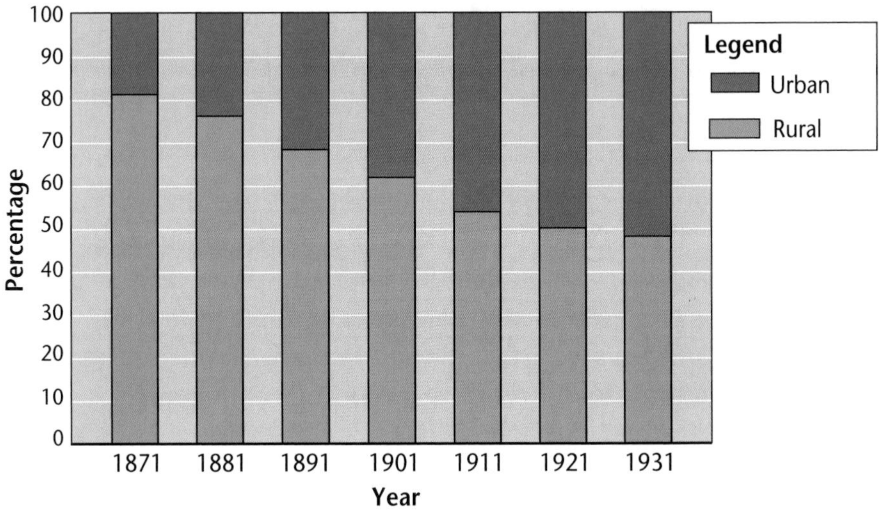

◀ **Figure 3-8** Canada, Rural and Urban Population, 1871–1931. During what decade did Canada's population become more urban than rural for the first time?

Education

Education changed with the growth of towns and cities. In the more farm-based economy of the 19th century, eight years of education was considered enough. But by the 1920s, about a third of students went on to attend high school for two or more years.

Most high schools were built in the growing towns and cities so that students could reach them more easily. Since there were no school-bus routes in the 1920s, rural students often spent less time in high school than urban students.

There were class differences too. Working-class children often left school between Grades 6 and 8, while those from middle- and upper-class families usually finished high school.

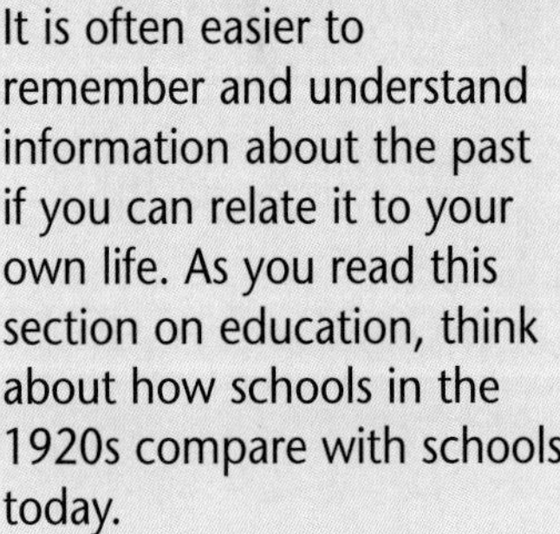

Literacy Hint

It is often easier to remember and understand information about the past if you can relate it to your own life. As you read this section on education, think about how schools in the 1920s compare with schools today.

Figure 3-9 In the 1920s, education was different for girls than for boys. What are these girls learning? Why do you think this skill was taught in school?

Did You Know?

Although more students attended school than ever before in the 1920s, only about 2 percent of those who started school would go on to college or university. Today, about 40 percent of the Canadian workforce has some post-secondary education.

If you look closely above the outside doors of some older schools, you will see that there are two main entrances—one for boys and one for girls. Not only did boys and girls enter through different doors, they often left school with quite a different education. Everyone in high school was required to take certain core subjects, such as English, History, Math, and Science. Beyond that, however, students were usually directed to different options according to their gender, such as mechanical trades for boys and secretarial classes for girls. Ella Trow, a 1927 Toronto high school graduate, remembers what girls' education was like at the time:

> Wives stayed home and looked after the house, and the girls were expected to learn how to do the same. Manners, behaviour, voice, and all of these things were taught in school. There were classes in home economics, in with cooking and everything else to do with running a household. In those days it was called domestic science where we'd also be taught subjects like food chemistry, etc. Many girls, who had no intention of going to college would specialize in domestic science as its aim was to make a girl a better housewife.

Ella Trow, quoted in Bill O'Neil, *Bill O'Neil Presents: Voice of the Pioneer* (Toronto: Doubleday Canada, 1988), p. 120

Employment

Jobs were plentiful throughout much of the 1920s, at least for men. Many of the jobs created during this period involved work in urban factories. The manual trades education that boys received helped prepare them for these jobs. About three-quarters of all the factory jobs in Canada were held by men in 1921.

Opportunities for young, urban women were more limited. After 1918, most women either left their wartime jobs or were laid off. Girls' education prepared them to work as secretaries, telephone switchboard operators, sales clerks, managers, and independent business owners in the growing towns and cities. The expansion of large department stores like Eaton's and Simpson's created thousands of jobs for women in all these categories. However, there were only a handful of female accountants, engineers, doctors, or lawyers.

For most urban women, a paid job was a temporary stage in life between their school years and marriage. Some women remained in the labour force for their entire lives, but most worked outside the home for only about eight years.

Figure 3-10 Elsie Highet, a telephone operator in Castor, Alberta. Why were women encouraged to take lower paid, unskilled jobs like this one?

Checkpoint ✓

7. Go round the class and take turns estimating what percentage of the Canadian population lives in urban areas today. Then check your answers at the Statistics Canada website. How close were you?
8. Create a chart to show similarities and differences between your high school and a high school of the 1920s, based on information in this section. Include the following categories: required subjects; years in school; gender differences.

The New Consumerism

In 1910, the tremendous power of Niagara Falls was first used to create hydroelectricity in Ontario. By the mid-1920s, electricity was transforming the way people lived—at least in urban areas. Families with steady incomes (or a good credit rating) could afford to buy new labour-saving appliances. Natural gas or electric stoves were advertised, along with electric toasters, vacuum cleaners, and washing machines.

Popular home entertainment equipment in the 1920s included radios and phonographs (record players). This simple audio equipment was quite expensive at the time. For example, a basic electric radio cost more than 50 dollars, at least two weeks' wages for most people! During the 1920s, many people went deep into debt to own consumer products.

Cheap electricity also helped automobile manufacturing expand in Canada. Owning a car in the 20s was a real status symbol. By 1926, cost-saving assembly-line production methods had lowered the price of a basic Ford or Chevrolet to less than $400. This meant that car ownership was within reach for about half of all Canadian families. The automobile made it easier for farmers to get into town, and allowed workers to commute from any part of the city. People began travelling by car for vacations, leading to the growth of summer cottages and camping parks in scenic locations.

LIVING LANGUAGE

One of the many new products in the 1920s was the Popsicle™. Originally, Popsicles were called Epsicles, after their inventor, Frank Epperson. Today, "Popsicle" is a trademark of the Good Humor Company.

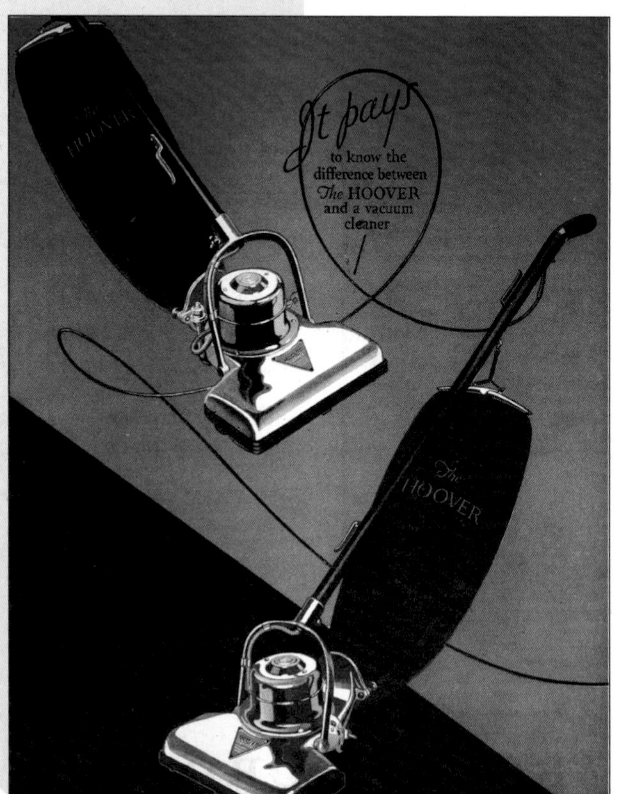

It pays
to know the difference between The HOOVER and a vacuum cleaner
The HOOVER
The HOOVER

◀ **Figure 3-11** In the first half of the 20th century, cheap electricity led to the development of many labour-saving devices and new consumer products. What technological development has had a similar effect in the second half of the 20th century and into the 21st?

Sports

With the new urban lifestyle, people found themselves with more leisure time than ever before. They could come home from an eight- to ten-hour office or factory workday and tune in to sporting events on the radio. People living near large cities could use a car to attend the game or travel in electric streetcars.

Lionel Conacher was the most popular sports hero of the day. Conacher seemed to do well in every sport he played. He won the Canadian Amateur Light-Heavyweight Boxing title in 1920, and the 1921 Grey Cup with the Toronto Argonauts Football Team. In 1925 he joined the NHL, and went on to win two Stanley Cups in the 1930s.

The 1928 Olympics marked Canada's best Olympic track-and-field performance up to the present day. Women competed for the first time ever, and the Canadian women's team ranked highest in the world. They set two new world records.

◀ **Figure 3-12** The Edmonton Grads women's basketball team won 17 North American championships in a row. Between 1915 and 1940, the Grads won 502 games and lost only 20. They successfully represented Canada at four Olympics, winning 27 games in a row. Can you think of a team in any sport today that has had this much success?

Until 1925, both amateurs and professionals played for the Stanley Cup. Later, though, the Cup was awarded only to National Hockey League teams. The (original) Ottawa Senators dominated the decade, capturing the Cup in 1920, 1921, 1923, and 1927.

For links to sites about sports heroes in the 1920s

Checkpoint ✓

9. Explain how new consumer products might have affected the following:
   a) family leisure time b) family social status c) family debt levels
10. Choose three moments in Canadian sport mentioned in this section and create a poster or newspaper headline for each.
11. The 1920s have been called a golden age for women's sport in Canada. Find evidence in this section to justify this label.

▲ **Figure 3-13** Agnes Macphail of Grey County, Ontario.

Changing Social Values

The years between the Great War and the Great Depression are often nicknamed "The Roaring Twenties." This term reflects the freedom and excitement that many people felt at the time. The economy was certainly roaring—at least for some people (more on this in Chapter 4). Along with this new wealth came a desire to break free of the past.

Women in Politics

Hopes for political reform were high in 1920. Five women ran for office in the 1921 election, and one was elected. In fact, Agnes Macphail was the only woman elected (and re-elected) to Parliament during the 1920s. She spent a quarter-century in politics, actively supporting women's issues and social reforms in Parliament. Macphail was an excellent public speaker, respected by all for her sincere interest in improving people's lives. Many of the changes that she fought for are still part of Canadian society today, including a minimum wage and social benefits, prison reform, and equal status for women.

Literacy Hint

To read a line graph, check the caption to see what information is being presented. Then look along the left-hand side for the scale, and along the bottom to find the time frame. Now look for a pattern in the line itself. Is it heading up or down? Are there spikes or dips or does the line move smoothly in the same direction? What is one general statement you can make about the trend shown in the graph?

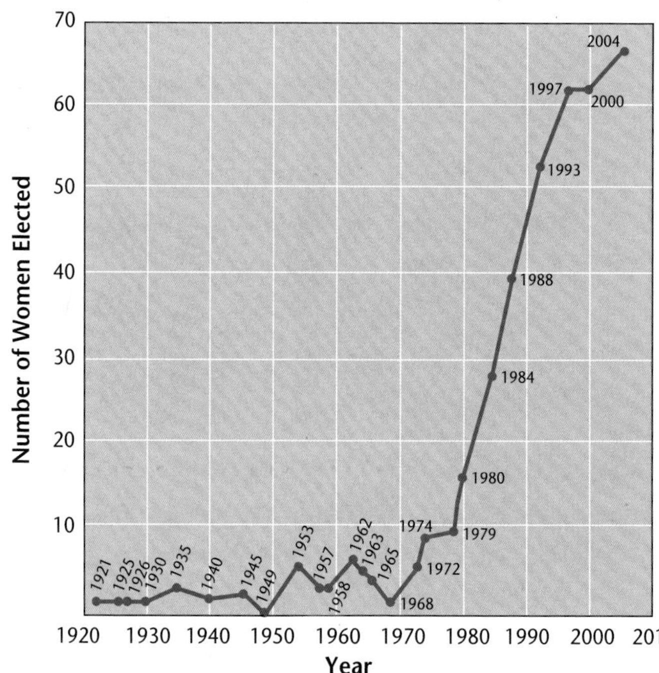

Figure 3-14 ▶ Women Elected to Federal Parliament, 1921–2004. When did the number of women in Parliament begin to climb quickly?

Source: www.parl.gc.ca/information/about/process/house/asp/WomenElect.asp.

The Persons Case

If someone asked you to decide if women should be counted as "persons" you would probably think the question was a little odd. But back in the 1920s, the definition of "person," at least in the legal sense, was the focus of a high-profile legal battle that came to be called the **Persons Case**.

Canada's laws were based on the British North America Act of 1867. The Act stated that only "fit and qualified persons" could be appointed to public positions, such as the Canadian Senate. A group of Alberta women, nicknamed the Famous Five, argued that "persons" included women, too. But the Supreme Court of Canada ruled that historically women were not included in the meaning of "persons" and thus had a "*legal incapacity to hold public office.*"

The Alberta women challenged this judgment at the higher court of the Privy Council of England. In 1929, it ruled that women were persons after all, and therefore eligible for public office. Now women legally had equal political status. The very next year, Cairine Wilson was appointed as the first woman to sit in the Senate of Canada.

The Famous Five

- Nellie McClung
- Emily Murphy
- Henrietta Muir Edwards
- Louise McKinney
- Irene Parlby

For links to sites about the Persons Case

Figure 3-15 This ▶ statue commemorates the Privy Council decision that recognized women as "persons." It depicts the Famous Five at the moment when they heard the court's decision. Why do you think the artist chose to depict the women this way?

Checkpoint ✓

12. Suggest three reasons for the increase in females in Parliament between 1921 and 2004. Which reason do you think is most important? Why?

13. Some groups and communities celebrate "Persons Day" on October 18. How would you celebrate Persons Day in your community? Brainstorm a list of ideas for a school or community-based celebration that would also help educate people about the importance of the Persons Case.

The New Popular Culture

We are surrounded by popular culture—movies and celebrities, music and dance, fashion and fads, and other interests made popular by the media. In the 1920s, the **flapper** became a symbol of popular culture. A flapper was a young woman who dressed and acted unconventionally. She was a new woman for a new time.

Flappers liked to have fun in ways that would have been unthinkable for women in the past. They drove cars. They did the Charleston, a popular, fast-paced dance accompanied by loud jazz. They even smoked cigarettes—a habit that was frowned upon, not because of the health risks (as it would be today) but because it was considered unladylike!

In the 1920s, radio was brand new. It quickly became a popular form of entertainment. Powerful transmitters broadcast American radio programs into Canada, sometimes drowning out smaller Canadian stations. By 1929, about 80 percent of the radio programs heard by Canadians came from south of the border. Along with American radio came American popular culture. A new kind of music called jazz filtered into Canadian homes. Radio announcers used the new American slang of the era. Some of these terms that originated in the 1920s are still used today—for example, do you know what a "gate crasher" is, or what it means to be "hip"?

Canada did have its own silent film industry in the early 1920s. However, after the "talkies" were invented in 1927, five major American studios soon produced about 90 percent of all feature films. Movie theatres sprang up across Canada to show these Hollywood productions.

Did You Know?

In the 1930s, the Canadian government created two institutions to lessen the American influence over Canadian media—the Canadian Broadcasting Corporation (CBC) and the National Film Board (NFB).

Figure 3-16 This fashion photo shows what flappers looked like in the 1920s. Flappers wore straight dresses that were very different from the long, full, tight-waisted styles of the past. Instead of long, curled hair, they wore a short, even cut, often tucked under a tight hat. Long beads, high heels, and plenty of makeup completed the look. Do you like it?

The End of Prohibition

Early in the 20th century, liquor was very cheap and problems caused by alcohol all too common. The **Temperance movement,** led by women's activists like Nellie McClung, worked to have alcohol banned or strictly controlled. During the war many people felt that it was wrong to drink when the troops were sacrificing so much. Between 1915 and 1917, every province except Quebec passed **prohibition** laws. They banned the sale of alcohol, except for religious or medical purposes. (One sympathetic doctor in Manitoba prescribed a daily dose of whisky to 5800 patients in one month!)

People tired of prohibition after the Great War, and one by one the provinces cancelled it between 1920 and 1930. However, prohibition remained in force in the United States until 1933. "Rum-running" between "wet" provinces and "dry" ones, and between Canada and the U.S., caused a crime wave in the 1920s. Chicago mobster Al Capone was a big player in the illegal liquor trade across the Canadian border.

Even with the easing of prohibition laws and the new, more open popular culture, the 1920s remained a much more conservative decade than we are used to today. For example, in Ontario a series of "Sunday laws" enacted before the Great War forbade people from working, shopping, selling goods, doing business, participating in sports, or even bathing in a public place on Sundays.

Did You Know?

Smugglers used many tricks to slip past police. One smuggler, Muskrat LaFramboise, used a boat with a plug in it, like a bathtub. When the police caught sight of him, he would pull the plug and let the boat sink. Later, LaFramboise would come back and dive for the sacks of liquor.

Checkpoint ✓

14. Take a survey in the class to find out people's favourite singer or group, actor, and movie. How many answers in each category are American? What do these results suggest about the influence of American popular culture on Canadians today as compared with the 1920s?

15. Use the catalogue picture in Figure 3-16 to compare women's fashions in the 1920s with today's fashions in clothing.

Figure 3-17 The cartoon illustrates how "big" organized crime grew during prohibition. Why was Canada important to Al Capone's Chicago gang?

An Inventive Era

Even before 1920, Canadians were known as inventive people. James Naismith invented the game of basketball, and Sandford Fleming organized the world into standard time zones. Reginald Fessenden's wireless radio broadcast showed Canadian leadership in communications technology. In the 1920s and 30s, Canadian inventors continued to come up with new ideas, especially in public health and consumer products.

Insulin

In 1921, Teddy Ryder was six years old and close to death. Teddy had diabetes, a disease that no one knew how to treat at that time. Diabetics cannot produce enough insulin to convert food into energy. Without treatment, victims waste away and die.

Teddy's mother brought him to Dr. Frederick Banting in Toronto. Banting, along with his graduate student, Charles Best, had found a way to inject insulin into humans. She begged Dr. Banting to treat her son. Luckily for Teddy, Banting agreed.

A few months later, Teddy returned home with his mother, a much healthier boy. Since then, millions of diabetics have been saved from an early death thanks to Banting and Best. In 1923 Banting won the Nobel Prize in medicine. He and Best generously turned over all rights to their discovery to the university and the Medical Research Council of Canada. Saving lives was reward enough for them.

▲ **Figure 3-18** Teddy Ryder in July 1922 (top) and July 1923 (bottom). What differences do you see in his appearance?

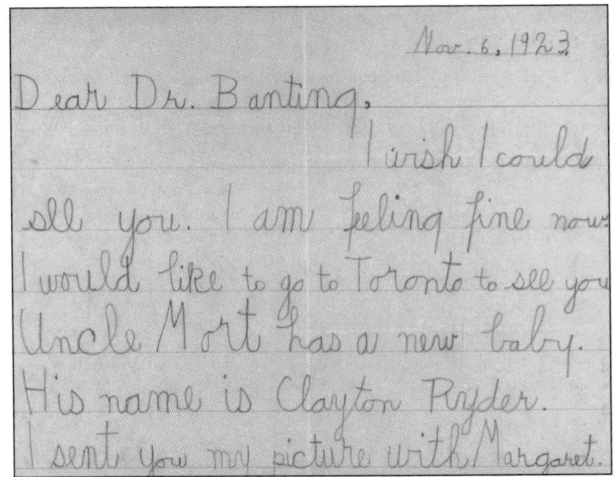

Nov. 6, 1923

Dear Dr. Banting,
I wish I could see you. I am feling fine now.
I would like to go to Toronto to see you.
Uncle Mort has a new baby.
His name is Clayton Ryder.
I sent you my picture with Margaret.

◀ **Figure 3-19** Seven-year-old Teddy Ryder wrote this note to Dr. Banting after his return home. How can you tell he feels grateful to Dr. Banting?

Plug-in Radio

Edward "Ted" Rogers always loved radios. In fact, when he was just 13 years old, he won a prize for the best amateur-built radio in Ontario. In 1927, Rogers obtained a patent for the world's first alternating-current radio. Before his invention, home radios were large, expensive pieces of furniture powered by bulky, acid-filled batteries. Rogers's radio did not need a battery—it could be plugged in. That meant radios no longer had to be so big, or so expensive. The same year, he also started the world's first electric radio broadcasting station, CFRB in Toronto.

Did You Know?

Ted Rogers's son, Ted Junior, went on to establish the Rogers Media empire, which today includes Internet, television, telecommunications, and video rental services.

Snowmobile

In 1934, Armand Bombardier's two-year-old son, Yvon, was very ill and needed a doctor. The nearest hospital was several kilometres away, but the roads were blocked with snow. For years Joseph-Armand had been working on a vehicle that could drive over snow, but when he really needed one, it wasn't ready. A few hours later, the little boy died.

Yvon's death pushed Bombardier to work even harder on his invention. In 1935 he came up with a new traction system, the sprocket wheel/track. The invention, patented in 1937, was the result of 10 years of intense work and effort.

Bombardier's inventions revolutionized winter transportation, especially in the North. In 1959, he used the same traction system, coupled with a smaller, lighter-weight engine, to create the modern two-passenger "Ski-doo."

▲ **Figure 3-20** An early snowmobile. Bombardier's machine may have looked like a cross between a car and a bulldozer, but it did the job better than any previous snow machine. How has this invention changed the lives of Canadians living in the far North?

Checkpoint ✓

16. Work in a group to rank the inventions discussed in this section from most to least significant. Compare your list with that of others, and be prepared to defend your choices.

17. Think of some modern technological changes. Which do you think might be most like the change from large battery-powered radios to Ted Rogers's plug-in radio? Explain your choice.

History Skill: Creating a Timeline

To create a timeline . . .

- ✓ decide on a theme and a title for your timeline
- ✓ consider the number of events you want to show
- ✓ place the events in chronological order
- ✓ consider what conclusions you can draw from your timeline

TIMELINE: Important Canadian Discoveries and Inventions, 1920–1939

- 1921 William Stevenson wire-photo transmitter
- 1921 Frederick Classens portable X-ray machine
- 1922 Frederick Banting and Charles Best insulin
- 1925 Wallace Turnbull variable-pitch propeller
- 1925 Arthur Sicard snow blower
- 1927 Ted Rogers, Sr. alternating-current radio
- 1928 Frank Morse Robb electronic organ
- 1928 Archie Huntsman quick-frozen foods
- 1931 T.G. Drake, A. Brown, F. Tisdall Pablum baby food
- 1935 J.A. Bombardier snowmobile

Arranging events in chronological (time) order is a good way to organize your thinking about past events. Timelines are an effective way to show this sequence. Here are the steps to follow when you create a timeline.

Step 1

Decide on the purpose or theme of your timeline and compose a title that reflects this theme or purpose. Always use dates in the title to show the beginning and end of the timeline.

Step 2

Decide how many events you'll include and how much space you'll need. You may need to make a rough copy first.

Step 3

Draw a single line down the page to the correct length. Make sure you leave enough space to write in the events beside the line. You might also find other creative ways to present your timeline.

Step 4

Write the dates to the left of the line. To the right, opposite each date, write the name of the event or a brief, point-form description of it. What conclusions can you draw from your timeline?

Practise It!

1. a) Read through this chapter again to identify the six most important events that took place from 1919 to 1929.
   b) Compare your timeline with that of a classmate. Did you choose the same items? Discuss any differences.
   c) How could the creation of timelines be a useful study skill?

Chapter Summary

The 1920s was a time of many new directions in society. As a result, Canada in 1929 was a very different place than it had been just 10 years before. In this chapter, you learned about the following changes in the Canadian way of life:

- Over a million immigrants arrived here, mostly from Europe.
- Canada became more independent of Britain and established its own national identity, for example, in art.
- Increasing urbanization had an effect on education, employment, leisure activities, and consumerism.
- Women gained recognition in sports and politics, and were finally recognized as "persons" in the law.
- American pop culture began to influence the lives of Canadians.
- Canadians made several important inventions and discoveries.

For many, the 1920s was a time of optimism. In the next chapter, you'll learn what happened in 1929 to end those good times.

a million immigrants arrive

Canadian identity established

women gain recognition

Wrap It Up

Understand It

1. Make a mind map to show at least three changes that affected women's lives in the 1920s.

Think About It

2. What conditions described in this chapter might help explain why the 1920s saw the creation of so many new inventions?

Communicate It

3. Choose one of the artists, politicians, athletes, or inventors named in this chapter. Write a first-person account (or present an oral report) on his or her most important accomplishment. Describe some of the experiences that led up to this accomplishment, as well as its effects.
4. If you were transported back to the 1920s, what aspects of teenage life at that time do you think you'd enjoy? What would you miss most about your life today? With a partner, prepare a skit based on your ideas.

Apply It

5. In your view, which one of the six points listed in the Chapter Summary has had the most important effect on Canada today? Explain.

Chapter 4

The Twenties: Boom and Bust

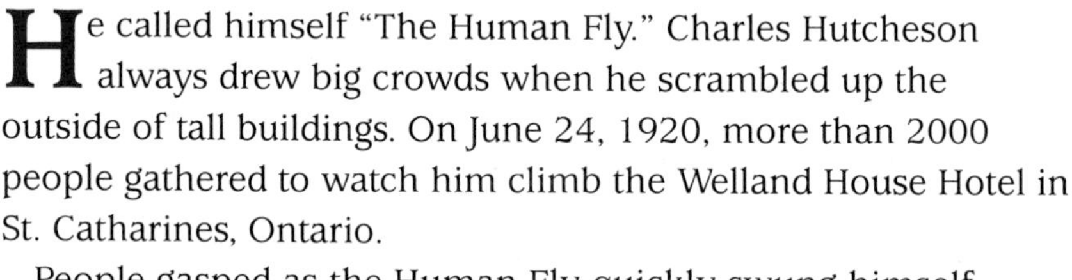

The Human Fly

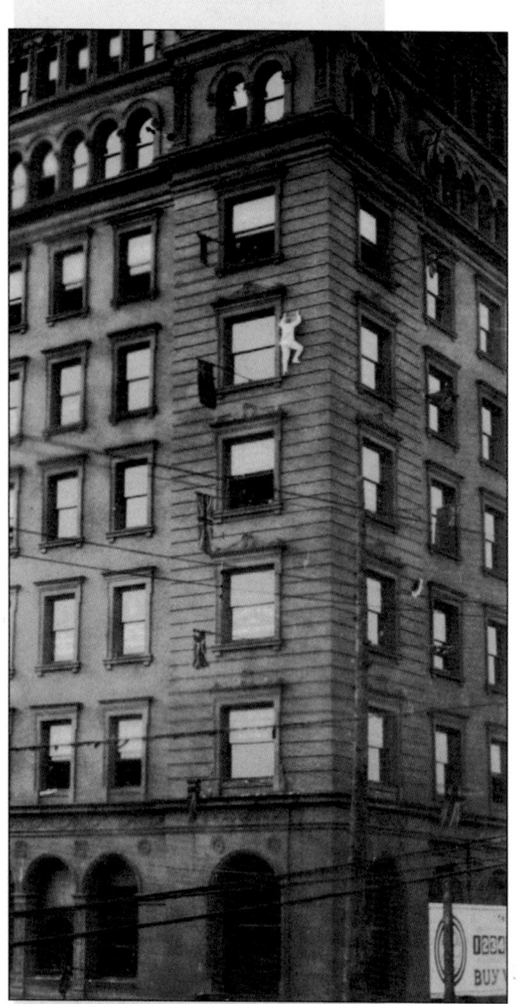

▲ **Figure 4-1** Daredevil stunts were popular entertainment in the 1920s. Why did people gather to watch such events?

He called himself "The Human Fly." Charles Hutcheson always drew big crowds when he scrambled up the outside of tall buildings. On June 24, 1920, more than 2000 people gathered to watch him climb the Welland House Hotel in St. Catharines, Ontario.

People gasped as the Human Fly quickly swung himself upward between window ledges with only a knotted rope. Hutcheson was so sure of himself that he didn't even use a safety harness or net. Maybe he was too sure. Suddenly, one knot came undone in his hand. Hutcheson dropped more than six storeys to a porch below, and lay there, seriously injured. He never fully recovered.

In many ways, the story of the Human Fly mirrors the economic story of the 1920s. Stock market prices climbed to dizzying heights, with no "safety nets" in place to protect investors. Then, on October 29, 1929, stock markets around the world crashed. The value of stocks fell so low that, like Charles Hutcheson, many investors and companies never recovered.

Checkpoint ✓

1. If the Human Fly were doing his stunts today, what reaction do you think he would get from
   a) the audience b) the authorities
   c) the media d) promoters and advertisers?
2. With a partner or small group, brainstorm ideas about the stock market. What is it? What do people buy and sell on the stock market? Why do people invest in the stock market?

Key Learnings

In this chapter, you will explore

- the advantages and disadvantages of American branch plants and foreign investment in the Canadian economy
- the contributions of the Billes brothers to the development of the Canadian economy
- why old age pensions were established in Canada
- the experiences of Atlantic Canadians, workers, Asian and Black Canadians, and Aboriginal peoples during the 1920s
- how economic conditions in the 1920s affected the daily lives of Canadian families, and what caused the Crash of 1929

Words to Know

foreign investment
tariffs
branch plants
unemployment insurance
social welfare programs
League of Indians
residential schools
stock market
buy on margin
Black Tuesday

The Economic Boom

In Chapter 3, you learned that a new and freer spirit emerged in North American society after the Great War. Underlying this new spirit was an economic boom—a period of rapid growth and high employment. The term "Roaring Twenties" is often used to describe both the economic and the social changes happening in society.

Developing Our Natural Resources

Growth in resource development and manufacturing led the boom. Investors poured money into energy, pulp and paper, and mining projects. In Alberta, the Turner Valley oil field was discovered, and began to provide a new source of energy. At the same time, mining exploration was opening up the Canadian North. Soon, new gold, silver, copper, and zinc mines dotted the bush country of the Canadian Shield.

Cheap hydroelectric power encouraged the growth of Canadian industry. More than $7 billion was spent during the 1920s to extract power from rivers. This water power was used to operate pulp and paper mills and mineral smelters across the Shield and through the mountain ranges of British Columbia. New resource-based communities sprang up overnight.

▲ **Figure 4-2** Bush pilots used small planes to carry prospectors, mail, and supplies north. They flew into regions that had never been mapped, using riverbeds and other natural features to find their way. Often they landed on bodies of water because there were no runways.

Checkpoint ✓

3. Imagine that you live in a small, isolated community in the far north. In winter, the only way in or out has been by dogsled, and few visitors have ever reached the community. What changes, for better and for worse, might the arrival of bush pilots in your community bring? Make a pro and con chart.
4. Draw a mind map to indicate how hydroelectric power led to the development of other industries in the 1920s.

	Britain	USA	Other
Exports from Canada	38.6	36.1	25.3
Imports to Canada	17.6	65.7	16.7

▲ **Figure 4-3** Canada's Exports and Imports, 1927 (as a percentage of total). Most Canadian exports were natural resources, such as minerals, wood products, and agricultural produce. Imports were largely manufactured goods such as cars and other consumer products. Which part of the diagram shows most clearly the importance of the U.S. to Canadian trade?

Source: *Sixty Years of Canadian Progress, 1867–1927* (Ottawa: Dominion Bureau of Statistics, 1927), pp. 98, 100.

Trade and Foreign Investment

By the 1920s the United States was already Canada's chief trading partner, and had been for a long time. This made sense, of course, because American businesses and customers were so much closer to Canada than those in Britain. In 1921, Canada exchanged two-and-a-half times more goods with the U.S. than with Britain. Many of the new consumer products and farm machinery that Canadians were so eager to buy during the 1920s came from the United States.

At the same time, the amount of U.S. **foreign investment** in Canada grew to match that of Britain. Between them, British and American investors financed most of the big development projects that jumpstarted Canada's economy around this time.

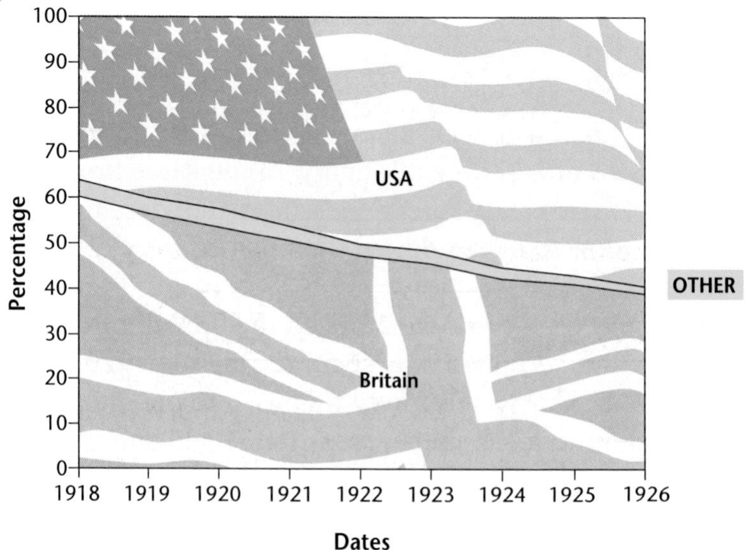

Figure 4-4 Foreign Investment in Canada, 1918–1926. Why did U.S. investment increase? ▶

Source: F.H. Leacy and M.C. Urquhart, eds., *Historical Statistics of Canada*, 2nd ed. (Ottawa: Statistics Canada, 1983).

American Branch Plants

American manufacturers had an advantage over Canadian manufacturers in the 1920s—the U.S. market was so much bigger than the Canadian market that American factories could make and sell their products for less.

To solve this problem, the Canadian government imposed taxes, called **tariffs**, on American imports. For example, in 1920 there was a 35-percent tariff on vehicles imported to Canada. This meant that Canadians had to pay $35 extra in taxes for every $100 they spent on a new American-made car. The tariffs allowed Canadian producers to sell more of their own goods within Canada. By protecting Canadian industries, tariffs also protected Canadian jobs.

Tariffs had another important effect. They actually led U.S. manufacturers to build factories in Canada in order to avoid the tariff. By 1913, there were already 450 **branch plants** in the country. A branch plant is a factory or business operating in Canada that is owned by a foreign company. Here's how one executive for the Studebaker car company explained his firm's decision to build a branch plant in Walkerville, near Windsor, Ontario:

> **We are in Walkerville purely because of the tariff. If it were not for the present tariff on the completed automobile, it would simply be a case of there being no advantage in being over here.**

W.P. Shillington, quoted in Michael Bliss, "Canadianizing American Business, Close the 49th Parallel Etc.," *The Americanization of Canadian Business*, Ian Lumsden, ed. (Toronto: University of Toronto Press, 1970), pp. 31–32

Did You Know?

At one time, as many as 70 Canadian companies were making or selling their own cars. But as the "Big Three" automakers—Ford, General Motors, and Chrysler—set up branch plants in Ontario, they drove these smaller Canadian firms out of business. The last to fold was the Brooks Steam Motor Company of Stratford, Ontario, which closed in 1926.

Advantages for Canadians	Disadvantages for Canadians
• large-scale industrial investments were made into Canada	• many small Canadian manufacturers were closed down
• lots of manufacturing jobs were created	• top management jobs were often held by Americans
• prices were lower because of large-scale production	• company decisions were made in the U.S. head office
• brand-name products were available for consumers	• profits went back to U.S. owners and investors

◀ **Figure 4-5** Pros and Cons of American Branch Plants.

Checkpoint ✓

5. Brainstorm a list of ways that Canada is affected or influenced by the United States today. Then choose one example from your list and draw a cartoon or make a collage to illustrate it.
6. Did tariffs accomplish what they were meant to do? Explain why or why not.
7. Write or role-play a conversation about the pros and cons of branch plants among the following three people in the 1920s:
   a) an industrial labourer
   b) a Canadian manufacturer
   c) a Canadian consumer

Profile: The Billes Brothers

The growth of the auto industry in Canada was sparked by U.S. investment, and most of the profit from the U.S. branch plants flowed back to shareholders in the United States. However, the popularity of automobiles after the Great War did encourage local automobile-related retail businesses to grow. One business that took root in the 1920s and is still thriving today is Canadian Tire Corporation.

In 1922, brothers J.W. (Bill) and J.A. (Alfred) Billes bought out a small firm, called Hamilton Tire and Rubber, where Bill had been sales manager. The next year they set up shop along Yonge Street, Toronto's major north–south route.

At first, the store specialized in selling and repairing tires. Soon, however, the brothers added other goods, such as batteries, radios, and auto parts to their stock. They named the business Canadian Tire "because it sounded big."

By the late 1920s, the little company had grown to match its big name. Buying at low prices helped the Billes brothers offer lower tire prices than their competitors. They also advertised heavily and offered an unconditional guarantee. In 1928 the first Canadian Tire catalogue was printed, establishing a national mail-order business for tires and auto supplies.

Two years later, the Canadian economy was sliding into the Great Depression—but not Canadian Tire. In 1934 the first Canadian Tire franchise opened in Hamilton, Ontario. Over the next five years, 70 more franchises would be sold to independent owners.

Today, Canadian Tire has more than 450 department stores, 40 auto parts stores, and 230 gas bars coast to coast. Its sales exceed $5 billion annually. The Billes brothers' little store has become one of Canada's most successful business empires.

Career Profile

Roger and Pauline Williams, Entrepreneurs

Have you ever thought about operating your own business? Roger Williams admits that he hadn't—until he was injured in a serious construction-site fall in 1997. After that he began carving, and discovered he had a creative talent that ran in the family. His grandmother wove traditional Ojibwe splint baskets, and his mother made and sold detailed beadwork. Today, his own talent is widely recognized: the guest book at the Williams shop has customer signatures from across Canada and around the world.

The Williamses are proud to make and sell their works. Pauline knows how important tradition can be. When she was a young child, the government required that she leave her family for much of the year to attend a residential school (see page 88).

Roger and Pauline produce more than 80 percent of the pieces that fill the shop's large display area. (The rest come from other First Nations crafters in Ontario.) Roger uses photographs and his imagination to create his specialty: detailed knives, wall hangings, and animals carved from moose and deer antlers. Pauline works on any items that require sewing.

The shop has many other objects the Williamses have made, including drums for ceremonial dances, carved cedar boxes for storing ceremonial feathers, and beautiful clothing pieces made from buckskin, bone, and brass. These items are used in traditional ceremonies. But first they must be "smudged"—purified by the smoke of the "four sacred medicines": cedar, sage, tobacco, and sweet grass.

Roger explains some secrets to their success in the shop: "I'm always seeking to make something different. I do this by researching new designs that people will want to own. It's so important to have a market for your talent, to be self-motivated, and to never quit on your dream."

1. In addition to their crafting skills and their knowledge of tradition, what skills do you think Roger and Pauline Williams need to run their business?
2. Which of these skills do you think you have and which would you need to acquire? How could you go about acquiring them?
3. If you were running your own business, what kind of business would you like it to be?

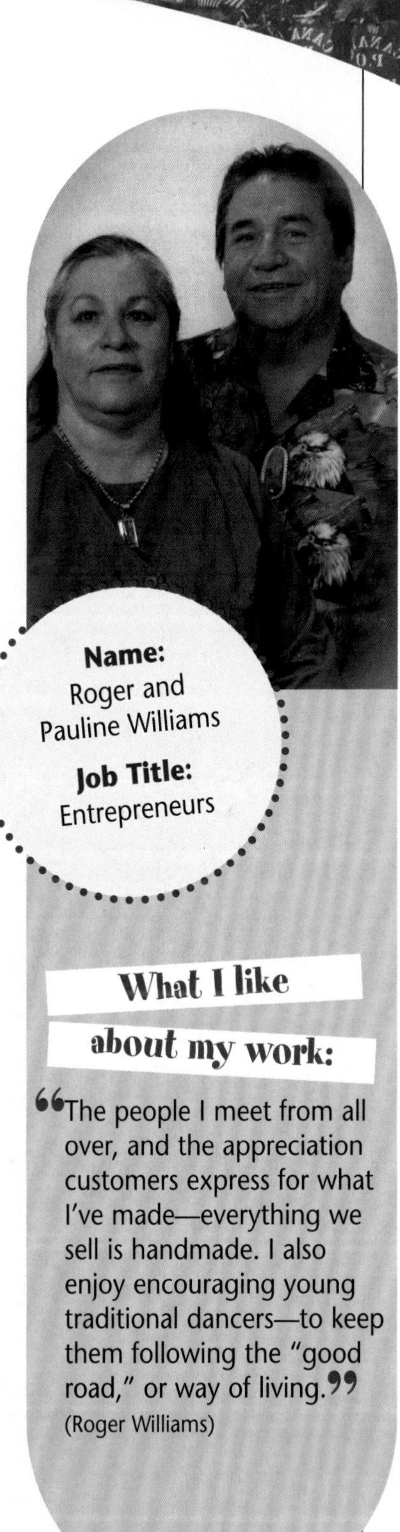

Name:
Roger and Pauline Williams

Job Title:
Entrepreneurs

What I like about my work:

"The people I meet from all over, and the appreciation customers express for what I've made—everything we sell is handmade. I also enjoy encouraging young traditional dancers—to keep them following the "good road," or way of living." (Roger Williams)

Did Everyone Benefit from the Boom?

As we have seen, times were good for many people during the 1920s. Unemployment was low and half of all Canadian families owned a car. But not everyone faced hopeful prospects. Many people in the 1920s were underpaid, underfed, and underemployed. Even within prospering regions, Aboriginal peoples and visible minorities lived on the margins of society, denied basic opportunities that others took for granted.

Maritimers and Newfoundlanders

While some regions, such as the West, Ontario, and Quebec, benefited greatly from the boom, the eastern provinces and Newfoundland were not doing as well. By the 1920s, the westward expansion of Canada had left the Atlantic region behind.

As more provinces joined Confederation, the midpoint of the country had shifted west, from Ottawa to Manitoba. The Atlantic region was located too far from the centre of the country to attract large manufacturers, such as carmakers, who planned to sell products Canada-wide. Coal shipments from Nova Scotia mines to the rest of Canada fell because of competition from Alberta's new Turner Valley oil and gas producers.

To make things worse, trading patterns had shifted too. The Atlantic region had been ideally located when Britain was Canada's major trade partner, but that advantage disappeared as U.S. imports and exports began to dominate the economy.

Literacy Hint

This section contains a lot of information. Slow down your reading speed as you work through the paragraphs. If necessary, reread parts of the text. Stop after each paragraph to summarize the information in your head.

For links to sites about Atlantic region mining

Did You Know

Newfoundland had an even more serious economic problem at this time. Financing both the Newfoundland Railway and the Great War had left Newfoundland deep in debt. Between 1918 and 1933, the government gradually slid toward bankruptcy.

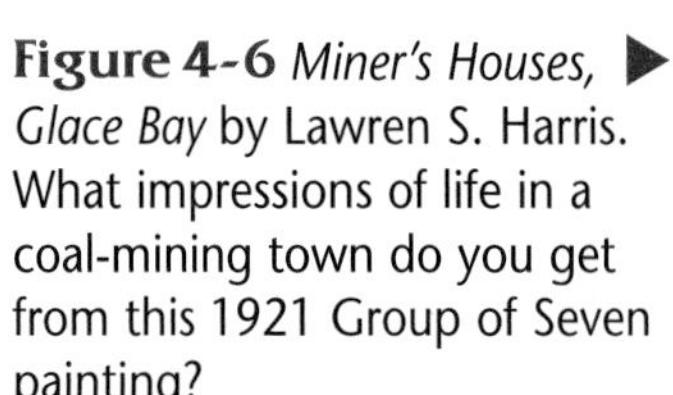

Figure 4-6 *Miner's Houses, Glace Bay* by Lawren S. Harris. What impressions of life in a coal-mining town do you get from this 1921 Group of Seven painting?

Workers

Business owners and investors made large profits during the boom, but their employees often worked long hours at low wages. In Quebec, most French Canadians worked for English-speaking bosses, with little chance for promotion. Immigrants sweated in dirty conditions in textile factories, metalworking foundries, and meatpacking plants.

As other forms of energy (such as oil and gas) became available, the market for coal dried up. Wages of Nova Scotia miners were cut by a third—and for dirty and dangerous work that already paid only about 25 to 30 cents per hour. Boys as young as 10 worked underground to help support their families.

From 1921 to 1925, violent strikes shook the coal districts. The Canadian army was ordered in to break them up. Unhappy miners either returned to work or left the region to work in textile factories in New England.

Today, there are government programs in Canada to help those in need. If we lose our jobs, we can claim **unemployment insurance** benefits. If we are sick, we can get free medical care. These **social welfare programs**, also known as social security programs, did not exist in the 1920s. Until 1927, there wasn't even a government pension plan for retired workers. Even then it took a political deal to force Mackenzie King's Liberal government to introduce Canada's first social welfare program. Here's how it happened.

After the King–Byng crisis (see Chapter 3) the Liberals won the most seats in the 1926 election. But they were six seats short of a majority. That meant they could rule only with the support of the small Progressive Party (the party Agnes Macphail belonged to). In return for their support, the Progressives demanded that the Liberals introduce an old age pension.

▲ **Figure 4-7** Women and older girls worked in this crowded Edmonton textile factory.

Did You Know?

When the Old Age Pensions Act became law, it paid only $20 per month to 70-year-old citizens who had been resident in Canada for at least 20 years. Only people with almost no income qualified for these pensions, and all money had to be repaid with interest after the pensioner died.

Checkpoint ✓

8. Suppose that you are a resident of Halifax in the 1920s. Write a letter to relative explaining why you have decided to leave the Atlantic region and where you plan to move.
9. a) How many social welfare programs can you think of that exist today? Work with a partner to list as many as you can.
   b) Which of the social programs we enjoy today do you think would be hardest to live without? Why? Discuss.

Visible Minorities

The 1920s certainly did not "roar" for many visible minorities in Canada. Instead, these minority groups faced political, social, and economic discrimination.

Did You Know?

In 1922 a strong anti-Chinese movement began in B.C., led by high-ranking politicians. They claimed that the Chinese were depriving White Canadians of jobs, business profits, and even seats in schools.

Asian Communities

By the 1920s, B.C. already had a large Chinese population. Many workers who came to Canada in the 1880s as railway labourers settled in B.C. Smaller groups of Japanese and Sikhs settled around Vancouver and Victoria.

All three groups faced discrimination. For example, many employers refused to hire Asian workers, or paid them lower wages. In response, many Asian Canadians set up their own small businesses, such as restaurants or laundries. Others fished or farmed. All three Asian cultures lived in close-knit communities, largely shut out from the rest of society but determined to build their lives here.

Black Communities

Most Blacks in Canada in the 1920s had come from the United States. Some were descended from 2500 Black Loyalists who migrated to Nova Scotia in 1783. Others were descended from escaped slaves.

Unlike many visible minority groups, Blacks gained the right to vote at Confederation. However, they were not treated as equals. For example, both Ontario and Nova Scotia set up separate schools for Black students, but did not fund them properly. This meant that most Black students got an inferior education and had fewer job prospects.

◀ **Figure 4-8** The great jazz pianist Oscar Peterson (right) was born in the 1920s in Montreal. His father Daniel (left) worked as a railway porter. This was one of the few jobs open to black men at the time. (Read more about Oscar in Chapter 14.)

Aboriginal Peoples

Ever since the Indian Act became law in 1876, the lives of First Nations peoples had been bound up in strict regulations enforced by the RCMP. For example, traditional ceremonies and dances were forbidden, and permits were required to sell farm produce and livestock. Government officials controlled (and sometimes stole) band money. First Nations peoples could not vote unless they left their reserve.

In 1919, Frederick Loft, a Mohawk chief from the Six Nations Reserve near Brantford, Ontario, organized the **League of Indians** to address some common First Nations issues:

- the seizure of their lands illegally and without consultation or negotiation
- the government's failure to sign treaties recognizing land claims
- government restrictions on traditional hunting and trapping rights
- policies that threatened First Nation languages and customs
- the poor economic and health conditions on many reserves

The Indian Affairs department did nothing to address these problems. Instead, Deputy Superintendent of Indian Affairs Duncan Campbell Scott tightened his control in order to stop any further attempts to organize.

Duncan Campbell Scott once admitted that the object of his department was "to continue until there is not a single Indian in Canada that has not been absorbed into [mainstream society]. . . ."

Figure 4-9 Frederick Loft continued his efforts to organize the League of Indians even after Scott threatened to cancel his status as an Indian. Why do First Nations people consider Loft a hero?

Residential Schools

Perhaps the most damaging government policy toward First Nations peoples was the creation of the **residential schools**. Starting in 1920, all First Nations children aged 7 to 15 were required to live most of the year in one of 80 government-funded schools. The aim was to remove children from their home and culture, and use the education system to assimilate, or absorb, them into Canadian society. Traditional languages, clothing, and religious practices were strictly forbidden. Instead, the children were required to speak English (French in Quebec), wear uniforms, and become Christians. There have been many proven cases of physical and sexual abuse at the residential schools.

First Nations people continue to struggle with the effects of the residential schools. Thousands of lawsuits have been launched against the federal government and many of the religious groups involved in the schools' administration. Official apologies have been issued by most of these groups. Here is part of what Bill Phipps, the moderator of the United Church of Canada, said in a statement made on October 26, 1998:

> On behalf of the United Church of Canada I apologize for the pain and suffering that our church's involvement in the Indian Residential School system has caused. . . .
>
> We know that many within our church will still not understand why each of us must bear the scar, the blame for this horrendous period in Canadian history. But the truth is that we are the bearers of many blessings from our ancestors, and therefore we must also bear their burdens.

▲ **Figure 4-10** The picture at the top shows a young boy named Thomas Moore before he entered a residential school in Regina. The picture at the bottom was taken after he had been in the school for a while. How has he changed?

For links to sites about residential schools

Checkpoint ✓

10. The expression "The Roaring Twenties" does not really fit the experience of some groups in Canada during those years. Choose one of the groups in this section and suggest an alternative description of the decade that expresses its experiences. Explain your description to a partner.

11. a) Create a poem, drawing, collage, or use another medium to illustrate the government's policy toward First Nations peoples in the 1920s.

b) Do you agree with the United Church that people today need to accept responsibility for injustices committed in the past? Is an apology enough, or must more be done? Discuss with a partner.

Playing the Stock Market

Stock markets played a big part in the economic boom of the 1920s. Let's take a moment to examine how stock markets work.

What Is a Stock Market?

If you wanted to start up a business, you would need to spend money. You might use your own, or get a business loan from the bank. Or, you could find partners and offer them a share in your profits in exchange for investing their money in your business.

Companies that need a lot of money can sell shares in their business on the **stock market**. They make ordinary people their business partners. Each share gives the owner a piece of the business. Shareholders are entitled to attend the company's annual general meeting and to vote to select top executives.

People buy shares (also called stocks) for two different reasons.

1. They hope that the success of the business will cause the value of each share to rise. Then they can sell the stocks for a profit.
2. If the company is doing well, shareholders may receive a portion of the company's profits. This payment is called a dividend.

Of course, there are risks involved in buying stocks. If the company does poorly, no dividends are paid. The value of the shares will probably fall too.

The idea of holding shares in a business dates back centuries, to a time when business owners in private clubs bought and sold portions of one another's companies.

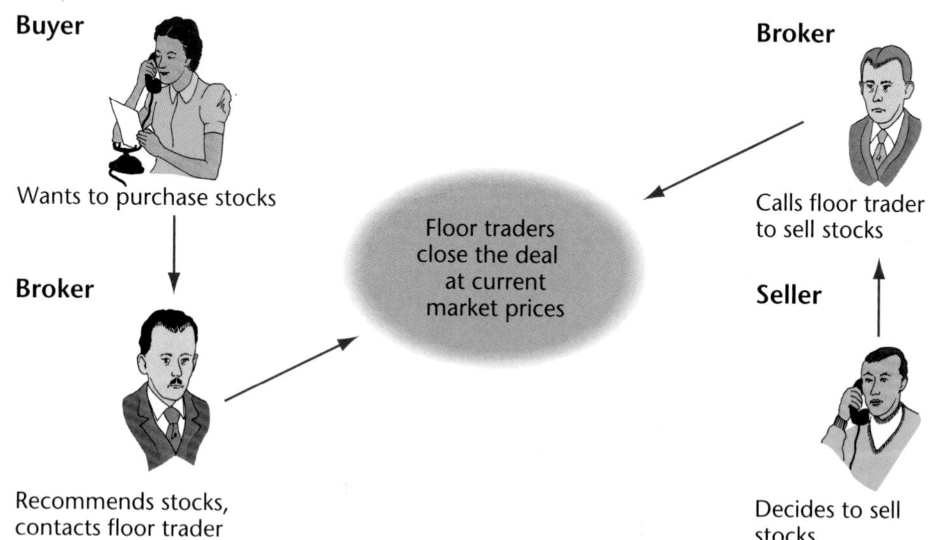

◀ **Figure 4-11** In the 1920s, floor traders handled Buy or Sell orders at the stock market. At the end of the day, the floor traders completed their orders, and then sent them back to the stockbrokers' offices. The stockbrokers notified their clients that the deals they requested had been completed. Today we use computers and telecommunications systems to handle the volume of stock trading, but the systems work basically in the same way.

The Stock Market Boom

About one Canadian in ten invested in stocks during the 1920s. Charlotte (Lottie) Nugent was one of them. Lottie was a bookkeeper at Monarch Brass in Toronto. Like most young women of the time, she hoped to marry someday and leave Monarch Brass to raise a family.

By the late1920s, Lottie had become the head bookkeeper at the firm. Over the years she had carefully saved up $3000. Lottie had a boyfriend too—a young stockbroker from a good Toronto brokerage firm. Stockbrokers advise clients who want to invest in stocks. He confidently advised her to invest in the booming Toronto Stock Exchange. Lottie trusted his judgment, and used all her savings to **buy on margin**—that is, she borrowed money from her boyfriend's firm to pay for her shares, and paid only a small percentage of cash up front.

Lottie's boyfriend assured her that she could easily pay off the loan—and still make a profit—as the stocks went up in value and paid dividends. Stock prices had been climbing since the mid-1920s and everyone said that the boom would continue.

Figure 4-12 Number of Shares Sold on the New York Stock Exchange, 1920–1929 (in millions). The New York Stock Exchange was so large that other markets usually followed whatever pattern it set. In what year did the stock market boom begin to accelerate?

NYSE Stocks

Year	Number of Shares	Year	Number of Shares
1920	227	1925	454
1921	173	1926	451
1922	259	1927	577
1923	236	1928	920
1924	282	1929	1125

Source: Derrik Mercer, ed., *Chronicle of the Twentieth Century* (Harlow, Essex: Longman Group UK, 1990), p. 383.

Checkpoint ✓

12. Why do some companies offer shares on the stock market? Give two reasons why investors buy these shares.
13. Describe a business that you might like to start up someday. Explain how you would get enough money to set up the business.
14. In your own words, explain the term "buying on margin." What financial benefits did this purchase plan offer? What problems do you think could arise from this practice? Use examples to explain your ideas.

History Game:

Manage Your Stock Investments

Required to Play:

- a balance sheet
- one die and pencil

Purposes:

- To keep a balance sheet based on buying and selling shares
- To calculate profit or loss after 15 turns (weeks) of play

Objective: To win the game by making the largest profit after 15 rounds, based on a starting balance of $100.

How to Play:

1. Before starting play, you must understand how to keep a balance sheet. The five-week sample shown below illustrates how the column on the right is calculated.
2. Take turns playing 15 rounds of the game, entering information on your own balance sheet after each round. On each turn, slowly roll one die three times for the following information:
   First roll: 1 or 2 means you must Buy stock; 3 or 4 means Sell; 5 or 6 means Hold
   Second roll: the numbers 1 to 6 give the stock price in dollars
   Third roll: determines the number of shares bought or sold
3. To keep things simple, you can sell any time you roll 3 or 4, even if you haven't bought that number of shares yet. This will be corrected at game end.
4. Here is how to decide the game winner after 15 rounds of play:
   a) Add up the total number of shares bought and the total number of shares sold to see which is bigger.
   b) *If you bought more shares than you sold*, you need to sell all your remaining shares at the price of $3 each. For example, if you bought 13 shares and only sold 2, you have 11 unsold shares. You must sell these, for a total income of $33. Add the total value of these unsold shares to your cash balance after 15 weeks.
   c) *If you have sold more shares than you bought*, you must subtract $3 for each extra share sold from your cash balance after 15 weeks. So if you sold 12 shares and bought 10, you need to subtract $6 ($3 x 2 shares) from your balance.
   d) Compare the final balance with your $100 opening balance. The difference is your profit or loss in the stock market.

Follow-Up:

1. Which class members were most successful? With a partner, discuss how the game compares to the stock market in real life.
2. Experts say that the secret to the stock market is to "buy low, sell high." In real life, why might it not always be easy for investors to follow this advice?

		Buy			Sell			Closing Balance
Week	Activity	Price $	Number shares	Spent (–$)	Price $	Number shares	Received (+$)	Balance $
								100
1	Buy	3	6	–18				82
2	Buy	1	3	–3				79
3	Sell				6	2	+12	91
4	Hold							91
5	Buy	5	4	–20				71
...15					3 [Set price]	11 [Unsold shares]	+ 33 [Stock value]	104 **Profit $4**

▲ **Figure 4-13** A sample balance sheet. Multiply the price by the number of shares to determine the amount spent or received. Adjust your closing balance after each turn.

Black Tuesday

For links to sites about the stock market crash

All through September of 1929, Lottie Nugent watched nervously as the stock market fell. Her boyfriend kept telling her to hang on. He was sure the stock market would soon head up again. "It always does," was his simple advice.

But he was wrong. Experienced investors had recognized that prices had gone as high as they were going to go, and that this was a smart time to sell. Many put large blocks of shares on the market. All these sell orders caused share prices to slip gradually downward.

In October, things slipped even further. Financial experts urged investors not to panic, but some did. Soon there were many more people looking to sell their shares than there were people interested in buying them. Finally, on October 29, **Black Tuesday**, share prices nose-dived. Desperate traders sold their shares for whatever they could get. Lottie's last hope of making any profit was lost.

Days later the news was even worse. Her boyfriend's brokerage company was bankrupt. It needed to close out her account to pay off debts of its own. She was given just six days to come up with the $4421.27 still owing on shares she had bought on margin. That was as much as Lottie could earn in five years' work at Monarch Brass.

Like many people, Lottie lost it all in the Great Crash. She could see no way out. Her plans for the future were in ruins. Lottie quietly went home and took her own life. This is a true story.

STOCK PRICES CRASH EARLY; SLIGHT RALLY LATER
Millions of Shares Valued in Billions Sold in Stock Break

WORLD MARKETS NOSEDIVE TO NEW DEPTHS
Worst Collapse in Canadian Financial History

BLACK TUESDAY
Wall Street Crashes

S-T-E-A-D-Y EVERYBODY
Trust Your Banker

◀ **Figure 4-14** These headlines from newspapers in 1929 tell the story of the stock market crash. What do you think the last headline means?

The same scenes were played out in other countries in North America and Europe. On "Black Tuesday," stock markets collapsed in New York, Toronto, Montreal, and around the world. Within a month, a typical share price of $10 was down to less than $5. By mid-1932, the same share was worth $1.50 or less. Some cases were more extreme; for example, Massey-Harris farm machinery shares fell from a high of $99.50 down to just $2.50 during this time.

It wasn't just investors who lost out. As shares lost value, companies had less money available. Most cut back on production or closed altogether. Soon, about one Canadian worker in four did not have a job, and many others were facing wage cuts. Since people had less money to spend, stores had to cut their prices and staff. This downward spiral quickly dragged entire communities along with it. The next 10 years became known as the Great Depression.

Did You Know?

Among those who lost heavily in 1929 was a prominent Quebec lawyer named Louis St. Laurent. Nineteen years later, when he became prime minister, he had just finished paying off these debts.

Checkpoint ✓

15. How were each of the following affected by the Crash?
a) stock investors
b) large companies
c) industrial employees
d) store owners

16. Choose one of the headlines in Figure 4-14 and write a brief news story describing the events on and leading up to Black Tuesday.

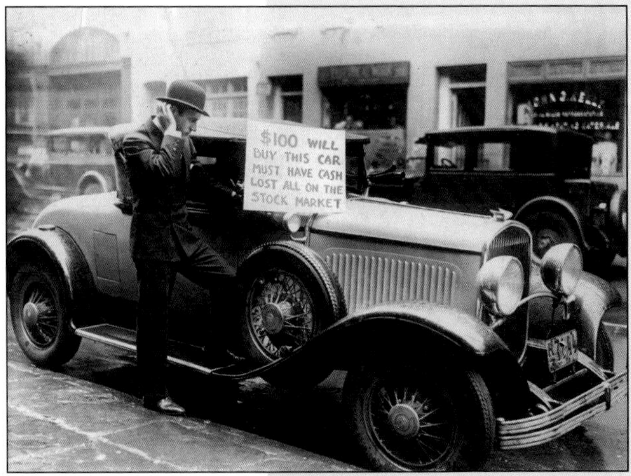

▲ **Figure 4-15** Would you pay $100 for this car?

Causes of the Crash

In a sense, the Crash was predictable. As the Human Fly found out, what goes up must come down—and the same holds true for the economy over time. The economy had been riding so high for so long that it was bound to face a downturn at some point.

But what caused such a sudden and severe crash? The stock market collapsed because of some serious weaknesses in the economy. Each problem was either a case of too much or not enough. There was too much margin buying, production of goods, and American economic influence. There were not enough wages for workers or protection for people's savings. These five problems caused an imbalance that eventually toppled the entire world economy.

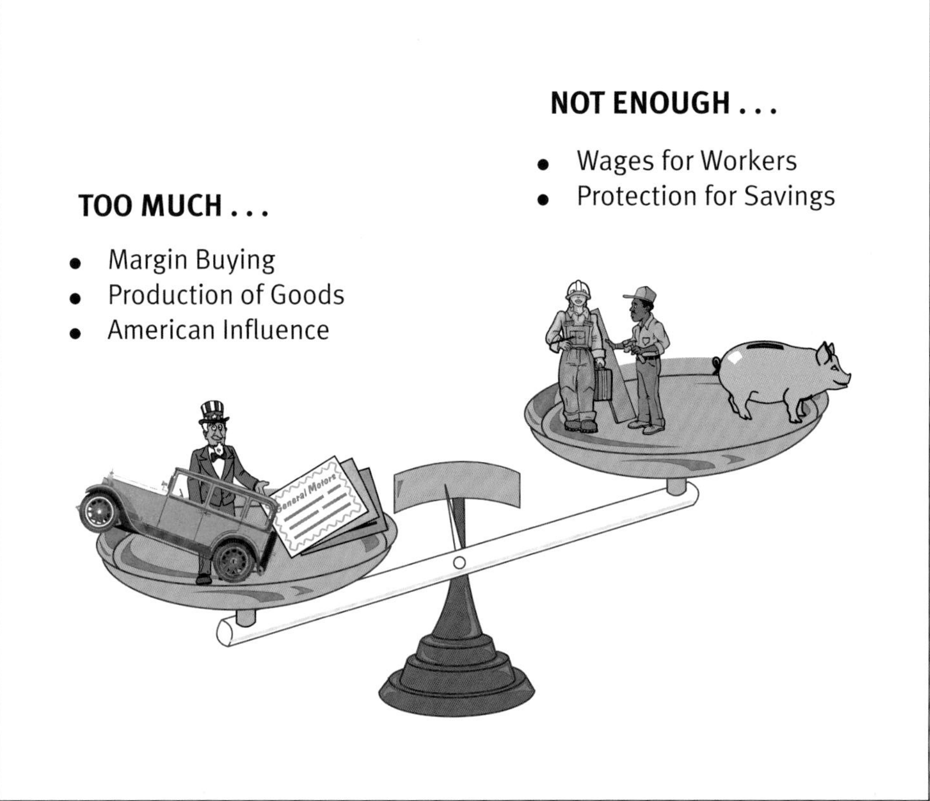

Figure 4-16 Causes of the Great Crash of 1929. Which of these factors do you think was most responsible for the severity of the crash?

The End of the Boom

The collapse of stock markets around the world marked the end of an era. For many people, the prosperity and optimism of the 1920s became a fond memory in tough times. Canadians suffered because of the stock market crash. Many lost their savings, their jobs, their automobiles, and their homes. Some people, like Lottie Nugent, the trusting Toronto bookkeeper, lost even more.

Checkpoint ✓

17. With a partner, role-play a conversation between a banker and a small investor. The banker has to explain to the investor that his savings have been wiped out by the stock market crash.
18. Look at the five causes of the 1929 Crash. Choose two of them and explain ideas for changes you would make to prevent such a large crash from happening again.

Chapter Summary

The Roaring Twenties was a time when the Canadian economy expanded faster than it ever had before and then contracted even more dramatically in the Crash of 1929. In this chapter you learned the following facts about the 1920s boom and bust:

- Natural resource industries and manufacturing grew very rapidly.
- American investment in Canada surpassed British investment.
- American manufacturers built branch plants here to avoid tariffs.
- The Atlantic region and several social and cultural groups in Canada did not share in the general prosperity of the 1920s.
- The Great Crash of 1929 affected economies around the world.

In the next chapter you'll explore the harsh world of the 1930s, a much more difficult period for many Canadians.

rapid economic growth

high employment

social welfare programs

Black Tuesday

Wrap It Up

Understand It

1. Explain what part each of the following played in the Roaring Twenties in Canada:
   a) consumer spending b) resource development
   c) foreign investment d) branch plants
   e) stock investment f) buying on margin

Think About It

2. In your opinion, do the benefits of American investment in Canada outweigh the disadvantages? Write a persuasive letter to the editor in which you use information and evidence to support your view.

Communicate It

3. Use at least three different information sources to find out about the origins and aims of the League of Indians. Prepare an interesting bulletin board display panel that highlights your research. Always include a detailed listing of your information sources.

Apply It

4. What other examples can you think of where people buy things on credit with a small (or no) down payment, as investors did when they bought stock on margin? What are the advantages and disadvantages of this practice?

5. Where did Lottie Nugent go wrong? How might her life have been different if she had made different decisions? Retell her life story with a happier ending.

Chapter 5
The Great Depression

Calling Superman!

> "The bread line! Its row of downcast, disillusioned men; unlucky creatures who have found that life holds nothing but bitterness for them."

Science Fiction Magazine #3, January 1933

Literacy Hint

If you were inventing a superhero who would appeal to people in today's society, what powers would you give him or her?

Words to Know

- recession
- business cycle
- depression
- Dust Bowl
- cash economy
- relief
- On-to-Ottawa trek
- New Deal
- Social Credit party
- Cooperative Commonwealth Federation (CCF)
- Union Nationale

This is the beginning of a story called "The Reign of the Superman," written in 1933 by Jerry Siegel and illustrated by his Canadian friend, Joe Shuster. In the story, an evil professor performs experiments on a down-and-out drifter named Bill Dunn, whom he finds waiting in line for a handout of food.

Needless to say, this story did not make Siegel and Shuster famous. But not long after it appeared, they began to think about creating a "Superman" who helped people instead. One day, Joe Shuster sketched a red-caped hero with blue tights—and the rest, as they say, is history.

The world certainly needed a friendly superhero in the 1930s. Cities were full of bread lines like the one in the story, where unemployed men lined up to get enough food to stay alive. In the countryside, things were no better. People were desperate for work, desperate for food, and desperate for an escape from their difficult lives.

Figure 5-1 The first Superman comic. Why do you think Superman has remained popular for so long?

Key Learnings

In this chapter, you will explore

- what life was like for Canadians during the Depression
- how the labour movements and governments responded to the Depression
- the founding of new political parties in the 1930s
- why unemployment insurance programs were established

Literacy Hint

Think about how the economy affects your own life. What happens when businesses stop hiring or lay off employees? How does unemployment affect individuals? Communities?

Life in a Time of Depression

Have you noticed a lot of Help Wanted signs in stores lately? Are new businesses opening up in your area? Are existing ones expanding? These may be signs that the economy is in a boom period. In Chapter 4 you read about a decade-long boom that occurred in the 1920s.

Perhaps, though, the news headlines talk of rising unemployment, and businesses are closing rather than expanding. If so, you may be in a **recession**. This rising and falling pattern in the economy is known as the **business cycle**.

If the cycle continues to fall, and lay-offs and production cuts become severe, the economy enters a **depression**. The depression of the 1930s was so severe it has become known as the Great Depression.

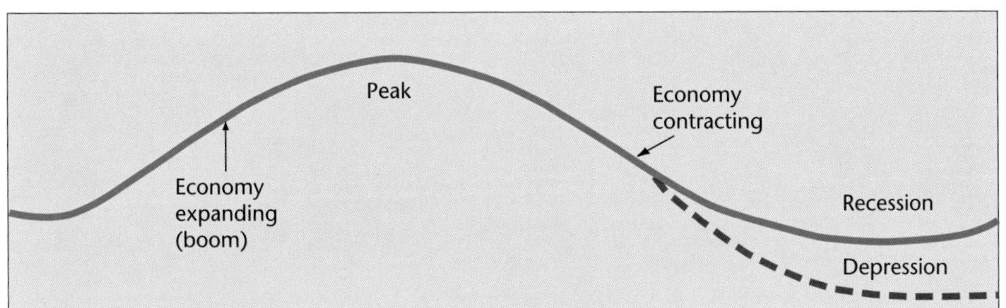

◀ **Figure 5-2** The Business Cycle. What types of jobs might be more deeply affected by these changes in the economy?

Checkpoint ✓

1. In your own words, explain the business cycle.
2. Do you think the Canadian economy is in an up cycle or a down cycle right now? Look for evidence in your neighbourhood and in the business section of a newspaper.

Life on Farms

While some people made it through the Depression without a major change in their lifestyle, most people suffered terribly. The letter below was written to R.B. Bennett by a woman living on a farm in Saskatchewan during the Depression. It is one of hundreds the prime minister received in the 1930s from desperate Canadians living in both rural and urban areas. You can tell from the letter that the woman writing it had nowhere else to turn.

Like the Hodginses, many farm families barely scraped by during the Depression. Falling demand for farm produce, lower prices, and crop failures made life next to impossible for many farmers.

Literacy Hint

You can often tell as much from the way a primary source is written as you can from what it says. What might the spelling mistakes and vocabulary tell you about the writer of this letter?

Perdue, Sask.
Sept. 28, 1933
Prime Minister R.B. Bennette
Ottawa, Ont.

Dear Sir

it is with a very humble heart I take the opportunity of writing this letter to you to ask you if you will please send for the underware in the Eaton order (made out and enclosed in this letter). My husband will be 64 in Dec. and has nuritis very bad at times in his arms and shoulders. We have had very little crop for the last three years: not enough at all to pay taxes and live and this year crops around here (West of Saskatoon) are a complete failure. My husband is drawing wood on the waggon for 34 miles, and had to draw hay too, for feed for horses this winter. He has to take two days for a trip, and sleep out under the waggon some times. He is away for wood today and it is cold and windy. So I am writing this in the hope that you will send for this underware, as we really have not the money ourselves. I have patched & darned his old underware for the last two years but they are completely done now, if you cant do this, I really don't know what to do. We have never asked for anything of anybody before. ... Thanking you in advance I remain yours truly

Mrs Thomas Hodgins
Perdue, Sask

National Archives of Canada, C-085866, C-043771, C-043772. © Unknown. Reproduced at www.collectionscanada.ca/primeministers/h4-150.09-e.html#a76

Did You Know?

Bennett bought the Hodginses the underwear. He often responded to letters like this by sending the writer two dollars of his own money.

◀ **Figure 5-3** Many farmers could not afford gas for their cars. Instead, they took out the engine and hooked the chassis to a horse or cow. Why do you think these "hybrid" vehicles became known as "Bennett Buggies"?

Why did demand for farm produce fall? In the 1920s, much of Canadian farm produce was exported to Britain, Europe, and the United States. When the Depression hit, governments everywhere tried to protect their own producers by limiting imports from other countries. International trade fell, and with it went much of the demand for Canadian farm goods.

When the export market dried up, farmers had to sell their products at home. But when more of any product is available than people are willing to buy, prices fall. As a result, total farm income fell by more than 60 percent between 1928 and 1933.

Did You Know

In 1928, Canadian farmers bought 17 143 tractors. Five years later, they bought only 777.

Year	Live cattle	Pork (tonnes)	Butter (tonnes)	Eggs (dozens)
1920	315 179	49 608	6 196	6 000 000
1925	267 292	67 953	11 114	2 691 000
1933	60 134	35 972	2 012	1 987 000
1938	179 224	80 965	1 766	1 842 000

Source: M.C. Urquhart and K.A.H. Buckley, *Historical Statistics of Canada* (Toronto: Macmillan, 1965), pp. 377–378.

▲ **Figure 5-4** Exports of Selected Agricultural Goods, Canada, 1920–1935.

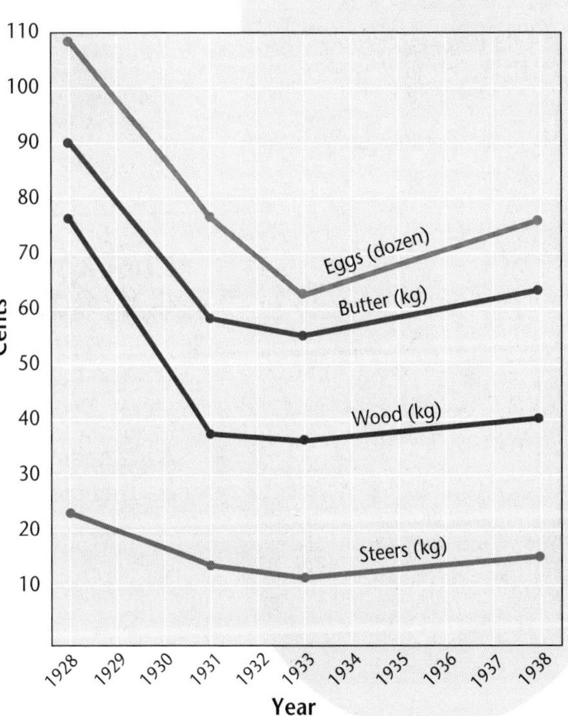

Source: *Historical Statistics of Canada*, pp. 359–360.

Figure 5-5 Wholesale Prices of Selected Farm Products, 1928–1938. ▶

The Dust Bowl

All these terrible conditions were made worse by a series of unusually dry summers. The lack of rain led to drought, a condition in which the land is too dry to grow crops. Eventually, the topsoil dries up and is blown away by the wind in huge dust storms. The whole phenomenon was known as the **Dust Bowl**. It was particularly severe on the Prairies, where plagues of grasshoppers ate any crops that did manage to push their way through the dirt.

The term "dust bowl" was unknown in the English language until 1936. Today, improved farming methods have reduced the drying out of the topsoil, and dust bowls have been largely avoided in Canada since the 1930s.

For links to sites about the Dust Bowl

▲ **Figure 5-6** Dust storms like this one were common during the Dust Bowl.

Checkpoint ✓

3. a) Explain what happened to exports of Canadian farm produce during the 1930s. (Use two figures to support your answer.)
   b) Explain what happened to prices of Canadian farm produce during the 1930s. (Use two figures to support your answer.)
4. Imagine you are R.B. Bennett. You receive letters all the time from desperate people asking for your help. You know you can't send money to everyone. How will you decide who to help? Discuss with a partner or in a small group.

Life in Towns and Cities

People who abandoned their farms and came to the city soon realized that they were no better off. At least on the farm they could grow their own food, or trade some cream from their cows for vegetables from another farmer. By contrast, urban areas ran largely on a **cash economy**. This meant that people had to have cash to buy the things they needed to survive. For most people, having a job was the only way to get cash. But jobs were in short supply, and more and more people were competing for each opening. Many unemployed workers ended up standing in bread lines like those described at the beginning of this chapter. With so many people chasing fewer jobs, workers had to accept pay cuts imposed by their employers.

Did You Know?

Aboriginal people who had retained their traditional hunting and fishing lifestyle tended to do better during the Depression than those who had moved into farming or the wage economy.

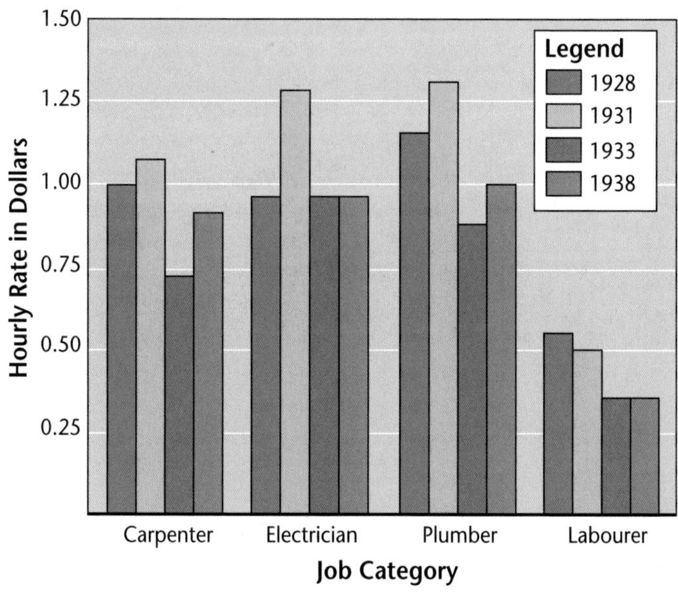

Source: Adapted from *Historical Statistics of Canada*, p. 86.

◀ **Figure 5-7** Hourly Rates for Men in Selected Building Trades, Toronto, 1928–1938. Which of the trades shown had managed to regain its pre-Depression wage level by 1938?

Checkpoint ✓

5. If you were alive in the 1930s in Canada, would you prefer to live on a farm or in the city? Discuss your reasons with a partner.
6. Write down three observations based on information in the bar graphs in Figure 5-7.
7. How do you think workers felt about their situation in 1933? Explain.

Responses to the Depression

Things were so bad for farmers and city dwellers alike that charity groups were having trouble helping all the people who came to them. The federal and provincial governments were reluctantly forced to contribute to **relief** programs. At the end of 1933, 400 000 people were relying on charity and federal and provincial relief payments to get by. Many more needed the help, but were too proud to accept it.

The details of government relief programs varied across the country, but they were never generous. The average weekly food allowance was $4.22 per person. Since milk cost 9 cents a litre, and beef cost 29 cents a kilogram, this amount would permit only a basic diet. In Newfoundland, things were even worse. Family relief there was just 42 cents a day.

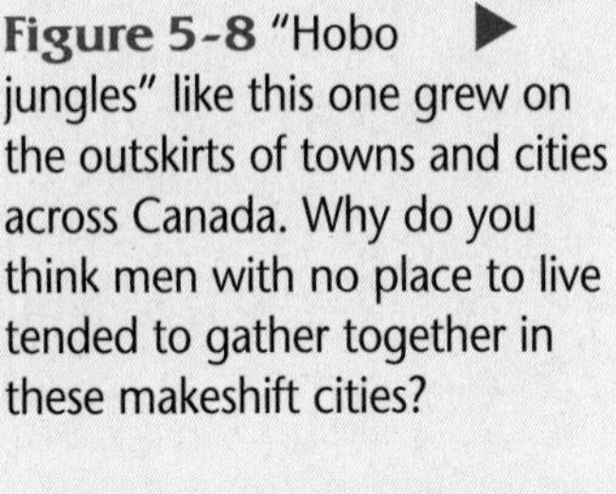

Figure 5-8 "Hobo jungles" like this one grew on the outskirts of towns and cities across Canada. Why do you think men with no place to live tended to gather together in these makeshift cities?

Worst off were young, single men. As soon as they turned 16, they were cut off relief and expected to find work. In some provinces, the government set up labour camps for these men, usually in isolated areas away from cities. Men at the camps were fed, clothed, and housed in exchange for doing public service work—such as building roads or cutting trees. Conditions in the labour camps were often terrible, and the pay was about one-tenth what a regular worker would make doing the same tasks.

Did You Know?

Homeless men travelling the country developed a kind of code to communicate with each other. For example, if a man came across a sympathetic woman who was willing to offer food or work, he would draw a cat in chalk on a gate post. The symbol for a vicious dog was

The On-to-Ottawa Trek

Labour unions were faced with many difficulties during the Depression. They wanted to press employers for better wages and working conditions, but they were not in a good bargaining position.

One of the most famous union protests was the **On-to-Ottawa trek**, which began in British Columbia in June 1935. The unions recruited frustrated unemployed workers from the relief camps for a trek to Ottawa. Thousands hitched rides on eastbound railway freight cars. Others joined them as they crossed the country.

When they reached Regina, the prime minister ordered the trek to be stopped. Negotiations with its leaders soon failed, so Bennett sent the RCMP and Regina police to break up the protest. On July 1, the police moved in and a riot followed. Hundreds were injured and a police officer was killed. Around 130 people were arrested.

▲**Figure 5-9** The On-to-Ottawa trek. Why do you think Prime Minister Bennett decided to stop the protest?

An official inquiry was held, which blamed the trek's leaders. It was a finding that only the most desperate were likely to disagree with.

Nevertheless, many people were sympathetic to the trekkers' protest, even while they condemned the violence that ended it. One woman wrote to Alice Millar, Bennett's personal secretary, a few days after the Regina Riot:

> **Young men of that age like to have money to spend, like to take a girl out, like to get married, like to build their homes. Like to dress nice and go to a dance occasionally. . . . So they are really tired of camp life. It is just like being in [jail]. It is the oneness of it all, the monotony if you get what I mean. No outlook . . . And I am heartily sorry for them.**

Jean McWilliam, letter to A. Millar, July 3, 1935. National Archives of Canada

For links to sites about the On-to-Ottawa trek and relief camps

Literacy Hint

Events in history are not always described in chronological order (time sequence). For example, this section begins by stating what happened in early 1935 and then goes back in time to explain what led up to this event. You can follow the sequence of events by

- comparing dates
- looking for clue words, such as *before, after, since, meanwhile*

In the 1930s the slang term "pokey" was used to describe the money given out by government to the unemployed and needy. Since then, the pronunciation has changed to "pogey"—but the meaning has stayed the same. Employment insurance is now a regular part of life in Canada, helping people over temporary periods of unemployment or lay-off.

Bennett's New Deal

In early 1935, with an election looming, Bennett realized he would have to do something to help end people's misery. Before that time, the government believed the best solution to the Depression was simply to wait for things to get better on their own; the business cycle would correct itself, the economy would begin to expand again, and unemployment would go down. This is how governments had always dealt with economic issues before.

But by 1935 it was clear that this Depression was different. It involved far more unemployment than ever before, and gave no sign of ending quickly. Bennett himself took much of the blame as people grew frustrated with the inaction of the government.

Bennett outlined a program of reforms, which became known as his **New Deal**. (President Roosevelt of the United States had begun a program of the same name in 1933.) The plan included measures to increase competition and to give the government more power over the economy. Bennett hoped these changes would boost production and create jobs. The Deal cut the work week down from 60 hours to 48. It also created an unemployment insurance program—the first in Canada's history.

These changes came too late to save Bennett. His government was soundly defeated in the 1935 general election, and Mackenzie King and the Liberals returned to power. Although the Liberals followed through on many of Bennett's New Deal promises, the climb out of the Depression was slow. In fact, employment started to rise rapidly only after 1938, when the military began recruiting people and factories began producing war materials for yet another war effort. You will read more about this buildup to World War II in Chapter 6.

Checkpoint ✓

8. Why were labour unions not in a good bargaining position with employers during the Depression?
9. If you were a young man during the Depression, do you think you would have chosen to work in an isolated labour camp or to live the life of a hobo? Discuss with a partner.
10. Using your own words, make a bulleted list that summarizes the measures contained in Bennett's New Deal. Which measure do you think the people would have found to be the most important, and why?

New Political Parties

At the beginning of the 1930s, the two largest political parties in Canada were the Liberals and the Conservatives. By the end of the decade, they had some competition.

There were two reasons for the rise of new parties at this time. First, the old parties (Conservatives and Liberals) seemed unwilling to find new ways of dealing with the Depression. Second, the old parties seemed to be controlled from the major cities in central Canada. People in other regions felt that their concerns were not being addressed. As you'll see, it was in these regions that most of the new parties had their beginnings.

For links to sites about Social Credit, the CCF, and their founders

Social Credit

William Aberhart was a teacher and preacher from Alberta. He believed that the reason for the Depression was that people—especially farmers—did not have enough buying power to purchase all the goods and services that industries could produce. The government, he felt, should give each citizen a monthly "Prosperity Certificate" worth $25, which would allow people to buy more products. As demand increased, companies would hire more workers to produce additional goods. Aberhart formed a new political party to press for these reforms. He called it the **Social Credit party**.

In 1935 the Social Credit party was elected as the provincial government of Alberta. The Prosperity Certificates were never paid out, but Social Credit remained in power in Alberta until 1971. In later years (1952–72; 1975–91), it also gained power in British Columbia.

◀ **Figure 5-10** William Aberhart, the founder of Social Credit. Why do you think Aberhart's idea of providing spending money to jumpstart the economy was so popular in the West?

The Cooperative Commonwealth Federation (CCF)

After the War, J.S. Woodsworth (the conscientious objector from Chapter 2) worked as a minister in Winnipeg. He was shocked by the poverty in his parish and came to believe that the private ownership system had failed. Woodsworth thought governments should take a greater role in the economy, especially by taking over key industries.

Woodsworth also believed that governments should provide more help to people. He wanted to see unemployment insurance, free medical care, family allowances, and better old age pensions. Woodsworth was one of the founders of the **Cooperative Commonwealth Federation**, a party formed in 1933 to fight for these programs. Many of the CCF's programs have since been adopted in Canada, as other parties have come to support them.

In 1961, the CCF changed its name to the New Democratic Party (NDP). As either the CCF or NDP, the party won power in a number of provinces. It formed the government in British Columbia (1972–75, 1991–2001), Saskatchewan (1944–64, 1971–82, 2001–), Manitoba (1969–77, 1981–88, 1999–), and Ontario (1990–95).

The Union Nationale (UN)

Maurice Duplessis believed that Quebec's problems in the Depression stemmed from the fact that its industries were largely owned by Americans and English-speaking Canadians. He founded the **Union Nationale** in 1935 to fight for stronger government involvement and to give Quebeckers more control over their economy.

In 1936, Duplessis led the UN to power in Quebec. He began the process of giving more economic power to Quebeckers, a practice that has continued to this day. The UN held power in Quebec for 22 years

Did You Know?

Some of Duplessis's policies were very controversial. In 1937 he passed a law that gave him the right to shut down any organizations or groups he considered a danger to the government. Duplessis used this "padlock law" to target Jews, Jehovah's Witnesses, and labour unions, as well as communists.

Checkpoint ✓

11. Create a chart to summarize the information in this section about the Social Credit, CCF/NDP, and Union Nationale parties. Include the name of the party's founder; the year it was founded; its main beliefs; and where and when it has been in power.
12. Of the three party platforms mentioned, which, if any, do you find most convincing? Debate with a partner.

History Skill: Preparing a News Story

News stories are an important source of historical information. Understanding how they're constructed makes it easier to identify the crucial facts they contain.

Step 1

Use the 5WH method to determine the key facts about the event. 5WH stands for *Who? What? When? Where? Why? How?*

Step 2

Write an opening paragraph that answers all or most of the 5WH questions. For example, the following paragraph answers *Who? What? When? Where?* and *Why?* about the 1923 Nobel Prize for Medicine:

> It was announced today in Sweden that University of Toronto researchers Frederick Banting and J.J.R. Macleod have been awarded the 1923 Nobel Prize for Medicine. Banting and Macleod earned the prize for their discovery of a new treatment for diabetes.

Step 3

In later paragraphs, fill in details about the main event. These paragraphs often elaborate on *How?* and *Why?* answers.

Step 4

Finish the story by explaining the significance of the event, describing people's reaction to it, or suggesting what will likely happen next. Add a headline that's short and describes the main event.

For example, here's how a reporter might use the 5WH method to write a story you read about in Chapter 3:

Who?	U of T researcher Frederick Banting and Dr J.J.R. Macleod
What?	Awarded Nobel Prize for Medicine
When?	1923
Where?	Sweden
Why?	For their discovery in 1921 of a new treatment for diabetes
How?	By extracting a hormone called insulin from the pancreas of a dog and injecting it into a patient

Note

The History Skill on the Inquiry Method, page xii, has more information on types of questions.

To write a news story . . .

- ✓ gather information using the 5WH method
- ✓ write a first paragraph that briefly answers most of the 5WH questions
- ✓ fill in details in later paragraphs
- ✓ end with the event's importance, people's reactions, or what will happen next
- ✓ write a short headline that focuses on the main event

Here's how the finished article might read:

Toronto Researchers Win Nobel Prize

The headline is short and explains the main event that happened.

It was announced today in Sweden that University of Toronto researchers Frederick Banting and J.J.R. Macleod have been awarded the 1923 Nobel Prize for Medicine. Banting and Macleod earned the prize for their discovery of a new treatment for diabetes.

The first paragraph answers *Who? What? Why? When?* and *Where?*

Diabetes is caused by an inability to produce insulin. If left untreated, it can cause blindness, loss of limbs, and even death. The new treatment was developed in 1921 by Dr. Banting and his assistant, Charles Best, under Macleod's supervision. It involves extracting a hormone called insulin from the pancreas of a dog and injecting it into the patient. Since then, the treatment has allowed many diabetics to live full, normal lives.

The second paragraph explains *How?*

The award marks the first time that the Nobel Prize has been awarded to Canadians. Dr. Banting has announced that he plans to share his prize money with his assistant, Dr. Best. Dr. Macleod will do the same with his colleague James Collip, who helped purify the insulin so that it could be injected. ■

The final paragraph explains how the recipients reacted to receiving the award.

Practise It!

1. Write a news article about one of the following stories (you may have to do some research to answer all the questions):
   a) the stock market crash
   b) the On-to-Ottawa Trek
   c) the founding of the Social Credit, CCF, or Union Nationale parties
   d) the announcement of Bennett's New Deal

Newfoundland During the Depression

In the 1930s, Newfoundland and Labrador was not yet part of Canada. Although it was a colony of Britain, it had run its own government since 1854. The only aspects of Newfoundland's government that the British controlled directly were defence and foreign relations.

When the Depression hit, Newfoundlanders were trying to pay off a debt of $35 million built up by their participation in World War I. Then, in the early 1930s, the price of fish collapsed. Fishing was the basis of the economy, and the falling prices hit Newfoundland's economy hard. The government struggled to pay the debt while the demand for relief payments from unemployed workers grew. A series of corruption scandals in government only made things worse.

Finally, in 1934, the Newfoundland legislature (the part of government that makes laws) made a desperate move. It handed itself back to the British government! The British took over the debt and continued to govern Newfoundland directly from London until it became a province of Canada in 1949.

Just three weeks after Black Tuesday, on November 18, 1929, a powerful undersea earthquake caused a tsunami, or giant wave, to hit the Burin Peninsula of Newfoundland. Over 40 communities suffered property damage and 27 people were killed.

▲ **Figure 5-11** A street scene in St. John's, Newfoundland, during the 1930s. Given what you know about conditions in Newfoundland and the Atlantic provinces *before* the Depression, do you think people living there noticed as much of a change in their way of life as people in other parts of the country did? Explain.

Checkpoint ✓

13. Based on what you know about the global economic conditions in the 1930s, why do you think the fish market collapsed during this period?
14. If you lived in Newfoundland in 1935, trying to survive on relief payments of 42 cents a day, how do you think you would feel when the government voted to hand control of the colony back to Britain? What advantages might this arrangement have for you?

The Legacy of the Depression

Do you think you would have been able to survive in the Depression? There's no doubt that the 1930s was a tough time to live through. Of course, people's troubles were made a bit easier to bear by the fact that so many others were also affected. Norman Jewison, the famous Canadian film director, was a boy in Toronto at this time. He recalls that kids didn't realize they were poor, so they didn't worry about it. All their friends lived the way they did, and accepted that it was normal.

Although it was a terrible experience for some, the Depression did have some positive and lasting effects. From then onwards, Canadians expected their governments to play a bigger role in keeping the economy strong. It was no longer enough to leave it to the business cycle and individual employers. They also expected governments to look after individual and family security. Unemployment insurance, welfare payments, better pensions, and children's allowances all had their origins in this period. The Depression has made a permanent impact on our history.

Did You Know?

Films offered a way to escape during the Depression. Even though people had very little money, box office receipts remained high through most of the 1930s. Norman Jewison recalls collecting coins from each of his friends to buy a ticket to the movies. Jewison would watch the film and then go back to his friends to retell it for them!

Figure 5-12 Norman Jewison is best known for films such as *Fiddler on the Roof, Moonstruck*, and *The Hurricane*, based on the biography of boxer Rubin "Hurricane" Carter.

Chapter Summary

Those who lived through the dark years of the Great Depression will never forget it. It certainly left its mark on Canada as a whole. In this chapter, you have learned the following things about Canada during the Depression:

- Lower prices, lower demand, and drought caused many farmers to lose more than half their income.
- Unemployment was at its highest in cities.
- What relief payments were available were in most cases barely enough to survive on.
- In 1935, unions organized an "On-to-Ottawa" trek by unemployed men from labour camps. The trek was stopped in Regina, where a riot left one police officer dead.
- Several new parties emerged during the Depression, including the CCF, the Social Credit party, and the Union Nationale.

In the following chapter, you will read about events that were unfolding in Europe during this same period—events that would lead to World War II.

Dust Bowl

New Deal

On-to-Ottawa Trek

Wrap It Up

Understand It

1. Explain the significance of each of the following during the Depression.
   a) the Dust Bowl
   b) relief camps
   c) Bennett's "New Deal"
   d) The On-to-Ottawa trek

Think About It

2. Imagine you were the head of a family in your community in the 1930s. Make a list of things you might do to make things better for your family as it tries to cope with the Depression.

Communicate It

3. Write a short letter to Prime Minister Bennett from someone who has been hurt by the Depression. Explain your situation and ask if there is anything he can do to help you.
4. Create a radio ad that one of the new political parties featured in this chapter might have used for an election in the 1930s. Perform your ad for the class either live or on tape.

Apply It

5. Find out more about the views of the Liberals, Conservatives, and New Democrats (NDP) regarding employment insurance and social assistance today. Create a chart or other graphic display to present your results.

Chapter 6

Canada and Events in Europe

Speaking Out Against Injustice

First they came for the communists, and I did not speak out—
because I was not a communist;
Then they came for the socialists, and I did not speak out—
because I was not a socialist;
Then they came for the trade unionists, and I did not speak out—
because I was not a trade unionist;
Then they came for the Jews, and I did not speak out—
because I was not a Jew;
Then they came for me—
and there was no one left to speak out.

Pastor Martin Niemoeller, 1933

Do you think you would have the courage to speak out against evil or injustice if doing so could hurt you? Martin Niemoeller did. Niemoeller was a submarine commander in the German navy in World War I and later a leading Protestant minister. In the 1930s he became an outspoken critic of the Nazi party and government in Germany—and paid a high price for it. Niemoeller lived through one of the darkest periods in the 20th century. As you read this chapter, think about how you would have reacted if you were watching events in Germany during this time.

▲ **Figure 6-1** Adolf Hitler rose to power in Germany in the 1930s.

Words to Know

hyperinflation
fascists
Nazis
Führer
public works
Nuremburg Laws
Kristallnacht
ghettoes
concentration camps
Final Solution
Holocaust
appeasement
anti-Semitism

Key Learnings

In this chapter, you will explore

- the events that led to Hitler's rise to power in Germany
- Hitler's economic and social policies in Germany
- Hitler's actions against the Jews, leading up to the Final Solution
- Western leaders' policy of appeasement toward Hitler
- the obstacles faced by Jewish refugees
- why Britain, France, and Canada declared war on Germany

Germany and the Rise of the Nazis, 1919 to 1933

Germany's Economic Problems

As you read in Chapter 2, the Treaty of Versailles ended World War I. The punishing terms of the treaty were designed to ensure that Germany could not pose a threat to other countries for decades.

After the war, every country in Europe was in terrible shape, economically, socially, and politically. With the added burden imposed by the Treaty of Versailles, Germany was in ruins. It was exhausted by the effort of fighting the war, and now it was saddled with an impossible debt to its enemies.

Germany was given a new constitution in 1919. It was known as the Weimar constitution. Everyone hoped that it would create a stable and democratic country. But it did not. Because so many parties got elected to the German Parliament, it was very divided. No one could agree on a plan to rebuild Germany's economy.

A series of weak governments followed. They tried to pay the reparations that the Treaty of Versailles demanded. When they did not have enough money to make the payments, they did two things that had dramatic results.

- They borrowed money, mainly from the United States, with a promise to pay back the loans in the future.
- They printed more German marks and used them to buy U.S. dollars to pay off the loans and reparations.

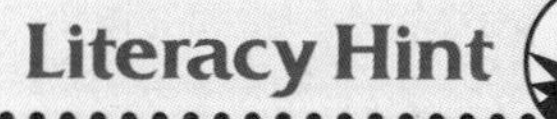

Literacy Hint

What do you know about Adolf Hitler already? Use the first column of a KWL chart to record any information that you already have about him. Write things you would like to know about him in the second column. As you read the chapter, look for answers to your questions, and fill in the third column of your chart.

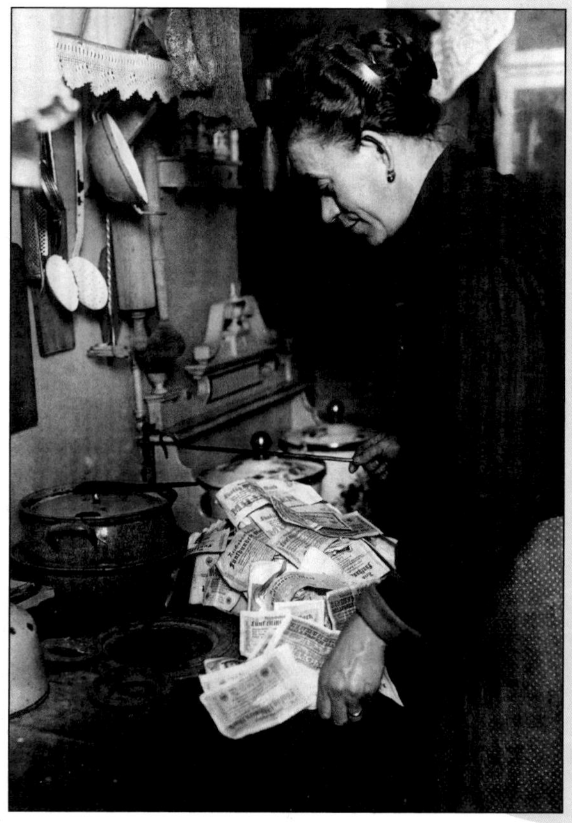

Figure 6-2 This woman is using paper money to light her stove in Germany in 1923. What does this tell you about the value of German money at that time?

As more marks went into circulation, each one became worth less. Businesses demanded more marks for their products. Workers demanded more marks for their labour. Prices rose, slowly at first, then at an alarming rate.

As the value of the mark went down, Germans could no longer afford to buy imports. Many companies went bankrupt and laid off all their workers. The situation became so bad that people needed shopping bags full of marks to buy basic groceries. Prices rising out of all control like this is called **hyperinflation**.

Did You Know?

During the period of hyperinflation, criminals were more likely to steal your clothes than your money, because money had so little value.

Year	Price	Year	Price
1919	0.26	1923 (Jan.)	700.00
1920	1.20	1923 (May)	1200.00
1921	1.35	1923 (Sept.)	2 000 000.00
1922	3.50	1923 (Nov.)	80 000 000 000.00

Source: Joel Anderson, "A Look at German Inflation, 1914–1924," www.joelscoins.com/exhibger2.htm, 1999, accessed February 15, 2005.

▲ **Figure 6-3** Price of a Loaf of Bread, Germany, 1919–1923. Which year saw the most rapid rise in prices?

Although a new version of the mark was introduced in 1924, and prices stabilized, the damage had been done. People had no confidence in German money or the German economy. Unemployment rose to very high levels.

Checkpoint ✓

1. a) Based on your experience, do prices of things you buy tend to rise quickly, or stay relatively stable these days?
   b) Do some research to find out the actual inflation rate in Canada today. Does what you found out correspond with your own experience as a consumer? Explain.
2. Create a graphic organizer to illustrate how the reparations imposed on Germany by the Treaty of Versailles led to severe hyperinflation.

The Rise of the Nazi Party

In this atmosphere, extreme parties began to gain popularity. They seemed to be the only ones offering a clear message and strong leadership. The Communists wanted to make Germany more like Russia. The **fascists**, or **Nazis**, on the other hand, supported dictatorship and an economy dominated by large corporations. They were also racist, and admired certain so-called "pure" races. Their leader was Adolf Hitler.

Hitler exploited people's bitterness over unemployment, poverty, and the Treaty of Versailles. He told the German people he had a plan to make Germany a great nation again. His plan included the following items.

- He would stop paying the reparations to other nations.
- He would invest in Germany's industries to create growth.
- He would build up Germany's military forces.
- He would end unemployment.

It was a powerful message. Even Martin Niemoeller was impressed. In his 1933 autobiography he looked forward to a "National Revival" that he hoped Hitler would bring about. Niemoeller would later regret this statement.

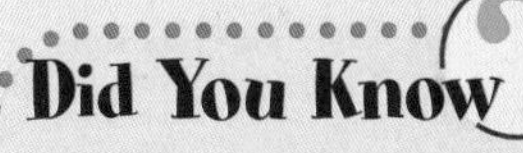

Did You Know?

The word "Nazi" is a shortened version of the first word in the party's German name—"Nazionalistische"—meaning national.

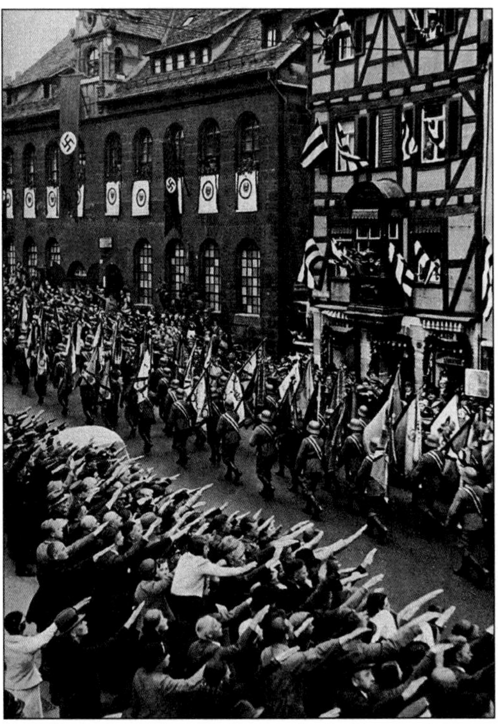

◀ **Figure 6-4** A Nazi rally in 1935. Hitler was a very effective speaker, who appealed to people's emotions more than their intellect. What dangers can you see in this approach to politics?

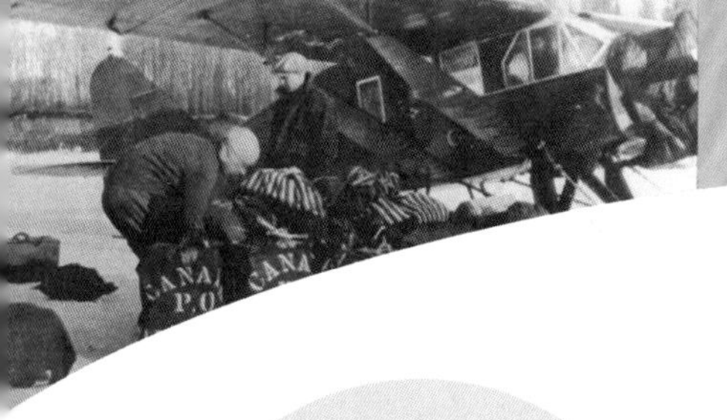

Literacy Hint

Whenever you notice a date in the text, flag it or make a note of what happened on that date. Later, you can go back and organize the events in a timeline (this will help you complete the first "Wrap It Up" activity).

Just before the election of 1933, the German Parliament Buildings burned down. Many historians believe that the Nazis themselves set the fire, but Hitler blamed the Communists—a tactic designed to scare people into voting for the Nazis.

Hitler also enlisted his supporters in the Storm Troopers to threaten voters with violence if they did not openly support the Nazi Party. Not surprisingly, the Nazis won the most seats in the German Parliament, and Adolf Hitler became Chancellor.

Once in office, Hitler asked Parliament for special powers to deal with the "enemies of Germany" who he claimed were trying to destroy the government. He pointed to the burning of the Parliament Buildings as proof that the threat was real.

As soon as Parliament had granted him these powers, he abolished the Parliament! Hitler would now rule as a dictator. He called himself the **Führer** (or leader) and his word was law. Anyone who opposed him would be imprisoned, tortured, or murdered.

Did You Know?

The Nazis never won a majority of seats in any election. But in 1933 they won a plurality—that is, they had more seats than any other party. The other parties were too disorganized to form an alliance against the Nazis. If they had, history might have taken a very different course.

◀ **Figure 6-5** Children as young as seven were expected to join "Hitler Youth" groups like this one. Why do you think Hitler was anxious to introduce young Germans to Nazi ideas at such a young age?

Checkpoint ✓

3. What aspect of Hitler's plan do you think Germans would have found most appealing before his election? Why?

4. Design a rough layout and text for a poster or advertisement that another party could have used to oppose Hitler in his election campaign in 1933.

Hitler's Economic and Social Policies, 1933 to 1938

At first, Hitler focused on building up Germany's economy and reducing unemployment. Like other Western nations, Germany began a huge program of **public works**—projects paid for by the government, such as road building and the installation of water and sewer pipes. Hitler also authorized the production of an affordable *volkswagen* or "people's car," for ordinary working families.

Hitler created hundreds of thousands more jobs when he began to build up the German military. The buildup was above the levels allowed by the Treaty of Versailles, but Hitler claimed that Germany had to protect itself against the Communists, and especially the Soviet Union, if it should attack.

At the same time, Hitler began to reduce people's civil liberties. (Civil liberties are the rights of people to do, say, and act as they please in society, as long as they're not breaking any laws or hurting other people.) Trade unions were banned, newspapers had to support Nazi policies, and teachers were expected to tell their classes how wonderful Hitler was. Books that did not conform to Nazi views were burned in huge bonfires.

Figure 6-6 Students and members of Hitler's Storm Troopers burn books in a public square in Germany. How do you think it would feel to witness an event like this? ▶

Did You Know?

The company that made the Volkswagen survived long after the war ended, and continues to make cars today. A modified version of the original Volkswagen is still sold as the popular "Beetle."

Checkpoint ✓

5. Identify two things that Hitler did to help the German economy after he came to power. Explain how these actions would have helped Germany's financial recovery.
6. What do you think would happen if a Canadian leader today tried to reduce people's civil liberties the way Hitler did?

Hitler and the Jews, 1933 to 1942

Hitler showed early on that he was an enemy of the Jewish people. He believed in the "purity" of what he called the "Aryan" races of northern Europe, including Germans. He believed that Jews, who were not Aryan, were an inferior race.

At first, the Nazis took small steps against the Jewish community. They banned displays of modern art and performances of modern music, claiming that these art forms had been influenced by Jews. Instead, the Nazis promoted traditional German artists and musicians, such as the operatic composer Richard Wagner. School textbooks were changed to portray Jews as evil, so that the youngest of Germans would be exposed to this racist message.

Did You Know?

Mein Kampf—a book Hitler wrote while in prison—contained vicious attacks on Jewish people. In the book, he claimed that Jews supported Germany's enemies in World War I, and thus contributed to its defeat.

The Nuremburg Laws and Kristallnacht

Things got much worse in 1935, when the **Nuremberg Laws** came into effect. The Jewish people in Germany could no longer

- attend a university
- teach in any school or university
- marry a person who was not of the Jewish faith
- hold a government job
- be the author of a book
- be a lawyer or doctor

The word *swastika* to describe the symbol adopted by the Nazi Party was first used in the English language in 1932. Originally an Indian word and symbol meaning "good luck," the Nazis turned it into an emblem of hatred and inhumanity. It is now against the law to display the Nazi swastika in Germany.

As shocking as these laws may seem today, other nations remained silent about them. And within Germany most people were too afraid to speak out. Martin Niemoeller was an exception. He started speaking openly against Hitler's policies in 1934. At a church service in 1937 he said this to a packed congregation:

> We have no more thought of using our own powers to escape the arm of the authorities than had the Apostles of old. [Nor] are we ready to keep silent at man's behest when God commands us to speak.

behest: order

Three days later he was arrested and sent to prison.

In November 1938, the Nazis launched a violent attack on German Jews. Jewish homes, businesses, and synagogues (places of worship) were attacked all over Germany. The event is known as ***Kristallnacht,*** or "night of the broken glass." Individuals and families were terrorized as Nazi-led mobs beat them up at will. Afterwards, the Nazis forced the Jewish people themselves to clean up the mess, and pay for its disposal.

Here's what happened to one young Jewish man named Kurt Weiss, who lived in Breslau.

> My grandmother woke me up, "Kurt, leave the house, the synagogue is burning, get out of the house." My grandfather already disappeared, he had German friends to hide him. He was gone. We lived close by the synagogue. It was a beautiful building, many meters high, with two domes, and had been newly renovated. So I ran out, but before I ran out, I grabbed my army pass and put it in my pocket. I thought it wouldn't hurt.
>
> At about 50 meters, I ran into two Gestapo SS men. They stopped me. 'Are you a Jew?' 'What are you talking about,' I replied. I took out my army pass and showed it to them, but not the inside page [which identified him as a Jew].
>
> On the street I passed only the smashed stores, a liquor store with everything poured on the street. Everything smashed, a crystal store. . . .

Kurt Weiss, quoted on www.hopesite.ca/remember/history/holocaust_victoria/toc_holocaust_victoria.html

For links to sites about anti-semitism

Gestapo SS: the German secret police

Figure 6-7 ▶ Jewish businesses destroyed during Kristallnacht.

Checkpoint ✓

7. If you were a Jewish person living in Germany in 1935 when the Nuremberg Laws were brought in, which of these laws do you think would affect you the most? Why? Discuss with a partner.
8. Today, we use the word "scapegoat" to refer to an innocent person or group that takes the blame for the mistakes or shortcomings of others. Use words or pictures to explain how the idea of the scapegoat applies to Hitler's treatment of the Jewish people.

Ghettoes and Concentration Camps

The situation in Germany got steadily worse. In 1939, the Nazis began moving Jews to special areas of cities, called **ghettoes**. The ghettoes were barricaded from the outside and guarded by soldiers to make sure no one escaped.

The Nazis also built **concentration camps** to imprison Jews, Roma (then called gypsies), Communists, Jehovah's Witnesses, mentally ill people, and other groups considered "undesirable." Prisoners were forced to do hard labour. If they grew too weak, they were killed. Among these prisoners was Martin Niemoeller. He spent the years 1938 to 1945 first in the Sachsenhausen and then in the Dachau concentration camps.

Did You Know?

Pastor Niemoeller survived the concentration camps and the war. He later became president of the World Council of Churches. Niemoeller died in 1984.

For links to sites about Martin Niemoeller

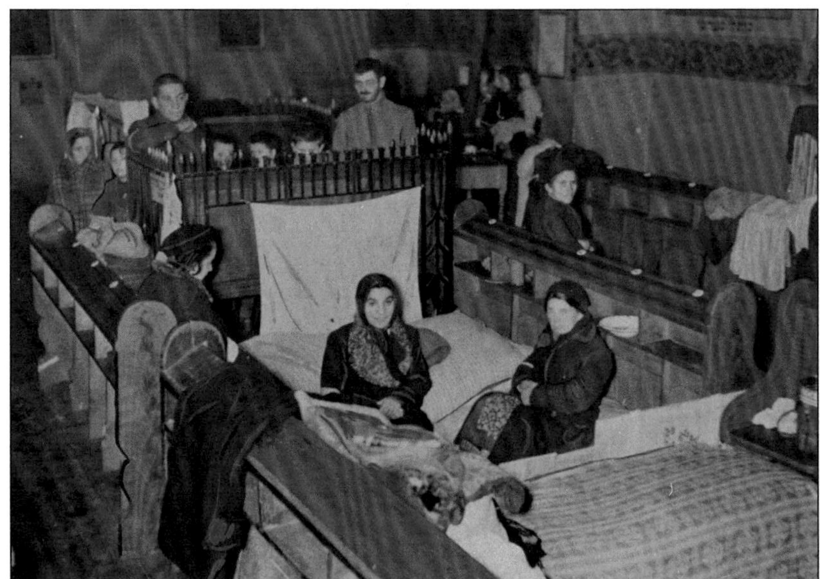

▲ **Figure 6-8** An overcrowded ghetto in Poland. How well would you manage under these circumstances?

Hitler's Final Solution

In January 1942, the Nazis secretly adopted a new policy. They called it the **Final Solution**. To carry out their plan, they built six special camps. These camps were designed not to imprison but to kill all the prisoners sent to them. It is estimated that about 6 million Jews and an additional 1 million people in other "undesirable" categories were exterminated at these death camps. This systematic destruction of human life has become known as the **Holocaust**.

How much of this was known outside Germany before the end of the war is not clear. Jews who managed to get out of Germany and Austria in 1938 and 1939 certainly told tales of terrible suffering and violence. But the Final Solution was not in place until 1942, and very few Jews managed to escape after that time. Nevertheless, many historians find it hard to believe that political leaders outside Germany did not know that Jews there were in very grave trouble.

For links to sites about Holocaust survivors

▲ **Figure 6-9** The barbed wire at the Auschwitz concentration camp in Poland. About 1.5 million prisoners were killed here.

Checkpoint ✓

9. Why do you think it's important for present and future generations to learn about the Holocaust? What lessons can we learn from this horrific incident that would affect our lives and actions today?
10. What situations exist in the world today that you feel Canada's leaders should be speaking out about? How could you encourage them to do so?

The World Reacts to Hitler, 1933 to 1939

At first Western leaders reacted favourably to Hitler's economic reforms and chose to ignore or did not realize the dangers of Nazi rule. The last thing they wanted was another war like the last one, especially in the middle of a Depression. Most leaders, including Mackenzie King, favoured a policy of **appeasement**—giving Hitler what he wanted in order to avoid another war.

Here's what Mackenzie King wrote in his diary in February 1938:

> "I believe Hitler was honest in what he said to me [in June 1937] and will control the situation for peace. He will, however, make known anew his purpose to have a real say in Europe. . . . [Hitler is] indicating real leadership in an appalling European situation. . . ."

National Archives of Canada, Diaries of Mackenzie King, February 20, 1938

But not everyone was in favour of appeasement. Winston Churchill, who became prime minister of Britain in 1940, once said, "An appeaser is one who feeds a crocodile, hoping it will eat him last!"

Literacy Hint

When you read these quotations, keep in mind the time and place in which they were written. What can you conclude from them about Hitler's personality and his ability to persuade people?

Figure 6-10 Prime Minister Mackenzie King meeting with Hitler in 1937. Many leaders seemed anxious to meet the German leader. Why do you think this was?

Checkpoint ✓

11. a) In your own words, explain what is meant by the term "appeasement."
    b) Is appeasement always a mistake? Or are there times when it's a good idea to meet our enemies halfway? Discuss with a partner.
12. Draw a cartoon to illustrate the meaning of Churchill's quotation.

Jewish Refugees

Events in Germany alarmed the Jewish community, and many German Jews tried to get out. Although some did manage to escape, many countries were unwilling to take in large numbers of refugees.

In March 1939, the SS *St. Louis* left Hamburg with 907 Jewish men, women, and children aboard. The ship sailed first for Cuba. When it arrived, however, the Cuban government would not let the passengers land. Neither would Argentina, Uruguay, Paraguay, Panama, or the United States.

A number of prominent Canadians sent a telegram to Prime Minister King, begging him to allow the ship into the country. But King refused. Frederick Blair, the prime minister's chief adviser on immigration matters, expressed the government's position this way:

> Canada cannot open its doors wide enough to take in the hundreds of thousands of Jewish people who want to leave Europe: the line must be drawn somewhere.

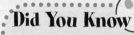

Did You Know?

From 1933 to 1939, Canada admitted only about 4000 Jewish immigrants. Compare this with the United States, which took in about 240 000.

Figure 6-11 Passengers on the SS *St. Louis*. Could you imagine something similar happening in Canada today?

It was true that unemployment was high, but this was not the only factor in King's decision. **Anti-Semitism** (prejudice against Jews) was widespread in many nations—including Canada. Many Canadian clubs and organizations would not allow Jews to become members. Jews were barred from some professions, and many Jewish people already living in Canada found it necessary to hide their identity in order to get work.

The SS *St. Louis* could find no country that would accept its human cargo, so it returned to Hamburg. Many of the passengers would later die at the hands of the Nazis.

Checkpoint ✓

13. Edmund Burke (1729–1797), a British politician, once wrote: "All that is necessary for the triumph of evil is that good [people] do nothing." How does this quotation apply to the SS *St. Louis* incident and to the plight of Jews in the 1930s in general?

14. a) What is your reaction to Canada's refusal to admit the refugees on the SS *St. Louis*?
    b) In your opinion, does Canada have a duty to accept refugees who are fleeing from dangerous situations? Discuss with a partner or in a small group.

Anti-aircraft gunfire became known as "ack-ack" in 1939. "Ack" was the military word to denote the letter "a" at that time, so "ack-ack fire" became established in the language. Today, incoming enemy planes are usually met with heat-seeking or guided missiles, and the letter "a" is now denoted by the word "alpha."

The Road to War, 1936 to 1939

While Hitler was pursuing his anti-Semitic policies at home, he was also plotting to extend Germany's borders. After gaining complete power, Hitler set out to build up the German military machine. The *Wehrmacht* (army), *Luftwaffe* (air force), and *Kriegsmarine* (navy) became fearsome weapons. The Treaty of Versailles said that this was illegal, but Hitler went ahead anyway.

Since the other nations did not try to stop the military buildup, Hitler decided to put it to use. Between 1936 and 1939 he began taking over more and more territory in Europe. Each time he did so, other nations failed to react. Hitler learned from this that he could get much of what he wanted without actually going to war. He got bolder and bolder, believing that the Western nations would never try to stop him.

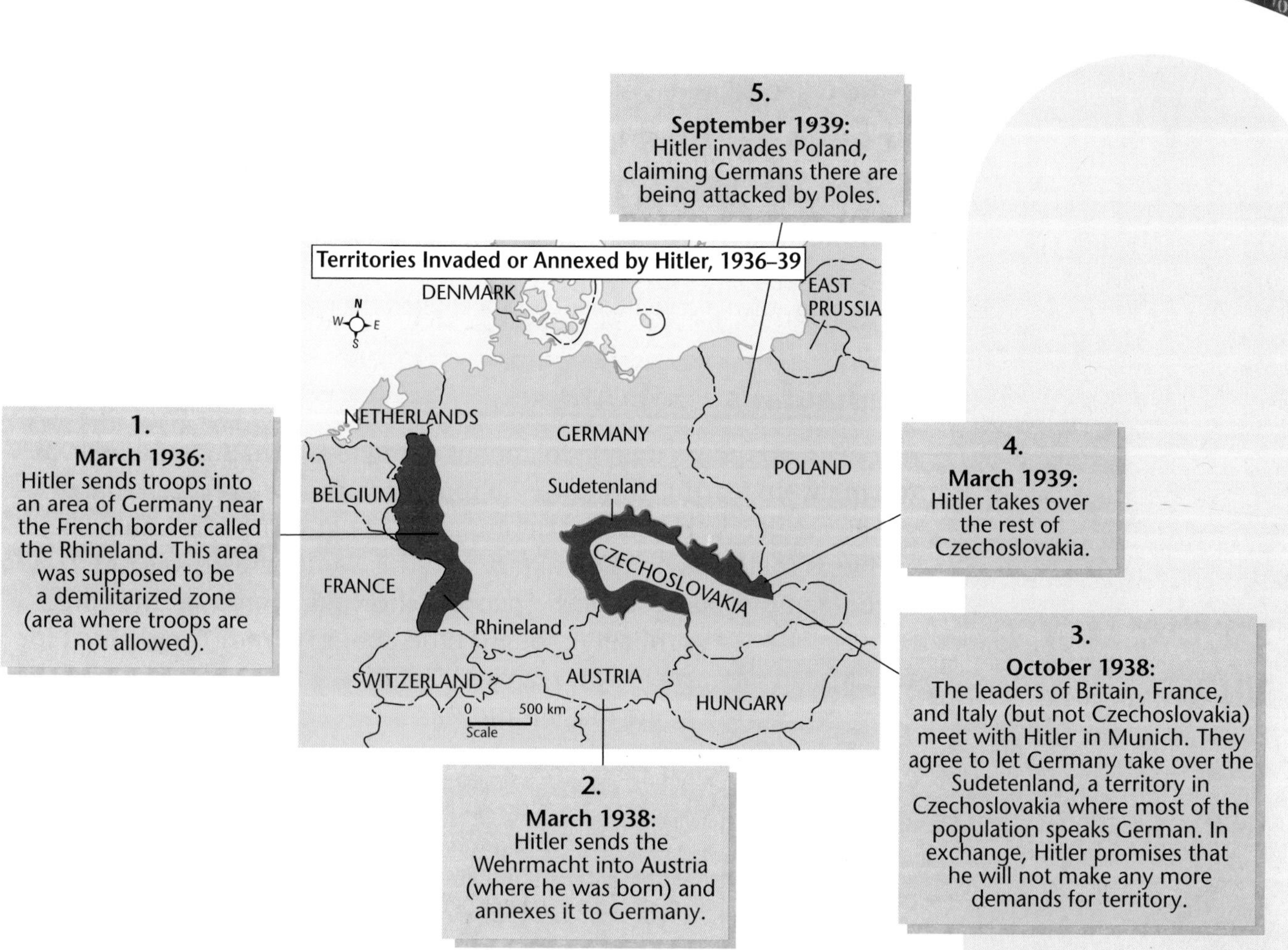

5.
September 1939:
Hitler invades Poland, claiming Germans there are being attacked by Poles.
Territories Invaded or Annexed by Hitler, 1936–39
DENMARK
EAST PRUSSIA
N
W
E
S
NETHERLANDS
GERMANY
POLAND
BELGIUM
Sudetenland
CZECHOSLOVAKIA
FRANCE
Rhineland
SWITZERLAND
AUSTRIA
HUNGARY
0
500 km
Scale
1.
March 1936:
Hitler sends troops into an area of Germany near the French border called the Rhineland. This area was supposed to be a demilitarized zone (area where troops are not allowed).
4.
March 1939:
Hitler takes over the rest of Czechoslovakia.
3.
October 1938:
The leaders of Britain, France, and Italy (but not Czechoslovakia) meet with Hitler in Munich. They agree to let Germany take over the Sudetenland, a territory in Czechoslovakia where most of the population speaks German. In exchange, Hitler promises that he will not make any more demands for territory.
2.
March 1938:
Hitler sends the Wehrmacht into Austria (where he was born) and annexes it to Germany.

▲ **Figure 6-12** Territories invaded or annexed by Hitler, 1936–39. Which three countries do you think Hitler attacked once war was declared? Check back once you've read Chapter 7 to see if you guessed correctly.

The invasion of Poland in 1939 finally forced Britain, France, and Canada to act. Britain and France demanded that Germany withdraw. Hitler never even replied to their message. On September 3, Britain and France declared war on Germany.

September 3 was part of the Labour Day weekend in Canada. Before war could be declared, Parliament had to be recalled. This took a week, because members had to travel from all across the country by train. Finally, on September 10, 1939, Canada, too, declared war. For the second time in a generation, Canada was at war.

Checkpoint ✓

15. Look at a map of Europe in an atlas. Compare Germany's boundaries today with those shown in Figure 6-12. Is it bigger or smaller? What other changes over time do you notice in the countries in this region?
16. As you read in Chapter 4, Canada had already made it clear to Britain that it would no longer automatically go to war to defend Britain's interests. Why, then, do you think Canada entered the war so quickly in 1939?

Canadians Look Ahead

How do you think people felt about going to war in September 1939? Some were fearful. Some were happy because they realized that it truly meant the end of the Depression. The government would spend billions of dollars on the military and this would create lots of jobs for the unemployed. Most of the people who volunteered for the Forces probably thought little about Poland. They joined for their own reasons. The following extract gives us some insight into this.

> I wasn't patriotic. None of my buddies were. I just wanted some good clothes and hot showers and three decent meals a day and a few dollars for tobacco and beer in my pocket, and that's about all I wanted. . . .

Quoted in Barry Broadfoot, *Ten Lost Years, 1929–1939* (Toronto: Doubleday Canada Ltd., 1973), p. 373

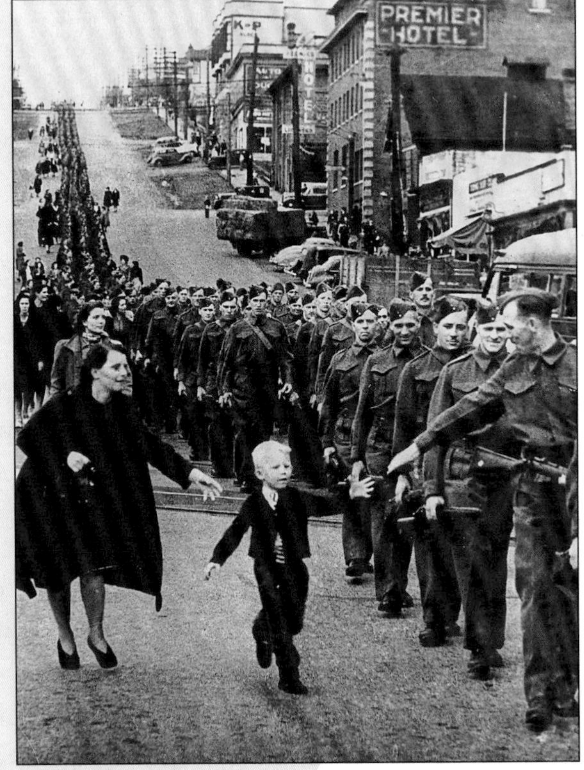

◀ **Figure 6-13** A young boy runs to say goodbye to his father, Private Jack Bernard. Imagine you are present at this scene. What do you think the father is thinking? How would this situation make bystanders feel?

History Skill: Evaluating Short- and Long-Term Consequences

Historians evaluate the significance of an event by considering both its short-term consequences (what happened right away) and long-term consequences (what happened over time). Often an event that has a negative effect at the time may have positive long-term consequences, and vice versa. A cause-and-effect chart can help to illustrate these connections.

Step 1

Decide what question you need to answer. For example, you might ask

- What is the connection between . . . and . . . ?
- What was the result of . . . ?
- How did . . . affect . . . ?

Let's use an event you're already familiar with to illustrate:

How did the stock market crash affect Canadians?

Step 2

Create a cause-and-effect chart to illustrate the short-term consequences of events.

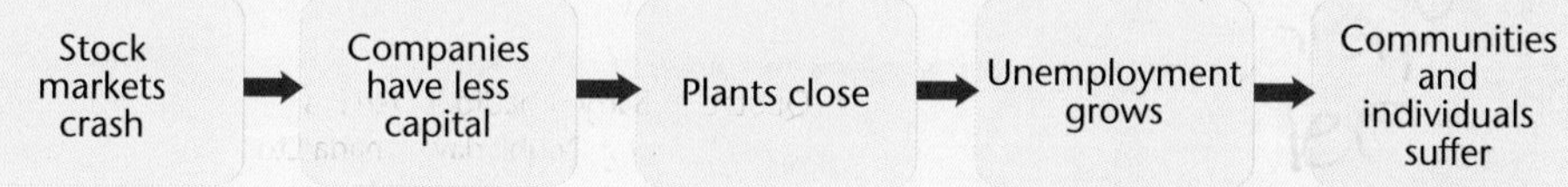

Step 3

Create another chart to illustrate the long-term consequences.

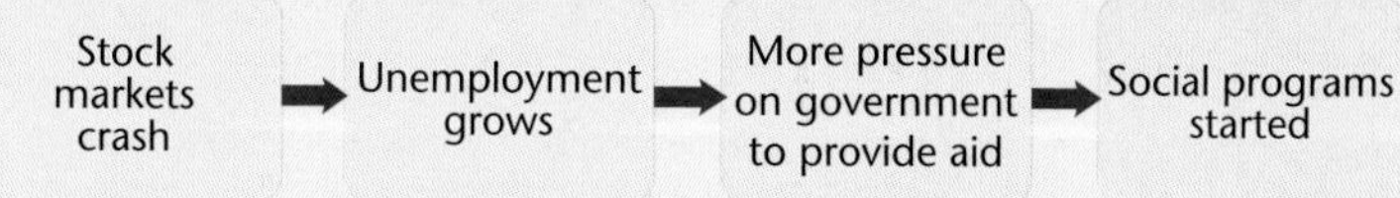

Step 4

Consider the two charts, and decide which has the greater historical significance. Did the event have a greater impact in the short term or the long term? Was one set of consequences positive and the other negative? What conclusions can you draw based on this information?

To evaluate the effects of an event . . .

- ✓ ask an appropriate question
- ✓ create a cause-and-effect chart to show short-term consequences
- ✓ create another chart to show long-term consequences
- ✓ ask: What conclusion can you draw based on this information?

Practise It!

1. Look at the two charts of the Great Depression above. Do you think that Canadians' suffering was outweighed by the long-term benefits for society? Give reasons for your answer in a paragraph.
2. a) Create a cause-and-effect chart to show the short-term consequences of the Treaty of Versailles in Germany.
   b) Create another chart to show how the Treaty of Versailles contributed to the rise of Hitler in the long term.
3. What is one conclusion you can draw about the treaty based on this information?

Chapter Summary

While Canadians at home were dealing with the Depression, even more devastating events were brewing in Europe. In this chapter you learned about the following:

- The terms of the Treaty of Versailles created great hardship and economic suffering in Germany, as well as feelings of humiliation.
- Adolf Hitler gained power through a combination of legal and illegal means. Once in power, he instituted programs to address Germany's economic problems and rebuilt the military. His anti-Semitic policies eventually led to the mass killing of Jews and other "undesirable" groups in death camps.
- Even after he began attacking other countries, Canada and other foreign governments favoured a policy of appeasement toward Hitler.
- Canada accepted very few Jewish refugees during the 1930s.
- In September 1939, Britain, France, and Canada finally declared war on Germany.

In the next chapter, you will read about what happened during World War II—the second great war of the 20th century.

1920 -1939

Nazis

Nuremburg Laws

The Holocaust

The West's reaction

Wrap It Up

Understand It

1. Make a timeline of the main political, economic, social, and military events described in this chapter.

Think About It

2. Research some of the people in Germany who spoke up against the Nazis in the 1930s. Choose one of these people and work on your own or with a partner to write a report describing what the person did, and why you think that person is a hero.

Communicate It

3. Work with a partner. Imagine it is 1938, and Hitler wants to take over the German-speaking parts of Czechoslovakia. Role-play a conversation between Prime Minister Mackenzie King and Winston Churchill in which each defends his own view on how to react to Hitler.
4. Imagine that you were one of the passengers on the SS *St. Louis*. Write a short letter to Prime Minister Mackenzie King in which you
   a) describe some of the things that have happened to Jews under the Nazis, and
   b) give reasons why he should allow all the passengers to settle in Canada.

Apply It

5. At what stage do you think Canada and other Western nations should have acted to stop Hitler? What actions could they have taken to avoid a world war?

Performance Task

Review Your Predictions

At the beginning of this unit, you made predictions based on three photos. Refer back to your predictions. How accurate were they? Make a list of three key things that you learned about each of the main topics in the unit.

Audiotape a Radio Show

In this unit you learned about life in the 1920s and 1930s in Canada. Since radio was one of the most popular forms of entertainment during the period (as well as a source of news and information), it's fitting to use this format to demonstrate what you've learned.

Step 1

Review the History Skills from this unit:

- Chapter 3: Creating a Timeline (page 76)
- Chapter 5: Preparing a News Story (pages 107–108)
- Chapter 6: Evaluating Short- and Long-Term Consequences (pages 127–128)

You'll be using these skills in the following activity.

Step 2

Review the Inquiry Method on page xii. Use these steps to guide your research for the activities in Step 3.

Step 3

Make a timeline of major national and international events that occurred during the 1920s and 1930s. Use the timeline to help you plan the contents of your radio show.

Work in a group to research, create, and audiotape a radio show from either the 1920s or the 1930s.

You should include the following features in your radio show:

- news stories about national events
- at least one news story about international events
- a commentary or interview predicting the likely short- and long-term consequences of one of the events you reported on
- a financial report

To complete your radio show, choose one or more of the following, or think of your own:

- advertisements for popular consumer items
- a sports report
- an interview with a prominent person
- a fashion report
- a farm report
- popular music from the period in question

Step 5

Audiotape your radio show and play it for your classmates.

UNIT 3 Coming of Age, 1939-1960

Your Predictions Please # 3

Study the three photographs. They show some features of Canadians' lives between 1939 and 1960. Consider the clues beside each one. Then make some predictions about what you think you'll discover in this unit.

Clue 1 How is she dressed?
Clue 2 What emotions do you think her face shows?
Clue 3 Why might she think, as a woman, that it was especially important to do her job effectively?

Prediction 1
Based on the clues, what do you think you'll learn about the role that Canadian women played in World War II?

◀ F.R. Kemp, a member of the Women's Royal Canadian Naval Service (WRENS), arrives in England to work as a radio operator.

Clue 4 How organized does the drill appear to be?
Clue 5 Do you think the table would protect the children from a nuclear bomb?
Clue 6 Why, in your opinion, would adults ask students to practise a drill like this?

▲ Children and their teacher practise "duck and cover" to protect themselves from a nuclear bomb attack.

Prediction 2
Based on the clues, what do you think you'll learn about Canadian reactions to the possibility of a nuclear war between the United States and the Soviet Union?

Clue 7 How does this group of teenagers reflect the increased wealth in Canada during the 1950s?

Clue 8 How do you think Canadians' lives were changed by more affordable products like cars?

Clue 9 Since there were more young people than ever before, how do you think this would affect society?

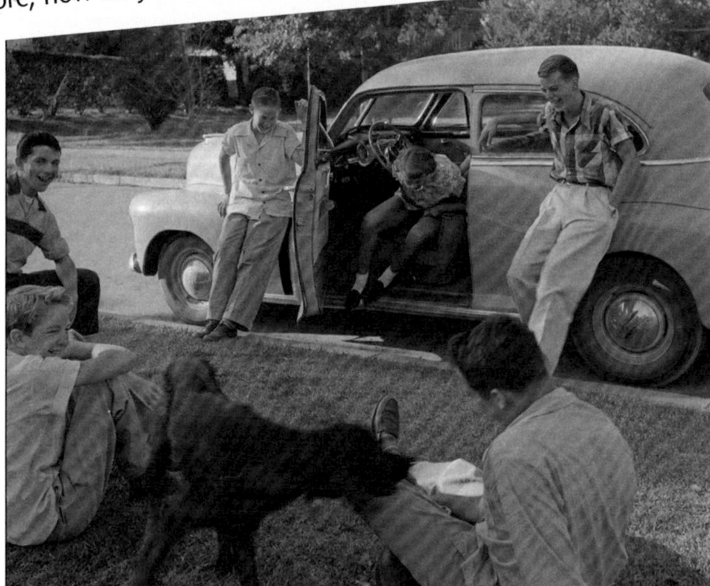

▲ A group of teenagers gathered around a car in 1953.

Prediction 3

Based on the clues, what do you think you'll learn about new consumer products and the lives of young people?

In this unit you will explore . . .

- some forces and events that have influenced Canada's policies and identity
- Canada's participation in World War II
- changes in Canada's international status
- changing economic conditions that affected Canadians
- using methods of research
- interpreting and analyzing information

Experience History

Some of the experiences people have are beyond their control. You know all about bad luck—but you also know that some of the things that happen today are a result of plans or decisions you made yesterday. Some of your experiences will be a result of what happened (or didn't happen) in the past. Similarly, events in history can help to shape present experiences.

Choose one of the three photographs to think about more carefully. What important events may have led up to the situation it shows? What important plans or decisions would the people in the photo have made earlier? Record your ideas in a list, with a short explanation of each point you make.

Unit 3 Performance Task

At the end of this unit you'll use what you've learned to **plan a "Then and Now" Local History Display.**

Chapter 7

Canadians Overseas in World War II

For links to general sites about World War II

The War, Year by Year

World War II lasted six years, from 1939 to 1945. It was fought in Europe, North Africa, the Atlantic, and the Pacific, and involved nations on all five continents. Battles were fought on land, at sea, and in the air. In this chapter we'll examine some of the important contributions that Canadians made to the war. First, though, here's a quick year-by-year overview of the course of the war.

1939 Germany signs a non-aggression pact (an agreement not to attack one another) with the Soviet Union, then invades Poland. Britain, France, and the Commonwealth countries, including Canada, declare war on Germany.

1940 In six months, Hitler's army overwhelms Denmark, Norway, Luxembourg, Belgium, and finally France. Italy joins the war on Germany's side. Britain and the Commonwealth now stands alone against the Axis powers. Germany launches massive air attacks against towns and cities in England in the Battle of Britain.

1941 Having failed to capture Britain, Hitler turns east, breaking his pact with the Soviets and attacking Leningrad and Moscow.

In August, the Allies launch a disastrous raid at Dieppe, France, after which more than half of the Canadian soldiers in the attack are captured, wounded, or dead.

In December, the Japanese air force captures Hong Kong in 17 days and destroys the American base at Pearl Harbor (in Hawaii). The Americans now join the Allies against Japan and Germany.

1942 The Allies win major victories in the Pacific (at Midway) and North Africa (at El-Alamein). German U-boats step up their attacks on convoys in the Atlantic in an attempt to cut Britain off from its supply route.

1943 The Soviets push German troops back at Stalingrad. In July, the Allies move from North Africa into Sicily and up the Italian peninsula.

1944 The Allies launch a massive campaign in Normandy, France, on June 6—D-Day. From there, they continue to push west, while the Soviet Union attacks from the east.

1945 Allied forces from the east and west meet in Germany. Hitler, recognizing that he's defeated, commits suicide. In May, Germany surrenders.

In August, the United States drops two atomic bombs on Japan, wiping out the cities of Hiroshima and Nagasaki in a matter of seconds. Japan surrenders.

Words to Know

Battle of the Atlantic
theatres of war
corvettes
D-Day
radar

Allied Side	Countries	Year of Entry
	Britain	1939
	France	1939
	Canada	1939
	Other Commonwealth members, such as Newfoundland	1939
	United States	1941
	Soviet Union	1941
Axis Side		
	Germany	1939
	Italy	1940
	Japan	1941

▲ **Figure 7-1** The Major Alliances of World War II. In what ways do you think Britain depended on its allies?

Checkpoint ✓

1. Based on this overview, in what year would you say that the tide of war turned in favour of the Allies? Why?

Key Learnings

In this chapter, you will explore

- Canada's military contributions in World War II
- how Canadians, as individuals and as communities, contributed to the war effort
- the advances in technology that have changed war

The War at Sea

When Canada went to war in 1939, its navy played a very important role. Britain could not defeat Germany unless food and military supplies were shipped in from North America. In fact, on its own, Britain could not produce enough food or military supplies to survive.

Since Britain is an island, Germany tried to form a blockade by surrounding the country with hundreds of U-boats (submarines). Individual submarines were vulnerable, especially when sailing on the surface, so they would hunt in groups called wolf packs to make it harder for Allied ships to sink them. They would surround their target and move in for the kill, just as wolves do in the wild.

To counteract the wolf packs, the Allies used a convoy system similar to the system used in World War I. The convoys often left North America from Canadian ports such as Halifax, sailing in groups of up to 30. The struggle between the wolf packs and the convoys became known as the **Battle of the Atlantic**. It was one of the crucial **theatres** (sites of action) of the war.

Frank Curry sailed on a **corvette** for five-and-a-half years as an ordinary seaman. He had spent his childhood in Winnipeg in the 1930s, listening excitedly to reports on the radio about events in Europe. When war was finally declared, he couldn't wait to sign up.

Figure 7-2 A convoy about to leave Bedford Basin, Nova Scotia. Would you have felt safe travelling aboard one of these ships?

Curry had a rude awakening when he found himself out in the North Atlantic in a corvette, seasick and shivering with the cold, searching hour after hour in the darkness for any sign of German U-boats. "It was a shattering experience," he wrote.

> The corvettes . . . were . . . marvellous ships for . . . escorting convoys. They could stay out for long periods of time. They were built simply as covers around engines and large oil tanks. The rest of the space—whatever was left over—was where they crammed in the crew. The only living space you could call your own was wherever you slung your hammock, and that could be anywhere, alongside a pipe or a boiler or a walkway. There weren't such things as cabins or sleeping quarters.
>
> . . . [When I was called to duty] I would slide out of the hammock to the steel deck, always awash with seawater. I'd still be bone-tired and half sick, clutching at the stanchions, as the ship plunged and rolled, and I'd glance at the weary off-watch sailors wedged, fully clothed, as I had been, onto the lockers or in their hammocks, with their lifejackets wrapped around them.

Frank Curry, quoted in Bill McNeil, *Voices of a War Remembered: An Oral History of Canadians in World War II* (Toronto: Doubleday Canada Ltd., 1991), pp. 291–292

Literacy Hint

As you read about the first-hand experiences of different World War II participants, try to put yourself in their place. Consider how they felt about their experiences and how they might feel about war in general.

"Corvette" is also the name of a popular sports car that debuted in the 1950s. Modern versions of the car are being driven to this day. They're known for their speed and sleek style.

stanchions: posts

◀ **Figure 7-3** Women didn't normally serve at sea, but they still played a vital role as part of the Women's Royal Canadian Naval Service. Wrens (as they were called) served in a variety of shore-based positions, including clerk, messenger, switchboard or teletype operator, wireless telegraphist, and motor-transport driver. These Canadian Wrens are about to leave Canada to serve in Britain. Why do you think the navy was anxious to recruit women to fill these positions?

Did You Know?

A German submarine, U-537, set up a weather station in Martin Bay, Labrador, to transmit weather signals to European stations. The signals were used to prepare weather forecasts for German ships and U-boats operating in the North Atlantic. The station was not discovered until 1980.

For links to sites about the war at sea

The War Closes In on Canada's Shores

At first, it seemed that the German U-boats might win. In 1942 alone, the wolf packs sank 1164 Allied ships. Britain's survival was on the line.

Some of the naval fighting took place close to Canada's shores. German U-boats were detected and sunk as they patrolled the mouth of the St. Lawrence River. Submarines were also sunk off the coast of Nova Scotia, where they waited for convoys to pass. The Allied side lost merchant ships in the waters off Bell Island in Conception Bay. A Nova Scotia–Newfoundland ferry was also sunk, and 137 people died, including many women and children.

Recognizing the strategic location of Newfoundland, both Canada and the United States established military bases in Newfoundland and in Labrador. The Americans built a naval base at Argentia in Placentia Bay, an army base at Pleasantville near St. John's, and an air force base at Stephenville. Canadians and Newfoundlanders could no longer think of World War II as a distant war. By 1943, the convoys and the corvettes had improved their efficiency. The U-boats were less successful. As the year wore on, the wolf packs were in retreat, and supplies began to get through more regularly. As Prime Minister Winston Churchill of Britain said at the time, the tide had turned.

During the five years of the war, 25 000 merchant ships were convoyed across the Atlantic. Only the British navy played a larger role in winning the Battle of the Atlantic and winning the war in Europe.

Checkpoint ✓

2. Draw a diagram that shows how the convoy system was able to defeat the German blockade around Britain during World War II.
3. Imagine that you are a member of the naval services. Write a short letter home describing how you feel you're helping the war effort.
4. Find Argentia, Pleasantville, and Stephenville on a map of Newfoundland and Labrador. Why were these good locations for American bases?

Did You Know?

The Canadian army took part in all the major campaigns of the war. At its peak, almost 500 000 soldiers were serving at one time. During the course of the war, it is estimated that 23 000 soldiers lost their lives and 58 000 were injured.

The War on Land

By June 1940, Britain was the only major power in Europe that Germany did not control. This meant that its overseas Commonwealth allies—such as Canada and Australia—had an especially important role to play.

Although Canada had a fairly small population, it was able to assemble a strong fighting force. Among those who signed up early on was 21-year-old Charlie Martin. Like Frank Curry, he'd heard the radio reports from Europe through the 1930s. Now, Hitler had most of Europe in his power, and Britain was in desperate need. In June 1940, Martin left the family farm to join the infantry, and was assigned to the Queen's Own Rifles. A little more than a year later, the battalion was shipped out to Britain. Losses occurred in both winning and losing campaigns. Here are just some of the major battles that Canadians participated in.

The Dieppe Raid, 1942

The first major mission for Canadian soldiers stationed in Britain was to raid the German forces at the French coastal town of Dieppe. Their goal was to make a quick landing, assess the strength of the German defences, and leave again.

The Canadians crossed the English Channel by boat on August 19, 1942. John Mellor of Kitchener, Ontario, was among those who fought at Dieppe. Here's how he described the landing:

As soon as [the Canadians] dropped into the water from their landing craft they ran into this murderous barrage of gunfire. Many died before they took even one step forward. Those that followed had to step over their bodies. . . .

If they managed to get on the beach at all, they found it totally strung with entanglements of barbed wire . . . and sown with mines. Even if they got across that, they came face to face with the actual sea wall itself, which was [about 2.5 metres] high. That was covered with rolls of barbed wire too, on the top, and there were machine-gun posts all the way along.

The whole front itself, [1.6 km] long and crescent shaped, had boarding houses and hotels that were filled with hundreds of Germans with machine-guns and mortars zeroing in on the main beach.

Voices of a War Remembered, pp. 269–70

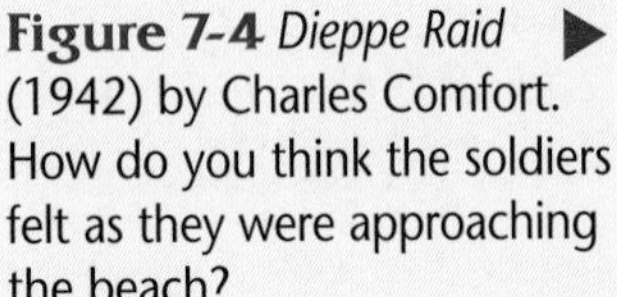

Figure 7-4 *Dieppe Raid* (1942) by Charles Comfort. How do you think the soldiers felt as they were approaching the beach?

Literacy Hint

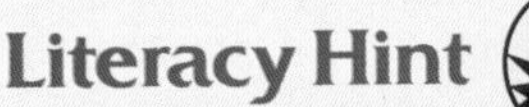

If you add the numbers in rows 2 to 5 of this table, the total (5577) exceeds the total shown in row 1 (4963). This is because some of the wounded in row 3 were also counted in rows 4 and 5.

Figure 7-5 Human Cost to Canadians of Dieppe Raid, 1942. Use these numbers to explain why the Canadian forces were so devastated by the Dieppe Raid.

Canadian Soldiers in Dieppe Raid	Number	Percentage
1. Total number of Canadians involved	4963	100.0
2. Killed	907	18.3
3. Wounded	586	11.8
4. Captured as prisoners of war	1874	37.7
5. Returned to England	2210	44.5

Source: Adapted from Gerald Hallowell, ed., *The Oxford Companion to Canadian History* (Don Mills, ON: Oxford University Press, 2004), p. 180.

The Allies' light tanks proved useless on the stony beach as rocks jammed their caterpillar tracks. German airplanes finished off the job by bombing the beach. Miraculously, John Mellor survived all this, but he didn't get off easily. A fragment of metal knocked his eye out.

Charlie Martin was not at Dieppe, but he benefited from the lessons learned there. Just two years later, he and the Queen's Own Rifles were part of another beach landing not far from Dieppe. As you will see, in 1944, the generals would deliberately select sandy beaches where there were no cliffs. The tanks and trucks could be driven straight out of the landing craft without getting jammed on the stony beach, and there was nowhere for defenders to hide. But there were people who wondered—John Mellor among them—why so many soldiers had to die at Dieppe in order to learn these lessons. Some felt that the military made excuses for a badly planned mission, and that the planners should have foreseen these problems before the raid.

Soldiers in the Pacific

So far we've looked at World War II in Europe. But Japan had been at war with its neighbours, especially China, since 1937. In 1939, Japan joined the Axis nations and continued its military operations in the Pacific. It was decided to send Canadian and other Allied soldiers to Hong Kong—a British colony at the time—to try to keep it from falling to Japan.

The Canadian troops saw little action there until late in 1941. At that time the British expected Japan to attack, so they urgently requested more troops. In October 1941, 1975 Canadian soldiers were shipped from Vancouver, arriving in Hong Kong in mid-November. They formed part of a total defence force of 14 000 troops.

On December 8, Japan attacked. It captured Hong Kong in only 17 days. By the time Hong Kong surrendered on Christmas Day, 290 Canadians had been killed and 493 injured. This was a total casualty rate of almost 40 percent. The survivors spent the rest of the war as prisoners of war (POWs).

The POWs in Japanese camps were badly treated. Many were not given enough food, were forced to do hard labour or to march long distances to new locations. POWs found to have broken camp rules were brutally punished. Certainly the conditions that the Canadians met in the Japanese POW camps were among the very worst in the war.

TIMELINE: Key Events in the Pacific War

- **1937** War between Japan and China begins
- **1940** Japanese troops occupy Malaya, Vietnam, and other countries in Southeast Asia
- **1941** Japanese troops capture Hong Kong, taking Canadian troops prisoner
- **1941** Japanese air force attacks American base in Pearl Harbor, Hawaii; United States declares war on Japan and Germany
- **1943** American forces begin to push back Japanese occupiers and liberate captured territory
- **1945** American planes drop nuclear bombs on Japanese cities of Hiroshima and Nagasaki; Japan surrenders

Figure 7-6 A group of Canadian and British prisoners being liberated from a POW camp, August 1945. What do you see in the picture that shows the prisoners have been mistreated?

John Ford, from Port-aux-Basques, Newfoundland, became a POW after being captured in Java in 1942. He was first held in Singapore, and then taken to Nagasaki, where he was put to work building ships.

> It was slave labour. . . . You'd have your breakfast (a small tin of rice) in the morning. You'd take your lunch with you, a little rice can. Then, when you'd go back to the camp again at night, the same thing, a little bit of rice. Occasionally, probably once a month or once every two months, you'd get a bit of cabbage stew. Nothing, only water.

Danette Dooley, "A-Bomb Survivor Wants Recognition," *St. John's Evening Telegram,* 20 August 2005

Checkpoint ✓

5. a) What reasons did the Allies give for the failure of the Dieppe Raid?
   b) As a class, discuss whether you think the Allies' explanation seems reasonable or whether they were making excuses for their mistakes.
6. Imagine that you were a prisoner of war in a Japanese POW camp. Outline three ways you would have tried to cope with the mistreatment.

History Skill: Reading and Drawing Maps

When you use or make a map in history, you need to recognize and apply some basic mapping principles: symbol, location, direction, and distance. Every map needs a clear title, as well.

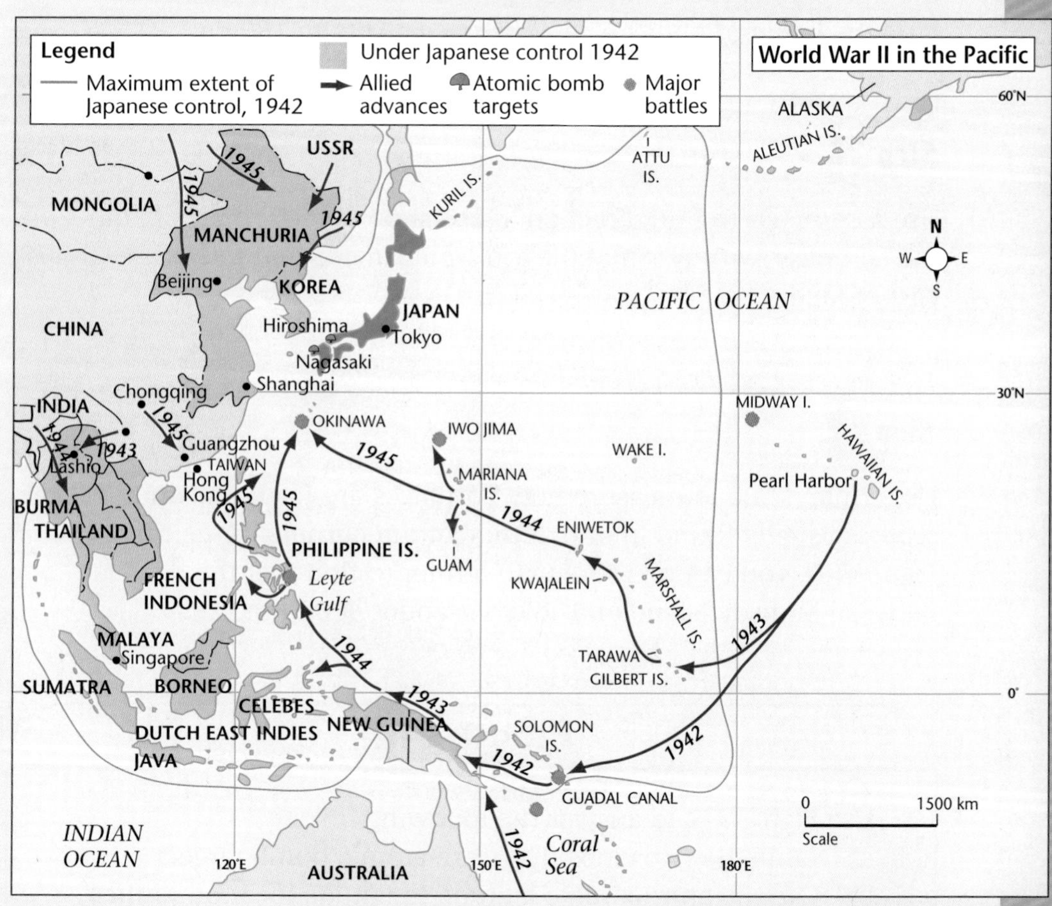

Source: Elisabeth Gaynor Ellis and Anthony Esler, *World History: Connections to Today, Teacher's Edition*, Prentice Hall (USA), 1997, page 805.

Figure 7-7 The War in the Pacific, 1942–45

Step 1

Use a legend to identify the meaning of symbols, lines, and colours that represent real things. The legend is usually found to one side or corner of the map. In Figure 7-7, the map legend shows that green areas and lines represent Japan. Red lines show the advance of the Allied forces, while orange and grey indicate battles and bomb targets.

Step 2

Identify the method used to show location. For example, road maps use a letter-number grid of crisscrossed lines. Figure 7-7 uses a grid of blue lines for latitude (across) and longitude (up and down). Look for the numbers of these lines along the bottom and the side of the map. Find the battle of Midway at 30 degrees north by 180 degrees east.

Step 3

Use a compass to find direction. Maps show direction using points of the compass, with north at the top. You can see that Midway Island is east of Japan.

Step 4

Use a map scale to measure how far places are from one another. The scale is usually found in one of the bottom corners of the map. On Figure 7-7, you can measure with a ruler to find that the distance between Midway Island and Tokyo is about 4000 km.

When reading or making a map . . .

- ✓ use a legend to identify symbols, lines, and colours
- ✓ identify the method used to show location
- ✓ use a compass to find direction
- ✓ use a scale to measure distances on the map
- ✓ include a clear title when you make a map

Practise It!

1. Use Figure 7-7 to answer the following:
   a) Name the two cities that were atomic bomb targets.
   b) Give the approximate latitude-longitude location of the battle of Guadalcanal.
   c) In what direction had the Allied fleet sailed from Hawaii to get to Guadalcanal in 1942?
   d) How large was the area controlled by Japan east and west along 0 degrees of latitude?
2. Use the map to describe the Allied plan to defeat Japan.

The Italian Campaign, 1943–45

One of Canada's successful campaigns was fought in Italy. In 1943 the Canadians made their way up the country's east coast, fighting battles at Ortona and Ravenna. This involved house-to-house fighting as the Canadians slowly pushed back the German occupiers. House-to-house can be a most vicious method of fighting because enemy troops are at close quarters and can quickly surprise and kill one another. In the Battle of Ortona, many troops were killed on both sides within only a few days. But by the spring of 1945 the Allies had liberated all of Italy, and a successful campaign came to an end.

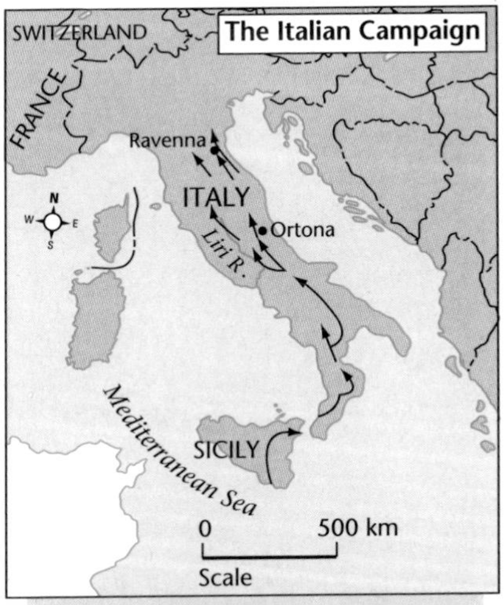

The Italian Campaign
SWITZERLAND
FRANCE
Ravenna
ITALY
Ortona
Liri R.
SICILY
Mediterranean Sea
0 500 km
Scale

▲ **Figure 7-8** The Canadian army's Italian campaign. What geographic features can you see that might make Italy hard to defend?

D-Day and Beyond, 1944 to 1945

In the early morning of June 6, 1944, Charlie Martin and the Queen's Own Rifles were on a landing craft heading for a strip of sandy beach in the Normandy region of France. The seas were rough, but Charlie, who was by now sergeant-major of A Company, felt calm. He and his men had been training for two years—and this was their chance to put what they had learned into practice.

Martin was about to take part in one of the most important battles of the war: the **D-Day** landing. The total Allied invasion force numbered 150 000 troops, of whom about 30 000 were Canadian. Their mission was to capture the beaches of Normandy, then push inland. Charlie's boat was the first to hit shore.

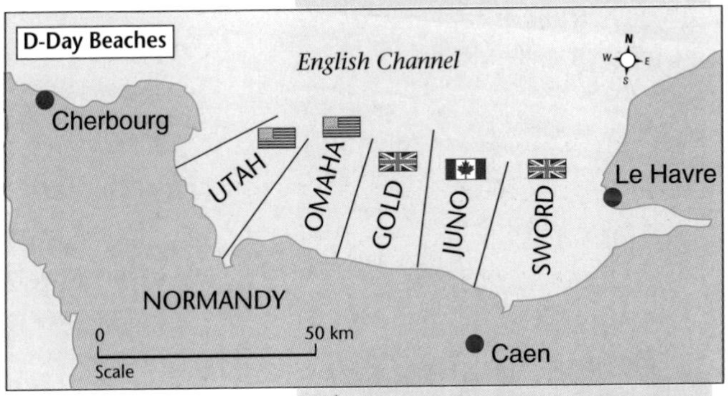

D-Day Beaches
English Channel
Cherbourg
UTAH
OMAHA
GOLD
JUNO
SWORD
Le Havre
NORMANDY
0 50 km
Scale
Caen

▲ **Figure 7-9** The attack took place along five beaches code-named Utah, Omaha, Gold, Juno, and Sword. Canadian troops were assigned to Juno. By the end of the first day, the Canadians had pushed farther inland than any of the other Allied forces. What lessons did the Canadians learn at Dieppe that helped them make the D-Day landing a success?

> The order rang out "Down ramp." The moment the ramp came down, heavy machine-gun fire broke out from somewhere back of the seawall. Mortars were dropping all over the beach. . . .

Charles Martin, *Battle Diary: From D-Day and Normandy to the Zuider Zee and Ve* (Toronto: Dundurn Press, 1994), pp. 6–7

By the end of the first day, A Company had advanced seven miles (11 km) and achieved their objective—but at a huge cost. Half the Company's members had been killed or wounded.

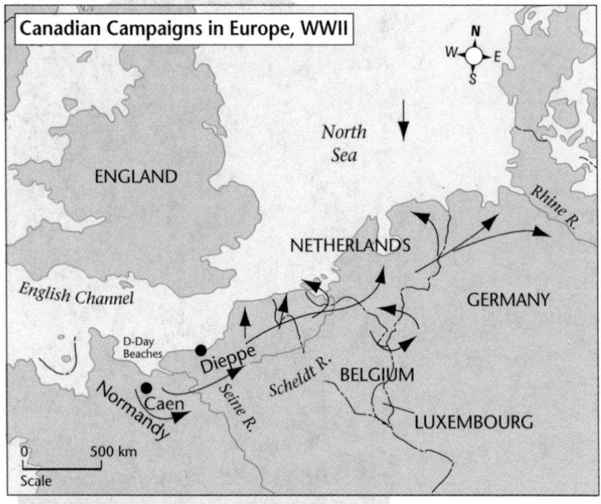

▲ **Figure 7-10** The Canadian army's campaigns in Europe. Approximately where on this map did the D-Day landings take place?

▲ **Figure 7-11** In May 2005 Canadian veteran Fred Kidd, 96, shakes hands with Dutch children after the special ceremonies in the Netherlands to mark the 60th anniversary of the liberation of the Netherlands. Why do you think the people in the Netherlands continue to honour these veterans so many years after the end of the war?

Did You Know?

Some Canadian soldiers married Dutch women, who came to Canada as "war brides." To this day, a special relationship exists between the Netherlands and Canada.

> The tears came. I went behind a wall. So many had been lost. I found myself questioning—idiotically—why war was conducted this way. Four years of training and living together, a common purpose, friends who became brothers—then more than half of us gone.
>
> *Battle Diary*, p. 14

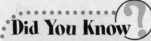

About 715 Canadians were injured and 358 lost their lives on D-Day, but the invasion was a huge success. From Normandy, the Allies worked their way north and east. The Germans gradually surrendered or fell back, and by early 1945 the Canadians had entered the Netherlands. Starving Dutch citizens welcomed their liberators, who brought much-needed food supplies.

Liberating Concentration Camps

Not all the liberation duties were pleasant ones. Some Canadian soldiers were assigned to liberate prisoners from concentration camps. Jim Anderson, from Ancaster, Ontario, described what he saw.

> There were great piles of bodies in several locations and, as you can imagine, an overwhelming stench. To this day I feel bad about the revulsion I felt towards some who came forward and put their arms out to hug and embrace us. Most of them were filthy, wasted, scabby, and toothless. . . .
>
> *Voices of a War Remembered*, pp. 210–211

Liberating the concentration camps was difficult for the liberators and prisoners alike. Although they were being freed, many of the prisoners had nowhere to turn.

> . . . Many of them were so anxious to get away from there that they were walking and crawling towards the gates and the holes in the barbed wire. We were trying to convince them to wait for the Red Cross and the other help that would be coming but it did no good. They just wanted to get away.
>
> *Voices of a War Remembered*, pp. 210–211

▲ **Figure 7-1 2** An Allied soldier at the liberation of a concentration camp. How do you think the soldiers felt entering these camps? How do you think the prisoners felt?

Checkpoint ✓

7. Look back at the quotations from John Mellor, Charlie Martin, John Ford, and Jim Anderson. Outline the challenges that each of these soldiers describes. Whose challenges do you think were the most difficult to face? Explain why you made this choice.

The War in the Air

The Allies realized at the outbreak of the war that air power was going to be a key factor. They needed both bombers (planes used to drop bombs on the enemy's targets) and fighters (planes used to protect their own targets).

When war broke out in 1939, the Royal Canadian Air Force (RCAF) had only 29 military aircraft. It was far from war-ready. The government rapidly converted existing factories to warplane production. New pilots and mechanics had to be trained quickly too.

By the summer of 1940, when the German *Luftwaffe* bombers attacked southern England in order to set up a Blitzkrieg, 80 Canadian pilots were already flying fighters against them. They helped the Allies successfully defend England in the Battle of Britain (see the timeline on page 134). But that was only the beginning. Each month, more and more Canadians were shipped to Britain to fly in fighters and bombers. More ground crew also went to service the aircraft.

LIVING LANGUAGE

Blitzkrieg means "lightning war." It was the term used to describe the all-out attacks on land and air used in Poland and France. Because Germany never landed troops in Britain, they were never able to establish a Blitzkrieg there.

Air Battles

Air crews from all over the Commonwealth trained and fought together in Britain's Royal Air Force. As a result, no famous raids are exclusively assigned to Canadian air crews (or any other nationality). But Canadians participated in almost all of the major air battles of World War II.

Both the Axis and Allied sides bombed targets that resulted in the deaths of civilians. John McQuisten spent his war years in the air force. After the war, he thought about the fact that human beings had died as a result of his actions.

> When we dropped those bombs we never had the feeling we were killing human beings. In fact, we hoped we weren't. We were just dropping bombs on military targets trying to destroy the enemy's capability to wage a war against us. Also, the very fact that we were being shot at ourselves while doing this was foremost in our minds. The truth is, it wasn't hard to push a button and not have to look the enemy in the eye. It makes it much easier to kill. That applies to any military [person]. You don't have to be a bad person to do it.

Voices of a War Remembered, p. 59

Did You Know?

Almost 250 000 people served in the Royal Canadian Air Force during World War II. Because of the nature of their service, 17 000 of the 18 000 people who were hurt eventually died from their wounds.

For links to sites about the war in the air

Checkpoint ✓

8. How did Canada's "air readiness" change between 1939 and 1940?

9. As a class, discuss the quotation from John McQuisten.
   a) How did he feel about his actions in the air force during World War II?
   b) How would you have felt in his place?
   c) Do you think it's ever justifiable to bomb targets where the risk of killing civilians is high? Explain.

The Air Transport Auxiliary Ferry Service

Many women would have liked to enroll as pilots in the RCAF when war broke out in 1939, but they were not allowed to. It was not until the 1990s that all restrictions based on gender were abolished in the Canadian military. But women did have the opportunity to fly.

The Air Transport Auxiliary Ferry Service was set up at the start of the war. Its role was to fly new warplanes built in Canada and the United States to Britain for service. Without the Air Ferry Service, delivery would have had to be made by ships, which were slow. Many of the pilots who delivered these planes were women.

Flights made their way to Gander in Newfoundland or Goose Bay in Labrador, where they were checked before flying over the Atlantic. The pilots then sailed back to Canada to make another delivery.

▲**Figure 7-13** Marion Orr (1918–1995) was a Canadian Ferry Service pilot who worked in England moving combat aircraft. She was discharged in October 1944, after flying 67 different types of aircraft for a total of over 700 flying hours. After the war she opened her own flight school, and later became Canada's first female helicopter pilot.

Radar

During the war the RCAF not only increased its personnel and aircraft, it also improved its technology. In 1941, a secret method of detecting airplanes with radio waves was perfected. It was called radio detection and ranging—**radar** for short.

Radar was important to the Allies because it allowed them to know how many Axis planes were coming before an attack. It also allowed the navy to "see" enemy ships at night and then send ships or planes to attack them. Battle planners could now give precise instructions about an enemy's position and what action to take.

Did You Know?

Radar works by sending out a *radio* beam. When the beam *detects* something, it bounces back to the radar instrument. Its position—its *range*—can be shown on a screen. If the object is moving—like a plane or a ship—the screen will show this movement. The object can be identified, and action taken against it.

The War's End

In Europe, the invading Allied armies moved steadily closer to Germany. Some Canadian troops, including Charlie Martin and the Queen's Own Rifles, crossed the Rhine into Germany at the end of March 1945, then headed up to the Netherlands. Just before they reached the North Sea, on April 16, 1945, Charlie Martin's war ended when he was shot in the chest and legs. He passed out in the army hospital.

> I did not recover consciousness until May 8. A pretty nurse was sitting beside me. Winston Churchill was announcing over the hospital radio system that the war was over.
>
> *Battle Diary*, p. 145

In the Pacific, the American forces were leading a massive assault on Japan. Then, in August 1945, American bombers dropped an atomic bomb on each of two Japanese cities, Hiroshima and Nagasaki. The effects were devastating. In Hiroshima alone, over 160 000 people were killed or seriously injured. August 15, 1945, marked V-J Day, or Victory in Japan Day—the day Japan surrendered and the war ended.

The Axis was defeated—and Canadians had played an important role in the victory. Although the population of the United States was 11.5 times the size of Canada's in 1940, the number of people who served in their army, navy, and air force was only 7.4 times larger. Included in these numbers are the 1660 men and women from Newfoundland who served in Canadian forces —120 of these Newfoundlanders died.

Did You Know

Canadian scientists were involved in the "Manhattan Project," which the United States government had started earlier in the war. This project's purpose was to develop a new type of bomb—an atomic bomb. The uranium used for the development models and the final bombs came from mines in Deep River, Ontario.

Checkpoint

10. How did female pilots contribute to the war in the air during World War II? Why were their missions so important?
11. Explain how radar technology gave the Allied forces an advantage in planning battles. You can use diagrams in your response.
12. Do you think dropping the atomic bomb on Japan in 1945 was justified? Present arguments for and against in a chart, then explain where you stand.

The term "atomic bomb" became commonly used for the first time in 1945. The bomb was named for the way it splits the centre—the nucleus—of uranium atoms in order to unleash their destructive power. In 1945 there were just two atomic bombs, which the United States used in Japan. By 2005 it was estimated that the United States had over 20 000 nuclear weapons and Russia had over 28 000. Several other countries, such as China, also have nuclear arms.

How Canadian Communities Contributed Overseas

At first, Canada's forces wouldn't accept "non-white" volunteers. But after three or four years of war, the forces began to open up. The contributions of Aboriginal people and people from other ethnic communities to the war helped to break down some of the barriers in Canadian society.

Aboriginal Peoples' Participation in the Military

Every major battle of the war—including Hong Kong, Dieppe, and D-Day—involved Aboriginal soldiers in the Canadian contingents. About 3000 Aboriginal people enlisted, along with over 10 000 people of part Aboriginal heritage.

When the war was over, many Aboriginal veterans were denied their benefits, such as free schooling to learn a trade. It wasn't until the early 2000s that the federal government finally compensated them or their descendants.

Aboriginal personnel received at least 18 bravery medals for their actions during the war. As well, in 1943, King George VI awarded British Empire Medals to four First Nations.

African Canadians' Participation in the Military

Many African Canadians served Canada with distinction in World War II. A large number of them were from communities in Nova Scotia, Montreal, and southern Ontario. Their service during and often after the war helped change attitudes in Canada. Leonard Braithwaite's experiences are typical of many African Canadians during World War II.

▲**Figure 7-14** On 21 June 2004, National Aboriginal Day, this monument to Aboriginal veterans was unveiled in Ottawa. It recognizes the contributions of the Aboriginal community in all 20th-century wars and peacekeeping missions that Canada has participated in. Why do you think it took so long for the accomplishments of Aboriginal veterans to be recognized in Canada?

Profile: Leonard Braithwaite—Fighting for Change

Leonard Braithwaite was born in Toronto in 1923. In 1942, after he turned 18, he tried to join the RCAF to become a navigator on a bomber. But they refused to accept him because he was Black. He later blamed this refusal on the prejudice of the recruiting officer, saying "He had no use for coloured people. It wasn't just him, but this was how society was then."

When a new recruiting officer took over in January 1943, he accepted Braithwaite at once. Unfortunately, Braithwaite's eyes weren't good enough for him to become a navigator, so he had to train as an aero engine mechanic. After his training was complete, he was posted to the 6th Bomber Squadron, based in Yorkshire, England. He worked on the bombers that participated in raids on Germany. He was honourably discharged from the RCAF in June 1946.

Braithwaite went on to attend the University of Toronto (1946–1950). He later became a lawyer. Much of his work involved helping fellow African Canadians break down the barriers of discrimination. He also served as a school trustee, a councillor on the Toronto City Council, and as a member of Ontario's Legislature.

Chinese Canadians' Military Contributions

It is estimated that over 600 Chinese Canadians served in uniform for Canada in World War II. At first, the Canadian government discouraged them from enlisting. But as the war in the Pacific raged, the Allies realized that Chinese Canadians had a special role to play in areas that were largely Chinese-speaking such as Hong Kong and Malaysia. Chinese-Canadian soldiers also fought in Europe. In 1947 the government finally extended the vote to Chinese Canadians, partly in recognition of the role they had played in the war effort.

For links to sites about how Canadian communities contributed overseas

Profile: Kam Len Douglas Sam (1918–1989)

Kam Len Douglas Sam was born in Victoria, the son of Chinese immigrants. In 1938 he went to England to join the Royal Air Force (RAF). He was rejected, though, because regulations didn't permit non-white members of an air crew. But when the regulations were changed in 1942, Douglas Sam joined the RCAF at once. He became a pilot of a Halifax bomber.

Douglas Sam was shot down over France in June 1944 and presumed dead. But he survived and became a spy for the French resistance against Germany. To give him cover, the RCAF reported his death, even though it knew that he was still alive. His family didn't know he was alive until he was safely back in England. After the war, he worked for British intelligence in Asia.

Checkpoint ✓

13. How did Leonard Braithwaite and Douglas Sam react to their experiences in attempting to volunteer for the military? How would you have responded if you were in their place?
14. How did the war efforts of individuals from different ethnic communities help change society's attitudes?

Chapter Summary

During World War II Canada became a more confident country. In this chapter, you have learned about:

- The role Canadian forces played in the war, and some of their major battles.
- The new technologies and how they affected warfare.
- The experiences and contributions of some Canadian individuals and communities in World War II.

The theatre of war may have been overseas, but as you will see in the next chapter, Canadians also served on the home front.

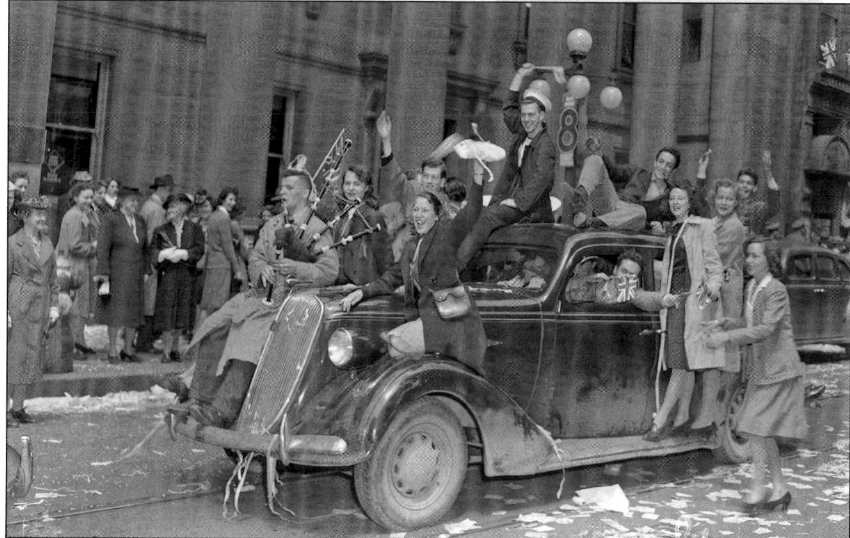

▲ **Figure 7-15** Canadians celebrating the end of the war in August 1945. What would you have done to celebrate such an important occasion?

Wrap It Up

Understand It

1. Using a graphic organizer, summarize the important military contributions that Canada made to the Allied victory
   a) on land b) on sea c) in the air

Think About It

2. Despite the hardships they endured, many people in Canada and Britain have fond memories of World War II. Based on Charlie Martin's experiences and what you've read about the war so far, why do you think this might be? Discuss your ideas with a partner or small group.
3. As a class, watch a movie about a World War II story. After the movie, debate with a small group of students whether or not the movie was realistic.

Communicate It

4. Find a picture that illustrates an interesting or significant Canadian contribution to the war overseas. Show the picture to the class and explain what it shows, why you chose it, and what we can learn about the war from it.

Apply It

5. Find out how your community assisted the war effort. Put together a poster that uses pictures and texts to summarize your findings.

Chapter 8
Canadians at Home During World War II

For links to general sites about the home front during World War II

Not all the people who helped win the war were in the armed forces. Many civilians played a valuable role in securing victory while never leaving Canada. These civilians and their war efforts are referred to as the **home front**. Below are some of the contributions Canadians made on the home front. Read through the list and think about what skills and sacrifices each contribution would involve.

a) working as support staff in a training camp for the forces
b) working in a factory to produce tanks, guns, or airplanes
c) raising money in the community to support the war effort
d) participating in scrap drives to collect discarded or broken equipment that could be recycled to make war goods
e) growing vegetables on land owned by the government to increase the supply for export to Britain
f) accepting the rationing of basic food items to leave more food available for people overseas
g) accepting that you have to give up some of your personal freedoms in order to increase Canada's security from enemies

▲ **Figure 8-1** People contributing to the war effort on the home front. What activities do you see people doing to help win the war?

Checkpoint ✓

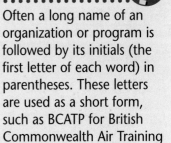

1. Rank the activities on the previous page from 1 (what I would be most prepared to do) to 7 (what I would be least prepared to do).
2. Explain why you'd be most prepared to do items 1 and 2. Why would you be least prepared to do items 6 and 7?

Key Learnings

In this chapter, you will explore

- how Canadians, as individuals and as communities, contributed to the war effort at home during World War II
- how Canadian women gained access to non-traditional employment
- economic conditions during World War II
- how conscription divided English Canada and Quebec
- how and why the Canadian government restricted certain rights and freedoms during the war and the effects of these restrictions

Words to Know

home front
British Commonwealth Air Training Plan
Camp X
munitions
plebiscite

Training Special Forces

One of the key roles Canadians played was to provide a base for Allied training in the air force and intelligence.

Air Force Training

In December 1939, an agreement called the **British Commonwealth Air Training Plan** (BCATP) was signed by Canada, Britain, Australia, and New Zealand. Volunteers came from all over the Commonwealth for air crew training at sites across Canada.

Canada was a natural location for this program. It was far from the military action, so there was no danger of trainee air crews being caught in air raids. Fog was relatively rare, especially on the prairies where many of the schools were, so flights were able to operate most of the time. The open terrain allowed crews to train for long-distance missions in safety. And once the crews completed their training they could get to Britain within two weeks.

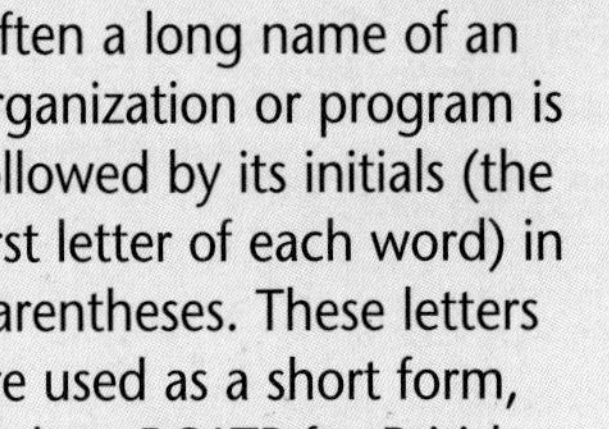

Literacy Hint

Often a long name of an organization or program is followed by its initials (the first letter of each word) in parentheses. These letters are used as a short form, such as BCATP for British Commonwealth Air Training Plan in this chapter.

Les Alexander from Flin Flon, Manitoba, trained as a pilot at a BCATP flight school. Here's how he described his experience.

iota: the smallest amount

attributed: recognized the cause of an effect

> Our task was to fly at night to bomb a specific target, or if that one turned out to be impossible, some alternate target. . . . I made 500 of these training flights and never had one iota of trouble with any of those machines—not even an uncalled-for flutter of an engine. I have always attributed this to those women who did much of the servicing. . . . Sure, the pilots and air crew did a great job but it's time now to give credit to those on the ground without whom we couldn't have kept those planes aloft.

Bill McNeil, *Voices of a War Remembered: An Oral History of Canadians in World War II* (Toronto: Doubleday Canada Limited, 1991), pp. 53–54

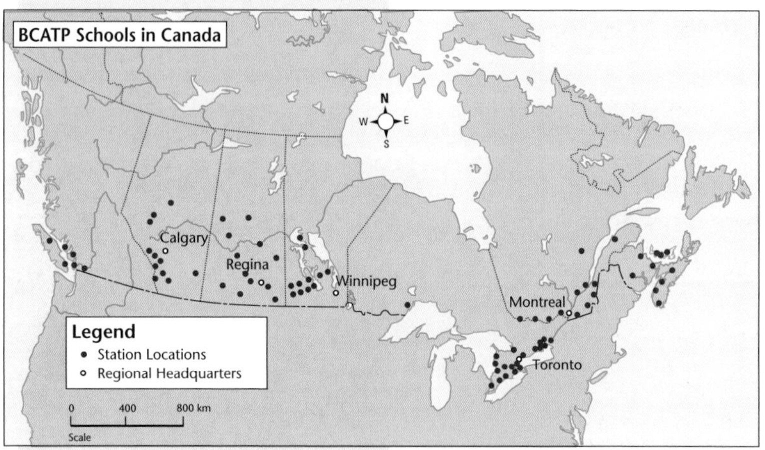

Source: Desmond Morton, *Victory 1945* (Toronto: Harper Collins, 1995), p. 94.

It wasn't just pilots who trained under the BCATP. There were training programs for navigators, bomb aimers, air gunners, paratroopers, and radio operators—all of whom were needed on long-range bombers. Many of the Plan's graduates went on to serve in the major air battles in the war.

◀ **Figure 8-2** BCATP schools in Canada. Why do you think these locations were selected?

Major BCATP Statistics	Figure
Number of trainees	131 533
Number of Canadian trainees	72 835
Number of trainers	10 906
Maintenance and support staff	104 113
Number of training schools and other sites (at peak)	231
Total cost	$2 100 000 000
Canadian share of total cost	$1 600 000 000

Sources: Adapted from *The Canadian Encyclopedia: Year 2000 Edition* (Toronto: McClelland & Stewart Limited, 1999), p. 306; Gerald Hallowell, ed., *The Oxford Companion to Canadian History* (Don Mills: Oxford University Press Canada, 2004), pp. 89–90.

▲ **Figure 8-3** The Size of the BCATP. What percentage of the trainees were Canadian?

Intelligence Training: Camp X

Another special facility set up in Canada was for intelligence training. This facility was established near Whitby, Ontario, in December 1941. Its official name was STS (Special Training School) 103, but it was generally known as **Camp X**. Intelligence services are in charge of secretly gathering information about the enemy. Their personnel require skills such as radio communication and survival training. The operations at Camp X were so secret that its existence wasn't officially acknowledged until the 1970s, over 30 years after the war ended!

Most of the graduates were Canadians and Americans who went on to operate missions in Nazi-occupied Europe. Although it was a British-run school, Camp X was headed by a Canadian. Sir William Stephenson, from Winnipeg, had worked for the British intelligence services since the war began.

It's difficult to separate fact from fiction when reading about Camp X. Stephenson claimed that it trained the agents who assassinated the German General Reinhard Heydrich in 1942. Later books on the subject, however, claim this wasn't true.

▲ **Figure 8-4** British pilots in the cockpit of a plane during training at Pearce, Alberta. How did training together help air personnel from different countries work as a team on war missions?

Did You Know?

Ian Fleming, the creator of the famous fictional spy hero, James Bond, taught at Camp X for a short time. Fleming was employed by British intelligence. Many of the James Bond adventures he wrote about were based on ideas that came to Fleming while teaching at Camp X.

Checkpoint ✓

3. Explain why Canada was a natural location for the BCATP.
4. Identify the group of people Les Alexander thinks were responsible for the BCATP's success. As a class, discuss reasons why you think they weren't given proper credit for their actions.
5. a) What was Camp X?
   b) Why do you think we're still not sure what went on there?

Producing War Materials: Increased Employment

During the Depression years, unemployed Canadians felt that the federal government was slow to boost the economy. Once the war broke out in 1939, however, it rapidly expanded the economy, placing special emphasis on the production of war goods. By any account, Canada's war effort was massive. The value of Canada's economic production increased from $5.6 billion in 1939 to $11.8 billion in 1945.

For links to sites about employment

Figure 8-5 Thousands of people from other regions, especially the Maritimes and Newfoundland, flocked to the war factories of Quebec and Ontario. What do you think it would be like to work in a factory like this?

The federal government gave money to established civilian businesses to turn their production over to **munitions**. Car factories became tank and military truck factories. Civilian aircraft plants turned out the Lancaster and Halifax bombers and ship-building yards produced naval boats. All of this created badly needed jobs.

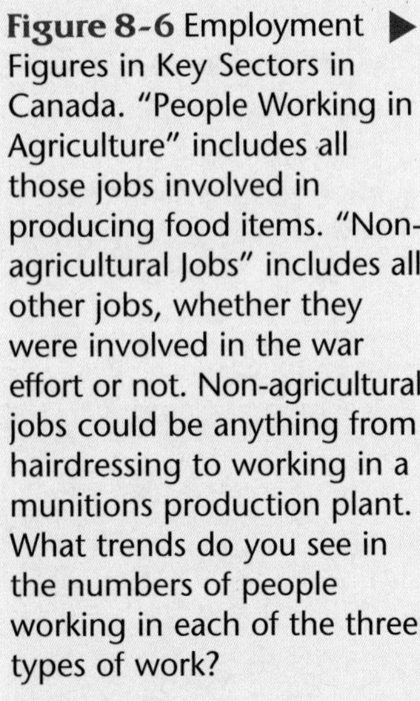

Figure 8-6 Employment Figures in Key Sectors in Canada. "People Working in Agriculture" includes all those jobs involved in producing food items. "Non-agricultural Jobs" includes all other jobs, whether they were involved in the war effort or not. Non-agricultural jobs could be anything from hairdressing to working in a munitions production plant. What trends do you see in the numbers of people working in each of the three types of work?

Year	Number of People Working in the Armed Services	Number of People Working in Agriculture	Number of People Working in Non-agricultural Jobs	Number of People Seeking Work
1933	5000	1 257 000	2 192 000	826 000
1935	5000	1 298 000	2 479 000	625 000
1939	9000	1 379 000	2 741 000	529 000
1941	296 000	1 224 000	3 047 000	195 000
1943	717 000	1 118 000	3 373 000	76 000
1945	736 000	1 144 000	3 303 000	73 000

Source: M.C. Urquhart and K.A.H. Buckley, *Historical Statistics of Canada* (Toronto: Macmillan and Company, 1965), p. 61.

Checkpoint ✓

6. Write down three facts or pieces of evidence that show that Canada's war production expanded significantly between 1939 and 1945.
7. Using the information from the non-agricultural column of Figure 8-6, draw a line graph or bar graph that shows how the number of workers in this category increased.

History Skill: Making Generalizations Based on Statistics

When historians study the past, they uncover a lot of facts and figures. Whether they're writing a book or paper or contributing to a website, they may have a limited amount of space.

To present their findings in a manageable form, historians often make *generalizations.* A generalization is a statement that summarizes evidence. The statement may not be true in absolutely every case, but it is accurate most of the time.

To make a generalization based on statistics . . .

- ✓ record the facts and figures you find
- ✓ look for a pattern in the information
- ✓ describe the pattern

Step 1

In making generalizations based on statistics, the first step is to record the information you've uncovered. Let's say that you've discovered the information about wages during World War II in Figure 8-6. As a historian, you would present the evidence as clearly as possible.

Step 2

The next step is to look for a pattern in the information you've found. For example, Figure 8-6 contains four separate sets of figures for six different years. Can you see a pattern there? Carefully look at Figure 8-6, then consider the answers to the following questions.

1. For what jobs did figures rise from 1933 to 1945? (Number of People Working in Non-agricultural Jobs; Number of People Working in Armed Services)
2. Which figures fell over this period? (Number of People Working in Agricultural Jobs; Number of People Seeking Work)

Step 3

Now that you see the pattern, you should be able to describe it. For Figure 8-6 the generalization is that "the number of people looking for work and the number of people in agricultural jobs decreased as the number of workers in the armed services and non-agricultural jobs went up."

Practise It!

1. Look for a pattern in the following table.

Year	Males		Females	
	With Jobs	Seeking Work	With Jobs	Seeking Work
1938	3 209 000	443 000	936 000	79 000
1940	3 273 000	355 000	979 000	68 000
1942	3 364 000	101 000	1 104 000	34 000
1944	3 098 000	39 000	1 411 000	24 000
1946	3 649 000	107 000	1 106 000	17 000

Source: *Historical Statistics of Canada*, p. 62.

▲ **Figure 8-7** Persons with Jobs and Persons Seeking Work, by Gender, Canada, 1938–1946.

2. Make your generalization.

▲ **Figure 8-8** Elsie MacGill was the first woman in Canada to graduate in electrical engineering from the University of Toronto. She later earned a degree in aeronautical engineering and became the first female aircraft designer in the world. During the war she was in charge of producing the Hawker Hurricane fighter plane.

Female Employment

During the war years another major trend developed. Many women replaced men who had joined the forces, answering advertisements such as the one below. The ad contains language that, though common for its time, would be considered sexist today. For example, women were often referred to as "girls."

Women between the ages of 18 and 35, and in good health, are wanted to work in eastern war plants. 'Keep 'em firing' is the motto used. The kind of girl we want is the girl with a good head on her shoulders. We take girls absolutely unskilled in war industries and train them right at the plant. A Saskatchewan girl—whether she's a farmer's daughter, domestic servant, waitress, clerk, stenographer, college graduate or debutante—if she is willing to learn—has the qualities of a good war worker. Wages are $0.35 an hour for a 48-hour week. Time and a half for all overtime. At the end of 4 to 6 weeks, the rate of pay will be increased according to the individual's ability. ∎

The Leader-Post, Regina, 5 December 1942

"Keep 'em firing": Give the troops enough war materials to fight the war

debutante: a young woman used to attending lavish social dinners and parties

time and a half: one and a half hours' pay for every hour of overtime work

a) Workers in a lumberyard in Queen Charlotte Islands, British Columbia.

b) Sixteen-year-old Rosina Vanier working in a Pictou, Nova Scotia, shipyard.

◀ **Figure 8-9** From coast to coast women took on a variety of non-traditional jobs to help the war effort. These jobs allowed them to show patriotism and gave them the money they needed to live. What kinds of challenges do you think they might have faced?

Wages for Male and Female Production Workers

The following graph shows some interesting trends in the wages of male and female production workers during the war years.

What patterns can you see? How can you explain them? It would take over 40 years before "equal pay for equal work" would become Canadian law in the 1970s. This meant that women and men doing the same work had to be paid the same. "Equal pay for work of equal value" was first introduced in the 1980s. This meant that job categories with the same responsibilities and requirements must be paid the same. (Previously it had been legal for an employer to pay male-dominated job classes, such as caretakers, more than female-dominated job classes, such as food preparation workers.)

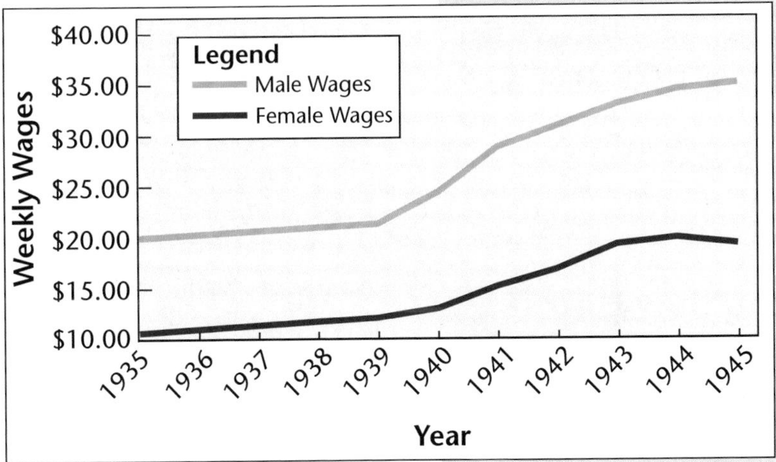

Source: *Historical Statistics of Canada*, pp. 99–100.

▲ **Figure 8-10** Weekly Wages for Male and Female Production Workers in Canada, 1935–1945. What generalizations can you make based on this graph?

Did You Know

Here are some average costs from 1939:

sirloin steak: $0.59/kg

1 polo shirt: $0.45

men's suit with two pairs of trousers: $20.00.

1 table radio: $9.00

dinner and dance to live music (2 people): $7.00

Source: Robert Bothwell, *Years of Victory, 1939–1948* (Toronto: Grolier, 1987), pp. 16–19.

Compare these costs with prices for the same products today.

Literacy Hint

The most important point in a paragraph is usually found in the first sentence. The sentences that follow give information to support that point. As you read, consider the main point in each paragraph.

Checkpoint ✓

8. Create a poster that would encourage women to become factory workers to help the war effort.
9. Look at Figure 8-10: did men's or women's wages rise more quickly during the war years?

Community and Individual Contributions

When a nation is involved in a major war, the government often calls on everyone to contribute. Military and factory workers are important, but so are the civilians who raise money and cut down on waste. Canadian communities and individuals did this and more during World War II.

Community War Efforts

Different communities contributed to the war effort in different ways. The Chinese-Canadian community in British Columbia is an example of how much money dedicated civilians could raise. This was very important because Canada was just coming out of the Depression when World War II began. The federal government didn't have all the money it needed to finance the war effort.

When China and Japan had gone to war in 1937, Chinese Canadians started to raise money right away to help China. So, unlike several other communities, they already had a fundraising structure in place that they used to contribute to Canada's war effort in 1939. Overall, it's estimated that over $5 000 000 was raised by the Chinese-Canadian communities across Canada during the war years.

But it wasn't just ethnic communities that were involved. Cities, towns, neighbourhoods, religious groups, schools, and many other groups of people organized to raise money for the war. In Newfoundland, for example, citizens banded together to fundraise. They developed the "One Percent Scheme," in which employees with salaries donated 1 percent of their wages toward the war. Such fundraising made a significant contribution to the cost of the war.

Then there were those who contributed through groups at work. Dorothy B. Inglis of Toronto describes how she and her co-workers supported the war effort.

> The Red Cross supplied us with wool and the whole lot of us set to work with our needles making socks for the men in the services. Throughout the war, we made literally thousands and thousands of pairs of socks. . . .
>
> In addition to the socks, the girls in our office also had a quilt project. The government gave us a room on the top floor of our old building and allowed us to set up a quilting frame there so that during our lunch hours, if we weren't knitting, we could be there working on a quilt. . . . It was always a proud day for us when we had one finished and ready to be packaged up and sent over to England for those people who spent many of their nights shivering in an air raid shelter.

Voices of a War Remembered, pp. 119–120

▲ **Figure 8-11** How did activities like knitting socks or quilting blankets help win the war overseas?

Checkpoint ✓

10. Why was fundraising important to the war effort?

11. As a class, brainstorm a list of fundraising activities that your school community might have run during World War II.

LIVING LANGUAGE

The saying "Loose lips sink ships" started on a propaganda poster that warned people to be careful when talking about anything to do with the war. The government didn't want anyone to supply information to spies who may be listening. Now the saying is generally used to warn people about the negative effects of gossip.

Individual and Family War Efforts

There were many ways for individuals and families to help out with the war effort. Their patriotic actions were encouraged by government propaganda. Propaganda persuades people to act in support of a cause. It's often used by governments during a time of crisis.

Posters and newspaper articles encouraged people of all ages to contribute—and they did. Children took part in scrap drives. They collected metal and rubber (such as bicycle tires) that could be recycled into new war products. Both adults and children tended "Victory Gardens"—plots of land, often in public parks, that had been dug up for growing vegetables. Older people helped out by packing food boxes bound for overseas.

People of all ages were careful with their food supplies. Britain couldn't grow enough food to feed its population, so Canada supplied it with large amounts of food. For example, 40 percent of Canadian beef production went to Britain in 1943. In addition, sugar molasses was needed to make ethyl alcohol, an ingredient for explosives. The government started to ration basic food items in 1942. Families were issued a ration book each month. In order to buy certain foods you would need money and a ration stamp or coupon. Figure 8-12 shows how much of certain types of food an adult was allowed under the rationing program in the middle of the war. The ration for children was smaller.

Restaurants were compelled to introduce "Meatless Tuesdays" in 1943 and "Meatless Fridays" as well in 1944. All rationing ended in 1947. Bill McNeil of Glace Bay in Cape Breton was 16 years old when the war broke out. He describes how his community adjusted to rationing.

Item	Allowance
Sugar	225 g
Butter	225 g
Tea or Coffee	30 g or 125 g
Beef, veal, pork, lamb	450 g to 1.3 kg depending on cut

Source: Joyce Blyth, "Food Rationing: A Part of World War II in Canada." *Wellington County History, Volume 8* (Wellington County Historical Association, 1995), p. 72.

▲ **Figure 8-12** Weekly Adult Ration Allowance for Selected Products, Canada, mid-1943. Do you think you would have found it easy to live on rations like these to support the war effort? Explain your reasons.

> You got used to the shortages of everything . . . butter, sugar, and even jam. There was a substitute jam that was made from flour sugar, water, and food colouring. Nobody could ever get used to that. The women got used to food rationing though, and they learned to trade coupons with neighbours . . . butter for tea, and meat coupons for sugar.

Voices of a War Remembered, pp. 4, 9–10

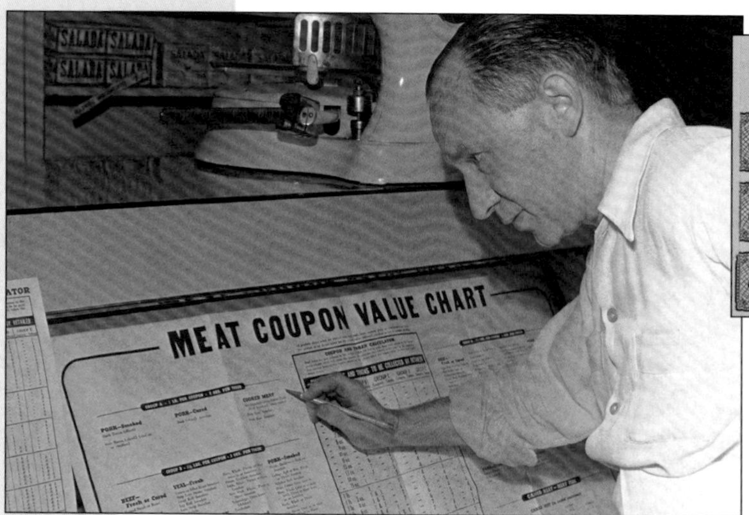

◀ **Figure 8-13** Using ration coupons and charts could make food shopping a complicated task. Which foods would you least like to see rationed? Why? Would this be possible in wartime?

Career Profile

Carol Radford-Grant, Archivist

Archives are places where historical documents are kept. Members of the public can go there to study these documents and find out about the past. Carol Radford-Grant is one of a number of archivists who works at the Archives of Ontario. Her job has two parts. First, she describes the variety of records held by the Archives by recording them in a computer database. Second, she makes the documents available for research by the general public, including family historians, teachers, and students. Carol preserves historical records of individuals, companies, and the government of Ontario. She also makes sure they're properly stored.

Name:
Carol Radford-Grant

Job Title:
Archivist, Archives of Ontario, Toronto

You might want to visit an archive if you need to find out about the history of your community, the growth of a company, or when your ancestors came to Canada, for example. Carol works to make sure you can quickly find records to help you if they're available in the Archives.

Carol believes that to do her job you have to have an appreciation for history. You have to like the challenge of trying to understand old documents and how and why they were created. It's also important to pay attention to details and to balance a variety of tasks. Finally, you have to be organized and to be able to complete tasks without someone constantly supervising what you're doing.

Carol studied for her diploma in the Archives Technician program at Algonquin College in Ottawa. She took two courses in Canadian history, and two courses in the history of archives.

1. What would you like and dislike about being an archivist?
2. What skills do you already have that might suit this career?
3. How could you develop some of the additional skills needed to become an archivist?

What I like about my work:

"I love collecting things. It's fun to collect letters, photographs, maps, and other documents. It's especially exciting knowing that these are originals, and that you can't find them anywhere else."

"It's helpful to know the basics of our history to do many jobs in Canadian archives. It helps you understand the background the documents were created in. That way, it's easier to describe them."

Checkpoint ✓

12. Pretend you are a teenager living during World War II. Describe how you and your family contribute to the war effort on the home front. How do you feel about the sacrifices you are making?
13. Imagine that you have to reduce the amount of sugar and sweeteners you eat by 25%. What choices would you make to do it?

Individual Freedoms in Wartime: Should They Be Restricted?

How much freedom should citizens have in a time of war? Should everyone be compelled to support the war effort? Should people be allowed to criticize the government about its actions when they think it's making a mistake, or should they be prevented from speaking out?

Some people have no difficulty answering these questions because they feel that war is a special situation. Others feel that human freedoms must be respected even during a war.

During World War II, individual freedom was definitely restricted. Everyone was subject to censorship, whether they knew it or not. The government had the power to prevent radio and newspapers from reporting news stories that might harm the war effort. In addition, the Canadian government had a powerful weapon in controlling the war effort—the War Measures Act, passed in 1914 during World War I (see Chapter 2). In Newfoundland, the authorities had similar powers. The War Measures Act gave police special powers to arrest and detain anyone they suspected of being disloyal.

▲ **Figure 8-14**
J.S. Woodsworth didn't want Canada to join World War II. Should he have been allowed to express his views? Explain.

Conscientious Objectors and Pacifists

The religious groups that were conscientious objectors to World War I (Mennonites, Quakers, Hutterites, and Doukhobors) were also opposed to Canada's participation in World War II. They believed war to be so wrong that Canada shouldn't defend itself even if it was attacked by a hostile power.

Other groups were pacifists. They were prepared to defend Canada against an invader, but believed that a peaceful solution could be found to the world's conflicts. These people were in the minority when war was declared in 1939. J.S. Woodsworth, founder of the CCF party, was the only member of Parliament who opposed Canada's participation. Although the pacifists were committed in their beliefs, their influence on the rest of society was limited.

The Conscription Crisis, 1943

During World War I the government introduced conscription—the compulsory enlistment of citizens into the armed forces. This issue arose again during World War II. Volunteer rates dropped off by 1943, so the military and government became worried that there wouldn't be enough troops to maintain an effective fighting force.

Prime Minister Mackenzie King preferred not to re-introduce conscription. He had seen how it had divided the nation in 1917. He always said "Conscription if necessary. But not necessarily conscription." He hoped the issue would just fade away. When it didn't, he decided to hold a **plebiscite** on the subject and ask everyone to accept the result. In a plebiscite, voters are asked a yes or no question. The government may choose to adopt or ignore the result.

◀ **Figure 8-15** An anti-conscription rally in Montreal. Why did Prime Minister Mackenzie King ask the people to decide this issue directly through a plebiscite?

Once again, the country was divided. The people of Quebec didn't support the war to the same extent as the rest of the country. Many Quebec citizens saw the war as a British war, and wanted no part of it—so it wasn't surprising when that province voted against conscription. In the other eight provinces (Newfoundland was not yet a province of Canada), a larger portion of population was of British origin: they voted in favour.

In the end, the government did introduce conscription, and young men were drafted into the forces. But by the time the conscripts were drafted, trained, and sent to a military unit, the European war was starting to wind down. They were never sent overseas, and were used for protecting Canada directly. So not only were conscripts limited in what they added to the fighting forces, the whole issue stirred up bad feelings within the nation.

Did You Know?

Some members of the Italian Canadian and German Canadian communities were interned early in the war. Included in their numbers were refugees who had fled Europe. In November 2005 the federal government reached an agreement with the Italian Canadian community recognizing its error. Negotiations are still underway with the German Canadian community.

Checkpoint ✓

14. If Canada went to war, do you think you'd be a) a conscientious objector, or b) a pacifist? For each one, explain why or why not.

15. Draw a political cartoon showing Prime Minister Mackenzie King's approach to the conscription crisis of World War II.

The Internment of Japanese Canadians

As a result of the War Measures Act, many people in Canada and Newfoundland with origins in the Axis nations were interned in camps for much of the war. The largest number of these were Japanese Canadians, most of whom lived in coastal British Columbia.

Japan attacked the American naval base at Pearl Harbor, Hawaii, in December 1941. Afterwards, both the Canadian and American governments interned people of Japanese origin living on the West Coast. Many of these people were Canadian citizens, born in Canada, but the government no longer trusted them.

Altogether, 21 000 people of Japanese origin were interned, 17 000 of whom were Canadian citizens. They were placed in camps, with armed guards, in the mountainous interior of British Columbia. They slept dormitory-style in wooden huts where conditions were primitive. They had no flushing toilets or running water. Hideo Kukubo recalled his experiences more than 30 years later:

> I was in that camp for four years. When it got cold the temperature went [way] down. . . . The buildings stood on flat land beside a lake. We lived in huts with no insulation. Even if we had the stove burning the inside of the windows would all be frosted up and white, really white. I had to lie in bed with everything on that I had. . . . At one time there were 720 people there, all men, and a lot of them were old men.

www.yesnet.yk.ca/schools/projects/canadianhistory/camps/internment1.html, accessed 27 June 2005

◀ **Figure 8-16** The community kitchen of a Japanese-Canadian internment camp. Do you think the Canadian government was justified in interning Japanese Canadians during World War II?

The federal government sold Japanese-Canadian property (houses, cars, boats, businesses) and used the money to pay for the internment. In many cases, the internees were virtually penniless when they were finally freed. Some of the families were moved to Southern Ontario, where they worked on fruit and vegetable farms. None of the interned people were freed until the war ended in 1945. The Canadian government did not remove travel restrictions and restore other citizens' rights until April 1, 1949.

As well as interning Japanese Canadians, the federal government offered all people of Japanese origin free passage to Japan. Some of the people who didn't accept this offer were interned. Then the government began a process of forceful shipment to Japan. This was devastating to families, some of whom were broken up in the process. Over 4000 Japanese Canadians were deported in this way to Japan, many of whom had never been there in their lives.

It now appears that the Canadian government was driven by racist fears. An RCMP report in 1942 stated that the Japanese Canadians did not threaten Canada's security in any way. There were even Japanese Canadians who served in the armed forces. Yet the government continued with its policies in what is now widely considered one of the most shameful events in Canadian history. In 1988 the Canadian government finally apologized to the Japanese-Canadian community and paid monetary compensation.

For links to sites about the Japanese internment and Joy Kogawa

Profile: Joy Kogawa, born 1935

Joy Kogawa was born in Vancouver in 1935. Along with her family she was interned in Slocan, British Columbia, in 1942. The family was later moved to Coaldale, Alberta, where she graduated from high school in 1953. She never forgot the injustices that her family experienced through internment, including the confiscation of their property under the War Measures Act.

As an adult, Kogawa used her writing to tell this terrible story. Her most famous book is *Obasan* (1981), which examines the injustices that Japanese Canadians experienced during and after World War II. The central character of the story, Naomi, reappears in a children's version of *Obasan* that Kogawa wrote called *Naomi's Road* (1986).

In the following excerpt from *Naomi's Road*, the young girl Naomi describes her feelings after being moved from her home in Vancouver to an internment camp in Slocan:

> *How gray everything is. There's a dead dried bumble-bee on the window sill. Dusty newspapers cover the walls instead of wallpaper. Everything looks gray. I've never seen such a dusty little house . . .*
>
> *Every morning I wake up in a narrow bunk bed near the stove. I wish and wish we could go home. I don't want to be in this house . . . I want to be in my own room where the picture bird sings above my bed. And the real bird sings in the peach tree outside my bedroom window. But no matter how hard I wish, we don't go home.*
>
> Joy Kogawa, *Naomi's Road* (Toronto: Stoddart Kids, 1986), pp. 24–25

In the 1980s Kogawa became involved with the movement to win justice for Japanese Canadians. Their work was largely responsible for winning compensation for the survivors of internment and their descendants. Kogawa's writing has earned numerous awards. She has also received the Order of Canada (Canada's highest honour for civilians) for her contributions to this country.

Checkpoint ✓

16. Imagine that you were a Japanese-Canadian teenager during World War II. Write a letter to the government describing your feelings about being sent to an internment camp.

17. The Canadian government apologized and gave monetary compensation to the families of the interned Japanese Canadians. Do you think these actions were enough to ensure that justice was done? Explain your answer.

18. Write down your opinion on each of the following questions. Give reasons for each answer.

- How much freedom should citizens have in a time of war?
- Should everyone be compelled to support the war effort?
- Should people be allowed to criticize the government's actions?

Chapter Summary

Winning World War II was regarded as every person's job. In this chapter, you have learned about:

- How Canada's location made it ideal for Allied air training and intelligence training.
- How the increased war production during World War II led to an overall growth in Canada's economy.
- The experiences and contributions of Canadian individuals and communities during the war.
- How the restrictions of certain rights affected individuals and communities.

People found that the war effort created a bond among them. They felt close to their neighbours, colleagues, and communities. Many people in later life looked back to their time working for the home front and regarded those years as the best of their lives. In the next two chapters, you'll learn about how the country changed after the war.

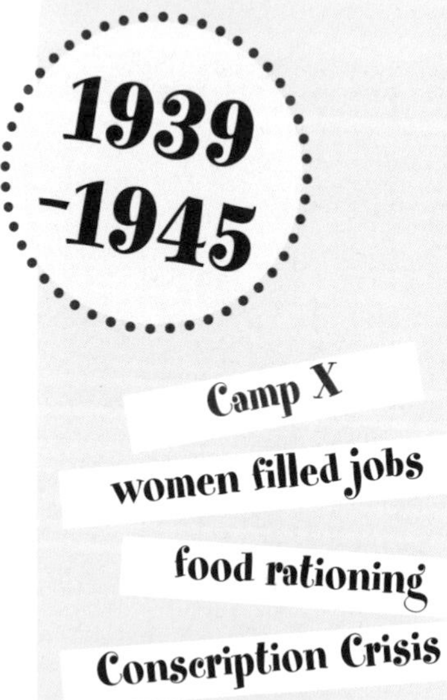

Wrap It Up

Understand It

1. As a class, discuss why many people considered their home front years the best years of their lives. Use examples from this chapter of activities they could be proud of.

Think About It

2. Imagine you were a newspaper reporter at the end of World War II. Choose either Dorothy Inglis or Bill McNeil to interview. Create 10 questions that you'd ask your subject. Be sure to follow the 5W + 1H model.

Communicate It

3. Create a collage that shows the efforts of people in your community who contributed to the war effort on the home front. Identify the role that seems most interesting to you and explain to your class why you have selected this role.

Apply It

4. Use the library or Internet to find out more about women who worked in factories during World War II. How did their efforts help change women's role in Canadian society?
5. After World War II, Canada participated in a number of United Nations missions to keep warring groups apart, and even to destroy terrorist camps in Afghanistan (2002). List three reasons why you think Canada's experiences in World War II made it a good choice to participate in missions like these.

Chapter 9

Canada and World Affairs, 1945 to 1960

Living next to the world's only superpower must be frustrating for the folks north of our border who don't share our views, values, and fears.

Yet the idea that Canada could demand America consult with its leaders before we shoot down a missile aimed at the United States that is over Canadian soil is the most ridiculous notion I have heard in some time.

That, however, is Canada's position . . . "This is our airspace: we're a sovereign nation, and you don't intrude on a sovereign nation's airspace without seeking permission," Canadian Prime Minister Paul Martin said.

His stance evidences a childlike quality. . . . This is one of those times when the United States must heed its national interest. If the Canadians don't like it, too bad. There is nothing they can do about it. ▪

Peter Brown, "It's Canadian Airspace, but Our Lives," *Orlando Sentinel* (Florida), 4 March 2005

◀ **Figure 9-1** These neighbours in Beebe Plain, Vermont, and Beebe Plain, Quebec, have the border running right through their street. Many Canadians and Americans live close to one another, but there are times when they don't share the same point of view. What problems do you think this might cause?

In this chapter you will consider critical Canadian and world issues of the past that are still very important today. When this article was written in 2005, Canadians were struggling to be heard by the United States. Fifty years earlier, the situation was, at times, much the same.

Checkpoint

1. a) Summarize the two differing opinions described in this article:
   i) Prime Minister Paul Martin's ii) American columnist Peter Brown's
   b) Which one do you agree with? Explain why.
2. Why wasn't Peter Brown's editorial opinion popular with most Canadians? List the specific comments that Canadians may have objected to.

Key Learnings

In this chapter, you will explore

- Canada's contributions to the United Nations
- how the experience and memory of the Holocaust helped shape Canada's role as a world leader in human rights
- the peacemaking and peacekeeping roles of the Canadian armed forces
- Canada's role in Cold War activities up to 1960
- how new technology has changed the way war has been fought

Words to Know

Universal Declaration of Human Rights
Iron Curtain
Cold War
NATO
peacekeeper
peacemaker
arms race
ballistic missiles
NORAD

Canada: A Middle Power

Canada came out of World War II as an important middle power. This means it was neither a superpower like the United States and the Soviet Union nor militarily weak like some developing nations. At the war's end, the Canadian navy was the world's third largest, while Canada's air force was the fourth biggest worldwide. Canada ranked behind only the United States, the Soviet Union, Britain, France, and China in international stature. As a middle power, Canada had a military with which to defend itself and the international reputation to influence foreign nations.

The United Nations

A new world order was emerging even before the war ended. The League of Nations set up after World War I had not worked. Its main tactic to prevent war was to use economic sanctions—its members wouldn't trade with aggressive nations. It did not use troops. Members also did not include all of the world's powerful countries. Although

Canada was a member, the United States was not.

By 1936 the League of Nations was largely ignored. Prime Minister Mackenzie King said that Canada would not automatically support its actions. Given its limited power, the League of Nations was unable to prevent World War II. So in the summer of 1945, 50 nations met at San Francisco to try once more to set up a powerful worldwide organization.

The United Nations (UN) that was established was a bigger, stronger organization than the League of Nations. For one thing, the United Nations included all of the world's leading powers. The United States showed its commitment to the new organization by locating the UN headquarters in New York City. The founding members, including Canada, committed not only to world peace and security, but also to economic development and human rights.

▲ **Figure 9-2** The flag of the United Nations. The olive branches on the flag symbolize peace. What is shown in the centre part of the flag?

Did You Know?

UNICEF stands for United Nations International Children's Emergency Fund. It was started in 1946 as a temporary way to help children uprooted by World War II. In 1953 it became a permanent part of the United Nations, assisting children and families in many nations.

Organization of the UN

Figure 9-3 shows how the United Nations is organized. All members send representatives to a General Assembly, but settling disputes is in the hands of a Security Council. This group has five permanent members, and another ten rotating members serving two-year terms. Each permanent member of the Council—the United States, the then Soviet Union, China, Britain, and France—must agree to decisions, such as sending armed forces to prevent or stop a war. Each one has veto power that can prevent any action from taking place. This veto power has often made it difficult for the United Nations to act quickly.

Several important United Nations institutions were also created to improve world living conditions. These include the Food and Agriculture Organization (FAO), United Nations International Children's Emergency Fund (UNICEF), and the World Health Organization (WHO). In July 2000 the United Nations established a Permanent Forum on Indigenous Issues. The Forum has representatives who advise the Economic and Social Council on a wide range of issues affecting Indigenous (or Aboriginal) peoples.

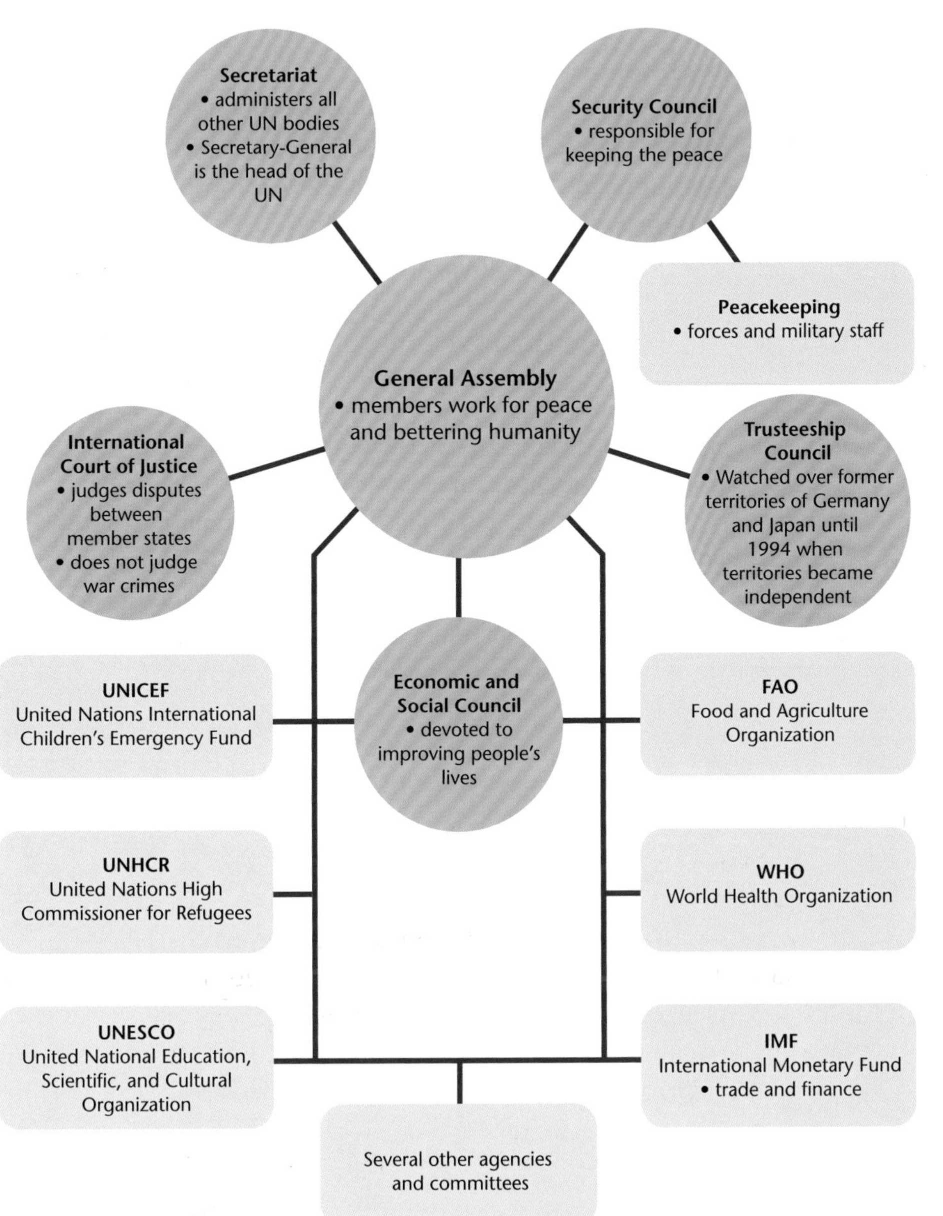

Source: Adapted from the *World Book Encyclopedia* (Chicago: World Book Inc., 1989), p. 71.

◀ **Figure 9-3** The structure of the United Nations and its agencies. Think about how each of these agencies might help increase world security.

Checkpoint ✓

3. Make a chart like this one to compare the League of Nations with the United Nations.
4. Brainstorm reasons why the United Nations is working to improve world living conditions. How is this connected to world peace and security? How is it connected to human rights?

Topic	League of Nations	United Nations
a) Purpose		
b) Membership		
c) Exercising Power		
d) Problems		

Did You Know?

The death toll from World War II far exceeded any previous global conflict. There were about 42 million military and civilian deaths—10 million more people than Canada's population in 2005. This figure included the deaths of more than 6 million Jews in the death camps.

DDT: a very powerful, odourless insecticide now banned in many countries. During World War II, the U.S. army used it to control body lice.

For links to sites about the United Nations and human rights

The Holocaust and Human Rights

When Allied troops marched into German territory in 1945, they came upon the Nazi death camps and saw the horrors of the Holocaust first-hand. René Lévesque was a Canadian news correspondent during World War II. He later became the premier of Quebec. Lévesque accompanied the American army when they liberated a concentration camp minutes after the Nazi guards had fled. He raised questions about responsibility for the Holocaust that are still debated today.

> Deloused and covered from head to foot in DDT, we retraced our steps to our billet [room] in the harmonious-sounding village of Rosenheim. On the way, passing through the quiet suburb with its kindly old people, we asked each other with our eyes, "Did they know? How could they not have? What was behind those good, old, pious-looking faces?" But what was the use questioning? We were beginning to wish we hadn't seen anything ourselves.

René Lévesque, *Memoirs* (Montreal: Amerique, 1986)

The Holocaust motivated the United Nations to protect human dignity and human rights immediately. In 1946 Montreal law expert John Peters Humphrey established the United Nations Human Rights Division. He served as the first director of the Division and worked with a small international group to prepare a statement of human rights that would be recognized by all member nations.

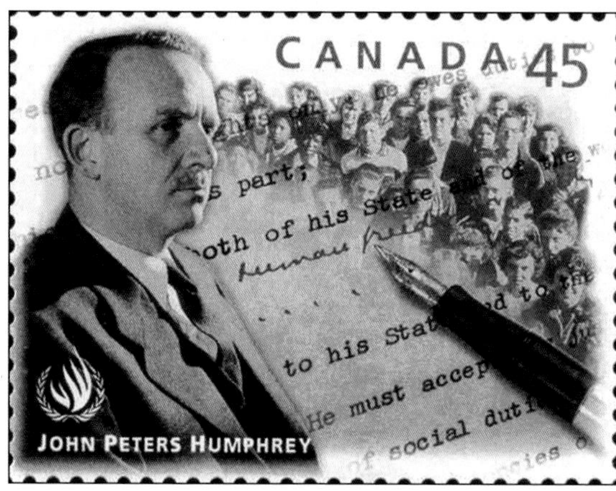

Figure 9-4 A Canadian stamp honouring John Humphrey. Why did Humphrey deserve to have his picture shown on a stamp?

On December 10, 1948, the United Nations adopted Humphrey's final copy of the **Universal Declaration of Human Rights**. Its 30 articles have been used as basic principles of law in many countries, including Canada. It was the foundation for Prime Minister John Diefenbaker's 1960 Canadian Bill of Rights and the 1962 Ontario Human Rights Code.

Excerpts from the Universal Declaration of Human Rights

Article 1: All human beings are born free and equal in dignity and rights. They are endowed with reason and conscience and should act towards one another in a spirit of brotherhood.

Article 2: Everyone is entitled to all the rights and freedoms set forth in this Declaration, without distinction of any kind, such as race, colour, sex, language, religion, political or other opinion, national or social origin, property, birth or other status. . . .

Article 3: Everyone has the right to life, liberty and security of person.

Article 4: No one shall be held in slavery or servitude; slavery and the slave trade shall be prohibited in all their forms.

Article 5: No one shall be subjected to torture or to cruel, inhuman or degrading treatment or punishment.

Article 6: Everyone has the right to recognition everywhere as a person before the law.

Article 7: All are equal before the law and are entitled without any discrimination to equal protection of the law. All are entitled to equal protection against any discrimination in violation of this Declaration and against any incitement to such discrimination. . . .

Checkpoint ✓

5. Discuss René Lévesque's comments about the concentration camp:
   a) Should people who knew about the death camps but didn't do anything about it share responsibility for the Holocaust?
   b) What do you think Lévesque meant by his last sentence: "We were beginning to wish we hadn't seen anything ourselves"?
6. Identify which articles of the Human Rights Declaration were clearly violated by the Nazis.

Did You Know?

Since 1993, the United Nations has been developing a Declaration on the Rights of Indigenous Peoples. Specific wording is still being negotiated. This will continue during the second International Decade of the World's Indigenous People, which began on January 1, 2005.

without distinction: without any difference

servitude: being forced to work for someone against your will

discrimination: treated unfairly based on race, gender, and so on

incitement: encouraging someone to take an action

Post-war Tensions

The United States and the Soviet Union were united against Nazi Germany. Beyond that, they were highly suspicious of each other. In the last months of the war in Europe, they advanced rapidly on Hitler's crumbling empire from opposite sides. Both emerged from the war as superpowers—one a capitalist democracy, the other a communist dictatorship. Figure 9-5 outlines some key differences between their societies.

Characteristic	Capitalist Democracy	Communist Dictatorship
1. Political decisions	Made by an elected government	Made by one person who rules the state by force
2. Economic decisions	Made by many investors and entrepreneurs	Made by one person who rules the state by force
3. Private property	Many individuals own private property	The state owns most property
4. Wealth distribution	Varies between different economic classes	Divided fairly evenly by the state

▲ **Figure 9-5** Look at the different characteristics of a capitalist democracy and a communist dictatorship. What type of society is Canada?

▲ **Figure 9-6** Though American soldiers (left) and Soviet soldiers celebrated their joint victory against Hitler, their alliance did not outlast the war. Why did the Cold War develop so quickly?

Soviet leader Joseph Stalin did not withdraw Soviet troops from Eastern Europe after the war. Instead, Soviet troops and Communist-controlled governments occupied a wide band of territory between the Soviet Union and democratic Western Europe. Stalin aimed to expand communism, an international movement, and more importantly, to protect the Soviet Union from possible invasion through Western Europe.

In 1946, Sir Winston Churchill, the former prime minister of Britain, called the dividing line between democratic countries and communism the **Iron Curtain**. Relations between the United States and the Soviet Union quickly chilled into the **Cold War**. The two superpowers would use any means, short of directly battling each other, in their struggle for world supremacy. This tension increased when the Soviet Union tested its first atomic bomb in 1949.

Cold War Spies in Canada

Canada was rocked by a Cold War spy scare as World War II ended. Igor Gouzenko, a clerk in the Soviet embassy in Ottawa, risked his life to offer top-secret documents to the RCMP in return for a new life in Canada.

His file was shocking. Canadian government employees and even a member of Parliament were passing atomic secrets through a Soviet spy ring. Eighteen people were arrested for espionage and eight were found guilty. The highest ranking spy was Fred Rose, the only member of Parliament elected as a communist in Canada's history.

Few Canadians were concerned that the Mounties secretly held all the suspects and didn't permit them to have lawyers before they were formally charged. Communism was a much greater fear than the powers of the RCMP.

The term "Cold War" was first used in 1945 to describe the conflict between the United States and the Soviet Union. It is now used to describe any lengthy period of hostile actions between nations that doesn't include armed battles. A cold war consists of threats, spies, and propaganda.

Collective Security

The Soviet Union had veto power at the United Nations Security Council. To the democratic nations, this meant that United Nations forces could never be used if the Soviets threatened to take over other nations to spread communism. Instead, they decided on a policy of containment to stop (or "contain") the spread of communism themselves. In 1949 Canada joined with the United States and Western European allies, including Great Britain and France, to form the North Atlantic Treaty Organization (**NATO**).

NATO was the first Cold War collective security agreement. Members of a collective security agreement all promise to protect one another if any of them are attacked. Canada played an important part in the creation of NATO, and in getting the United States to become part of this peacetime military arrangement. All members stationed troops and air force squadrons in Europe to meet their obligations. It was the first time Canadian military personnel had been stationed abroad during peacetime.

▲ **Figure 9-7** In order to protect himself, Igor Gouzenko hid his face when making public appearances. How do you think Canadians felt when they discovered that spies were working for the Soviets in Canada?

In 1955 the Soviet Union organized communist Eastern Europe into its own alliance, the Warsaw Pact. Both of the superpowers were surrounded by their own armed camps. The Cold War was heating up.

Source: Jarvis et al., *War and Peace (Canada 21 Series)* (Scarborough: Prentice-Hall, 1996), p. 64.

Figure 9-8 The Iron Curtain: NATO and Warsaw Pact countries, 1955. What image does the term Iron Curtain create in our mind?

Checkpoint

7. Explain how each of the following increased post-war world tensions.
   a) the superpowers
   b) the Iron Curtain
   c) espionage
   d) collective security
8. a) Locate each of the following on the map: NATO members, Warsaw Pact members, the Iron Curtain. Why do you think the countries in Eastern Europe were important to the Soviet Union?
   b) Now locate Turkey on the map. Why do you think NATO built a large military base there?

International Conflict

International conflict occurred less than five years after World War II. Canada became involved in the war in Korea and the crisis over the Suez Canal in Egypt. Both situations were made worse by the Cold War. In Korea, Canada served with the United Nations as a **peacemaker**—using military force to establish peace. In the Suez, it acted as **peacekeepers**—separating two sides at war while helping to work out a settlement and then monitoring a temporary truce or peace agreement while keeping the two opposing sides apart.

War in Korea

Japan seized Korea before World War II and then occupied it afterwards. Korea soon became a centre of conflict. The Soviet Union held the north, while the United States supported the south. Then, in 1949, communist forces in North Korea attacked South Korea. The United Nations Security Council voted to help South Korea defend itself. The Soviet Union was refusing to attend the Security Council at the time because of other political issues, so it wasn't present to veto the decision.

Canada was one of 14 countries who pledged troops to help the United Nations in Korea. Within weeks, Canadian navy destroyers joined with the United States Pacific fleet, and troops were trained for combat.

In Korea the United Nations troops were under American command, and used military force to support the small South Korean army. They aimed to make peace by pushing back the Communist invasion. Canada's first soldiers arrived late in 1950. By then, China was backing North Korea.

Neither side could make any real advances during this three-year war. About 27 000 Canadian military personnel served bravely in this war. More than 1200 were wounded and 516 killed in action. In the end, a truce was called and the border drawn close to where it was three years before. North Korea and South Korea remain divided enemies to this day.

◀ **Figure 9-9** *Welcome Party* (1978) by Edward F. Zuber. Imagine yourself in the middle of this scene. Describe the difficulties of fighting in the Korean War.

The Suez Crisis

Africa and Asia are joined by a thin sliver of land at the top of the Red Sea. Between 1859 and 1869, private investors from Britain and France constructed a 190-km canal through this land to connect the Red Sea to the Mediterranean Sea and create a shipping shortcut between Europe and Asia. When the canal was built, the region was dominated by Britain and France. But by 1956 Egypt was an independent nation, and President Nasser took over (nationalized) the canal. This angered Britain and France, who worked together with neighbouring Israel to attack the Canal Zone.

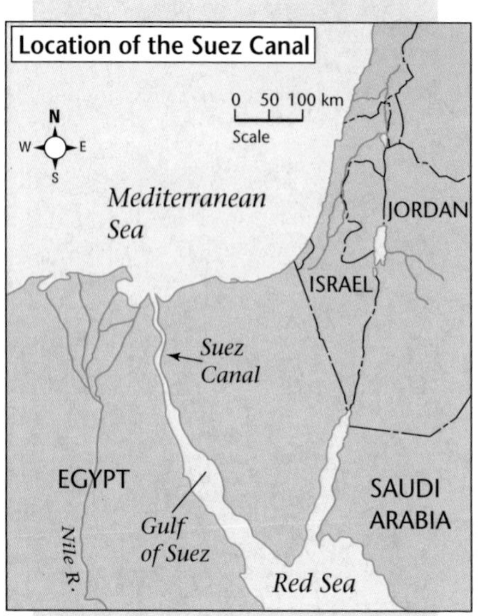

Location of the Suez Canal
0 50 100 km
Scale
N
W
E
S
Mediterranean Sea
JORDAN
ISRAEL
Suez Canal
EGYPT
SAUDI ARABIA
Gulf of Suez
Nile R.
Red Sea

▲ **Figure 9-10** Suez Canal, Middle East. Why did the location of the Suez Canal make it so important to so many different nations?

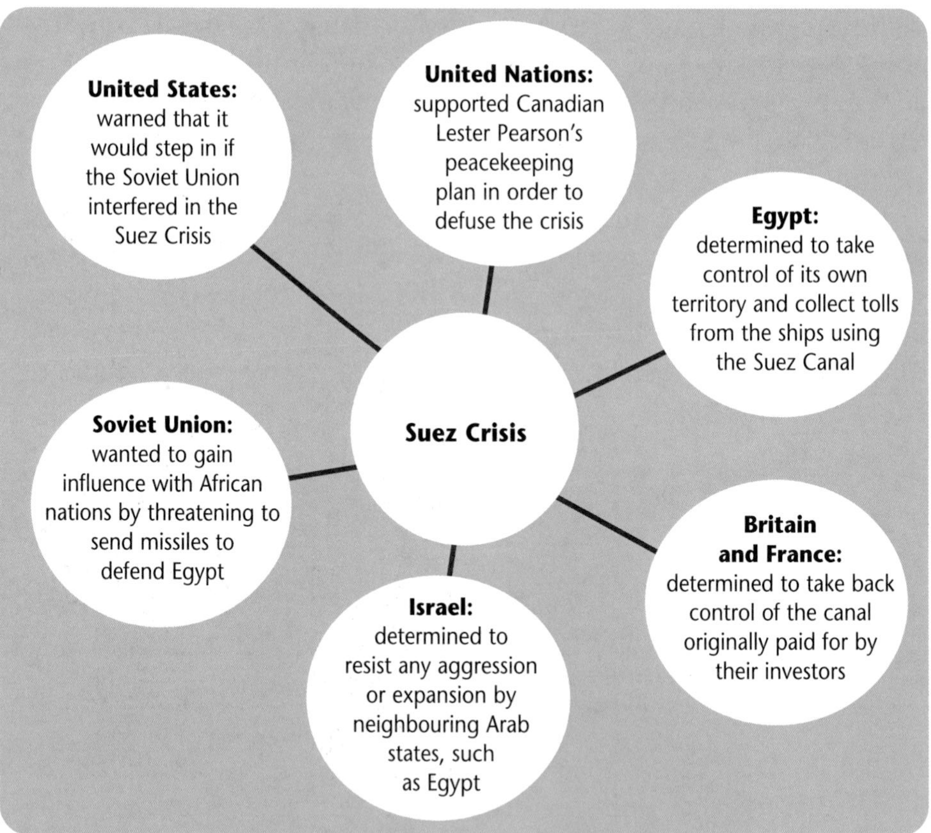

United States: warned that it would step in if the Soviet Union interfered in the Suez Crisis
United Nations: supported Canadian Lester Pearson's peacekeeping plan in order to defuse the crisis
Egypt: determined to take control of its own territory and collect tolls from the ships using the Suez Canal
Suez Crisis
Soviet Union: wanted to gain influence with African nations by threatening to send missiles to defend Egypt
Britain and France: determined to take back control of the canal originally paid for by their investors
Israel: determined to resist any aggression or expansion by neighbouring Arab states, such as Egypt

▲ **Figure 9-11** The Suez Crisis: Points of View. Why did this conflict turn into a Cold War conflict?

Lester B. Pearson was Canada's top government official in the External Affairs Department. Among his previous experiences was a term served as president of the UN General Assembly. Pearson drew up a plan to send an international peacekeeping force to the Canal Zone. The United Nations readily accepted it, setting up an Emergency Force (UNEF) under a Canadian commander. Six thousand peacekeepers, including 1000 Canadians, acted as observers and mediators, shooting only if attacked.

While there had been small UN missions used to keep the peace as early as 1947, the UNEF became the new model for UN peacekeeping operations. As a result of this mission, future peacekeepers served under the UN flag and wore the trademark light blue beret.

The peacekeeping force was successful. Egypt agreed to pay for the canal, and the crisis passed. In 1957 Lester Pearson was honoured with the prestigious Nobel Peace Prize for his efforts. He humbly called the award a tribute to Canada as a whole, not just to him personally. The Suez Crisis marked the beginning of Canada's distinguished record of United Nations peacekeeping missions. It also showed that Canada was willing to make a foreign policy decision that opposed that of Britain.

For links to sites about the Korean War and the Suez Crisis

Figure 9-12 Lester Pearson and his wife, Maryon, with the Nobel Peace Prize. Why do you think Lester Pearson deserved this prize?

Checkpoint

9. Why did the United Nations decide to get involved in the Korean War? Was its attempt at peacemaking successful? Explain your answer.
10. How did Lester Pearson's plan differ from the approach the United Nations took in the Korean War? In small groups, discuss which method is more effective: peacemaking or peacekeeping. Use examples.

Literacy Hint

Use the Checkpoint questions to help you recall and think about what you've read. You can also use them to help you study if you're tested on the information in the textbook.

History Game: *Island in Crisis*

Required to Play:
Figure 9-3: United Nations diagram

Purpose:
To apply the United Nations organizational chart to solving international and humanitarian crises

Objective: To win the game by having the class vote for your group plan

How to Play:
1. Examine Figure 9-3, the diagram showing the structure of the United Nations.
2. Form groups of five, with each person representing a permanent member of the Security Council (Britain, China, France, Soviet Union, and the United States). Make a name tag identifying your role.
3. Carefully read the scenario below. Although the country it describes is fictional, the situation is based on real events from different parts of the world in the post–World War II era.
4. In your group, meet as the Security Council to decide what should be done to keep the peace. Remember, each permanent member has veto power.
5. In your group, meet as the Economic and Social Council to decide what should be done to improve people's lives. Which agencies and committees should be involved? No one has veto power at this council.
6. In what order should the total UN plan proceed? Prepare a one-page report to the UN Secretary-General to summarize your decisions.
7. As a class, compare the solutions proposed by different groups in the class. Choose the winning group by voting as the UN General Assembly might do.

Follow-Up:
1. What differences of opinion, if any, arose in your group? How did you resolve them?
2. Do you think the United Nations should be involved in humanitarian assistance, or should this be supplied by wealthy nations such as Canada? Explain your views.

The Scenario

Lorfan is a heavily populated island, strategically positioned for Cold War air and naval bases. American and Soviet intelligence have each worked secretly to gain control of the small kingdom. Now, both superpowers are ready to use troops to rid the island of the other's agents. Aircraft carriers and troop ships from both nations are headed for the island, and Lorfan's king has appealed to the United Nations for help.

Lorfan is also one of the least developed nations in the world. Life expectancies are short because of malnutrition and deadly diseases from unclean water. Most people must work hard to scratch out a living on tiny farms or fishing boats. The island needs money and assistance to improve farming, fishing, and local communities. Most schools are overcrowded and poorly equipped. The children can't learn because they're hungry and sick. Can the United Nations help solve this humanitarian crisis?

▲ **Figure 9-13** A vote being held at the UN Security Council in 1953. Why do you think it would be difficult for so many to agree?

Living in America's Shadow

Canada's cooperation with the United States extends back to World War II. First, the 1941 Lend-Lease Act allowed the United States to supply Britain with war materials through Canada. Then, in 1942, the United States built and paid for the Alaska Highway to protect itself against Japanese attack. Part of the highway crossed northwestern Canada. The Americans turned over control of that portion of the highway after the war. Since that time, Canada has been under pressure to cooperate with the United States to defend North America.

North American Defence

When the Soviet Union exploded its first atomic bomb in 1949, the Cold War rose to a new level of fear and suspicion. The **arms race** was in full swing as each side built more powerful nuclear weapons. This led to the Joint Defence Agreement of 1950, which combined the defence resources of Canada and the United States. The shortest route from the Soviet Union to the United States is over the North Pole and across Canada so Americans were given permission to use Canadian airspace to intercept incoming planes and missiles, cushioning the United States from attack.

By 1953 both the United States and the Soviets had developed the hydrogen bomb, an even deadlier weapon. Cold War tensions were so high that many believed a Soviet invasion of North America was a real threat. During the 1950s, Canada worked with the United States to construct three different lines of radar stations to detect incoming planes and missiles shown in Figure 9-14.

Increasing Cold War Security

In 1957 the Soviet Union used a rocket to launch the first satellite, called *Sputnik 1*, into space. Military leaders on both sides realized that nuclear weapons could easily be fired with large missiles instead of being dropped from aircraft. They called these new weapons **ballistic missiles** with nuclear warheads and they rushed to produce them. It was estimated that a Soviet missile could reach American cities in just 30 minutes.

Literacy Hint

While reading, keep asking yourself questions about the topic. For example, ask yourself: Whose point of view is being presented? Do I agree with this point of view?

Did You Know

The Melville Air Force Station in Goose Bay, Labrador, was part of the Pinetree Line of radar stations. Its construction began at the outset of the Cold War in 1951 and was completed in 1954. The station was totally self-contained, and included messes (areas where the staff ate together), staff quarters, and even a bowling alley. It was in operation until 1988.

For links to sites about radar stations

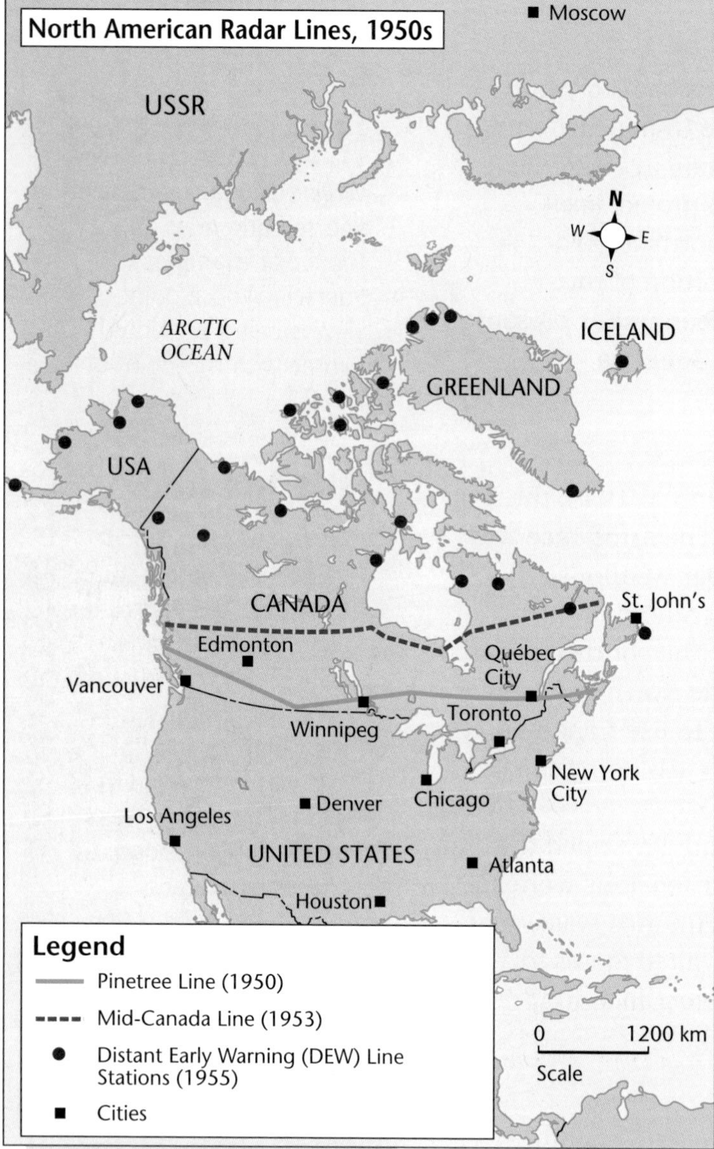

▲ **Figure 9-14** Three North American radar lines. Why were Canadians worried about Soviet nuclear weapons aimed at American cities?

Canada decided early on not to develop nuclear weapons, but Canadians were still concerned about security. During that same year, 1957, the North American Air Defence Command **(NORAD)** was formed. This agreement between the United States and Canada joined Canadian and American radar, fighter jet, and missile units under a single command to protect the continent. NORAD headquarters were in Colorado, and a major air base was built in North Bay, Ontario.

Continental defence drew Canada and the United States closer together, but Canadians were clearly the junior partners. In NORAD, the highest-ranking Canadian officer was the deputy commander. In an attack, the United States Air Force General at NORAD headquarters didn't need to talk to Canadian officials before ordering planes from American and Canadian bases to intercept the enemy.

Canadian Concerns in a Cold War Era

Canadians had serious concerns during this era. Nationalists felt that Canada had given up too much control over its own military forces and airspace to the United States. They felt that Canada should try to be as independent as possible. But many other Canadians felt that Canada's military could not offer enough protection. They felt that Canada should work with its traditional allies—the United States and Western Europe—to improve security. There were also Canadians concerned about nuclear weapons at Canadian NORAD bases. Finally, almost everyone was concerned about a nuclear attack and nuclear fallout. Schools practised air raid drills where students would huddle under their desks to protect themselves. An underground nuclear fallout shelter, nicknamed the "Diefenbunker" after Prime Minister Diefenbaker, was built near Ottawa. If a nuclear attack occurred, key government officials would be rushed there to safely direct the country. The Diefenbunker is now a museum that focuses on the Cold War.

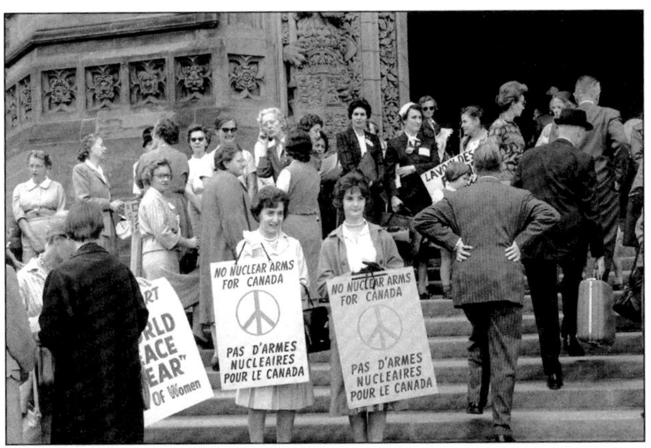

◀ **Figure 9-15** Many Canadians were opposed to a 1958 plan to arm missiles at a Canadian NORAD base with nuclear warheads. Despite anti-nuclear protests held across the country, these warheads were installed in 1963. Should citizens be allowed to protest against their government's policies?

For links to sites about the effect of the Cold War on Canadians

Source: Emergency Measures Organization (Ottawa: The Queen's Printer, Cat. No. Id 83-1/4, 1959).

◀ **Figure 9-16** Government agencies distributed plans to construct fallout shelters. Tens of thouands of these shelters were completed. What emergency supplies can you see?

"Nuclear fallout" is the radioactive dust created by atomic bombs. It contaminates air, land, and water and can poison people long after a nuclear explosion. Cancer and birth deformities are two of the serious health risks caused by radiation.

Checkpoint ✓

11. Locate each of the radar lines on the map in Figure 9-14. Use the text to compare their locations with the time they were built.
    a) What pattern do you see? b) Suggest reasons for this pattern.
12. In a chart, identify the benefits and problems for Canada of entering into continental defence agreements with the United States. Give examples from the text for each point you record.
13. Create a timeline for U.S.–Canada continental defence. Use information from the text about the following years: 1949, 1950, 1953, 1955, 1957, 1958, and 1963.
14. Draw a poster either for or against Canada's plans to arm missiles with nuclear warheads. Include reasons for your view on the poster.

Profile: The Avro Arrow

During the 1950s, a British aircraft company, A.V. Roe, designed and built fighter planes in suburban Toronto. In 1958 their new fighter, the Avro CF 105 Arrow, passed its test flights with flying colours.

The Arrow was the most technologically advanced jet of its day, capable of reaching speeds of almost 2500 km per hour. It was designed to overtake and destroy any Soviet warplanes that might enter Canadian airspace. More than $300 million had been spent on its development, much of it by the Canadian government.

But less than a year later, Prime Minister Diefenbaker announced the cancellation of the Avro Arrow project. He told the press that missiles rather than enemy aircraft had become the main security threat to Canada. He also pointed out that the United States refused to purchase the Arrow, instead favouring their F-101 Voodoo fighters.

Nearly 14 000 engineers and plant workers at A.V. Roe lost their jobs. Many of the firm's top scientists and engineers left for the United States, where they became leaders in American space programs.

Most Canadians heard only part of the story. What the prime minister didn't say was that the Avro Arrow had become too expensive. Originally, the planes were expected to sell for about $2 million each. But by the time development costs were added up, six Voodoo fighters could be purchased for the $12 million price tag of just one Arrow!

In fact, after cancelling the Arrow, Diefenbaker's government turned around and bought the cheaper Voodoos for the Royal Canadian Air Force. This had been recommended by the Chiefs of Staff Committee of Canada's armed forces. They were alarmed that the rising costs of the Arrow would take up a large part of Canada's entire military budget.

The plans were destroyed and all the planes were scrapped. Some bits and pieces from an Avro Arrow are displayed at the National Aviation Museum in Ottawa. Otherwise, there's almost nothing left of these airplanes.

Lou McPherson, who worked at Avro, described how he felt when he was ordered to cut up the planes:

> *"It just broke me up to do it. I hated the idea of cutting up this dream we all had. But we had to do it," said the now-retired welder.*
>
> *"We just started cutting. When I dropped the nose off with the arc welder* (a machine that uses electricity to melt metal), *someone tapped me on the shoulder and said I just caused $1 million damage. It was like a bad dream."*

Canadian Press/*Belleville Intelligencer*, "Search to Begin for Avro Arrow Models," *Windsor Star*, 10 August 1998

Checkpoint ✓

15. Why did Prime Minister Diefenbaker cancel the Arrow project? How accurate was his press statement? Explain further.

Chapter Summary

The post-war years were a major turning point in Canadian foreign policy. Fears of Soviet expansion and atomic weapons caused Canada to link more closely with the United States and the United Nations than with Britain. In this chapter, you learned about:

- Canada's role as a middle power after World War II, particularly in the United Nations.
- Canada's involvement in peacemaking and peacekeeping missions.
- The effects of the Cold War on Canada and the world, including the threat of nuclear weapons.
- How Canadian foreign policy was influenced less by Britain and more by the United States.

In the next chapter you'll explore the rapid economic growth of the 1945–1960 era and learn more about the everyday life of Canadians at that time.

Wrap It Up

Understand It

1. List three examples from the text that show how Canada developed a close relationship with the United States during the early years of the Cold War.

Think About It

2. Use information in this chapter to make a concept map about Canada's relationship with the United States between 1945 and 1960. Start with "Canada and the U.S." in the centre of a page, then branch outward with different ideas from there. Use lines to make connections between related ideas.

Communicate It

3. Today many Canadians believe that the Avro Arrow should never have been scrapped. Work together with a small group to find information and opinions about the Arrow not presented in the textbook. Use this information to discuss whether or not the Avro Arrow should have been scrapped.
4. What are your views on the issue of American missiles being used over Canada today? Write a reasoned reply to Peter Brown's editorial on the first page of this chapter.

Apply It

5. Watch a classic film about nuclear fears in the Cold War era. Record some impressions of this era that you get from the film. Compare these impressions with information in this chapter.
6. Either design a plan or construct a small model of a basement fallout shelter that could protect your family for a month. Include a list of food, water, and other supplies you would need to survive in the shelter.

Chapter 10

Canada in the Post-war Era

How much do you know about the popular culture, such as fashion and music, of the late 1940s and 1950s? Test your knowledge of 50s pop culture by examining each picture below. In your notebook, jot down the best answer from the four possible choices. Read through the rest of this chapter to see if you're correct.

① During the 1950s many Canadian families bought their first television. What was the popular TV series shown in this picture called? ▶
a) *Father Knows Best*
b) *The Plouffe Family*
c) *Leave It to Beaver*
d) *I Love Lucy*

◀ ② Beginning in the late 1940s, the number of babies born skyrocketed. Toy manufacturers profited by using television ads to sell toys. What was the name of this popular toy?
a) Slinky
b) Hula Hoop
c) Whirly-gig
d) Loop-D-Loop

③ During the 1950s many teenagers identified with a new type of music called rock 'n' roll. Do you know which rock 'n' roll idol from the 1950s is pictured here? ▶
a) Paul Anka
b) Little Richard
c) Frankie Avalon
d) Elvis Presley

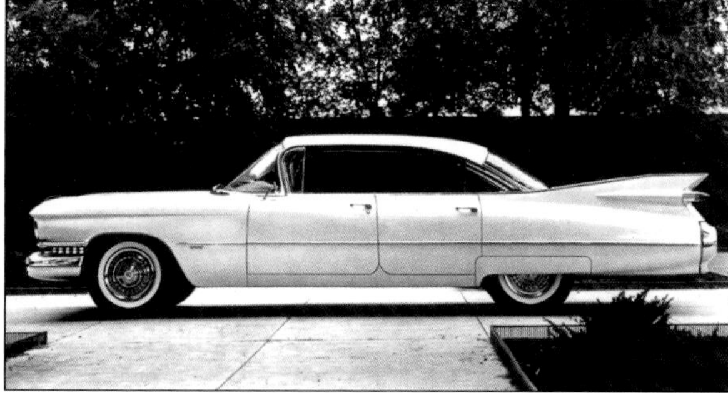

▲ ④ During the 1950s cars became longer, lower, and wider than ever. This 1959 car was the largest mass-produced car ever made. What make was it? a) Cadillac b) Chevrolet c) Chrysler d) Ford

Checkpoint ✓

1. Make a list of five different sources you can use to get an impression of life in the 1950s. Which of these information sources do you think is most reliable? Why?
2. From what you see in these pictures, do the 1950s appear to be a period of economic prosperity or not? Explain your answer.

Key Learnings

In this chapter, you will explore

- how Canada's population changed in the post-war baby boom
- how the lives of teenagers and women changed in the years following World War II
- changes after World War II that tied the Canadian economy closer to the American economy
- why social support programs were established in Canada

Words to Know

refugees
baby boom
birth rate
death rate
stereotype
credible
social security

Canada's Population Explosion

There was tremendous growth in Canada's population during the post-war era. In just 15 years after 1945 the number of Canadians increased by 50 percent, from about 12 million to 18 million. Two key factors accounted for this population explosion: immigration and the baby boom.

Immigration

Two million people immigrated to Canada between 1945 and 1960. They had been driven from their homelands by World War II, politics, and unemployment, and came for a new life and economic opportunity. Before the war Canadian immigration policy was restrictive. It favoured applicants from Britain, from other countries in the British Commonwealth and Western Europe, and from the United States. But with the huge number of displaced people in European refugee camps, Canada changed its immigration policy in 1946.

Canada began to accept **refugees**, people who were left homeless as

Did You Know?

Over 30 000 of the refugees who arrived in Canada were from Ukraine. They were assisted by the Ukrainian Canadian Relief Fund, which led the movement to transport displaced refugees from Ukraine to safer countries.

a result of war and political upheaval. Between 1947 and 1952, 186 000 refugees moved to Canada. Among them were Holocaust survivors, since Canada had reversed the discriminatory policy that had severely limited the number of Jews allowed into the country before World War II.

For links to sites about Canada's population explosion

The first period on the graph in Figure 10-1 covers the period up to 1952, when European refugees and immigrants entered Canada. About 20 percent of the bachelors in the Canadian forces married while overseas, and the thousands of war brides and their children are included as 1945–1952 immigrants.

Figure 10-1 Immigrant Arrivals to Canada, 1945–1960. Did the rate of immigration remain steady over this time? Which half of the graph had more immigration?

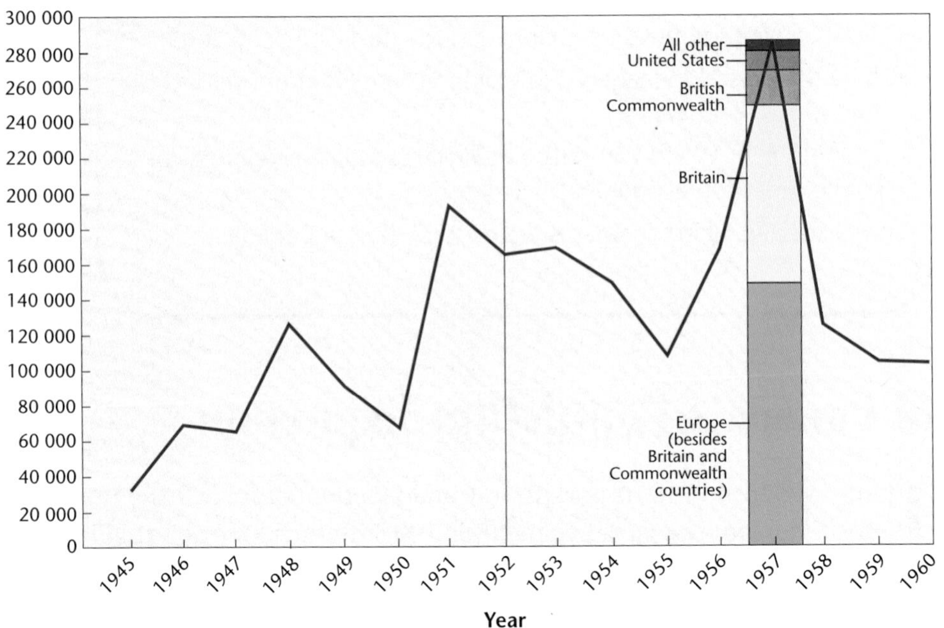

Source: F.H. Leacy and M.C. Urquhart, eds., *Historical Statistics of Canada* (Toronto: Macmillan and Company, 1965), Series A350.

Literacy Hint

This graph shows how immigration rose and fell between 1945 and 1960. The line that runs from the top to the bottom of the graph breaks the information up into two sections. Look at one section at a time to identify short-term trends.

The second period, from 1952 to 1960, mostly includes economic migrants seeking a better life. The year 1957 was the peak immigration year for the era, boosted by 38 000 Hungarian refugees who fled from a failed anti-Communist revolution the year before. The steady drop in immigration from 1958 to 1960 reflects a slow economy that led Canada to accept fewer applicants.

Immigrants' Challenges

New arrivals to Canada had a number of obstacles to overcome, including fear, loneliness, and, in many cases, language barriers. Margaret Brown, a war bride from England, describes her first experiences in the country:

> When I did get into Vancouver all dressed up, there was nobody to meet me, and I started to cry. I knew I was pregnant, and I thought Bob was married to someone else, or had a girlfriend and didn't want me. I was terrified. The Red Cross nurse came to me and gave me a cup of coffee. Someone said, "We should phone the other station," and sure enough Bob was waiting for me there. I was supposed to come on the CPR [Canadian Pacific Railway].

Cited in Mark Kingwell and Christopher Moore, *Canada: Our Century* (Toronto: Doubleday Canada, 1999), p. 263

▲ **Figure 10-2** War brides arriving in Canada. How do you think these women felt arriving in a new country far from their families?

Checkpoint ✓

3. Read Margaret Brown's comments.
   a) What were her fears?
   b) Why do you think she felt that way?
   c) Where did she find assistance?

4. Either take on the role of a new immigrant to Canada, or recall your own experiences in coming here. Role-play the problems and feelings that you face upon arriving in this country.

The Baby Boom

When the war ended the baby boom began. The **baby boom** refers to the rapid increase in births between 1946 and 1965. Canadians were eager for the security of home and family after six years of uncertainty between 1939 and 1945. Marriage rates soared to record levels immediately after Canadian servicemen returned from overseas.

The social and economic factors that fuelled the baby boom included the following:

- Most couples wed in their early twenties—almost a decade younger than today's newlyweds—and they were usually ready to start a family right away.
- Post-war couples were young enough to have many children.
- The Canadian economy boomed for a good part of the post-war era, making it easier for many young couples to feed and clothe an average of three children.

Toy manufacturers benefited from the increased number of children in North America. The Hula Hoop was one toy that became very popular in 1958. It was named for the motions made by people who spin this plastic hoop around their waists. These moves are similar to those of a traditional Hawaiian dance called the hula.

The Canadian **birth rate** (the number of births per 1000 people) jumped sharply in the late 1940s and remained high for 20 years. In fact, between 1946 and 1965, the years of the baby boom, almost 9 million children were born in Canada.

At the same time, the **death rate** (the number of deaths per 1000 people) steadily dropped because of a booming economy and better health care. This combination of rising birth rate and falling death rate caused a huge natural increase in Canada's population. (The "natural increase rate" is the excess of births over deaths in a year.)

Time Period	Population Growth by Natural Increase (Births minus Deaths)
1931–1941	1 222 000
1941–1951	1 972 000
1951–1961	3 148 000
1961–1971	2 607 000
1971–1981	1 913 000
1981–1991	1 974 000
1991–2001	1 528 000

Source: Population and Growth Components (1851–2001 censuses), www.statcan.ca.

▲ **Figure 10-3** Changes in Population Through Natural Increase, 10-Year Periods. When did the natural increase rate peak?

Checkpoint ✓

5. Make a list of at least three reasons to explain why a baby boom occurred in Canada. Which reason do you think was the most important? Why?
6. a) Use the number table to draw and label a bar graph of natural increase from 1931 to 2001.
   b) On your graph, label the baby boom, 1946–1965.
   c) Do you think your generation will have large or small families? Explain your thoughts.

Canada's Economic Boom

Just as the population was increasing, so was the Canadian economy. It was much healthier in the 1950s than it had been 20 years before. The following chart compares the economies of the 1930s and the 1950s.

Figure 10-4 Canada's ▶ Economy, 1930s and 1950s. Why had Canada's economy improved since the war?

1930s	1950s
Severe drought destroyed the crop and grazing lands of western Canada	Major resource discoveries such as oil, gas, nickel, and uranium
Few jobs available	Many jobs available
Varied working conditions (based on the attitude of the boss)	Improved working conditions (more unionized labour)
Low wages	Rising wages
Prairie farmers left windblown lands	Families moved to the Prairies and Canadian Shield

The new economy was built on natural resources ranging from oil in the West to iron ore in the East.

In 1953 Alberta seemed to be balanced between its past and a new future. Bob DesRivieres describes his experiences in Alberta during this time:

> It was tough finding a good job in Ottawa after the war. Sherritt-Gordon Mines opened a nickel processing plant at Fort Saskatchewan, Alberta, so many families drove West to get jobs. We left in October, 1953.
>
> Moving to Alberta was like pioneering. Our houses weren't ready yet, so we spent the winter in cabins at Elk Island National Park. There was no insulation and an oil stove barely heated our place. Buffalo sometimes stared into our windows! We were really roughing it that winter.

Bob DesRivieres, 2005

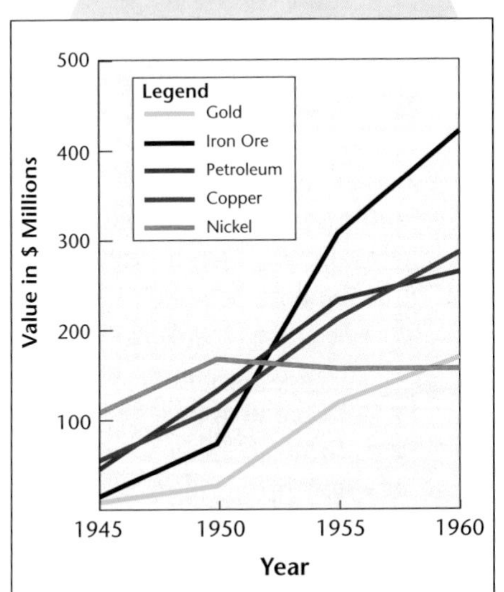

▲ **Figure 10-5** Canadian Mineral Production (Value in $ Millions). Describe the overall pattern of mineral production between 1945 and 1960.

Industrial Growth

Development of mineral wealth quickly spread through the economy. For example, as the output of iron ore in Wabush and Carol Lake, Newfoundland, increased, it went to steel mills in Hamilton to be refined and then manufactured into cars and trucks. Likewise, the oil and natural gas wealth of western Canada affected industrial production in Ontario.

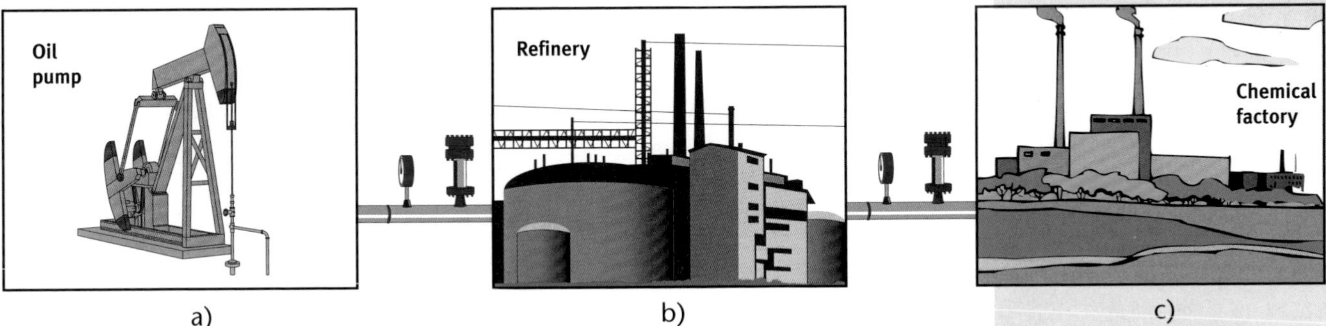

▲ **Figure 10-6** a) Newly discovered oil and natural gas wells in western Canada were linked to the east by pipelines. b) Big international oil companies built refineries in Southern Ontario to refine crude oil into its many byproducts, such as gasoline and motor oil. c) Other American-owned firms opened chemical plants nearby, to further process petroleum byproducts into plastics, and chemicals. How did the production of these goods further increase Canada's economy?

Checkpoint ✓

7. Look at the graph in Figure 10-5. Rank the production of each mineral from 1 to 5, with 1 as the fastest rate of increase and 5 as the slowest.
8. Describe how Alberta seemed to be caught between the frontier and the modern world in 1953. Explain your opinion about living there at that time.

Did You Know?

Canada and the United States cooperated in joint investments, such as the St. Lawrence Seaway Agreement of 1954. A system of canals and locks that allowed large ships to reach Lake Superior through the St. Lawrence Seaway and Great Lakes system was completed five years later.

American Ownership

Much of Canada's post-war economic growth was financed by foreign investment—money from outside the country used to earn a profit here. The Liberal governments of Mackenzie King and his successor Louis St. Laurent encouraged American investment. Between 1920 and 1950 American investment had grown from 44 to 76 percent of total foreign investment in Canada.

In 1956 the government appointed the Royal Commission on Economic Prospects. It made several recommendations for Canada's growth. One was key: the government should limit foreign ownership to keep control of its own economy. At that time, though, Canadians welcomed the jobs that foreign investment created. The report gathered dust for the next 10 years before the issue came up again.

Figure 10-7 Percentage American Ownership of the Canadian Economy, 1926 and 1957. Which parts of the economy attracted increased investment from the United States between 1926 and 1957?

Economic Sector	U.S. Owned, 1926	U.S. Owned, 1957
Oil and Gas	not available	58
Mining and Smelting	28	46
Manufacturing	30	39
All Industry and Retail	35	27
Railroads	15	11
Other Utilities	23	12

Source: Ian Lumsden, *Close the 49th Parallel: The Americanization of Canada* (Toronto: University of Toronto Press, 1970), p. 24.

Checkpoint ✓

9. Discuss why most Canadians weren't concerned about foreign investment in 1956. Do you think most Canadians feel the same way today? Why or why not?
10. Percentages of foreign investment have increased even further since 1957. Either draw a cartoon or make a collage to express your thoughts on foreign ownership of Canada's economy.

The Effects of Economic Growth on Everyday Life

Rising wages and population growth unleashed a spending spree in the 1950s. Disposable income—the money left after basics like food, clothing, and shelter are paid for—increased by 43 percent between 1945 and 1959. More families had money for cars, TVs, appliances, furniture, figure skates, and hockey equipment.

A new automobile was the most desired consumer product of all. Vehicles were not only essential transportation, but status symbols as well. To entice people to buy new cars more often, General Motors, Ford, and Chrysler introduced new designs and colours every two years during the 1950s. During this era, cars grew longer, lower, wider, and more powerful. Gasoline cost only about eight cents per litre, so no one worried if they used a lot of fuel.

The popularity of cars shaped the communities of the 1950s. Few new houses had been built in Canada since the prosperous 1920s, but a growing population and a reviving economy kick-started housing construction. The suburbs—the communities beyond the old community core—emerged. Many suburbs grew haphazardly, and lacked services like schools and shopping. But residents could use the family car to get to work and to the new shopping malls that developed in the late 1950s.

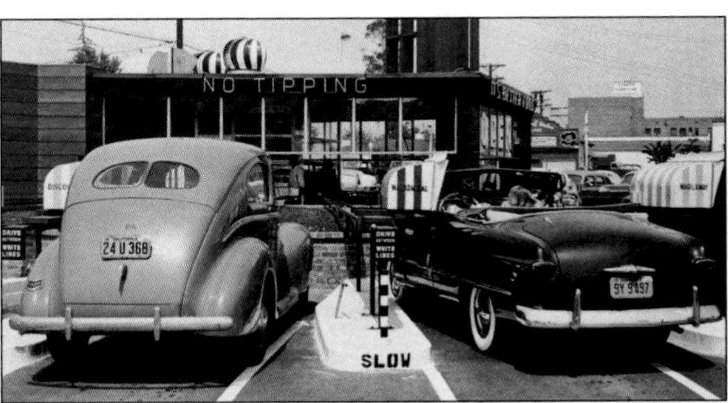

Figure 10-8 The popularity of drive-in restaurants and drive-in movie theatres showed how important the automobile had become to Canadians. Why do you think drive-in restaurants were popular with the young families of the 1950s?

Checkpoint ✓

11. List the factors that led to the development of post-war suburbs. Expand on each point by using an example.
12. a) What's meant by the term "disposable income"?
    b) List five items that disposable income was spent on in the 1950s and today.

Did You Know

The 1959 Cadillac took auto design to extremes. It stretched more than six metres, and had the largest tailfins in the industry. This Cadillac was loaded with heavy chrome bumpers and trim, and weighed as much as a truck. It was the largest mass-produced car ever made.

TIMELINE: The Growth of Television in Canada

- 1946 The first American TV stations begin broadcasting
- 1951 About 35 000 Canadians have televisions, all tuned to U.S. networks
- 1952 CBC-TV (Canadian Broadcasting Corporation) begins programming
- 1956 More than half of all Canadian homes have a television set
- 1959 Very few Canadian families own a colour television set because of its high price and the lack of programming

For links to sites about the history of television

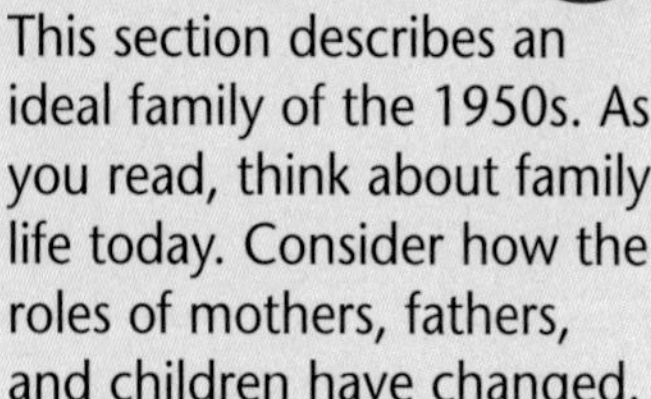

Literacy Hint

This section describes an ideal family of the 1950s. As you read, think about family life today. Consider how the roles of mothers, fathers, and children have changed.

The Spread of Television

Another big influence on life in the post-war era was television. Only a few Canadian families could afford black-and-white televisions in the early 1950s, but over time, mass production made them fairly cheap and widely owned.

Television quickly began to change family life. Children took to TV immediately, often rushing home after school to watch American-made cartoons and adventure series. A 1952 survey by the Toronto Women Teachers Association expressed concern that kids were watching 25 to 30 hours a week.

There were very few channels, and little need for parental controls. It was common for the whole family to watch television together after supper. Most of the popular family sitcoms were produced in the United States and shown either on American channels available in Canada or on Canadian channels that purchased them. CBC Television offered more dramatic, educational, and artistic programming, along with *Hockey Night in Canada* on Saturday evenings.

Family Life

Have you ever heard of the Cleavers: Ward, June, Wally, and Clarence ("the Beav")? In *Leave It to Beaver*, they were the perfect television family, competing for ratings with other similar shows. These American shows all projected a happy stereotype of 50s family life. A **stereotype** is a generalized mental image of a place, time, or social group that doesn't always match reality. In this case the stereotypical family consisted of a White married couple with a father working to support the family, and a mother who stayed at home baking cookies and looking after polite, obedient children.

The Role of Women in the Post-war Era

Though women handled all types of work during the war, most gave up their non-traditional jobs to returning servicemen. Some women continued as teachers, hospital workers, and sales clerks, but very few married women held jobs outside the home. For one thing, day care was generally available only from relatives. But more important was the social pressure for women to stay home that came from their husbands, who didn't want people to think they couldn't support their families.

Suburban women often felt the need to break out of the tight grip of family life. Their limited outlets included gathering for coffee and card parties and volunteering in neighbourhood schools and places of worship. Some women weren't happy with this confined role.

▲ **Figure 10-9** For many Canadians, including working class families, new immigrants, and visible minorities, this image was not a reality.

Teenagers

The prosperity of the 1950s helped create a new population group—teenagers. Their spending allowances and part-time jobs gave them the buying power to satisfy their own tastes. Girls often wore their hair in a ponytail, and many guys used plenty of hair cream to comb their hair back in the so-called "greaser" style.

In music, rock 'n' roll developed in the United States in the early 1950s and quickly spread to Canada. Since many adults disapproved of the beat and the lyrics, the music became a symbol of teenagers' growing independence. Elvis Presley was the king of rock 'n' roll. In 1957 about 24 000 screaming teenagers filled Maple Leaf Gardens in Toronto for two of his shows. Some adults were shocked by Presley's suggestive gyrations on stage. Of course, this made Presley even more popular with his fans. One successful Canadian performer was Paul Anka. Though his songs were more pop than rock 'n' roll, they were top sellers in both Canada and the United States.

- **In 1955 there were 1.6 million Canadians between the ages of 15 and 19.**
- **About 70 percent of these teenagers had their own bank account.**
- **As a group, they spent about $100 million per year.**
- **As a group, they bought more than 4 million music records per year.**

Checkpoint ✓

13. As a class, discuss whether television shapes society or simply reflects it. Explain your views, using *Leave It to Beaver* and modern television programs to support your opinion.

14 a) Why were some women unhappy with their role in the 1950s?

b) Compare women's role in the 1950s with their role today.

15. a) What similarities and differences do you see between Canadian teenagers in the 1950s and those of today?

b) How important do you think music is in reflecting teenagers' independence today? Explain.

History Skill: Judging the Credibility of Information

Credible means that something is believable. When you judge the credibility of information, you're deciding whether or not to accept it as true and accurate.

Whether gathering information from the library, the Internet, or any other source, it's important to judge its credibility. The interpretation of current events and past situations should be based on reliable facts.

Step 1

Check whether or not the source is credible.

- Where does the information come from? For example, some Internet websites are more credible than others. Sites with a " ~ " in the address are usually hosted by individuals. Better choices are sites sponsored by universities (.edu) and governments (.ca) or well-known media outlets.
- Who has written the information? Look for information about the author on the website or book cover. For example, the excerpt about teenage dating is from a book called *Canadian Families: Past and Present*. Its back cover states that in 1988, author Emily Nett was a professor in the Sociology Department at the University of Manitoba, where she taught courses on the family, courtship, and marriage. She seems qualified to write about 1950s dating.
- Are the author's facts carefully documented? In *Canadian Families: Past and Present*, Emily Nett carefully notes all her sources within each chapter, then provides a 26-page list of research references at the end of the book. This adds credibility to her book.

Teenage Dating in the 1950s

Dating was highly formalized in the 1950s; a series of stages from casual to steady dating to engagement and marriage were each marked by an exchange or gift which symbolized the degree of "seriousness" in the relationship.

. . . Since the 1960s, few young persons do anything so formal as "date" in the original sense of the word, although in many sectors of the society the word continues to be used. Others say that they "hang around together" and "get together."

Emily M. Nett, *Canadian Families: Past and Present* (Toronto: Butterworths, 1988), pp. 179 and 181

Step 2

Check whether or not the information presented is out of date.

- How old is the information? For example, Nett's book was written in 1988, almost 30 years after the 1950s dating patterns she describes. This allows her to use the many professional studies carried out during those years. However, her comments about teenagers just "hanging around" and "getting together" since the 1960s may be out of date by now.

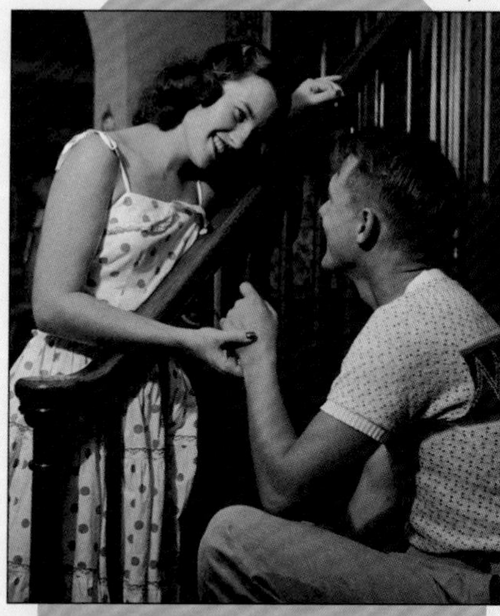

▲ **Figure 10-10** According to Emily Nett, this teenage couple is just one of many who were "going steady" in the 1950s. Do teenagers still "go steady" today?

Step 3

Check whether or not the information presented is credible.

- Are emotionally charged words and phrases used to present people or events in a certain way? For example, some sources have used phrases such as "insecure and spoiled" and "youth run wild" to describe teenagers in the 1950s. Instead, Emily Nett writes in a detached, scholarly style, without emotion.
- Is there information missing? Some sources leave out information that supports an opposing opinion.
- Does the information show stereotypes of gender, religion, race, culture, or nationality? Is the information prejudicial, sexist, or racist?

To judge the credibility of information . . .

✓ determine whether the source is credible

✓ determine whether the information is out of date

✓ evaluate the material for bias and stereotypes

Practise It!

Locate information about teenage life in the 1950s.

1. Determine how qualified the author is to write on this topic by answering the following questions: a) What's the author's professional background? b) How much research did the author do? c) Did the author cite sources?
2. Check the date when the article was written. Is the information outdated or still valid?
3. Check the material for bias or stereotypes: a) Does the author use emotionally charged language? b) Is the information prejudicial, sexist, or racist?
4. a) Write down the title, author, date, and source of the article.
   b) Using your answers to questions 2 to 4 above, explain whether the article is credible or not.

A Time for Nation Building

For links to sites about nation building

The period after World War II was a time of nation building. The government of Canada invested in major social systems. The nation also expanded as Newfoundland entered Confederation.

Government Social Investments

The Great Depression taught Canada that governments must play a stronger role in supporting people's lives. And so, after 1939, a series of **social security** programs were introduced to help people who are unemployed, elderly people, youth, and children. These measures were further increased during the 1960s (see Chapter 11). The result was the "cradle to the grave" network of social services which help to support the quality of life that we enjoy in Canada today.

Figure 10-1 1 Canada's Social Security Programs, 1940–1960. Why are these programs called a social "safety net"?

Year	Social Security Program
1940	**Unemployment Insurance** Both workers and their employers contributed to this insurance plan, which paid unemployed workers while they were looking for new jobs.
1944	**Family Allowance Benefits** Better known as the "baby bonus," these monthly benefits were paid for basic food and clothing for each child in the family. Every family was eligible.
1952	**Old Age Security** This plan improved upon the 1927 Old Age Pension by extending it to all Canadians aged 70 or older. The payment was also increased to $40 per month, and didn't have to be repaid.
1948, 1957	**Canada Hospital Insurance Plan** The federal government first gave the provinces money for health care in 1948. Payments were increased to cover about half of the provinces' health care costs in 1957.

Profile: Tommy Douglas: A Great Canadian

During 2004–2005, CBC-TV held a nationwide contest in which the Canadian public was asked to vote for "The Greatest Canadian." The winner was a man previously unknown to many people but highly respected by others for his important contributions to social security in Canada.

Tommy Douglas (1904–1986) is known as the father of Canadian medicare, that is, government hospital insurance.

Douglas was born in 1904 and grew up in Winnipeg, Manitoba. When he was 10 he experienced a serious bone infection in his knee. Since his parents couldn't afford the operation, doctors were ready to amputate his leg so that the infection wouldn't spread. But then a visiting surgeon offered to operate for free, and saved the boy's leg. Later, Tommy Douglas said that this incident inspired his dream for accessible medical care for all.

After training as a minister, Douglas moved to Weyburn, Saskatchewan. The Great Depression hit that province especially hard, and Douglas was determined to help the province's people. In 1935 he was elected to Parliament. Nine years later he left federal politics and was elected premier of Saskatchewan, a position he held from 1944 to 1961.

During those years, his government put Saskatchewan back on its feet with social and economic programs to improve the quality of life there. Most important, in 1947 Premier Douglas introduced Canada's first government-sponsored health care plan. Then, in 1961, this limited plan was expanded to full medicare, with complete medical and hospital care for everyone in the province. By 1966 Lester Pearson's federal Liberals had extended this popular program to the entire country.

Did You Know?

Final results of the public's vote for The Greatest Canadian, 2005:

1. Tommy Douglas
2. Terry Fox (Chapter 11)
3. Pierre Elliott Trudeau (Chapter 12)
4. Dr. Frederick Banting (Chapter 3)
5. Dr. David Suzuki, scientist
6. Lester Pearson (Chapter 9)
7. Don Cherry, hockey broadcaster
8. John A. Macdonald, first prime minister
9. Alexander Graham Bell, inventor
10. Wayne Gretzky, hockey star

Checkpoint ✓

16. Canada's social security system has often been described as "cradle to grave." Read the descriptions of the programs listed in Figure 10-11 and explain why this phrase is used.
17. As a class, discuss why Tommy Douglas was voted the Greatest Canadian.

▲ **Figure 10-12**
Joey Smallwood (right), Newfoundland's first premier, shakes hands with Sir Albert Walsh, the province's first Lieutenant-Governor. Why do you think Smallwood was elected the first premier of Newfoundland?

TIMELINE: Canada's 10th Province

- 1763 Newfoundland becomes a British colony
- 1824 Newfoundland is made a British Crown Colony
- 1855 Newfoundland gains responsible government
- 1869 Confederation talks fail
- 1895 A second round of Confederation talks fail
- 1934 Newfoundland gives up responsible government to Britain
- 1949 Newfoundland becomes Canada's 10th province
- 2001 Official name becomes Newfoundland and Labrador

The 10th Province

Newfoundland was the last province to join Confederation. In 1914 it was an independent former British colony with its own prime minister and government. Twice during the 19th century there had been discussions about Newfoundland joining Confederation, but Newfoundland had strong trade ties to Britain.

However, during the Great Depression, Newfoundland was almost broke. In fact, its government offered to sell Labrador outright to Canada, just to meet expenses. In 1934 British and Canadian governments agreed to help Newfoundland meet its financial obligations. It had to agree to a royal commission to study its economic and political affairs. It was a bitter pill for the independent country to swallow.

After World War II, with their debt paid off, Newfoundlanders had the opportunity to decide their own future by voting for one of three options:

- remain ruled by the British government commission
- return to self rule, the situation before 1934
- negotiate with Canada to become a province

Newfoundlander Joseph "Joey" Smallwood worked very hard for the Confederation option. In mid-1948 Confederation was chosen, but only by 52 percent of Newfoundland voters. The Canadian government, however, was satisfied with their choice. The province joined Canada the next year and Joey Smallwood was elected as its first premier.

Checkpoint ✓

18. Use the timeline to determine how long Newfoundland was an independent country. Why did Newfoundland resist joining Canada during the 19th century?

19. Use what you've learned about Canada's economic and social investments in the 1950s to draw a poster or create a pamphlet convincing the people of Newfoundland to join Confederation.

Chapter Summary

The post–World War II era featured rapid economic growth, a population boom, and the spread of American popular culture in Canada. In this chapter you learned about:

- Canada's population growth through immigration and the baby boom.
- Canada's economic growth after World War II.
- The effect of economic growth and television on Canadian lifestyle.
- How Canada expanded through economic and social programs and the addition of Newfoundland to Confederation.

automobile

TV

rock 'n' roll

Next, you'll examine Canada between 1961 and 1980, a time with dramatic changes for social groups that had been left on the fringe of Canadian society during the 1950s.

Wrap It Up

Understand it

1. Copy and complete this organizer chart to summarize the ways in which the United States influenced Canada socially and economically between 1945 and 1960. Review this chapter to find the information.

Social Influences	Economic Influences
1. Television: 2. Music: 3. Automobiles:	1. Natural Resources: 2. Manufacturing: 3. Transportation:

Think About It

2. Discuss whether or not the television families of the 1950s are like the television families today. As a group, try to agree on a few present-day television families that you think are true representations of modern Canadian families.

Communicate It

3. With a partner, select one social security program in Figure 10-11. Together, research the program and develop arguments to explain
a) why the program must be kept, and
b) why you think it should be phased out.
You and your partner should be prepared to debate either side in class.

4. Prepare a bulletin board display entitled Canadian Society in the 1950s. Include such topics as Music, Television, Movies, Fashion, Automobiles, Teenagers, Roles for Women, and the Baby Boom.

Apply It

5. Watch excerpts from popular movies about the 1950s. Keep a record of film images that remind you of things you learned about in this chapter. Are these images realistic compared with what you've learned in this chapter?

Performance Task

Review Your Predictions

At the beginning of this unit you made predictions based on three photos. Refer back to your predictions. How accurate were they? List three key things that you learned about each of the main topics in the unit.

Plan a "Then and Now" Local History Display

Every community has people and places that reflect its history. Suppose you've been hired to create an interesting display for an upcoming school or community reunion. Many of those who will be attending the reunion haven't been in the area since the 1940s or 50s. The theme of your display will be "Our Community Then and Now."

Step 1

Review the History Skills from this unit:

- Chapter 7: Reading and Drawing Maps (pages 143–144)
- Chapter 8:Making Generalizations Based on Statistics (pages 159–160)
- Chapter 10: Judging the Credibility of Information (pages 200–201)

You'll be using these skills in the following activity.

Step 2

Review the Inquiry Method on page xii. Use these steps to guide your research in Step 3.

Step 3

Work in groups of three or four to research, plan, and present a display, highlighting what your community was like in the 1940s and 50s and how it has changed.

Step 4

Combine your work with those of other groups to create a class display. Use photographs, oral presentations, audiotaped interviews, and "then and now" photos or video clips. If possible, invite parents or other members of the community to view your display.

Your display should include the following:

- at least one graph based on statistical information about the local community or region (you may use statistics that go further back than the 1940s and 50s). Include a caption that makes at least one generalization about these statistics.
- a brief written history of your community and how it has changed since the 1940s
- copies of old photos of the community (with captions) taken in the 1940s or 50s, alongside current photos of the same locations today (include such places as businesses, schools, places of worship, and other local landmarks)
- a large map (with legend) to show where the places in the "then and now" photos are located and to highlight other parts of the community that reflect the 1940s and 50s (e.g., World War II memorials, neighbourhoods built between 1945 and 1960, businesses and industries that existed then and still exist today)
- an interview with at least one person who lived in the community during the period you're researching
- a list of the sources you used, with a brief analysis of how credible you believe each source is, and why

To get started, check some basic community information sources:

- visit local museums or cultural centres
- check the Chamber of Commerce for information on what local businesses or industries existed during this period
- ask at your local library for historical photographs, statistics, and information about community history
- ask family or friends if they have any photos or memories they'd like to share
- look for facts about local history on the community's official website
- consult local street maps and the provincial road map for site locations

You might ask your interview subject to . . .

- comment on what the community was like back then
- explain how and why it has changed
- tell a story or anecdote about living in the community at that time

Growing Confidence, 1960–1980

Your Predictions Please # 4

Take a look at these three pictures—images of life in Canada between 1961 and 1980. Use the clues to guide you in looking more closely. Then predict what you might discover in this unit.

Clue 1 How can you tell that the participants were proud of their Aboriginal heritage?

Clue 2 What Aboriginal issues that you learned about earlier might have been discussed?

Clue 3 How might participants respond to a government proposal to end the Indian Act?

◀ Harold Cardinal, author and First Nations leader, attending a 1969 conference on the rights of Aboriginal peoples.

Prediction 1

Based on the clues, what do you think you'll learn about Aboriginal rights and issues in this unit?

Clue 4 What group of workers is demonstrating? Look closely to see what P.E.A.C.E. means on their signs.

Clue 5 What gender are the majority of people in the demonstration? Suggest their types of jobs.

Clue 6 What are the concerns of this particular group of workers?

clue

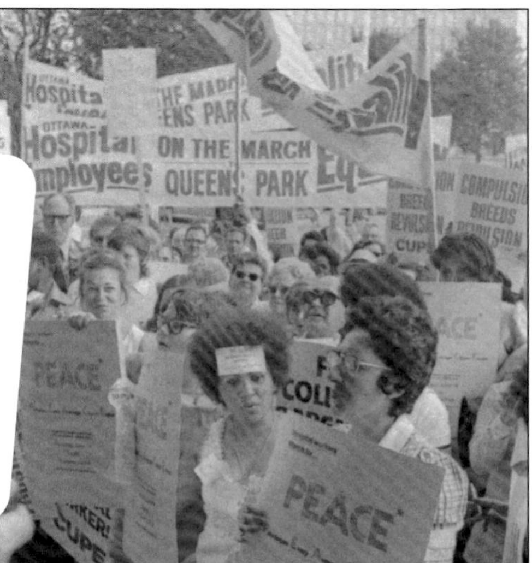

▲ Labour demonstration in Toronto, 1973.

Prediction 2

Based on the clues, what do you think you'll learn about working people in the period 1961–1980?

Clue 7 What seems to be happening in the photo? How can you tell?

Clue 8 What emotions do you think the participants would be experiencing?

Clue 9 How does this event reflect changes in Canadian society since World War II?

Prediction 3

Based on the clues, what do you think you'll learn about changes in Canadian immigration policy in this unit?

▲ Toronto's Caribana festival.

In this unit you will explore . . .

- some forces and events that have influenced Canada's policies and identity
- some influences on French–English relations in Canada
- ways Canada's population has changed
- changes in Canada's international status and role
- the impact of some political and social movements
- the contributions of some Canadian individuals to our identity
- changing economic conditions
- changing role and power of the federal government
- interpreting and analyzing information
- communicating the results of historical inquiries

Experience History

History teaches that some experiences can have important effects down the road. For example, in the 1950s teenagers emerged as a distinctive social group—and have helped shape society ever since. In your own life, you know that heading down the wrong track with the wrong friends can have negative results. Similarly, the actions that people and groups take today can affect Canadian society tomorrow.

Choose one of the three photos shown here, and consider how society can benefit from the actions it shows. Write a thoughtful journal entry in which you develop your ideas on this theme more fully.

Unit 4 Performance Task

At the end of this unit you'll use what you've learned to **hold a "sit-in" to protest issues from the 1960s or 70s.**

Chapter 11

A Changing Society

1960–1980 Trivia Quiz

The years between 1960 and 1980 featured many bold achievements in Canada. You may already know about some of them from family members or older friends. For this quiz, record your response to each question, then check with the teacher to see how you did. Take an educated guess if you aren't sure. More information about most of these questions appears in this chapter.

1. **Who scored the winning goal in the first Canada–USSR hockey tournament in 1972?**
   a) Paul Henderson b) Phil Esposito c) Ken Dryden
2. **Who ran the first Marathon of Hope for cancer research in 1980?**
   a) Steve Fonyo b) Rick Hansen c) Terry Fox
3. **Who first made the song "American Woman" a huge hit?**
   a) Neil Young b) The Guess Who c) Lenny Kravitz
4. **Who emerged in the 1970s as one of Canada's most famous authors?**
   a) Margaret Atwood b) Pauline Johnson c) Lucy Maud Montgomery
5. **Who became the first Canadian to win a Formula One Grand Prix race? (His son became the world champion.)**
   a) Scott Goodyear b) Gilles Villeneuve c) Paul Tracy
6. **Who wrote *The Unjust Society* criticizing Prime Minister Pierre Trudeau's "Just Society" program?**
   a) Stephen Lewis b) Joey Smallwood c) Harold Cardinal

▲ **Figure 11-1** The first Canadian to win a Formula One Grand Prix Race, in Montreal, 1978. Do you know who he was?

Checkpoint ✓

1. For your answers to the quiz, how many times can you say each of the following?

   a) I knew it for sure. b) I just took a guess.

   How did you know the answers for some of the questions?
2. Choose two of the people who you find the most interesting. Why would you like to learn more about them? What would you like to know?

Key Learnings

In this chapter, you will explore

- the impact of the baby boom generation
- how the lives of adolescents and women have changed
- why social support programs were established in Canada
- some factors shaping the experience of Aboriginal peoples
- how American culture and lifestyle have influenced Canada

Words to Know

counterculture
youthquake
lobby group
status Indian
Just Society
Aboriginal land claims
Can-con
equalization payments

Social Change in Canada

The years between 1961 and 1980 were an exciting time in Canada's history. Canadians and their government were finding new directions to take on issues connected to youth, women, Aboriginal policy, and government programs. These are the key topics of this chapter.

Literacy Hint

This chapter begins with the 1960s. As you read, recall television shows, movies, or photographs you've seen that are from, or about, that decade.

Canada's Birthday Party

The year 1967 was special for Canadians. Citizens' groups had been working with the federal government since 1961 to make sure everything was ready for the country's 100th birthday celebration. Musician Bobby Gimby had written a catchy jingle, sung by children, that was taught in schools and played endlessly that year. The sentiment was clear:

It's the hundredth anniversary of
Con-fed-er-a-tion.
Ev-'ry-bo-dy sing, together!
Ca-na-da, we love you . . .

For links to sites about Canada's centennial year, Expo 67, and Canada in the 1960s

Our centennial year celebrations highlighted many of the social changes and trends emerging during this era.

After much debate, the Maple Leaf design had become the national flag in 1965. It was flown widely in Montreal, where a world exposition called Expo 67 opened that spring. The huge exhibition featured impressive pavilions representing many different countries and themes. Despite the Cold War, both the United States and the Soviet Union were among them.

Everyone wanted to be there in Canada's magical summer of 1967. Attendance on the third day alone was 569 500! During its six-month run, an incredible 50 million people visited Expo 67. Here's one person's account of the event.

▲ **Figure 11-2** What is the purpose of large exhibitions like Expo 67? What do they do for the community that hosts them? What do they do for the people who visit them?

My parents, who hardly went anywhere, drove to Montreal for a week with my aunt and uncle. They just raved about Expo 67 when they got home, so my cousin and I decided that we had to go too. After all, we were mature 18-year-old girls and could look after ourselves. They were still in a good mood about their trip, so pretty soon we were on the train. Neither of us had been allowed to travel alone like this before.

We stayed with a family friend in Montreal, and enjoyed a week of freedom. Expo was like Disney's EPCOT, packed with pavilions from many countries. Canada's was beautiful—like a crystal pyramid turned upside-down. But we liked Czechoslovakia's the best because inside were some of the traditions we grew up with. We were born in Canada, but that was part of our heritage too. Expo 67 was something to remember!

Shirley Tripp

Did You Know?

Expo 67 was built on islands in the St. Lawrence River. One of them, Île Notre Dame, is an artificial island, built using earth excavated during construction of Montreal's subway system. Later, it became a Formula One racing circuit named after Gilles Villeneuve.

Checkpoint ✓

3. Would you like to visit something like Expo? If so, how might you arrange it (e.g., travel by train, stay with a family friend)? Suggest two such trips you might like to take.
4. When will Canada celebrate its 150th anniversary? How old will you be? Suggest ideas for celebrating this occasion in your community or in Ottawa.

The Youthquake

Since the baby boom had started in 1946, by the summer of Expo 67 the "early boomers" were already reaching adulthood. Many wore long hair, peace symbols, and colourful clothing, reflecting a strong focus on personal freedom. Sociologists call this the **counterculture**. The baby boom created a large group of young people who had a very different outlook from their parents'. They seemed to question and want to change everything the older generation believed in. The media termed it a **youthquake**—a large group of young people eager to shake the world.

The prosperity of the 1950s had given baby boomers comforts not known to their parents. Boomers watched television from an early age, and developed their own ideas about the world. For example, during the 1960s and early 70s, daily television news brought America's war in Vietnam into Canadian homes. Many popular songs carried strong anti-war messages, including tunes by Bob Dylan and John Lennon. Opposition to the war and to the older generation's values united many baby boomers.

Some baby boomers did set about changing the world in constructive ways. In fact, social activism by young people was greater between 1960 and 1980 than at any other time in Canadian history.

Did You Know?

John Lennon's song "Imagine" has become an anthem for peace. Canadian Neil Young sang it at a tribute to the heroes of the September 11, 2001, terrorist attack on the U.S. Lennon is said to have written the song on the back of a hotel bill while on an airplane.

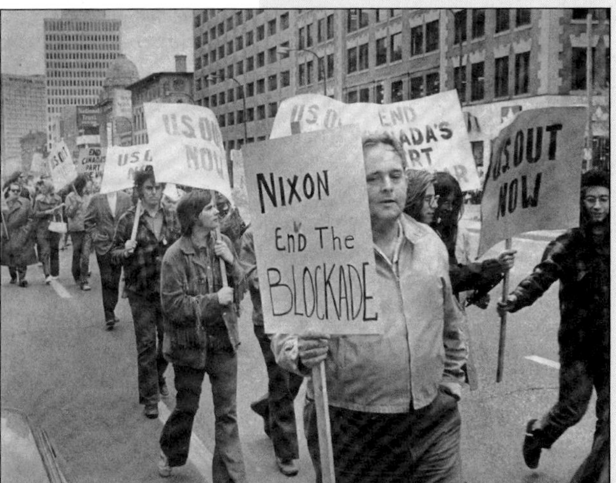

Figure 11-3 Several protests against the Vietnam War and other issues took place at Canadian schools and universities like this one at the University of Manitoba. It isn't surprising, because the baby boom had more than doubled Canada's university population between 1957 and 1967. What would inspire you to take part in a protest today?

Checkpoint ✓

5. Explain the terms "counterculture" and "youthquake." Why did many baby boomers hold the attitudes related to these movements? Do you think your generation has similar traits?
6. Consider the positive changes that young people tried to make in this era. Which of these causes, or others, do you think young people should be involved in today?

Did You Know?

The Greenpeace organization started in Vancouver in 1970 with a small group of people. They called themselves the "Don't Make a Wave Committee" and protested against nuclear testing in Alaska. Today, Greenpeace is a large international group that works to protect the environment.

Social Activism

Community Service: the Company of Young Canadians (CYC) worked to improve social services in low-income communities across Canada

International Service: Canadian University Students Overseas (CUSO) worked in developing nations in Africa, Asia, and Latin America

Environmental Movement: Vancouver-based Greenpeace and Toronto-based Pollution Probe attracted plenty of young people

Women's Movement: the United Nations declared 1975 International Women's Year, and many young women became activists

Aboriginal Movement: youth joined the National Indian Brotherhood and the Inuit Brotherhood to support their treaty rights and heritage

Profile: Terry Fox (1958–1981)

◀ Do you know anyone else who could do what Terry Fox did? What personal characteristics would it take? Why do you think he holds such an important place in people's memories?

Terry Fox is one Canadian baby boomer who may never be forgotten. His cause was a personal as well as a social one. He wanted to raise awareness of cancer and promote cancer research.

Terry was born in 1958, at the peak year of the baby boom. He was a competitive runner in high school, but in 1977 doctors found cancer in his right knee. His leg was amputated to prevent the disease from spreading. In 1980, Fox decided to run his own cross-country marathon to raise money for cancer research. At the time it seemed like a crazy idea. His parents and his doctor were opposed, but Terry had made up his mind, and he lined up a friend with a camper van to come along.

He started his Marathon of Hope at St. John's, Newfoundland, on April 12, 1980. Every day he ran a 42-km marathon on an artificial leg. Terry became a celebrity after he met Prime Minister Trudeau and the Marathon of Hope swung through Southern Ontario. Canadians watched him battle on for four months and 5373 kilometres. But he was forced to stop near Thunder Bay, Ontario, because cancer had spread to his lungs. Terry died just months later, and the whole country paused to mourn.

His courage and determination continue to inspire Canadians. More than $360 million has been raised for cancer research in the runs (and walks) dedicated to this Canadian hero.

Women in Society

Female baby boomers were the most educated generation of women ever. Many wanted professional careers, so they delayed marriage and family. The birth control pill, introduced in Canada in 1961, resulted in a steady decline in the birth rate that continues to this day. During this era, many young women adopted the "you can have it all" idea—that is, having both a family and a full-time job or career. More Canadian households than ever before were two-income families. This new outlook differed from the "single-income, stay-at-home-mom" family of the 1950s.

But in the 1960s Canadian women still didn't have equality with men, and many were disadvantaged economically. It was assumed that men were the main family providers. Married women without a job usually found it impossible to open a bank account, get credit, or even get a library card without their husband's signature. Professional women found it harder to get jobs and promotions than men with the same training did. In every single job category, women earned less.

Type of Work	Male Earnings	Female Earnings
Manufacturing	$112	$63
Senior Bookkeeper	$126	$99
Senior Office Clerk	$119	$93
Junior Office Clerk	$73	$65

Source: F.H. Leacy and M.C. Urquhart, eds., *Historical Statistics of Canada* (Toronto: Macmillan and Company, 1983), Series E60-68 and E326-375.

◀ **Figure 11-4** Average Weekly Earnings, Toronto, 1967. What percentage of male earnings did women make in 1967? To find out, add up each column, then divide female earnings by male earnings.

Political Action

Laura Sabia was a married Ontario mother with four children and an interest in community activism. She eventually became the leader of the Canadian Federation of University Women (CFUW). Sabia knew that women weren't getting a fair deal in many aspects of work and the law.

A determined organizer, she united the CFUW and 32 other groups to press Prime Minister Lester Pearson for a Royal Commission on the Status of Women. In 1967 Pearson reluctantly agreed, and three years

later the Commission reported to Parliament. Its conclusions don't seem as radical now as they did in 1970:

- Society should provide daycare services so that women with children can work outside the home.
- Employers should provide paid maternity leaves.
- Government should help eliminate discrimination against women in every aspect of life and work.

Judy LaMarsh was a cabinet minister in Prime Minister Pearson's government—only the second female to hold that position, after Ellen Fairclough. LaMarsh helped organize Canada's 100th birthday celebrations and set up the Royal Commission on the Status of Women. As Minister of National Health and Welfare, LaMarsh introduced the Canada Pension Plan and drew up Canada's medicare system.

During the 1960s only six women were in Parliament. LaMarsh knew how difficult it could be to interest politicians in acting on any tasks that weren't what she called "the big, shiny jobs." She wrote:

> The dirty jobs of politics, the ones of no glamour, often fell to me. Like a good soldier, I did my part. Women are much more realistic about this than men—we know that much of life is made up of dirty, tough jobs that someone has to do. . . . Women understand that men must often be kept from soiling themselves with the little dirty details of life in order to accomplish the big shiny jobs unimpeded. . . . Pity the Party without enough woman power. . . .

Judy LaMarsh, *Memoirs of a Bird in a Gilded Cage* (Toronto: McClelland & Stewart), 1968

Laura Sabia and Judy LaMarsh both knew that the male-dominated Parliament would need to be pressured to act on the Royal Commission's recommendations. So Sabia responded to Parliament's two years of delay by uniting many groups to form the National Action Committee on the Status of Women (NAC). This was a **lobby group**—people who try to convince politicians to take a particular point of view on issues. The NAC has been very important; for example, in 1982, it ensured that women's equality was clearly guaranteed in Canada's new Charter of Rights and Freedoms (more on this in Chapter 17).

◀ **Figure 11-5** Laura Sabia (left) and Judy LaMarsh (right). These were two of the most politically important Canadian women of the 1960s. How far do you think women have come in politics since then?

Checkpoint ✓

7. a) Summarize four examples of the inequalities faced by Canadian women in the 1960s. Which one do you think is the worst? Why?
   b) Do you see any inequalities for women today? How strongly do you feel about women's issues? Explain.
8. What similarities do you see between Judy LaMarsh and Laura Sabia? Give examples of what each woman achieved.
9. Examine the quotation from Judy LaMarsh more closely. In your own words, explain her views about men and women. To what extent do you agree with her? Why?

Aboriginal Peoples

The years from 1960 to 1980 brought great changes for Aboriginal peoples. First Nations, Métis, and Inuit groups organized and pressured government to recognize the unique needs of their societies, including the need to address land claims and treaty obligations.

The Indian Acts

In Chapter 4 you learned that the original Indian Act of 1876 put the Canadian government in charge of virtually every aspect of First Nations peoples' lives.

When the Indian Act was revised in 1951, several restrictions on First Nations cultural practices were removed. However, many government officials believed that the reserves helped protect First Nations cultures, so new rules were introduced to speed up assimilation. Any woman who married a non-Aboriginal man was no longer considered a **status Indian**

Did You Know?

The term "Aboriginal peoples" includes First Nations, Métis, and Inuit. The term "First Nations" came into use in the 1970s to replace the word "Indians," which many found inappropriate. The term "First Nations" doesn't have a legal definition, but is generally used to mean both status and non-status Indians. It doesn't include Métis and Inuit. Many First Nations use "First Nation" to replace the Indian Act word "band" in the name of their community.

For links to sites about the Indian Acts

(a person registered under the Indian Act). Nor would any of the children from this marriage be allowed to live on a reserve or to have legal status. The fight by First Nations women to have this law repealed continued until 1985 (see Chapter 17).

In 1960 First Nations women and men finally received the right to vote in federal elections. But their reaction to this surprised the government. Many Aboriginal leaders and organizations saw it as another trick to assimilate their people. There was great distrust. One reason was that, in the past, many First Nations war veterans who had voted weren't allowed to return to their reserves. To this day, First Nations participation in federal and provincial elections falls far below the overall Canadian average.

Did You Know?

When Newfoundland joined Canada in 1949, the Terms of Union contained no specific references to the Aboriginal peoples in Newfoundland and Labrador (Mi'kmaq, Innu, Inuit, and Métis). Nor were there any previous treaties between Aboriginal peoples and the Newfoundland government, and no reserves. The governments did not consider recognizing or extending rights to Aboriginal peoples in the new province as an important concern.

Checkpoint ✓

10. Explain how the Indian Act of 1951 was both an improvement and a step backward from the original Act.
11. Draw a mind map to show the challenges that Canada's Aboriginal peoples had to deal with up to the 1960s.

The "Unjust Society"

Pierre Elliott Trudeau was elected prime minister in 1968 on the promise of a **Just Society** (with "just" meaning "fair"). This political slogan meant that his government would support equality for every Canadian. For example, laws were changed so that homosexuality was no longer a deviant crime in Canada. As well, the laws regulating divorce were made more liberal. Talks were also started with First Nations representatives aimed at addressing issues affecting their lives.

These leaders clearly restated similar concerns about land claims, treaty rights, and economic issues that Chief Frederick Loft had outlined 50 years before (see Chapter 4). So they were shocked, then angered, when the Indian Affairs minister, future prime minister Jean Chrétien, presented the government's plan for a new policy in 1969. This discussion paper, called a White Paper, seemed to ignore everything the First Nations leaders had said.

Instead, it proposed assimilating their peoples into Canadian society within five years by getting rid of both the Indian Act and the Indian Affairs Department. The federal government would no longer be responsible for Indians as a legally identifiable group. Indian status would no longer exist, and the importance of any land claims or treaties signed in the past was downplayed.

The White Paper rallied First Nations, Métis, and Inuit communities across the country, and regional and national organizations were formed. Their leaders soon produced a counter-proposal entitled *Citizens Plus*. This proposal restated their demands for land and treaty rights and for special status as the original peoples of Canada. Increased self-government was a major theme of their plan. Harold Cardinal, president of the Indian Association of Alberta, led the attack on the government. His 1969 book, titled *The Unjust Society*, sharply criticized the views of Trudeau and Chrétien. Cardinal wrote:

▲**Figure 11-6** The 1970s saw increased activism and debate about Aboriginal issues. Frank Calder, a Nisga'a leader and the first First Nations member of a Canadian legislature (B.C.), is shown here in 1973 after a meeting with Prime Minister Trudeau and Indian Affairs Minister Jean Chrétien. (Read more about the Calder Case on page 222.) How can citizens make their voices heard?

> The history of Canada's Indians is a shameful chronicle of the white man's disinterest, his deliberate trampling of Indian rights and his repeated betrayal of our trust. . . .
>
> The new Indian policy . . . is a thinly disguised programme of extermination through assimilation. For the Indian to survive, says the government in effect, he must become a good little brown white man. . . . The Americans to the south of us used to have a saying: "The only good Indian is a dead Indian." The . . . Chrétien doctrine would amend this but slightly to, "The only good Indian is a non-Indian."

Harold Cardinal, *The Unjust Society* (Toronto: McClelland & Stewart), 1969

The government quietly dropped its White Paper. But the outcry against this proposal had sparked the political rebirth of the First Nations, Métis, and Inuit. Debate about government policy made the general public more aware and supportive of Aboriginal issues. Across Canada, governments began to consult with high-profile political groups. One of these was the National Indian Brotherhood, which became the Assembly of First Nations (AFN) in 1980. The AFN represents the elected governments of 633 First Nations across Canada.

Another example is the Inuit Brotherhood, which was formed in 1971 to speak with one voice on issues related to northern development and Inuit culture. Today it is known as the Inuit Tapiriit Kanatami (ITK), and continues to work for the following goals:

- to preserve Inuit language and culture
- to promote dignity and pride in Inuit heritage
- to identify Inuit needs and promote their well-being
- to improve communications among Inuit communities
- to help Inuit participate fully in Canadian society

For links to sites about the National Indian Brotherhood, the Assembly of First Nations, and the White Paper

The Métis

The Métis originated in the 17th century as the children of First Nations women and European men. They became a distinct people of mixed ancestry with their own culture.

Métis communities grew in the Upper Great Lakes area and westward throughout the Prairies and Northwest. The Métis played a key role in the fur trade. They also developed a unique culture and way of life, including skills in trade and transportation. Throughout their history, they have pressed for both their rights to land and the preservation of their language and culture.

Did You Know?

According to the 2001 census, Alberta has the largest Métis population, with 66 055. Manitoba follows with 56 795, and Ontario has 48 345.

Checkpoint ✓

12. Summarize the following in a T-chart: three changes proposed by the Canadian government's White Paper and three main points made by First Nations leaders in their reply in *Citizens Plus*.
13. Why do you think Harold Cardinal was so angry? Outline examples of positive effects that came about at least partly because of his book.

Land Claims

The Canadian government recognizes two types of **Aboriginal land claims**: specific and comprehensive (meaning "covering a wide area or a lot of things"). They are compared in the following chart.

	Specific Claim	Comprehensive Claim
Definition	made when the government fails to meet an obligation to First Nations people or Inuit either under treaty or in law	deals with lands where First Nations people and Inuit have continuing rights not given up by a treaty or other legal means
Example	reserves established by treaties were sometimes not made as large in size as what the treaty said	these claims often involve very large tracts of land, e.g., much of British Columbia is subject to comprehensive claims
Status, 1973–2003	252 claims settled	10 claims settled

◀ **Figure 11-7** Specific and Comprehensive Land Claims. What is your response to the number of claims that were settled in a 30-year period?

Did You Know?

The federal specific-claims policy was put into place in 1973. But over the next 30 years, only about 20 percent of 1201 specific claims were settled. Some of the unsettled issues have been disputed for 200 years.

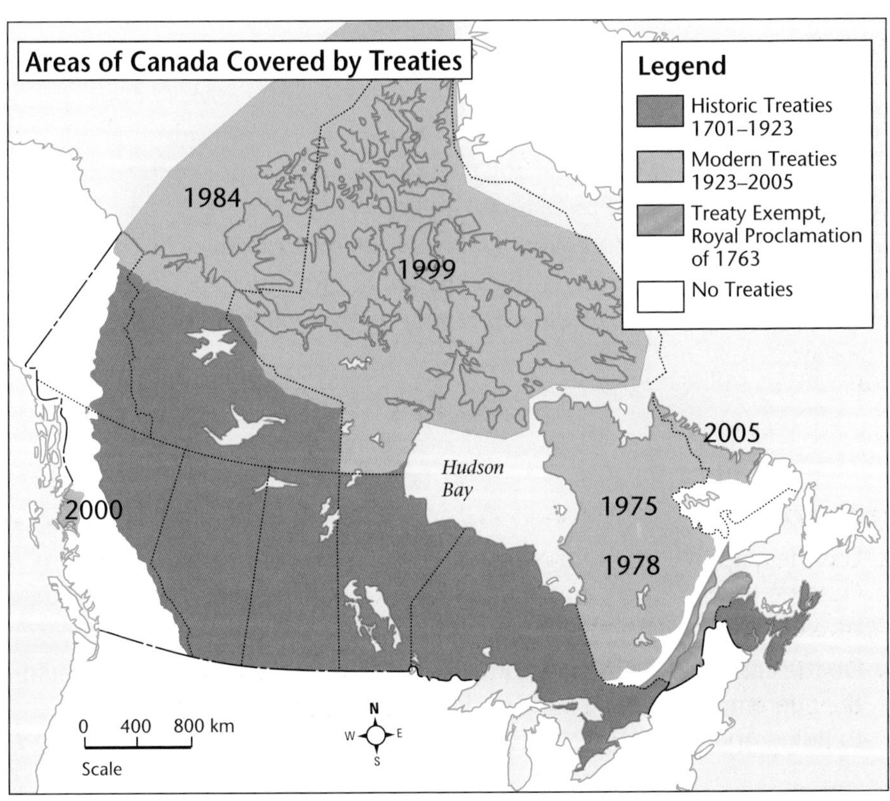

◀ **Figure 11-8** Areas of Canada Covered by Treaties. Find the area where you live. Is it covered by a treaty with First Nations or Inuit peoples?

The Supreme Court of Canada made a landmark land claims ruling in 1973 called the "Calder Decision." It stated that the Aboriginal right of first occupation gave them a legal claim to land where no treaty had ever been made to give up Aboriginal ownership. This important ruling, combined with the political organization of First Nations and Inuit, has led the government of Canada to make modern treaties. All the "modern treaties" shown on the map in Figure 11-8 were signed after 1973.

The map also shows large areas still without treaties in parts of Atlantic Canada, Quebec, British Columbia, and the Yukon. While there are First Nations reserves in these regions, there are also many unsettled comprehensive land claims and disputes about traditional hunting and fishing rights. The one exception is the island of Newfoundland. The Beothuk people who lived there before Europeans came have been extinct since the early 19th century.

The Calder Decision was based on the British monarch's Royal Proclamation of 1763. All land claims currently being researched will be judged according to the following standards from that Proclamation:

> . . . And whereas great frauds and abuses have been committed in purchasing Lands of the Indians. . . . We do, with the advice of our Privy Council [of Britain], strictly . . . require, that no private person do presume to make any purchase from the said Indians of any Lands reserved to the said Indians. . . . But, that if at any time any of the said Indians should be inclined to dispose of the said Lands, the same shall be purchased only for Us [the Crown], in our Name, at some public meeting or assembly of the said Indians. . . .

Did You Know?

According to the Royal Proclamation of 1763:

- Lands must be bought, not just taken from, First Nations peoples.
- Only the Crown (and its official agents) can buy First Nations lands.
- The Crown can buy only when the first occupants are willing to sell.
- The purchase must be made at a public meeting, not in private.

Checkpoint ✓

14. Use the map to compare the area of Canada without treaties to the areas of "historic treaties" and "modern treaties." Rank them first, second, and third by area. Why have so many treaties been made in the past 30 years or so?

15. Do the conditions of the Royal Proclamation seem fair to you? Why would the Supreme Court have gone back so far in history to find rules by which to judge Aboriginal land claims?

The James Bay Project

During the 1970s two huge energy developments were proposed for northern Canada: the James Bay Power Project in Quebec and the Mackenzie Valley Pipeline in the Northwest Territories. Both developments threatened the traditional way of life of the Aboriginal peoples in those areas.

At James Bay, the Quebec government planned to develop the largest hydroelectric power project in the world. However, officials did not consult with, or even inform, the Aboriginal people living in the project area.

Figure 11-9 The James Bay Power Project. Note the photograph in the centre showing Cree fishers of the James Bay area. How would the power project affect their livelihood?

1

The James Bay power project would allow Quebec to sell large volumes of electricity to the U.S., especially to neighbouring New York State and New York City.

2

The $21 billion project would redirect the flow of three large rivers into La Grande Rivière, doubling its water volume. Eight giant dams and power installations would be built, and huge areas would be flooded behind the dams.

3

No treaties had been made with the Cree First Nation and Inuit that lived there. They strongly objected because the project threatened their hunting and fishing livelihood. The Assembly of First Nations and many environmentalists supported them.

4

Treaties signed in 1975 and 1978 recognized Aboriginal claims to the land. In all, about $500 million was promised to protect the cultures and livelihoods of Cree and Inuit peoples in the area.

5

The first surge of hydroelectric power flowed from the project in 1979, although the overall plan wasn't finished for several more years.

Checkpoint ✓

16. Locate the two James Bay treaties on the map in Figure 11-8. How did the Royal Proclamation of 1763 help solve some of the controversy about the James Bay project?

17. Society has a huge "energy appetite." In your opinion, should governments and corporations build huge projects to produce more energy? What are some of the other answers to current energy shortages?

Government and Society

During the 1960s the federal government spent heavily on a wide range of social and economic programs. In this section, you'll learn about two particular government programs of the era: one to protect Canadian culture and the other to create jobs in low-income regions.

Protecting Canadian Culture

Literacy Hint

Before reading, figure out what the topic is and then think about what you already know about it. The two questions in this paragraph help you do that.

What types of music do you like to listen to? Do you know how to tell whether or not music is considered "Canadian"? Government regulations control much of what you hear and see in the Canadian media. Like them or not, these content regulations have been very important to the careers of many Canadian-born performers.

Tough Rules Stand Guard Over Canadian Culture
by Anthony DePalma

Lenny Kravitz's raunchy remake of the '70s classic "American Woman" had been thoroughly dissected, and the music director of Toronto's CHUM-FM radio station was satisfied that it was, indeed, Canadian. Surprising, since neither the singer nor the subject of the song has a direct connection to the Great White North.

But the music and anti-American lyrics—reflecting common Canadian views—were written by members of the Guess Who, a popular Canadian band of the 1970s. That gives "American Woman" the two points it needs under Canada's intricate system of rankings to help meet CHUM-FM's government-imposed requirement that 35 percent of its daytime playlist be devoted to Canadian content. . . .

The point system for determining Canadian content goes by the acronym MAPL—music, artist, production, lyrics—and assigns one point for each category where a Canadian is predominantly involved. At least two points are required for a record to be treated as Canadian.

So while Rod Stewart's "Rhythm of My Heart" is accorded the two points because the music and lyrics were written by Mark Jordan, a Canadian, Celine Dion's hit "My Heart Will Go On" from the movie "Titanic" cannot be counted in a radio station's quota for Canadian content because it gets only one point, for the artist. ■

In Chapter 10 you saw that most Canadians didn't seem concerned about growing American ownership of the economy during the 1950s. That changed after 1960, as many people saw that U.S. music, television, movies, and magazines dominated Canadian pop culture.

Talented Canadians couldn't be successful in the entertainment world unless they went to America. Politicians decided that it was time to protect Canadian culture.

So, in 1968, the federal government created the Canadian Radio-television and Telecommunications Commission (CRTC). Every radio or television station in Canada needed a CRTC licence, and to keep it, the station had to follow strict regulations. These included the Canadian content rules that you just read about. Broadcast rules were meant to support Canadian writers, producers, and performers by requiring

- 30 percent Canadian content ("**Can-con**") in the daytime music on radio stations
- 60 percent Can-con in prime-time television programming

Over the years these percentages have been changed a bit, and, of course, they apply only to radio and TV stations located in Canada.

Between 1960 and 1980, Ottawa made several other moves to promote and protect Canadian culture. Billions in tax dollars went to support Canadian movies, books, theatre, and history. Chapter 14 explores more of these government plans.

For links to sites about Can-con and the CRTC

Checkpoint ✓

18. Review the requirements for music to be classified as Canadian. Use these requirements to show why three examples of current songs are classified as Canadian.

19. Who are some of your favourite Canadian musicians? How much does it matter to you to hear Canadian musicians on the radio?

20. Discuss this question with a partner: "Does Canadian culture need government protection?"

The Atlantic Revolution

Walter Gordon's 1957 Royal Commission on Economic Prospects (see Chapter 10) proved that the four Atlantic provinces were rapidly falling behind the rest of Canada. Average incomes were far below richer provinces such as Ontario and British Columbia. With continued migration to Ontario and the West, people were becoming the region's major export.

The Atlantic region needed rapid social and economic change, and the federal government was ready to use **equalization payments** to help. These transfers of money from Ottawa to lower-income provinces are part of Canada's social security network.

Did You Know?

In 1974, $23 million went to U.S. promoter Malcolm Bricklin to build his exotic plastic gull-wing sports car in New Brunswick. Only 2854 Bricklins were built before the company went bankrupt.

For links to sites about the Atlantic Revolution and the Newfoundland Resettlement Program

During the 1960s and 1970s, billions were spent on what historian W.S. MacNutt called the "Atlantic Revolution." Hundreds of projects were introduced to upgrade transportation, create jobs, and generally improve people's lives. Many possibilities were considered. For example, both New Brunswick and Nova Scotia attracted auto assembly plants (which, in 2005, no longer exist). One 1968 study even recommended unifying New Brunswick, Nova Scotia, and Prince Edward Island into a larger, more efficient province. But a hundred years of provincial status proved too hard to give up, and the advice was ignored.

Newfoundland Outports

One of the biggest projects was Premier Joey Smallwood's plan to move 30 000 people from about 250 small communities along the

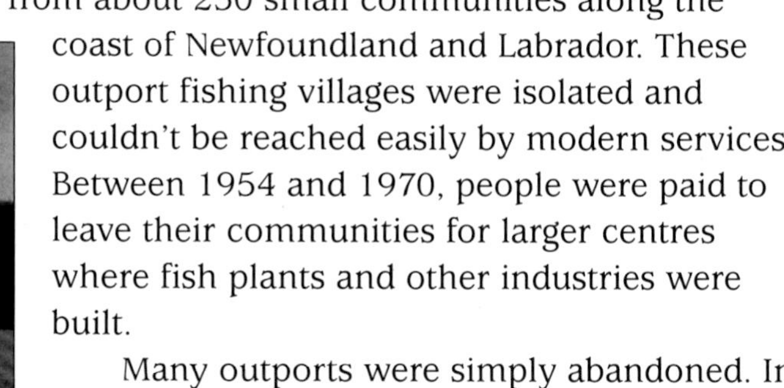

coast of Newfoundland and Labrador. These outport fishing villages were isolated and couldn't be reached easily by modern services. Between 1954 and 1970, people were paid to leave their communities for larger centres where fish plants and other industries were built.

Many outports were simply abandoned. In other cases, people were able to tow their homes along the ocean shoreline to the new location. The destruction of traditional outport life was difficult for many Newfoundlanders, especially older residents.

▲**Figure 11-10** Two programs—the Newfoundland Resettlement Program and the earlier Newfoundland Centralization Program—were among the largest government-sponsored resettlements in Canadian history. How would you react to being told you had to move to a larger centre?

Checkpoint ✓

21. Suppose you're a Maritimer on the commission studying Maritime unification.

a) Use an atlas to find recent population figures for Canadian provinces. Add up the areas and the populations of the three Maritime provinces. Then compare these figures to the other provinces. What do you observe?

b) List three reasons why it might be wise for these provinces to unite.

c) Suggest three reasons why these provinces didn't want to unify.

22. Discuss your feelings about abandoning your community and moving to a larger centre. How might your parents and grandparents (and other family members) feel about such a move?

The years between 1960 and 1980 brought about much social change in Canada as the federal government introduced policies and programs. In this chapter, you have learned:

- How the baby boom generation affected Canadian society up to 1980.
- How the lives of adolescents and women changed after the 1950s.
- How Aboriginal peoples persisted to gain land and treaty rights.
- How the federal government has tried to protect Canadian culture.
- Why social and economic support programs were established.

The next chapter discusses language and cultural issues. Its focus is on Quebec separatism and Canada's new multicultural policy.

Expo 67

Just Society

Can-con

Wrap It Up

Understand It

1. Show your understanding of Can-con regulations by keeping track of a Canada-based radio station's playlist. Use the MAPL point system. Create a chart to show the station's Can-con points for one hour. Did that hour meet the 35 percent requirement?

Think About It

2. Find out more about the Mackenzie Valley pipeline proposal, and the Berger Inquiry that resulted. What views were expressed by Aboriginal peoples? How did this inquiry reflect a different attitude by the government than it showed with the Indian Acts? Prepare a brief report.
3. Think about the issues that people fought for in the 1960s and 1970s. Write a letter to the editor about an issue worth supporting today.

Communicate It

4. Research the National Action Committee on the Status of Women during the 1970s. Then, with a partner, prepare and present a realistic conversation between Laura Sabia and Judy LaMarsh about NAC.
5. Communicate your knowledge of the social changes that took place in the 1960s by researching and presenting information on some of the popular protest songs and musicians of the era, including Canadians.

Apply It

6. How would you rule on the following specific-claim case? Identify the sections of the Royal Proclamation that seem to apply.

Band A asked for compensation for a small area of land in Southern Ontario now covered by the edge of a growing city. About 150 years ago, their chief personally sold this portion of the reserve directly to an individual investor. Since then, the land has been subdivided into land for homes, schools, businesses, and farms.

Chapter 12

Language and Culture

Terrorism in Canada

Sometimes you may think, "Canadian history is so boring—nothing ever happens!" We live in a normally quiet country, dedicated to the idea of "Peace, Order and Good Government," a phrase from our Constitution. But during the October Crisis of 1970, Canada faced terrorism head-on.

A radical group called the FLQ—Front de Libération du Québec—kidnapped James Cross, a British diplomat living in Montreal. They demanded freedom for 23 FLQ members jailed for bombing and other terrorist acts. The Canadian government, however, refused to negotiate. Five days later, Pierre Laporte, a Quebec cabinet minister, was kidnapped at machine-gun point. In response, Prime Minister Trudeau proclaimed the War Measures Act and sent Canadian troops in to guard government buildings and officials. The FLQ was made illegal, and anyone suspected of connections to it was held without charges. A day after the Act was put in place, police got a printed message from the terrorists about Pierre Laporte:

valet: French for servant or slave

chômage: French for unemployment

Bourassa: the Quebec premier

Dieppe cell: one of the branches of the FLQ

BECAUSE OF THE ARROGANCE OF THE FEDERAL GOVERNMENT AND ITS VALET BOURASSA. . . . PIERRE LAPORTE, MINISTER OF CHÔMAGE AND ASSIMILATION WAS EXECUTED THIS EVENING AT 6:18 BY THE DIEPPE CELL. YOU WILL FIND THE BODY IN THE TRUNK OF A GREEN CHEVROLET 9J-2420 AT ST. HUBERT BASE.

Translated copy of the kidnappers' note, in Pierre Elliott Trudeau, *Memoirs* (Toronto: McClelland & Stewart, 1993), p. 145

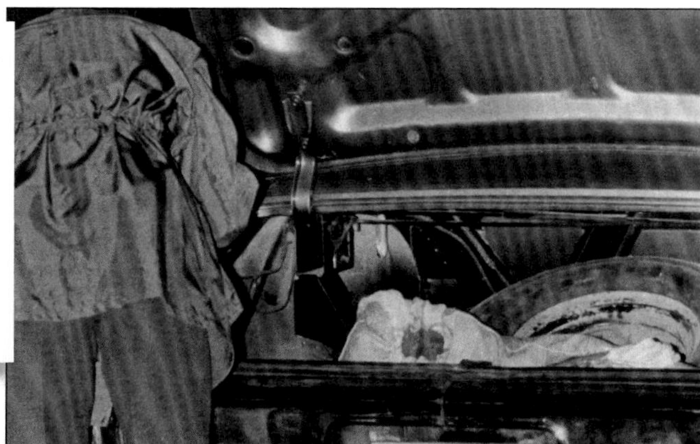

▲ **Figure 12-1** The body of Pierre Laporte, found near St-Hubert airport. How do you think Canadians reacted to seeing this news photo?

Laporte was dead, and there was still no word about James Cross. Then, two months later, intense police work located the kidnappers' hideout. Cross was released unharmed in exchange for an airplane to fly the kidnappers and their families to Cuba. Later in December, the crisis ended when three FLQ members accused of murdering Pierre Laporte were captured and brought to trial.

And you may have thought that Canadian history is boring!

Checkpoint ✓

1. Why do you think the FLQ kidnapped the second victim, Pierre Laporte? Why do you think they executed him and then led police to the body?
2. Should a government negotiate with terrorists? What approach do you think is the best? Explain your ideas with examples.

Key Learnings

In this chapter, you will explore

- the growth of Quebec nationalism and the separatist movement
- some key responses to the Quebec separatist movement
- efforts of French Canadians outside Quebec to get recognition
- contributions to Canada's multicultural society by some of its regional, linguistic, ethnic, and religious communities

Words to Know

patronage
Quiet Revolution
official languages
separatists
federalism
Parti Québécois
sovereignty-association
Bill 101
referendum
multiculturalism
points system
refugee status

Quebec and Canada

Many changes took place in Quebec after 1960. These changes created great tension between the province and the rest of Canada.

Literacy Hint

Before you read this section, jot down anything you already know about Quebec's relations with the rest of Canada. Add to your list as you read, and also write down any questions you want answered.

The End of an Era in Quebec

When Quebec premier Maurice Duplessis died in 1959, it was the end of an era. His very conservative Union Nationale (UN) party had ruled the province for most of the time since 1936. The party's aim was to uphold traditional rural French-Canadian values focused on church,

home, and family. Under the Union Nationale, the Roman Catholic Church was very powerful. Few things happened in Quebec without Duplessis's approval. The Union Nationale operated through corruption and **patronage** (the privileges or positions given by a politician to selected people).

Did You Know?

A 1949 strike in Asbestos, Quebec, rallied labourers, union activists, the Church, and intellectuals against the Union Nationale. Strikebreakers were brought in after 5000 miners walked off the job. Serious violence broke out as Quebec police cleared picketing miners out of the way. Duplessis's tough anti-union stance was not forgotten, and the seeds of change were planted.

The Quiet Revolution

Jean Lesage's Liberals were elected in Quebec in 1960 on their promises of political and economic change. This period of change in Quebec was called the **Quiet Revolution**. Premier Lesage gathered people around him who saw the need for change. They believed that corruption must go, education must be reformed, and Quebec must become more independent.

In 1962 the Lesage government was re-elected under the slogan "Maîtres Chez Nous." This means "masters in our own house" (meaning Quebec). The aim was to make the province stronger and more economically independent from Canada. For example, the province "opted out" of certain federal programs, such as family allowances, and set up its own pension plan. Quebec borrowed from the pension fund for major investments, like Hydro Quebec. The province also set up a department of cultural affairs to support French language and culture.

▲ **Figure 12-2a** Before 1960, few Quebec students graduated in science, technology, and business. Lesage introduced CEGEPs (pronounced *say-jeps*)—technical schools that are similar to community colleges. Why do you think he did this?

▲ **Figure 12-2b** To strengthen Quebec, Lesage's government bought out local electricity companies to form huge, provincially owned Hydro Quebec. How is the production and sale of electricity handled in other provinces?

Checkpoint ✓

3. What is meant by the term "Quiet Revolution"? Connect the Quiet Revolution to the Asbestos strike.
4. Identify each of the following and explain how it was part of the Quiet Revolution: a) CEGEPs b) Maîtres Chez Nous c) Hydro Quebec

The Bi and Bi Commission

By 1963, Prime Minister Pearson was worried about Quebec's new mood. He set up a Royal Commission on Bilingualism and Biculturalism (nicknamed the "Bi and Bi Commission") to gather opinion from across Canada about relations between the English and the French. Members of the Commission especially wanted to hear from francophones (people whose first language is French) outside of Quebec. These included the Acadians in the Maritimes, Franco-Ontarians, and francophones in the West.

Francophones had struggled for years to preserve their French language and culture. They believed that losing their language would soon spell the end of their distinctive cultures. Yet, in many provinces, people were strongly opposed to operating French-language schools with public funds. Even Bi and Bi Commission co-chairperson André Laurendeau was surprised by the anti-French feelings he heard.

The Commission completed the first part of its report in 1967. It made several recommendations, which soon became the Official Languages Act:

- French and English should be made **official languages** in Parliament and federal offices. (An official language is the one the government uses for its citizens.)
- As national capital, Ottawa should be declared officially bilingual.

Did You Know?

The Acadians were French-speaking people who settled in the Maritimes in the early 1600s. They were innovative in farming marshy land along the Bay of Fundy. During war with France, the British expelled them from the region, but afterwards many returned. Today there are almost 300 000 Acadians in the Maritimes.

Figure 12-3 Davidson Dunton (left) and André Laurendeau, co-chairs of the Bi and Bi Commission. Why would French groups outside Quebec want French-language schools?

- French and English should be official languages in provincial legislatures and offices where the minority group is at least 10 percent of the population (currently New Brunswick, Ontario, and Quebec).
- Bilingual language services should be available in districts where the minority group is at least 10 percent of the population.
- All parents should have the right to educate their children in either official language, French or English.

Parliament adopted the first two points very quickly, and New Brunswick soon declared itself officially bilingual. This was a victory for the centuries-old Acadian culture.

In 1983 the French-speaking minority in Manitoba successfully pressured the province to adopt both official languages. Three years later, Ontario agreed to provide government services in French and English, though it stopped short of declaring official bilingualism. Many provinces do offer French-language services in francophone districts, and provinces have established language immersion programs, where students use French all day.

▲ **Figure 12-4** The recent opening of Collège Boréal in Sudbury helped meet Franco-Ontarians' need for higher education in their first language. What French-language schools are located in or near your community?

For links to sites about the Bi and Bi Commission and francophones in Canada

Francophone Facts

- About 7 million Canadians have French as their first language.
- Almost 1 million Canadian francophones live outside of Quebec.
- About 500 000 francophones live in Ontario.
- About 240 000 Acadians live in New Brunswick.
- More than 55 000 Albertans are francophone. In 1999 the Alberta government formed a Secretariat of Francophone Affairs.
- Most provinces have organizations for francophone communities. For example, Newfoundland and Labrador has the *Fédération des francophones de Terre-Neuve et du Labrador* to promote French heritage and language.

Checkpoint ✓

5. How did the Bi and Bi Commission become a victory for francophones in New Brunswick, Ontario, and Manitoba?
6. Are there francophone areas in or near your community? How could you find out about the history of French settlement in your area or province?

FLQ Terrorism

Encouraging the use of the French language did not interest the Front de Libération du Québec (FLQ). This small Quebec terrorist group wanted primarily one thing—Quebec independence. At first, most Canadians didn't take them very seriously. After all, they specialized in street fighting and blowing up mailboxes. But by 1969 the FLQ had stepped up the violence, with bombs targeting the Montreal Stock Exchange and wealthy Quebec businesspeople. Several members were captured, tried, and imprisoned for these acts.

France's president, Charles de Gaulle, helped make the FLQ bolder. In a 1967 visit to Quebec, de Gaulle gave a spirited speech about Quebec's special connections to France. **Separatists** (people who wanted an independent Quebec) went wild when de Gaulle ended his speech with the dramatic cheer: *"Vive Montréal! Vive Québec! Vive Québec libre!"* This angered the Canadian government, and Prime Minister Pearson bluntly ordered de Gaulle to leave the country.

Literacy Hint

As you read this section, recall the opening page of this chapter. Writers sometimes start with a gripping story and then describe the details that led up to it. In this section, we return to that opening story.

◀ **Figure 12-5** President de Gaulle giving his controversial speech in Montreal. Why did it cause such an uproar? What is your opinion of what he said?

Checkpoint ✓

7. What did the FLQ want? Outline how President de Gaulle may have contributed to their increasing violence.
8. Think of another example of a speech that stirred up strong feelings in people who heard it. What is something you've said that led others to action?

Federalism and Separatism

For links to sites about separatism and federalism, and the Parti Québécois

By the late 1960s two strong positions about Quebec had emerged. One argued that Quebec should become independent from Canada (separatism), while the other called for a strong central government to hold the country together (**federalism**). It didn't take long for them to come into direct conflict.

Two Tough Opponents

Canada got a new leader in 1968. Prime Minister Pearson had announced his retirement, and his Liberals unexpectedly chose Pierre Elliott Trudeau to lead. Trudeau had been in Parliament for only a few years, serving as justice minister. He believed that a strong federal government in Ottawa should use its policies and spending for the good of the whole country. He was French Canadian, and a politician the Liberals felt would understand Quebec but speak for all of Canada.

Most important of all, Trudeau knew how to play to crowds and the media. He was single, and was very popular with female supporters. He once joked that he didn't really like kissing babies, but couldn't say the same thing about kissing their mothers! In 1968, "Trudeaumania" swept Canada, and he was elected prime minister.

Quebec got a new political party that same year. René Lévesque was a former journalist (see Chapter 9) dedicated to separatism by peaceful methods. He led the formation of the provincial **Parti Québécois** (PQ) in 1968. Ten years earlier, he and Trudeau had been friends with opposite ideas, but soon the federalist and the separatist became bitter opponents. Lévesque was a passionate politician, a dynamic speaker who appealed to voters' emotions. His new party spoke for an independent Quebec, and its popularity steadily increased until the PQ was elected to power in 1976.

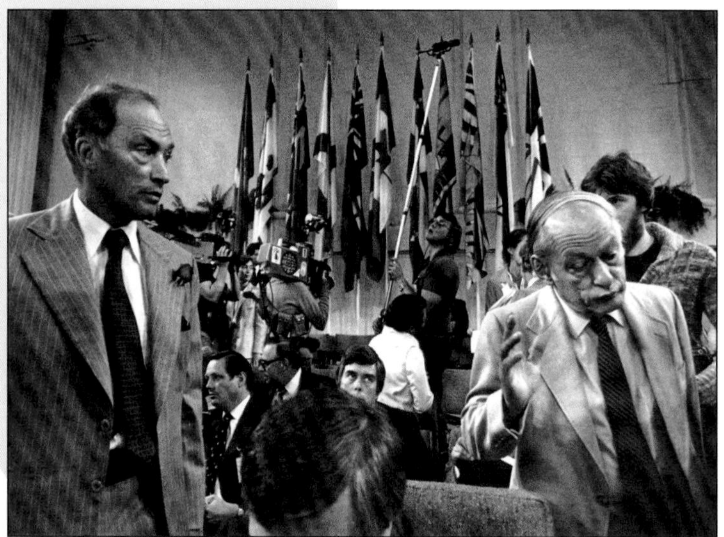

◀ **Figure 12-6** Trudeau and Lévesque. Why do you think these former friends became so opposed?

The October Crisis

In the chapter opening, you read that in October 1970, FLQ terrorists kidnapped British diplomat James Cross and Quebec Labour Minister Pierre Laporte. The terrorists demanded the release of FLQ prisoners, half a million dollars, and a plane to Cuba. Meanwhile, separatists demonstrated in the streets in support of the kidnappers and their cause. Trudeau flatly refused to negotiate with the terrorists and sent in Canadian soldiers.

Quebec premier Robert Bourassa and Montreal mayor Jean Drapeau urged Trudeau to declare the War Measures Act. This Act had been used only twice before, to give the government emergency powers during both World Wars. But Trudeau knew that it took away some freedoms of Canadian democracy, and so he waited a little longer. Then, six days after the second kidnapping, Trudeau put the Act in place.

A news reporter questioned the prime minister about these emergency powers, asking, "How far will you go?" Trudeau snapped back, "Just watch me!" About 450 people with suspected links to the FLQ were quickly rounded up and jailed without arrest for more than the 48-hour limit normally used under the Criminal Code. Some spent weeks in jail. Mistakes were made too, as some people with no FLQ connections at all were held. They were later compensated by the Quebec government for this violation of their civil rights. The War Measures Act itself remained in effect for about two and a half weeks.

Did You Know?

Five of James Cross's kidnappers were flown to Cuba. Later they turned up in Paris. Homesick, they finally returned to Quebec between 1979 and 1981 to face criminal charges. Another was arrested in Canada and tried 10 years after the October Crisis. All six spent a few years in jail.

▲ **Figure 12-7** The military was brought in to stand guard in Montreal during the October Crisis. How does the inclusion of children affect the meaning of this photograph?

Checkpoint ✓

9. a) What is meant by "Trudeaumania"? Explain why Canadians voted for Trudeau in 1969.
   b) How do Canadians view their politicians today? Do any enjoy the level of popular support Trudeau received?
10. Why was Trudeau not eager to declare the War Measures Act? How did it violate some people's rights?

Conflicting Views on the War Measures Act

1. René Lévesque, Leader of the Provincial Parti Québécois

Quebec no longer has a government. . . .

Bourassa's cabinet has turned in its hand and is no longer anything but a puppet of the federal rulers.

It is now clear that from the very beginning of this tragic period marked by the kidnapping of Mr. Cross, this government has only had a bit player's part. During the pseudo-negotiations initiated last Sunday by Mr. Bourassa, we were, alas, obliged to conclude that it had accepted to serve simply as the instrument of a policy conceived and determined outside its control [that is, in Ottawa] . . . and finally, it was this government that backed the extreme move of the Trudeau regime in placing the whole of Quebec under military occupation. . . .

René Lévesque, *Journal de Montréal*, October 16, 1970

bit player: an actor who doesn't play major roles

pseudo: not real

regime: a period of rule by a harsh or oppressive government

2. Pierre Trudeau, Prime Minister of Canada

Was I wrong in acceding to the reasons they [Premier Bourassa and Mayor Drapeau] presented to me? I don't think so. And I am certain that, had I not declared the War Measures Act when I did, I would be accused today of . . . ignoring the repeated appeals of the premier of Quebec and the mayor of Montreal, thus demonstrating my contempt for the competence of the government of Quebec as well as the administration of Montreal, and finally acting as if the federal government knew the situation better than anyone else, as if we alone were capable of rational judgment. And at the same time, I would be held responsible for the eventual death of Pierre Laporte.

Pierre Trudeau, *Memoirs* (Toronto: McClelland & Stewart, 1993), p. 142

acceding: agreeing to

contempt: a feeling of scorn, or that someone is worthless

Checkpoint ✓

11. In a dialogue with a partner, summarize Pierre Trudeau's reasons for declaring the War Measures Act and René Lévesque's reaction to the prime minister's actions.
12. From what you've read, do you think Trudeau's use of the War Measures Act was acceptable? Explain your views by referring to information in this section. What would you have done if you were prime minister?

The PQ Plan: Sovereignty-Association

Unlike the outlawed FLQ, René Lévesque wanted neither outright independence nor the use of violence. The Parti Québécois plan called for **sovereignty-association**, meaning that Quebec would be a politically independent province, with links to Canada's economy. For example, Quebec would have its own prime minister, but would still use Canadian currency.

In the 1976 provincial election Lévesque was elected premier. He didn't want to move too quickly on sovereignty-association. At the same time, he knew that many Québécois who weren't separatists worried that Quebec immigrants were learning English rather than French. To get their support, he would highlight French-language issues.

NOW REMEMBER, I'VE CHANGED THE OPERATION FROM COMPLETE SEPARATION TO SOVEREIGNTY ASSOCIATION... THAT MEANS WE'LL BE COMPLETELY SEPARATE ... EXCEPT FOR WHERE I'M ATTACHED TO YOUR WALLET...

▲ **Figure 12-8** Here's how one political cartoonist pictured Lévesque, Trudeau, and sovereignty-association. How does the cartoon show the idea? What does the cartoonist think of the idea?

Bill 101: Language Issues Heat Up

In 1977 the Parti Québécois passed **Bill 101**, the Charter of the French Language. It made French the province's only official language of government, and limited the use of English in many ways. For example, all outdoor advertising signs must use only French. Minority groups in Quebec protested that Bill 101 took away their civil rights. Prime Minister Trudeau was angry about the bill, but powerless to stop it. Lévesque had prepared the foundations for his next big step—Quebec independence.

Checkpoint ✓

13. Complete a chart to review terms from the section above:

Term	Meaning	Importance
Parti Québécois		
sovereignty-association		
Bill 101		

14. How was Bill 101 linked to the PQ's plan for sovereignty-association? In your opinion, was Bill 101 a good strategy for the PQ? Explain.

First Separatist Referendum

How does a **referendum** differ from an election? A referendum is a type of election, but instead of voting for people, electors vote on a question. In 1979 René Lévesque and the Parti Québécois knew that a referendum on separation from Canada would be a big decision for voters. Instead, they decided to ask voters to take the first step.

Voters would choose whether or not to begin talks with Canada about sovereignty-association for Quebec. That was Lévesque's plan: political independence, with economic ties to Canada. The idea was so complicated that the voting ballot had four paragraphs of explanation! After that, it was simple: marking "Oui" meant "start the negotiations with Canada," while "Non" meant "don't separate from Canada."

Separatism was very popular with Quebec baby boomers, a large group in 1980. Lévesque toured the province, using his convincing style in support of "Oui." Prime Minister Trudeau was worried enough to enter the campaign himself. He promised that a "Non" vote from Quebec would start a process to give Canada a new Constitution, a new deal between the provinces.

In the end, a small majority of the French-speaking Quebec voters said "Oui" to sovereignty-association. But most of the English minority, Aboriginal peoples, and immigrants in Quebec voted "Non." The final results weren't as close as expected: "Oui" was 40 percent, and "Non" was 60 percent. Canadians were relieved, but another independence referendum in 1995 would be much closer.

▲**Figure 12-9** Yes or no to sovereignty-association? Both sides campaigned heavily. How might any referendum affect neighbourhoods and even households?

Checkpoint ✓

15. What were Quebec voters being asked to decide in the 1980 referendum? How did Trudeau and Lévesque each get involved in the campaign?

16. With a partner, create a dialogue between two family members—one who voted "Oui" and one who voted "Non."

Immigration and Multiculturalism

During the period 1960 to 1980, changes in immigration policies altered Canada's population. This made it necessary to recognize the importance of many different cultures within our nation. By 1971, Parliament approved a policy of **multiculturalism** that has become a key feature of Canadian identity today.

For links to sites about Canada's immigration and multiculturalism policies

Immigration Changes

Canadian immigration was changing. For almost a century, Canada welcomed Britons, Europeans, and Americans, while virtually banning all others. By 1962, however, the Canadian government recognized that this policy was clearly discriminatory and out of date.

New rules were introduced that year, and later fine-tuned in the Immigration Act of 1978. A **points system** was used to score immigrant applications from around the world—almost like a test in school. Points were given for English or French language skills, and for the education and experience needed to work in Canada. Age, family sponsors, and other criteria also helped officials decide who could start a new life in Canada.

Year	Total Immigrants*	Europe (incl. Britain)	U.S.	Asia	South and Central America	Caribbean	Africa and Oceania
1960	104	83	11	4	2	2	3
1965	147	108	15	11	3	3	6
1970	148	76	24	21	5	13	7
1975	188	73	20	47	13	20	12
1980	143	41	10	72	5	8	7

Source: John Robert Colombo, *The Canadian Global Almanac, 1994* (Toronto: Macmillan Canada, 1994), p. 64, from Immigration Canada.

▲ **Figure 12-10** Origins of Immigrants to Canada, 1960–1980 (in thousands). When was the peak year for immigration in the years shown in this chart? What country or area had the biggest change in number of immigrants?
* Numbers may not add up to the total because of rounding off.

Checkpoint ✓

17. Work with a partner to construct two line graphs based on Figure 12-10 as follows. Then compare the graphs and discuss: To what extent did Canada's 1962 policy change immigration?

    Graph A: For each year, add the numbers for Europe and the U.S. (Canada's traditional sources of immigration). Make a line graph for the five dates.

    Graph B: For each year, add the numbers in the four columns on the right (few immigrants to Canada before 1962). Make a line graph for the five dates.

Refugees

In 1978 Canada accepted the United Nations' definition of refugees as people who are unwilling or unable to return to their homeland due to persecution, which means cruel or unfair treatment. Their situation must be based on race, religion, nationality, political ideas, or social class. Since 1978 about 650 000 people have used **refugee status** to resettle in Canada, an average of about 25 000 annually. Worldwide, Canada ranks second only to the U.S. in the resettlement of refugees.

The "Boat People"

In 1975, near the end of the Vietnam War, the former South Vietnamese capital city of Saigon fell to the communists. Refugees began to escape in small boats or overland to neighbouring Cambodia. In all, more than 6.5 million refugees fled the country between 1975 and 1980. Canadians saw their plight on television news and responded with an outpouring of support.

Figure 12-11 More than 60 000 Vietnamese people were admitted to Canada between 1979 and 1981. The new immigration laws had made this possible. Canadians donated money, clothing, and furniture to help resettle the "boat people." What conditions had the refugees experienced on the escape boats?

Trent Kilner remembers very little about the fall of Saigon. He was one of 57 Vietnamese children airlifted from the city by missionaries on April 10, 1975, just as the Communist forces prepared to enter. Trent was only about two and a half years old. He's not really sure of his age because there are no records of his birthdate or his birth parents. Trent was immediately adopted by the Kilner family of Sarnia, Ontario, where he grew up.

As a young adult, Trent spends hours trying to piece together his early years. Information flooded in when CBC-TV picked up his story from the local newspaper. Bob Nicholson, who piloted the Saigon rescue flight, e-mailed Kilner with this:

I have fond memories of the orphans in four rows of cardboard boxes, extending the length of the Hercules cabin. . . . Everyone pitched in to ensure that no baby died of dehydration en route to Hong Kong.

Trent Kilner's search for his origins continues. To date, he's linked up with half the Vietnamese orphans on that flight. ■

Adapted from Sarnia *Observer*, April 19 and April 26, 2005

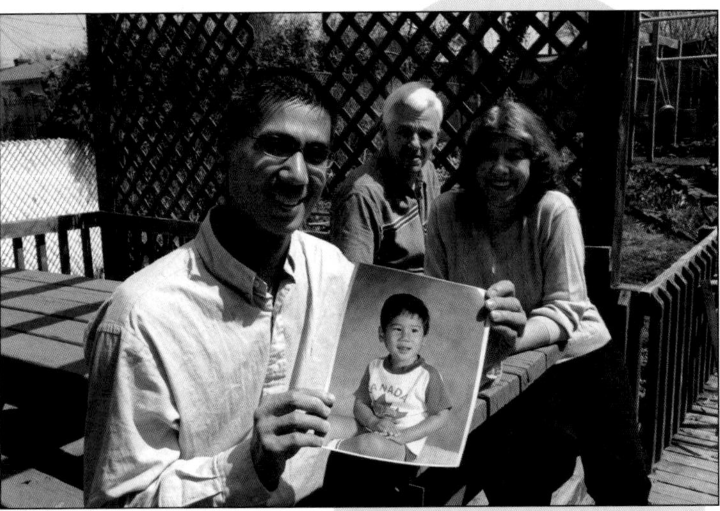

▲ **Figure 12-12** Trent Kilner with his adoptive parents. Do you know of any groups in your community that assist immigrant or refugee families? What types of assistance might be needed?

Checkpoint ✓

18. Compare the "points system" to "refugee status." Why does Canada make use of two different systems for classifying immigration applications? Why did many Vietnamese qualify for refugee status?

19. Brainstorm five different examples of the ways your community has helped people in need. Include at least one example based on new immigrants or refugees.

Multiculturalism Recognized

Let's go back to the "Bi and Bi Commission." It wasn't just about French and English. The Commission was also told to consider the contributions of other ethnic groups to the culture of Canada. At the time, it was little more than an afterthought, but it soon became as important as the rest of the study!

Gertrude Laing, from Calgary, was the first woman ever appointed to a Canadian royal commission. Her role was important, because pioneer

Did You Know?

The first enforceable human rights code in Canada was established in Ontario in 1962. The Ontario Human Rights Code prohibits discrimination on the grounds of race, creed, colour, nationality, ancestry, or place of origin. A Commission makes sure that the code is followed.

ethnic groups from western Canada—the Ukrainians, for example—wanted their contributions as "founding peoples" in the region recognized right alongside the English and French. A new idea called multiculturalism emerged from this part of the Royal Commission.

Many ethnic groups were eager to talk to the commissioners about the value of their culture to Canada. Up to this point, minority groups had simply been expected to assimilate—to fit into majority ways and learn English or French. Otherwise, cultural practices and customs were considered a personal matter, not of any interest to governments. "Hyphenated Canadianism," meaning thinking of oneself as Italian-Canadian or Chinese-Canadian, for example, was accepted but not officially encouraged. But the Bi and Bi Commission's massive report changed all that.

Checkpoint ✓

20. Explain each of the following terms, using an example from Canada:
a) bilingualism b) biculturalism c) assimilation d) hyphenated Canadianism e) multiculturalism

Canada's Multiculturalism Policy

On October 8, 1971, Prime Minister Trudeau presented the Commission's multicultural report to Parliament with these words:

> It was the view of the royal commission, shared by the government . . . that there cannot be one cultural policy for Canadians of British and French origin, another for the original peoples [Aboriginals] and yet a third for all others. For although there are two official languages, there is no official culture, nor does any ethnic group take precedence over any other. No citizen or group of citizens is other than Canadian, and all should be treated fairly. . . . A policy of multiculturalism within a bilingual framework commends itself to the government as the most suitable means of assuring the cultural freedom of Canadians.

Hansard, October 8, 1971

In a rare display of unity, all the Opposition parties supported Prime Minister Trudeau's policy of multiculturalism. There was no point in thinking of English and French as Canada's leading cultures any more. These were simply the official languages, spoken by many different ethno-cultural groups. Parliament voted to accept four key principles of Canada's unique multicultural policy:

- to financially assist cultural groups to grow and contribute to Canada
- to assist members of cultural groups in Canada to fight discrimination
- to promote exchanges between cultural groups to increase national unity
- to help immigrants learn at least one of Canada's official languages, English or French

Since then, Canada's multicultural policy has been widely accepted, but not by everyone. At first, there was some resentment about focusing on Canada's cultural variety. Today, intolerant individuals remain hostile toward Aboriginal peoples, immigrants, and a variety of religious and ethnic groups. Extremist hate groups use the Internet to deliver their white-supremacy messages. But many mainstream groups, such as the Canadian Labour Congress, are strong supporters of Canada's multicultural policy.

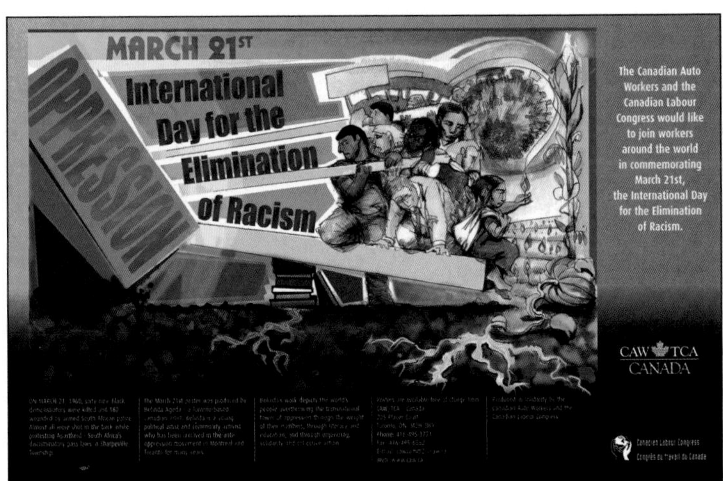

◀ **Figure 12-13** Canadian Auto Workers/Canadian Labour Congress anti-racism poster by artist Belinda Ageda. Which principles of multiculturalism does this poster represent?

Checkpoint ✓

21. Summarize Prime Minister Trudeau's views on the cultural variety of Canada in your own words. Do you agree with him? Explain.

22. Why do you think some people are intolerant of other cultures? What actions can you suggest to help solve the problem of racism?

History Skill: Recognizing Fact, Opinion, and Inference

When you're reading or discussing, you should be able to distinguish fact, opinion, and inference. This skill helps you to analyze information effectively.

Step 1

Understand the terms:

- A *fact* is something that can be proven to be true or false. It is specific information, such as names, numbers, dates, or events.
- An *opinion* is a judgment about something. It can be argued.
- An *inference* is a conclusion based on facts.

Step 2

During your reading or discussion, ask yourself:

- Is there hard evidence, such as dates, numbers, or names? Can much of this be proven? If yes, then the material is factual.
- Does the author seem to have an opinion about the subject? Is the author trying to convince me? If yes, then the material is an opinion.
- Are there facts that support a point? Have conclusions been made from facts? If yes, then the author has made inferences.

Step 3

To be sure that the information is correct, look up the topic in other sources to compare.

To recognize fact, opinion, and inference . . .

- ✓ recall that a fact is something that can be proven to be right or wrong; an opinion is a person's judgment; an inference is a conclusion based on fact
- ✓ question yourself about the writer's intent
- ✓ if you want to be sure the information is correct, check it in other sources

Practise It!

1. Read the following sentences. For each one, decide whether it is fact, opinion, or inference.
   - The 1970s was the best decade in Canada's history.
   - Immigration statistics show the effects of Canada's new immigration policies.
   - Pierre Trudeau declared the War Measures Act in 1970.
2. Review at least two excerpts in this chapter and note the facts, opinions, and inferences in each one.

Chapter Summary

Issues of language and culture were very important between 1960 and 1980. Great changes occurred in the relationship between Canada and Quebec, and in Canada's acceptance of the wide variety of cultures within the country. In this chapter, you have learned that:

- The "Quiet Revolution" reflected many changes in Quebec.
- Quebec had two separatist movements—one violent, one peaceful.
- Canadian federalism was determined to hold the country together, as shown in the October Crisis of 1970.
- The Official Languages Act supported the language and culture of French minorities outside of Quebec.
- Changes in immigration led to Canada's multiculturalism policy.

In the next chapter you'll explore the economic developments that Canadians experienced during the same time period.

FLQ

Official Languages Act

1980 referendum

multiculturalism

Wrap It Up

Understand It

1. Make a summary chart to show the effects of the Bilingualism and Biculturalism Commission, as follows:

A. Official Languages Act	B. Multiculturalism Policy

2. a) Compare the similarities and differences of the separatist views held by the FLQ and the Parti Québécois.
   b) Summarize the idea of sovereignty-association in your own words. Then outline the strengths and weaknesses of this idea in a paragraph, chart, or radio commentary.

Think About it

3. Think about how Canada might be affected by Quebec's separation. Consider political (e.g., boundaries), economic, social, and international effects. Then prepare a one-page report that expresses your thoughts on the topic in words or images.

Communicate It

4. Create a music and word collage on the theme of multiculturalism, using samplings from recorded music or original songs.
5. Investigate either Pierre Trudeau or René Lévesque, and prepare a brief biography using this textbook's Profile features as a model.

Apply It

6. Conduct a classroom referendum on an important issue in your school. First, carefully develop the wording. Conduct the vote, and then display and discuss the results.

Chapter 13

Economic Expansion and Crisis

As you'll read in this chapter, the 1970s were a period of economic uncertainty. It was difficult for investors to know what to do.

History Game: *What Should I Do with My Savings?*

Required to Play:
- one deck of cards
- paper and pencils
- one calculator (optional)

Purpose:
To help you understand some of the uncertainties of investing. Can you beat the inflation rate?

Objective: To win by having the most money at the end of the game.

How to Play:
1. Play with a partner. The game has 10 rounds.
2. On a sheet of paper, write the players' names across the top and the numbers 1 to 10 down the left-hand side.
3. Each player starts off with an imaginary $100.
4. One player (the dealer) shuffles the cards and deals the top card, face down. The other player (the investor) looks at the card to see what it's worth. This card represents the interest rate. The cards are valued as follows.

   Ace = 1 point
   2 to 10 = 1 point for each number
   Face cards = 10 points

   The investor may keep the card or return it to the deck. If the investor returns the card, the dealer deals a second card, face down. *The investor must keep the second card.*
5. The dealer takes the next card and places it face up. This card represents the rate of **inflation** (rising prices). The investor then turns her or his card face up.
6. The players then calculate the difference between the two cards. Follow the example in the table below.

   The difference between the two cards represents the real rate of interest received on a Guaranteed Investment Certificate. For Player A in the table, the interest rate is 7 percent and inflation is 2 percent. This gives a real interest rate of 5 percent.
7. The average investor adds the difference (if a positive number) or subtracts it (if a negative number) on his or her running total and writes that figure on the score sheet. Players both begin the game with $100. So, in the example, Player A would write "$105 ($100 + $5)" under his or her name on the score sheet for Round 1.
8. Switch roles to complete Round 1. In the example, Player B got a negative 7, so would write "$93 ($100 – $7)" on the score sheet.
9. Complete rounds 2 to 10, adding or subtracting to the running totals. The player with the most money is the winner.

Follow-Up:
1. When you were the investor, what factors helped you decide whether to keep or replace the first card you were dealt?
2. When was it easy to know whether to keep the first card? When was it difficult?

Player	Investor's Card (Interest Rate)	Dealer's Card (Inflation Rate)	Difference (Investor's Minus Dealer's) (Real Interest Rate)
Player A	7 of hearts = 7	2 of clubs = 2	5
Player B	3 of spades = 3	10 of hearts = –10	–7

Key Learnings

In this chapter, you will explore

- economic conditions of this time and their impact on families
- Canada's changing relationship with the U.S. and U.S. participation in the Canadian economy
- effects of freer trade and globalization on Canada's economy
- key struggles and contributions of the labour movement
- contributions of some Canadian entrepreneurs

Words to Know

inflation
oil crisis
embargo
Auto Pact
Foreign Investment Review Agency (FIRA)
globalization
civil servants
public employees
entrepreneurs
private companies
public companies

The Economy Races (1960s), Then Limps (1970s)

From 1960 to 1980 the Canadian economy grew tremendously. International trade expanded, with Canada offering much that the world wanted. We can see this rapid expansion in whatever part of the economy we examine—agriculture, natural resources, or manufacturing.

Economic Expansion

This table illustrates how significant the economic expansion was.

Year	Minerals ($ billion)	Manufactured Goods ($ billion)	Agricultural Exports ($ billion)	Total Exports ($ billion)
1960	140	24	1.6	5 390
1970	300	47	2.9	16 820
1980	1 600	170	12.7	76 158

Source: *Canadian Oxford School Atlas*, 5th ed., 1985, pp. 16A, 18A, 19A.

Figure 13-1 Value of Production of Selected Items, Canada, 1960, 1970, 1980. How would you describe the change in figures between 1960 and 1980?

Literacy Hint 

Skim through the chapter to see what the main topics are. As you read, keep a graphic organizer such as a web or a simple list to keep track of the main points and the key terms.

The figures in this table show a massive expansion. If, for example, you divide the 1980 figure for minerals by the 1960 figure, you get the following result: 1600 ÷ 140 = 11.4

This seems to suggest that mineral production rose by 11.4 times between 1960 and 1980—a huge amount for a 20-year period. But the price of minerals went up. Each tonne of coal and barrel of oil increased in value between 1960 and 1980. So the *value* of mineral

production went up by 11.4 times, but the *amount* of mineral production went up by a smaller amount.

Employment Growth

The growth of the economy created employment. The number of jobs rose, especially during the 1960s. Let's look at some statistics.

Figure 13-2 Total Number Employed, Male and Female Unemployed, Canada, 1966, 1972, 1980. Note that the number of employed people rose, but so did the number of unemployed. In other words, after 1966, the number of jobs available didn't rise as fast as the number of people seeking them. What might be some reasons for this?

Year	Total Number Employed (000)	Male Unemployed (%)	Female Unemployed (%)
1966	7 242	3.3	3.4
1972	8 344	5.8	7.0
1980	10 708	6.9	8.4

Source: *Canadian Oxford School Atlas*, 5th ed., 1985, p. 20A.

The Oil Crisis

The economy moved ahead in stops and starts. Although it varied across the country, the economy generally raced throughout the 1960s, slowed in the early 1970s, and hit some rough spots in the late 1970s.

In 1973 the first **oil crisis** occurred. Industrialized countries like Canada and the U.S. had become more and more dependent on cheap imported oil. Oil-producing countries, especially in the Middle East, demanded more money. They started an **embargo**—they deliberately shipped less oil to force prices up. In the international market, a barrel of oil rose from about US$2.50 in 1972 to US$7 in 1974. Then, after a second oil crisis in 1979, oil rose to US$15.

Figure 13-3 Lining up for gas, New Jersey, 1973. Scenes like this were also common in Canada. If we were to experience an oil shortage now, how would it affect you? What do you think the government would do?

The increased oil price made it more expensive for Canadian businesses to operate. They were forced to raise their prices, and then the demand for their products slowed. This caused companies to lay off workers, and the unemployment rate rose. You can see the rising unemployment rate in the previous table.

People who lived through this period tend to have fonder memories of the 1960s than the 1970s. By the late 1970s, you could get over 10 percent interest a year if you put your money into an investment certificate in a bank. But prices were rising at around 12 percent a year, and mortgage rates were very high, so you were no further ahead. The period from 1960 to 1980 was one of unevenness. The economy expanded, but it also had some serious problems.

The term "energy crisis" was first used in 1970. It meant a shortage of fuels created by too much demand. It led to rapidly increasing energy prices in the 1970s, and contributes to rising prices today.

Checkpoint ✓

1. Look at the way the mineral production figures were compared in order to calculate that they expanded 11.4 times between 1960 and 1980. Use the same method to calculate the expansion of a) manufactured goods and b) total exports. Did they expand more rapidly or more slowly than minerals? Explain.
2. What's the cost of gas in your community today? What effect do increased fuel prices have on prices for groceries, clothes, and other consumer goods? Why? If the prices of goods rise, what will workers say to their bosses about wages? If bosses give workers pay raises, what are they likely to do to the price of the goods they sell? Do you think this kind of pressure exists today? Explain.

Canada-U.S. Relations: Deepening Ties

Since Canadians live next door to such an economic giant as the United States, it's natural that the two countries have a strong economic relationship. The U.S. is the largest economy in the world. Transport links between the two countries are good. Each creates products that the other wants to buy.

Tariffs and Branch Plants

In the early 1900s the Canadian and American economies became more closely related. Mineral operations such as those in Sudbury, Ontario, and Labrador City, Newfoundland, were producing top-quality

For links to sites about the 1973 oil crisis and Canada–U.S. economic relations

product, and American factories were hungry for the nickel, copper, and iron. The U.S. was interested in Canada as a source of natural resources.

But Canada offered another opportunity. It was part of the British Commonwealth. This allowed it to sell manufactured goods in other Commonwealth countries at reduced tariffs. You may recall from Chapter 4 that a tariff is a tax on imports. Let's take the example of Britain. By 1910 it was producing a range of cars. It also allowed other countries to export their cars to Britain and sell them there. To make these imports more expensive (which would encourage people to buy British cars), the government placed a tariff on them. But it charged a lower tariff on cars and other products that were made in the Commonwealth. So, in Britain, a car made in Canada carried a lower tariff than one made in the U.S.

American car manufacturers saw that if they set up assembly plants in Canada, the cars they produced would qualify as Canadian. Cars that were exported to Britain and other Commonwealth countries would have the lower tariff. So a number of American companies established branch plants in Canada. You read about these plants in Chapter 4; they were controlled from American headquarters (in this case, Detroit).

Let's look at a brief history of the "Big Three" automakers in Ontario.

- The Ford Motor Company of Canada Limited was established in 1904. It opened its first automobile assembly plant in Windsor, and produced many of its groundbreaking Model T Fords there. After World War II it built a large complex in Oakville, Ontario, where much of its production is done today. Ford now employs about 10 000 people.
- General Motors of Canada Limited was established in 1918. It began production at Oshawa, Ontario, where its headquarters remain. It currently employs about 35 000 people.
- The Chrysler Corporation of Canada was established in 1925, and opened its first assembly plant in Windsor in 1929. It has gone through a number of reorganizations, and is now known as Daimler-Chrysler Canada Inc. It is still largely centred in Windsor, and has about 17 000 employees.

In the 1980s, Japanese companies like Honda and Toyota also opened plants in Ontario. But this wasn't to make it easier to sell them in Commonwealth countries; it was to make them easier to sell in the U.S.

The Auto Pact

Eventually, as Canadian car and parts production grew, Canadian factories could produce a surplus of goods. But it was expensive for automobile companies to have an assembly plant in Michigan and another in Ontario that produced the same vehicles for their local markets. So, in 1965, the Canadian and American governments signed an agreement popularly known as the **Auto Pact**. The Pact allowed producers to ship parts and finished vehicles across the two countries' borders free of tariffs. This meant that an Ontario plant could sell its vehicles anywhere in the U.S. without restriction. (The reverse was true as well.)

The Auto Pact was significant because it allowed producers to use fewer but larger plants to supply the whole North American market. Canada benefited enormously from the Auto Pact. After 1982 it exported more automotive products to the U.S. than it imported. The Pact helped make automotives the largest manufacturing sector of the economy.

Study the following steps and the map on the following page for an example of cross-border trade.

1 Rough castings for engine pistons are produced at a foundry in Pennsylvania. They're sent to an automobile parts manufacturer in Windsor.

↓

2  The rough castings are machined and assembled into finished pistons, placed in sets, and shipped to an engine assembly plant in Ohio.

↓

3  The pistons are assembled into an engine, which is then shipped to Oakville, Ontario.

↓

4  The engine is assembled into a car at the Oakville plant.

↓

5 

The finished car is shipped to Florida for sale.

In 2002 Canadian light vehicle (cars and light trucks) assembly was 2.6 million units. Light truck production has grown to almost equal that of passenger cars.

Literacy Hint

This is a sample of a flow chart printed on a map. Note its parts: numbers and arrows that give an order of events; locations; and diagrams. Use the list on the previous page with this map to work out the series of steps.

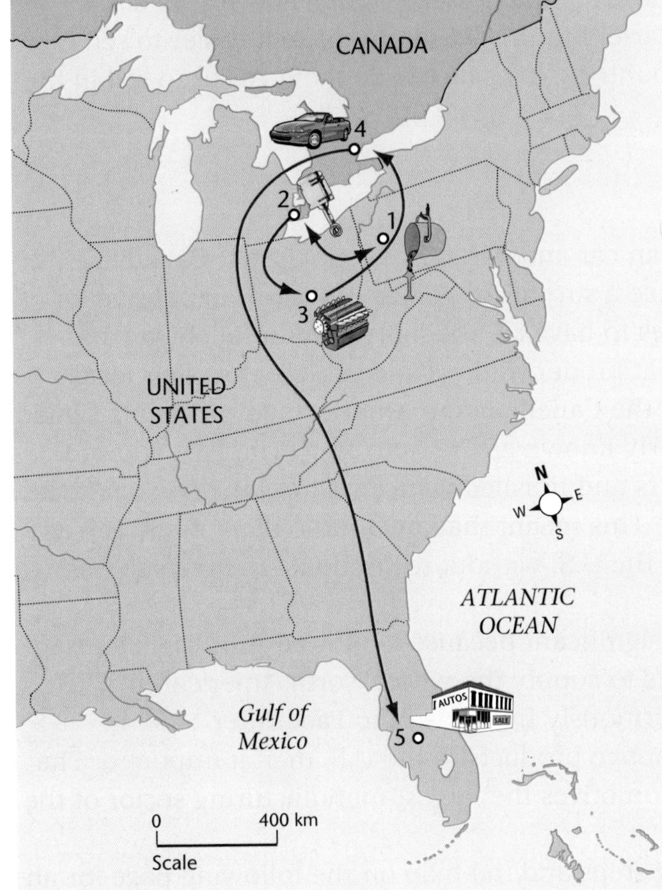

◀ **Figure 13-4** How the Auto Pact increased cross-border trade. How many times do the piston assemblies cross the border?

Protecting Canadian Ownership

Not all Canadians think that a close economic relationship with the U.S. is a good idea. Some politicians felt that it would lead to American domination of Canada. So in 1973 Parliament created the **Foreign Investment Review Agency (FIRA)** to approve or reject foreign takeovers of existing Canadian companies. But FIRA had many critics, who said that it approved too many takeovers. It was abolished in the late 1980s.

Special laws protect Canadian ownership in such areas as airlines, newspapers, magazines, television stations, and movie production. But the general trend now is toward more economic **globalization**. In such a world, our economic relationship with the U.S. may get even deeper. (You will read more about globalization in Chapter 15.)

Did You Know

The Auto Pact made Canada a manufacturing powerhouse. In 2004, Ontario produced more finished automobiles than Michigan—the headquarters of the U.S. automobile industry!

Checkpoint ✓

3. Some people say that Canada's close trade relationship with the U.S. makes us too dependent on that country. They add that we'd be better off finding other large markets for our products and therefore reducing our American influence. Do you agree or disagree? Explain your reasons.
4. How did the Auto Pact lead to increased cross-border trade between Canada and the U.S.?
5. What's likely to happen to Canada's economic relationship with the U.S. in a world of increasing globalization? Explain.

Did You Know?

In 1870, workers in the manufacturing industry typically worked 64 hours per week. They led the fight for fewer hours—and by the end of World War II the average work week was 40 hours.

The Growth of Labour Unions

Labour unions have been around for hundreds of years in Canada, beginning in the early 1800s. Trade unions were legalized in 1872. Union activity grew during the two world wars, especially after World War II, and strikes were common. Many employers, however, strongly resisted even recognizing the unions.

In 1944 the Liberal government passed a law that protected workers' right to organize. The law required employers to recognize and bargain with legal, certified organizations of their employees. Union membership increased, and by 1949 Canada had over 1 million union members. Then, in 1956, the Canadian Labour Congress was formed as an overall organization to which labour unions could belong. In this way, labour in Canada grew stronger.

But the laws also placed many restrictions on union members' rights. For example, federal and provincial **civil servants**—people who worked for the government—weren't allowed to go on strike. Their union leaders felt that this made it impossible to bargain successfully with their employers. Postal workers were federal civil servants, and they became increasingly frustrated with this law. In 1965 they held an illegal two-week walkout to demand the right to strike. Two years later the laws were changed across Canada to allow civil servants to strike, except those who provided safety (police, firefighters) or public health services (nurses). Provinces later changed their laws along similar lines for workers governed by provincial law.

◀ **Figure 13-5** Madeleine Parent was a union organizer during the 1940s textile strikes in Quebec—and ever since then she's fought for social justice. She was a founding member of the National Action Committee on the Status of Women in the 1970s. Parent also fought for pay equity and for the rights of Aboriginal and immigrant women. What social issues do you feel strongly about?

Literacy Hint

Expert readers arrive at conclusions based on facts they read. This is called making inferences. You can infer from this paragraph that public employees include teachers and public health care workers. You can infer from the name "Canadian Union of Public Employees" that it was a national organization.

Did You Know

One of the longest strikes in the world—13 years—took place in Fiji. Seven hundred miners went on strike against Australian Emperor Mines in February 1991. The employer fired the strikers, but 370 of them continued to strike. Finally, in June 2004, an Australian judge ruled that the government did not have to study the official report on the situation. The ruling crushed the strikers' last hope.

During the 1960s the federal and provincial governments expanded the range of services they offered. Public health care services, for example, were set up, and the number of civil servants in this sector increased greatly. As more baby boomers entered the school system, the number of employees in the education sector also rose rapidly. **Public employees**—another name for civil servants—became one of the largest employee groups in the economy. By the mid-1980s, the Canadian Union of Public Employees (CUPE) had become the largest single union, with 330 000 members.

The federal government had appointed a Royal Commission on the Status of Women, which you read about in Chapter 11. Its job was to investigate women's positions and opportunities in Canadian society. In 1969 it reported that women faced severe disadvantages in the workplace. They were generally paid less than men. They held few management positions. They weren't entitled to maternity leave, and couldn't claim sick leave when pregnant, because pregnancy isn't a disease! Labour unions generally responded to the report by taking up the cause of equal pay for women. Then, in 1980, Public Service Alliance of Canada (PSAC) workers went on strike against the federal government demanding equal pay for women and men.

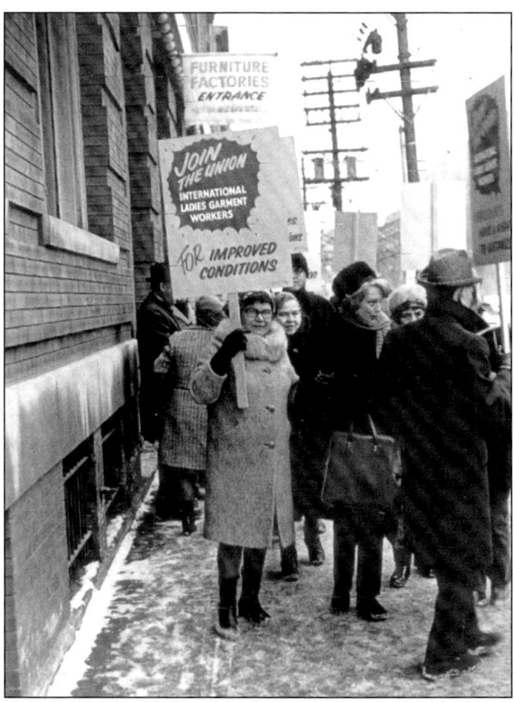

Figure 13-6 CUPE said the following about women's rights during the 1968 Royal Commission on the Status of Women: "CUPE does not feel that the labour movement does enough to fight discrimination against working women. We will readily admit that there is discrimination against women in all sections of the labour movement. To hide the fact will only prevent the solving of the problem. . . ." How could labour unions address women's disadvantages in the workplace?

Labour conflicts flared throughout the 1970s. For example, in 1972 the Common Front—a Quebec organization of labour unions—carried out a series of work stoppages across the country that saw 250 000 public employees walk out. In 1976 more than 1 million workers walked out in a National Day of Protest against the federal government's Wage and Price Controls program. The workers believed that the program would hold down wages more effectively than it would prices. In the same year, Jean-Claude Parrot, the leader of the postal workers' union, was jailed for refusing to order his striking members back to work after a court demanded that he do so.

Some changes came as a result of strikes and lockouts. A lockout occurs when an employer prevents workers from entering the workplace, in an attempt to force them to agree to new work terms like wage rates. Others came from quiet negotiations between workers and employers. Slowly, labour laws were changed.

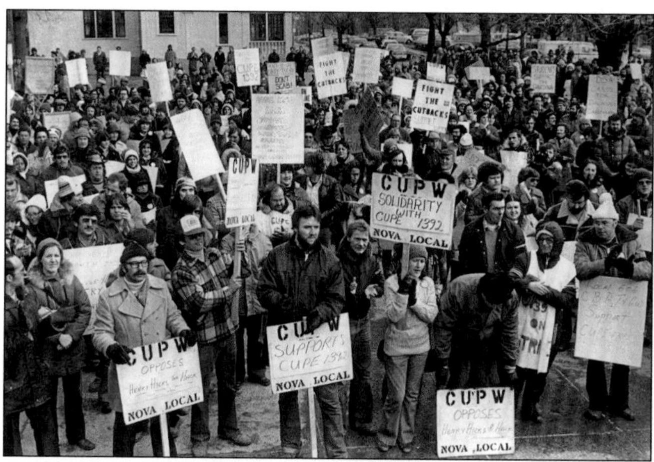

◀ **Figure 13-7** A day of protest in Halifax, 1979. Workers and supporters were protesting the handling of a strike by cleaning staff of Dalhousie University. How effective do you think these types of demonstrations are?

Checkpoint ✓

6. Why did the postal workers go on an illegal two-week walkout in 1965? What right did civil servants (public employees) win, which many other employees already had, in 1967?
7. What did the Royal Commission on the Status of Women report about women in the workplace? How did the Public Service Alliance of Canada (PSAC) react?

Let's finish this section by looking at profiles of two famous labour unionists from the period.

For links to sites about the growth of labour unions and the National Day of Protest

Did You Know?

The 1970s were a critical time for fishers and fish plant workers in Newfoundland. The Newfoundland Fish, Food and Allied Workers Union (NFFAWU) was formed. Their first strike at the Burgeo fish plant in 1971 resulted in legislation (the Fishing Industry Collective Bargaining Act) allowing fishers to bargain for the price of fish. The strike was an important milestone in the province's labour history.

Profile: Dennis McDermott (1922–2003)

Under Dennis McDermott, the two-million-member Canadian Labour Congress (CLC) became "one of the leading forces in Canada." He was a highly effective labour leader.

After serving in World War II, McDermott became an assembler at a Massey-Ferguson tractor plant in Toronto and was a member of the United Auto Workers (UAW). Some of the employees were from racial minorities, and felt there was racism in the workplace from both management and workers. McDermott joined a Joint Labour Committee to Combat Racial Intolerance. It pressured the Ontario government to pass anti-racism laws, leading to the Fair Employment Act of 1948.

After being a local UAW representative at the plant for a number of years, in 1954 McDermott became a UAW employee. In 1968 he became the UAW's vice president and a director of the CLC. Then, from 1978 to 1986, he served as the CLC's president.

McDermott was famous for a number of initiatives. In the 1970s, for example, he threw the CLC behind the attempts of California farm workers to form a union. And in 1981 he organized a rally on Ottawa's Parliament Hill to defend government programs such as health care and unemployment insurance against cutbacks. The rally drew over 100 000 participants—and still ranks as the largest ever held there.

From 1986 to 1989 McDermott served as Canadian ambassador to Ireland. He was awarded the Order of Ontario in 1988.

Profile: Shirley Carr

When Shirley Carr was elected president of the Canadian Labour Congress (CLC) in 1986, she was the first woman to hold that position. That achievement also made her the first woman in the world ever to become head of a national labour body.

Carr first became active in a union during her years as a city hall employee in Niagara Falls, where she was born. She was a member of Local 133 of the Canadian Union of Public Employees (CUPE) and later served on its executive (1970–1974). She became an officer in the Ontario Division of CUPE, and rose further to become a general vice president of CUPE. She went on to serve as executive vice president in the CLC. As president of CLC, she served for six years (1986–1992).

Carr took a strong stance for women's rights in the workplace and for women's right to be involved in decision making about social and economic issues. In 1994 she won a Governor General's Award in Commemoration of the Persons Case (see page 71), given every year to "individuals who have made an outstanding contribution toward promoting the equality of women in Canada."

While head of the CLC, Carr developed ties with the New Democratic Party and with community groups such as the United Way. She also served in the International Labour Organization, which promotes social justice and defends human rights and the rights of workers around the world.

The 1960s and 1970s saw a lot of turmoil. There were demonstrations in support of greater personal freedom. There were struggles to ensure fair treatment for women and minorities. There were protests for higher wages as prices of products went up, especially after the oil crisis of 1973. Labour unions participated in all these battles. Not everyone in Canadian society appreciated their efforts at the time. But in the long run, they did help win fairer treatment for working people.

Checkpoint ✓

8. Union leaders believe that employees can win fairer work conditions if they join together and have their representatives negotiate directly with employers. Critics believe that unions force companies to pay wages that are too high and that make their finished products too expensive for consumers. What do you think? Would you be better off in a union or non-union workplace? Explain your reasons.
9. Reread the profiles of Dennis McDermott and Shirley Carr. Explain how both were interested in not only winning higher wages for their union members, but also in society's larger issues.

Letting employees go to cut costs became so common in 1970 that two new words were invented. "De-hire" and "outplace" were used as less harsh ways of describing the process. "Downsize" was added in 1979.

Some Famous Entrepreneurs

Many of Canada's largest companies were originally founded by **entrepreneurs**. These are individuals who start a company, usually on quite a small scale and often with a new idea or approach. Many of these companies last only a short time. Some of them grow and are passed on to succeeding generations of the founder's family.

Companies that last through generations are often **private companies**; that is, companies in which all the owners are members of an individual family or a small group of friends. Sometimes they decide to sell shares in the company to anyone who wants to buy them, becoming what are known as **public companies**. The founding family often keeps more than 50 percent of the shares in the company. In this way, it can still control any decisions the company makes.

By providing employment, creating goods, and meeting needs, entrepreneurs can contribute greatly to Canada's economy. They can create social change through innovative ideas, awareness of cultural and social issues, and charitable donations. Let's look at some profiles of Canadian entrepreneurs.

Did You Know?

McCain Foods of Florenceville, New Brunswick, is an example of a private company founded by an entrepreneur. Automobile parts manufacturer Magna International of Aurora, Ontario, is an example of one that has become public.

Profile: K.C. Irving (1899–1992)

Kenneth Colin Irving (always known as "K.C.") was born in Bouctouche, New Brunswick, in 1899. His father was a prominent businessperson and ran a sawmill. K.C. became a skilled mechanic, and saw that the automobile offered great potential for the future.

By the early 1920s he'd set up a gas station and auto repair business, a Ford dealership, and a general store—all before he was 25! Then, in 1929, he established Irving Oil Limited to refine and distribute petroleum products. He also established a ship building company. When his father died in 1933, K.C. took over the lumber business.

Irving believed that companies should keep expanding into new areas of business. So by the 1960s he'd moved into television, radio, and newspapers. His companies employed about 8 percent of the entire labour force of New Brunswick!

In 1971 K.C. moved to Bermuda because he felt that taxes were too high in Canada. He transferred the daily running of his companies to his three sons, James, Arthur, and John Irving. In 2005 their total assets were estimated at $5.3 billion.

Despite his vast wealth, K.C. never really sat back and rested. He believed that we should accomplish something every day. Even at the end of his life, he was constantly active.

Profile: Rita Shelton Deverell, born 1945

Rita Deverell has had a distinguished career in Canadian broadcasting. As a founder of Vision TV—the world's first multi-faith and multicultural broadcaster—she is one of Canada's television pioneers.

Born in Texas, Deverell moved to Canada in 1967. She began her career in television by creating a children's program. She has been an actress, journalist, television host, producer, and program creator. During her years at the University of Regina, from 1983 to 1988, she was the first woman of colour ever to head a Canadian journalism school. She has also worked at CBC, and most recently at Aboriginal Peoples Television Network.

Deverell's entrepreneurial spirit is reflected in the new ideas and perspectives she's brought to broadcasting. Many of her projects have involved looking at the moral and ethical sides of current events. In her volunteer work and her membership on boards and committees, she has promoted racial and cultural diversity.

Rita Deverell is a member of the Canadian Association of Broadcasters Hall of Fame and of the Order of Canada.

Profile: Willard Garfield Weston (1898–1978)

W. Garfield Weston, son of George Weston, was born over his father's Toronto bread factory in 1898, and worked hard during his lifetime to become a leading Canadian industrialist.

At school, he played football and hockey, and got his best marks in public speaking. Eager to take part in the First World War, he enlisted with the Royal Canadian Corps of Signals, and helped drive a six-horse wagon in the frontlines of France, laying telegraph cables for battlefield communications. He spent his army leaves visiting English bakeries to learn more about the business in which he had grown up and would join on his return home.

At the end of the war, Garfield went back to Toronto and at age 21 joined the small family company, George Weston Limited. Only 26 years old when his father died, Garfield became president and general manager, soon expanding the business by buying smaller bakeries in Canada and the United States. In 1935, he expanded the business to Great Britain, later moving into Australia, South Africa, and Europe.

Throughout his life, Garfield remained passionately committed to Canada and its citizens. For instance, to assist prairie farmers devastated by the Depression, Garfield worked successfully to persuade British bakers to use Canadian wheat in their bread.

In 1972, Garfield Weston handed over control of Canadian operations to his son W. Galen Weston, also a successful entrepreneur with grocery and retail operations in Ireland. The younger Weston proceeded to restructure North American grocery operations. Today, Galen Weston leads one of Canada's most successful food corporations and largest private sector employers. Through the W. Garfield Weston Foundation, the Weston family continues to generously support environmental projects and educational scholarships across Canada.

Checkpoint ✓

10. Which of the entrepreneurs described do you find the most interesting? Explain your reasons.
11. What do you think it takes to be a successful entrepreneur?
12. Do some further research into one of these entrepreneurs. Imagine that you were applying for a senior job in that person's organization. What do you think are some of the personal qualities you'd stress about yourself? Explain why you think the person would find these qualities interesting.

History Skill: Identifying Point of View and Detecting Bias

When you research or discuss issues and events from history, you soon realize that people can have widely different opinions. That's because people naturally have their own points of view. We see things our own way because of who we are and what we've experienced.

When you are trying to learn about an event or issue, it's important to be able to identify these varying points of view, what might be behind them, and when you should look for additional information.

You have probably heard of the word "bias." Bias is a preference or a tendency to be for or against a person or thing. (It's possible to have a good or positive bias about something. You could have a bias in favour of multiculturalism. But the word is more commonly used in a negative way.) Bias can be hard to detect, since sometimes the person with the bias isn't aware of it. Here are some tips for being aware of points of view and bias in your reading, viewing, and discussing.

Step 1

Use the following questions:

1. Who wrote or produced this material? What might have influenced this person's point of view?
2. Think about the topic. What are some possible points of view on this topic? Are these other points of view presented?
3. Does anything seem to be missing or overlooked? (This is called "bias by omission.")
4. Look for word clues:
   - words that sound judgmental, such as "This decision was completely ridiculous."
   - exaggeration, such as "Never has there been such an evil act."
   - words that appeal to emotions, such as "How can anyone who believes in freedom and justice accept this idea?"
   - word choices (for example, choosing words that paint groups or individuals as all good or all bad—a "terrorist" to one person might be a "freedom fighter" to another)
5. Are there facts to support the point of view?

6. If it's a visual, why was that particular visual chosen? Is it meant to make you feel a certain way about the subject? Is it flattering or insulting to the subject?

Step 2

If you're studying different points of view held by historical figures, keep track of the differences in a chart like the following. The chart can help you identify the differences and consider the reasons for them, such as a person's background or other influences.

Person's Name	Person's Belief or Opinion	Person's Background and Influences

Step 3

Once you've identified a point of view or bias, analyze it. If you're researching, decide how much of the material you can use or accept. If you're reading about historical figures' points of view, interpret them by considering all the factors. Check other sources and compare the information.

Practise It!

1. Choose one of the following and develop two or more supported points of view for the issue.
   - locker searches at school
   - whether it should be a crime to share music from commercial CDs on the Internet
   - compulsory drug testing for professional athletes
   - tariffs on goods imported to Canada
2. Choose three or four newspaper headlines that deal with any significant issue and rewrite them to give a different slant on the stories.

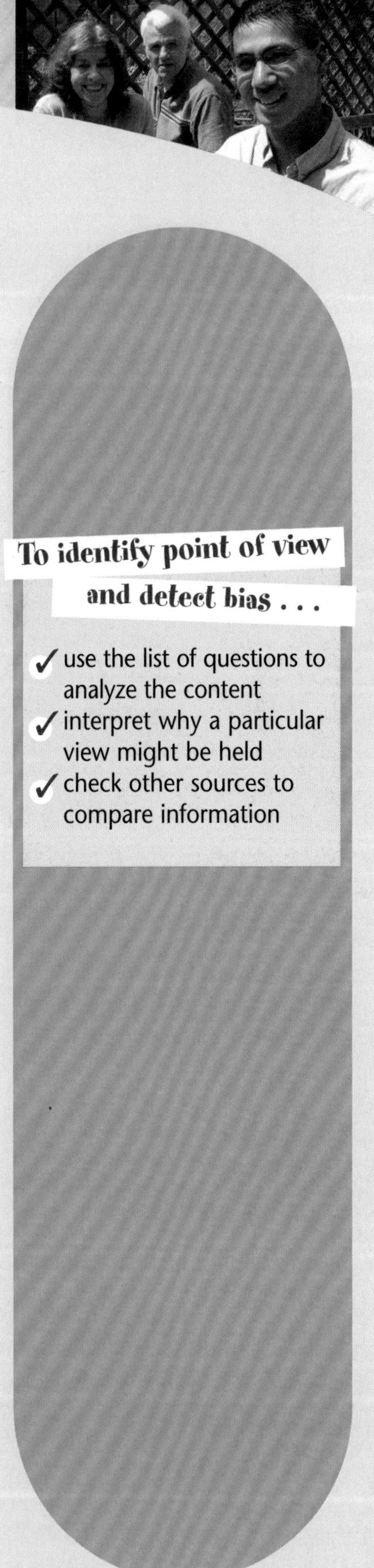

To identify point of view and detect bias . . .

- ✓ use the list of questions to analyze the content
- ✓ interpret why a particular view might be held
- ✓ check other sources to compare information

Name:
Shannon Prince

Job Title:
Museum Curator,
Buxton National Historic
Site & Museum

What I like about my work:

"Sometimes when I tell a story to an audience, some of them become a bit choked up. (I do, too.) I remember a 13-year-old boy who'd been reluctant to come to the museum in the first place because it would be 'boring.' He started to cry uncontrollably when he held a set of original child-sized shackles that had been used to restrain a child slave. This is very powerful history."

Career Profile

Shannon Prince, Museum Curator

Shannon Prince is a sixth-generation descendant of slaves. Her ancestors came to North Buxton (near Chatham, Ontario) from the United States in the late 1850s. When her children were young she used to volunteer at the museum. Her husband, Bryan, wrote a number of true stories about some of the former American slaves in the area who escaped to freedom in Canada. Prince herself became a storyteller, sharing stories with students who visited the Buxton museum in school groups. She believed passionately that everyone needed to hear about what these escaped slaves had accomplished,

When the position of museum curator became available in 1999, Prince applied for and got the job. In this position, she tries to make the museum relevant to people of all ages who visit. She supervises the collection, preservation, and display of the museum's artifacts (the historical objects in the museum). She also travels to schools and community groups to talk about the museum and the work it does.

Prince obtained her certificate of museum studies through the Ontario Museums Association. She travelled to various centres to take her classes. (The two-year program is also available through some community colleges.)

Shannon Prince's love for her work is obvious: "I'm passionate about this history. We have to recognize that so many cultures have contributed to Ontario and Canada and made them what they are today. Looking at the histories of all the people who came here will help us understand each other better."

1. What would you like and dislike about this job?
2. What skills do you think you'd need for this job?
3. What steps could you take to develop these skills?

The 1960s and 1970s were a period of great economic change in Canada. In this chapter you learned that:

- The 1960s had a roaring economy; the 1970s saw it decline.
- Canada's economic relationship with the U.S. deepened.
- Labour unions grew, and labour laws changed through the efforts of workers and union leaders.
- Canada's entrepreneurs contribute to the economy in many ways.

In the next chapter you'll look at other aspects of Canada's relationship with the U.S.

1973 oil crisis

FIRA

labour unions

Wrap It Up

Understand It

1. Find out how many of your classmates have a family member who belongs to a labour union and write down the unions' names. Organize them into company unions and public sector unions. Write down two observations about union membership among the families in your class.

Think About It

2. In 1963 gasoline sold for 8.8 cents a litre. In 1975 the price was 15.4 cents, then in 1985 it was 45 cents.
   a) Create a bar graph showing the price of gasoline from 1963 to the present.
   b) How do you think increased prices have affected our use of gasoline and related products? Identify three ways in which families today are trying to adapt to higher energy costs.

Communicate It

3. Find out from your local Chamber of Commerce or municipal office who some of the entrepreneurs are in your community. As a class project, invite an entrepreneur to speak to you. Arrange the visit and create a student panel to ask questions of your guest.

Apply It

4. Look at your own household (or an imaginary one, if you prefer). Consider five consumer products that are important to it. (For example: a vehicle, television, refrigerator, telephone, and camera.) What's the name of the company that manufactured each item? Find out how many of these are American-owned. What can you conclude about your household's economic closeness to the U.S.?
5. Find out how the economy of your community has changed since the 1960s and 1970s. Have employment and income risen, fallen, or remained steady?

Chapter 14

Canada and the World

The Great Flag Debate

A country's flag is the face it shows to the world. In 2005 Canada's flag celebrated its fortieth anniversary as one of the most recognized and respected national symbols in the world. But back in the 1960s, when the red maple leaf design was introduced, it created a huge debate that divided the nation. Here are some facts about the Great Flag Debate:

- Of the 3541 suggestions submitted to the flag committee, 2136 contained maple leaves, 408 contained union jacks, and 389 contained beavers.
- Some Canadians, including Progressive Conservative leader John Diefenbaker, felt strongly that the flag should reflect Canada's ties to Britain.
- Others, including Liberal Prime Minister Lester Pearson, felt just as strongly that the flag should reflect Canada's independence from its old colonial ties.
- Parliamentary debate on the flag issue lasted a record 210 days because the Progressive Conservatives refused to stop debating the issue.
- Feelings about the new flag ran so high at the time that the man who designed it, George Stanley, received death threats.

- Lester Pearson actually favoured the design shown at left, which became known as the "Pearson Pennant."

Literacy Hint

Make connections: this chapter is about the years 1960 to 1980, but some of the issues are ongoing. As you read, think about how the issues are similar to what's happening in Canada and the world today, and how they affect you.

Checkpoint ✓

1. a) Why do you think people felt so strongly about changing the flag back in the 1960s?
   b) Do you think the issue would be as controversial if it were being debated today? Why or why not?
2. a) Why do you think Pearson wanted three maple leaves on the flag instead of just one? What do you think they represented?
   b) Which flag design do you prefer—the Pearson Pennant or today's single maple leaf? Discuss with a partner.
3. Besides the maple leaf, what other symbols, attitudes, and traits do you think people in other countries associate with Canada? Create a class list that you can add to as you read this chapter.

Key Learnings

In this chapter, you will explore

- why social support programs were established in Canada
- the contributions of some Canadians to the Canadian identity
- how the federal government has used the media to promote a common identity
- changes in Canada's international status
- Canada's role in some key Cold War activities
- Canada's participation in war and contributions to missions and security

Words to Know

distinctiveness
collectivist society
individualistic society
unification of the armed forces
global village
middle power
development aid

Literacy Hint

During reading, ask yourself questions. For example, ask: Does this make sense to me? What does the writer mean? What does this make me remember or think about?

Promoting Canadian Distinctiveness

Before a nation can play a major role in world affairs, it must have a strong sense of its own **distinctiveness**. In other words, it must understand what its strengths and weaknesses are, and how it differs from other nations. This has sometimes presented a bit of a problem for Canadians. After all, in many ways we're similar to Americans. So how can others really understand us if they see us as too much like Americans?

Canadians and Americans differ about the type of society they're trying to develop. Canadians have more of a **collectivist society**. This means that we believe government has a role in looking out for

◀ **Figure 14-1** Prime Minister Pierre Trudeau famously described Canada–U.S. ties as being like a mouse sleeping next to an elephant. How does this cartoonist use that comparison? What do you think of the comparison?

everyone's personal welfare. Americans tend to support a more **individualistic society**—one in which people are individually responsible for their success in life.

It's important for a nation to understand its own distinctiveness before it tries to play an international role. If it has a positive vision of itself, is a nation more likely to be able to help others on the world stage?

For links to sites about some of Canada's social programs

Social Programs

We can see Canada's collectivist nature in the way our government pensions work. The federal government first established the old age pension in 1927. It was $20 a month for people 70 and over. But in order to collect it you had to prove that you didn't have any other income, and that was regarded as humiliating. So Old Age Security (OAS) was set up in 1952. It provided $40 per month for people over 70, and they no longer had to prove their need for it.

Then, in 1966, the federal government introduced the Canada Pension Plan (CPP). (Quebec adopted a similar plan, called the Quebec Pension Plan.) People made payments, called premiums, into the CPP, and could collect a retirement pension at age 65 (later reduced to 60). Finally, in 1967 the Guaranteed Income Supplement was introduced. It is part of the OAS, and provides a monthly payment for low-income pensioners.

The OAS and GIS are good examples of the way Canadians have decided that all senior citizens should have a basic income.

The same ideas were behind the establishment of medicare, or government-run health care. The federal and provincial governments gradually created medicare from the 1950s to the 1970s. By 1972 all provinces offered coverage for hospital visits and physician care. This coverage was paid out of taxes. Before medicare, families had to either insure themselves with private insurers or pay cash for medical expenses. Many poor families couldn't afford such care. But medicare was founded on the idea that no one should be denied medical care because of their income.

Canadians, then, were expressing their distinctiveness through their social programs. It's interesting to note that in the U.S., government old age pensions (or "social security," as it's called there) and Medicare programs are more restricted than they are in Canada.

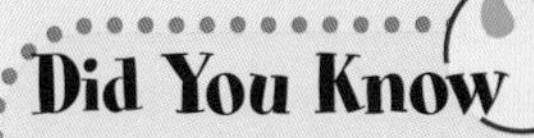

There are rules of etiquette for the Canadian flag. For example, if it's hanging vertically, the upper part of the leaf should point left when the observer is facing it. Nothing should be sewn or pinned to the flag.

The Flag Debate

Promoting Canadian distinctiveness was very much the focus of the 1960s flag debate. You may recall from Chapter 3 that, before the 1960s, Canada didn't have an official flag of its own. After World War I Britain granted Canada the right to use the Red Ensign—a red flag with the Union Jack (from the British flag) in one corner and the Canadian coat of arms on the other side. This was the flag that Canadians followed in World War II. But by the 1960s many people felt that it wasn't distinctive enough—especially at a time when more and more Canadians were from non-British backgrounds.

After a long debate, the current Canadian flag was adopted and first flown in February 1965. It was highly distinctive. It used only the official colours of Canada—red and white—and featured a single maple leaf, which had been a Canadian symbol for a long time.

Figure 14-2 The inauguration of Canada's national flag, February 15, 1965. At the ceremony Prime Minister Lester B. Pearson said, "Under this Flag may our youth find new inspiration for loyalty to Canada; for a patriotism based not on any mean or narrow nationalism, but on the deep and equal pride that all Canadians will feel for every part of this good land." When have you felt the most proud of Canada?

The Canadian Armed Forces

Another example of Canada's distinctiveness is its **unification of the armed forces**. The Canadian Army, the Royal Canadian Navy (RCN), and the Royal Canadian Air Force (RCAF) had always existed as separate services. But in 1968 this system was abolished and replaced with the unified Canadian Armed Forces (CAF). The old uniforms of the three services were replaced with a green uniform—the same for everyone. All ranks also became defined in army terms; for example, the person in charge of a military ship would be a colonel, not a commander.

The idea was that a unified force would be more efficient than three separate ones. But many problems arose, partly because pride in the individual services was lost when the single uniform was adopted. So, in the early 1990s, the land, air, and sea divisions adopted new uniforms based on those of the army, navy, and air force uniforms of the 1960s. The Canadian Forces, as they're now called, are still a single united military force. But the three services wear distinctive uniforms, and the old naval ranking system has been restored to the sea division.

Did You Know?

The colour of berets now worn by Canadian forces signifies their branch, mission, or "environment." For example:

all army: rifle green

armoured corps: black

airborne (parachute unit): maroon

navy: black

air force: blue

search and rescue: orange

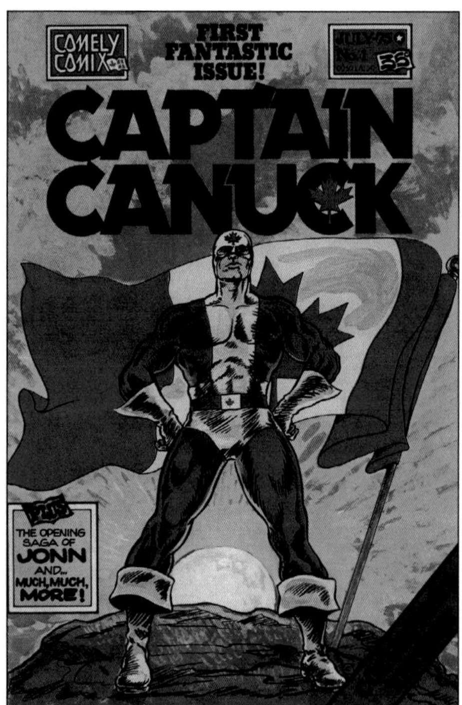

◀ **Figure 14-3** Cover of a 1975 Canadian superhero comic created by Richard Comely. Captain Canuck's adventures were set in the future (the 1990s!). He was an agent for the fictitious Canadian International Security Organization (CISO). What characteristics would you give a modern Canadian superhero?

Protecting Canadian Identity

The federal government has long recognized that it should be involved in promoting a common Canadian identity. One way it has done this is by supporting cultural institutions. From the time it launched the Canadian Broadcasting Corporation in the 1920s, the federal government has supported the creation of a distinctively Canadian "brand." Look at the timeline below for a summary of some of its efforts.

TIMELINE: Protecting Canadian Identity in Media

1960 A Royal Commission on Publications makes recommendations to ensure that Canadian books, newspapers, and magazines can survive against American competition.

1965 Changes to the Income Tax Act mean that, when calculating their income tax, companies can deduct advertising costs from their profits only if the ads appear in media that are substantially Canadian-owned.

1968 The Canadian Broadcasting Act confirms the CBC as a provider of national broadcasting to "enrich and strengthen the cultural, political, social and economic fabric of Canada." The Act also sets up the Canadian Radio-television and Telecommunications Commission (CRTC) as the regulating body.

1968 The Canadian Film Development Corporation (CFDC) is created to promote the movie industry. (As a result of the CFDC's work, today many American movies are shot in Canada, where costs are cheaper.)

1971 New regulations require minimum levels of Canadian content ("Can-con") on Canadian radio and television stations. (This has led to the growth of Canadian record and television production.)

1972 The Canadian Federal Book Publishing Policy brings in financial support for Canadian publishers.

1974 CBC Radio-Canada, the French radio network, acquires an Edmonton station and extends its coverage of western Canada.

1978 The *Anik B* satellite and the Inukshuk Project link six Inuit communities through video and audio—the roots of the Inuit Broadcasting Corporation.

Literacy Hint

After you've read a section of text, stop to list the main ideas. Use questions such as, What was the purpose of this section? What was the main message? What was the most important point?

Checkpoint ✓

4. Why is it important for a nation to have a strong sense of its own distinctiveness?
5. What's the difference between a collectivist society and an individualist society? According to the text, which type of society is Canada?
6. Make a list of three events that helped make Canada more distinctive. After each event, explain how it strengthened this distinctiveness.
7. What other things about Canada are unique or distinctive? Make a list of three items you can think of.

Famous Canadians and Our Identity

During the 1960s and 1970s a number of people showed Canada's best face to the world. In this section, you'll read about some of them.

Profile: Miyuki Tanobe, born 1937

Artist Miyuki Tanobe arrived in Quebec from Japan in 1971—and within a year she began to display her colourful paintings in a Montreal gallery. Today, she ranks among Canada's most sought-after painters. Her work also includes book illustrations, posters, screened prints, and film. In creating her own unique style, she has successfully combined the cultures of Japan and French Canada.

Tanobe was born in 1937 in Morioka, Japan, where she showed artistic talent as a child. Later she studied a wide range of artistic styles at Tokyo's fine arts school, but focused on the traditional *nihonga* techniques. (*Nihonga* simply means "Japanese painting.") She learned to brush coloured powders mixed with glue and water onto wooden panels—a very difficult style of painting to master.

In 1963 Tanobe went to Paris and continued her studies at France's national school of fine arts. There she became friends with a French Canadian named Maurice Savignac, whom she later married. When she returned to Japan he wrote to her about the lively neighbourhoods of his native Montreal, and in 1971 she came to see them for herself and started painting.

Miyuki Tanobe quickly adapted her Japanese training to French-Canadian culture. She began creating colourful street scenes of old Montreal neighbourhoods, each picture filled with interesting people and events. She combined her precise *nihonga* techniques with the simple, bold, bright style of an untrained folk artist. While the public enjoys her lively and humorous works, critics appreciate her superior technical abilities. Today, her unique style is taught at universities in Canada and the U.S.

Miyuki Tanobe has received many awards. Museums, galleries, and corporate head offices strive to include her paintings in their collections. Perhaps her highest honour came in 2003, when she was inducted into the Order of Canada by then–Governor General Adrienne Clarkson.

Profile: Rosemary Brown, 1930–2003

Rosemary Brown was a prominent Canadian politician and supporter of human rights. She was also the first Black woman to be elected to office in Canada and the first to run for the leadership of a political party.

Brown was born in Jamaica and moved to Montreal in 1951 to attend McGill University. After graduation she moved to Vancouver, where she worked with the Children's Aid Society and in children's hospitals. She later became a counsellor at Simon Fraser University.

After a number of years in social work she decided to run for political office. In 1972 she was elected as a member of the British Columbia parliament. She served until 1986. In 1975 she finished second in the race to win the leadership of B.C.'s New Democratic Party.

Upon leaving politics in 1986, Brown became a professor of Women's Studies at Simon Fraser University and worked for an organization that strove to increase the status of women in developing countries. From 1993 to 1996 she was chief commissioner of the Ontario Human Rights Commission—a government agency that tries to obtain fair treatment for all residents of the province.

Rosemary Brown was successful in her work in politics, the struggle for human rights, and international aid. She fought for those who were sometimes shut out of power and opportunity. She had received 15 honorary degrees from universities across Canada, and honours from the governments of Canada and Jamaica. She never lost sight of the fact that all people deserve to be recognized.

Profile: Oscar Peterson, born 1925

World-renowned jazz musician Oscar Peterson was born in Montreal. As a child he showed talent as a pianist and was given a lot of instruction in classical music. By the 1940s he'd been signed up by CBC Radio to perform in a number of popular entertainment shows.

But it was jazz that really inspired him. He performed at Carnegie Hall in New York in 1949 and formed his own jazz group in 1951. He toured the world with this group. Readers of *Down Beat* magazine voted him Best Jazz Pianist in 1952, and he won this award every year for the next 12 years. In 1958 he settled in Toronto, where he has lived ever since.

Peterson worked tirelessly for decades, and composed many jazz numbers. He's performed on television for the CBC, CTV, and the British Broadcasting Corporation. He's also written the score for movies such as *Big North* and *Fields of Endless Day*. To celebrate his lifetime achievements, the National Film Board made a film entitled *In the Key of Oscar*. He was appointed to the Order of Canada in 1972, and in 1989 the government of France appointed him an Officer of Arts and Letters. He's won seven Grammys and been nominated for 11 others.

Profile: Chief Dan George (1899–1981)

Chief Dan George was a famous actor, writer, and spokesperson for Aboriginal peoples. His work helped build cultural understanding. He was born on Burrard Reserve No. 3, a Salish community on Vancouver's north shore. His birth name was Geswanouth Slahoot, but he was named Dan George when he went to a residential school at the age of five. He left school at 17 and worked for many years as a labourer in the bush and as a dockworker in Vancouver. He became chief of the Burrard band in 1951 when he took over from his father. He continued in that role until his acting career began in 1963.

George had always been interested in acting. After being badly injured in a dock accident, he eventually drifted into television dramas with the CBC. In 1965 he was cast in the Hollywood movie *Smith*. Then, in 1970, he was invited to play the role of Old Lodge Skins in the film *Little Big Man* starring Dustin Hoffman. He was nominated for an Academy Award in the Best Supporting Actor category.

He didn't win the Oscar, but he'd become famous, and likely the most recognized First Nations person in Canada at the time. He did some stage acting, and became a spokesperson for Aboriginal peoples through the books and speeches he wrote. He promoted peace in his messages and appealed for fairer treatment for Aboriginal peoples. As he said to a rally of 35 000 people: "I shall grab the instruments of the white man's success—his education, his skills, and with these new tools I shall build my race into the proudest segment of your society."

George was also an author whose books projected his spirituality and Salish cultural teachings. His books include *My Heart Soars, My Spirit Soars,* and *You Call Me Chief: Impressions of the Life of Chief Dan George*. His lifelong work earned him many honours, including an honorary Doctor of Laws from Simon Fraser University.

Dan George made other movies throughout the 1970s, but stardom never changed him. Until his death, he lived on the Salish territory where he was born.

Profile: Pitseolak Ashoona (1904–1983)

Pitseolak Ashoona was an Inuit graphic artist who created more than 7000 drawings over her career. Her prints depict the North and the way of life and culture of the Inuit. She's one of Canada's best-known artists, and her works are shown in art galleries throughout the country. As a child, Ashoona lived on the south coast of Baffin Island. She moved to live in Cape Dorset permanently in the early 1960s. Cape Dorset, in Nunavut, has become known as the capital of Inuit art—it is the home of an Inuit artists' collective that focuses on graphics and carvings. Some of Ashoona's children and grandchildren have also become artists. She produced a book called *Pitseolak: Pictures Out of My Life* in 1971, and the National Film Board of Canada later made a film based on it. In recognition of her work, Ashoona was elected a member of the Royal Canadian Academy of Arts in 1974. She received the Order of Canada in 1977.

Profile: Marshall McLuhan (1911–1980)

Marshall McLuhan was a teacher and philosopher known throughout the world for his studies in media and communication.

He was born in Edmonton but moved as a child to Winnipeg. From 1946 to 1979 he taught at the University of Toronto.

McLuhan was interested in the way people communicate their ideas. He was particularly fascinated with electronic media. In his day, these were television, radio, and newspapers. He believed that print media (newspapers and magazines) and radio were "hot" media. They're of a high intensity, and contain lots of information, but they don't allow the reader or listener to feel emotionally about the content. He felt that television was a "cool" medium, of a lower intensity. It doesn't contain lots of information, and viewers have to fill in what's missing. Viewers tend to feel emotionally about what they see. They might feel anger, pity, horror, or admiration, depending on the program.

He summed up these ideas with the phrase "the medium is the message." By this he meant that individual media are designed to communicate particular messages. Telephones communicate information and ideas. Television communicates feelings. (Think about commercials, so many of which are designed to appeal to our emotions.)

Although many of McLuhan's ideas were criticized by other professors, his idea of the world as a **global village** is widely accepted. This is the idea that electronic communications have made the world smaller and more similar. So people tend to dress more alike (baseball caps, for example) than they did a hundred years ago. Young people in all parts of the globe now tend to listen to similar types of music. And because of instant communications, ideas spread quickly.

Marshall McLuhan became famous throughout the world. He received awards and honours from the United States, Great Britain, Italy, and the Vatican. In his own country, he received honorary degrees from many universities and was appointed to the Order of Canada.

Many other famous Canadians made their mark during this period. Like the people described in this section, they were famous in many different fields. Canada was becoming a more varied nation, and its reputation was spreading throughout the world.

Checkpoint ✓

8. Which of the profiles of famous Canadians most interested you? Why?

9. a) Make a list of five questions that you might ask the famous Canadians. (Example: How did you contribute to Canadian society?)

b) Explain why you think your questions—and the answers they might get—would help you understand their lives better.

10. Imagine it's 2020. You're developing a history project about Canada today. Identify three famous people you would include as representing Canada. Explain why you'd include each one.

Supporting International Military Organizations

In Chapter 9 you learned that Canada is a **middle power**—it doesn't have, or want, the military power to invade foreign nations, but it does play a role in international affairs. Throughout the 1960s and 1970s Canada's military strength was declining. The federal government wanted to put more money into social programs, and cutbacks were made in the military. By 1980, Canada's ability to defend itself had been greatly weakened—and it needed powerful allies.

Literacy Hint

Draw conclusions when you read. Read a section, think about it, and come to some conclusions. For example, after you read these examples of Canada's responses to military incidents, make some conclusions about what those responses say about Canada.

Figure 14-4 A 1961 editorial cartoon showing U.S. President Kennedy, Soviet Premier Khrushchev, and Prime Minister Diefenbaker. What flag is Diefenbaker carrying, and what does it mean about Canada's role?

For links to sites about Canada's NATO involvement and events on page 275

NATO Involvement

As you may recall from Chapter 9, Canada was a member of the North Atlantic Treaty Organization (NATO). The decades after World War II were a time of Cold War, and the threat of war between some communist and NATO countries was very real. After the Korean War, Canadian troops were stationed in West Germany to defend against the Soviet Union, if necessary. In the 1970s, however, Canadian troops in Europe were reduced and eventually withdrawn from Europe. After that time, Canada still contributed to NATO and remained a member.

Canada–U.S. Relations

In the early 1960s, during the arms race and the threat of nuclear war, Canada–U.S. relations were strained. For example, Prime Minister Diefenbaker's government wasn't as hostile to communist nations as the U.S. was. And so, when the U.S. tried to stop American-owned companies in Canada from trading with Communist China, the Canadian government objected. The following are other examples of the different positions taken by the Canadian and American governments.

The Cuban Missile Crisis

In 1962 the threat of a nuclear war became very real. American surveillance discovered Soviet missile sites in Cuba—missiles that could attack the U.S. and Canada. U.S. President John F. Kennedy ordered a blockade of Cuba so that the nuclear warheads and other military supplies from the Soviet Union couldn't get in. After many days of tense negotiating, the Soviet Union agreed to remove the missiles. Diefenbaker had delayed putting its NORAD military forces on high alert during this time, which angered the U.S.

The Vietnam War

As you read in Chapter 11, the U.S. entered a war in 1965 as allies of South Vietnam against North Vietnam. The war was brutal, with millions of civilian and military casualties, and was strongly protested in the U.S. American troops pulled out in 1975. Canada was officially a "non-participant," but it did send aid and supplies to South Vietnam (which indirectly helped the U.S. effort). Prime Minister Pearson tried to be a mediator, angering U.S. President Johnson, who wanted more support. During the war Canada received many American draft dodgers and deserters. Overall, Canada's international reputation and sense of independence increased as a result of its refusal to give blind support to the U.S.

Détente

"Détente"—a French word meaning a release from tension—was used to describe the improvement in relations between the U.S. and the Soviet Union in the early 1970s. President Richard Nixon met with Leonid Brezhnev, the Secretary-General of the Soviet Communist Party, and they signed a number of agreements. Strategic Arms Limitation Talks (SALT) were also underway. For Canada, it meant that the federal government could reduce the defence budget, support arms control, and focus more on social programs and nationalism.

Cruise Missiles

In the 1970s and 80s the U.S. was developing cruise missiles (rocket-powered bombs that travel low for long distances and guide themselves to a target). They asked for permission to test them in Canada. Many Canadians were opposed to the arms race and to American interference, and so they protested. However, in 1983 Canada signed an agreement allowing cruise missile testing over Canadian (mainly Albertan) airspace. (The landscape there is similar to that of the Soviet Union, where the real missiles might be used.) The U.S. used cruise missiles in later years in Afghanistan (2001) and in Iraq (2003).

Figure 14-5 A protest against cruise missiles on Parliament Hill, 1983. If the United States asked to do testing in Canada today, what would your response be?

Checkpoint ✓

11. Think about the above examples of Canada's position in international military matters. Do you think Canada should have responded differently to any of them? Explain why.
12. What's your opinion of Canada's position on U.S. military involvements today?

Supporting International Peace Organizations

Canada contributed to 16 different United Nations missions during the 1960s and 70s. You can see the major details of these missions on the next page.

Canada's contributions to these missions was part of its "middle power" strategy. If Canada played a role in maintaining peace around the world, it hoped to have an influence on such great military powers as the U.S.

For links to sites about Canada's role in UN missions and development aid

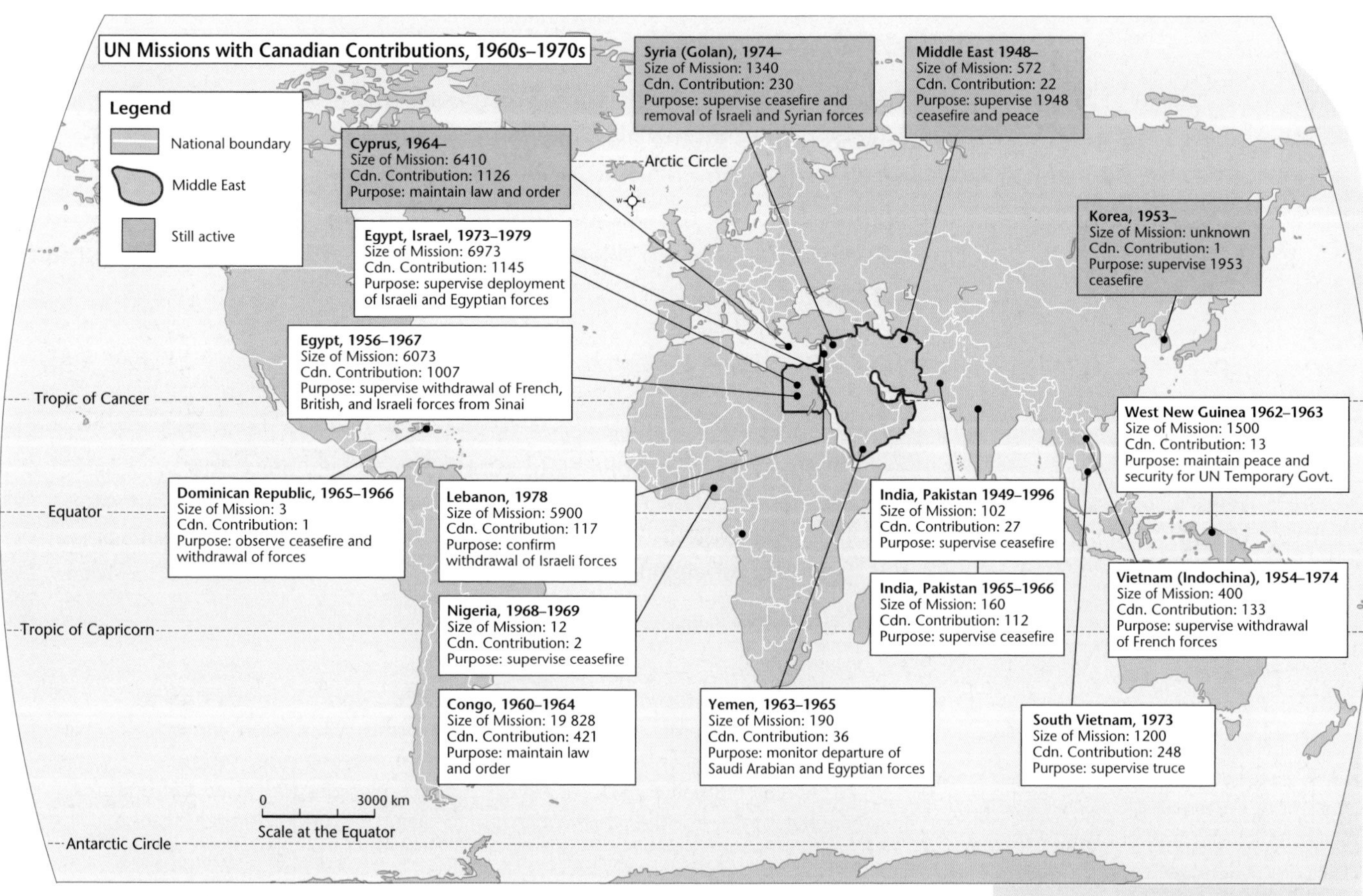

Source: Adapted from Department of Foreign Affairs and International Trade (DFAIT). 2003a. *Peacekeeping Operations over the Years and Canada's Contribution*. www.dfait-maeci.gc.ca/peacekeeping/missions-en.asp, accessed March 15, 2005.

▲**Figure 14-6** Summary of UN Missions with Canadian Contributions, 1960s and 1970s. Were you aware of Canada's role in any of these UN missions? What does Canada's role usually involve?

Canada has been elected six times as a member of the UN Security Council—the most powerful UN body. Two of these terms (1967–1968 and 1977–1978) occurred during the decades you're studying in this chapter. These events show that Canada was recognized as an important contributor to international peace. They also show that the "middle power" strategy seemed to be working.

Development Aid

Canada's international strategy involves more than keeping the peace. It also requires giving assistance to countries that need aid to develop. The Canadian International Development Agency (CIDA) is the organization that looks after **development aid**—giving money, advice, and assistance to help developing countries. Here's how CIDA explains its mission:

Development Results

All our lives we've dipped into our pockets to help our world neighbours. Many of us also devote time and energy to organizations that fight injustice, or build schools, or work to improve the health of people in developing countries.

Let's take a look:

- **You are reading this article.** That makes you a member of a remarkable club: the literate. It's not an exclusive club—or not any more. In 2000 the world reached a milestone when, for the first time in human history, literate people outnumbered the illiterate. More people than ever before are going on to higher education too.
- **You probably took a drink of water today**. In 1980, only 40 percent of the world's people had access to clean, safe drinking water. By 1990, 80 percent had access, and that figure continues to improve.
- **You don't fear starving to death**. Starvation was once among the most serious challenges addressed by foreign aid. Although hunger is still a problem in many parts of the world, the global food supply has improved so much that in 2004 the United Nations declared its concern over a new threat to world health—obesity.

These improvements are directly due to the international development programs supported over the last half century by the citizens and governments of democratic countries like Canada. . . .

Development Results, Canadian International Development Agency (CIDA), 2004.
www.acdi-cida.gc.ca/index.htm, accessed March 15, 2005.

Tremendous progress has been made in eliminating, or severely reducing, diseases. Smallpox, polio, cholera, and leprosy have been entirely or almost eliminated. According to CIDA, in 1970 the life expectancy in developing nations was only 55 years. By 2000, it had risen to 64 years.

The extract on the previous page comes from a Canadian government report about foreign aid, so you'd expect it to paint a fairly positive picture. But neither Canada's—nor the world's—aid programs are perfect. The United Nations has set an aid target for all developed nations. It is 0.7 percent of GDP—a figure first suggested by Lester Pearson in his work with the UN. Here's how you'd calculate a nation's target:

- Take the value of everything produced in the nation in one year (GDP).
- Calculate 0.7 percent of that figure: that's your target.

Only the Scandinavian nations (Sweden, Norway, and Denmark) have reached their target. And since 1985 Canada's international aid has steadily moved away from its own target.

Canada's international role in support of peace and assistance was strong throughout the 1960s and 1970s. You'll see later that this support declined in the 1990s. We'll return to these themes in Chapter 16.

▲**Figure 14-7** In 2000, CIDA sponsored this watershed management project in Brazil to help control pollution. If you worked for CIDA or another aid agency, what type of project would you like to work on? How would you involve the people of the countries in which you worked?

Checkpoint ✓

13. Look at the map of UN missions in Figure 14-6. Write down three observations that you can draw from the map. (Hint: You could look at where the missions were, how long they lasted, and how many Canadians were assigned to them.)

14. a) What have been some of the benefits of international assistance such as CIDA's?

b) Calculate Canada's 2004 foreign aid contribution as a percentage of its GDP. Use the following numbers:

(foreign aid spending \$2.9 billion ÷ GDP \$1324 billion) x 100

c) What conclusion can you draw about our contribution? (Remember that the international target is 0.7 percent of GDP.)

History Skill: Writing a Thesis Statement and Opinion Piece

An issue has at least two sides. In an opinion piece, you choose one side of the issue (your thesis) and try to prove its value. You also use supporting evidence and persuasive language as you make your points.

Example:

- **Think**: Canada's aid level to developing countries seems low.
- **Read**: I found out that some other developed countries give more.
- **Ask**: Should Canada give more?
- **Jot** down your feelings about the issue.
- **Gather**: Three nations have already reached the target.
- **Write**: Canada should take immediate steps to increase its foreign aid spending to the United Nations target of 0.7 percent of GDP.

Step 1

Your first task is to develop a clear thesis statement—a position you're going to defend in your writing. To get there, you should go through a number of steps.

- **Think** about the issue.
- **Read** about it.
- **Jot** down your feelings about the issue.
- **Gather** some facts that support your position.
- **Write** down a clear, personal position on the issue.

Step 2

Do some research to gather evidence for your opinion. Consider what arguments could be made against your thesis, and plan to counter them in your opinion piece.

Step 3

Create an outline of your piece. Introduce the thesis statement in the first paragraph, and then state your supporting reasons clearly. In the last paragraph, summarize your thesis.

Step 4

Use persuasive writing—choose strong verbs and convincing words such as "should," "obviously," or "it must." Appealing to the reader's emotions is also effective.

To write a thesis statement and opinion piece . . .

✓ use the think-read-ask-jot-gather-write process

✓ do some research to support your thesis

✓ make an outline: introduce, support, summarize

✓ use persuasive writing

Practise It!

Look back at the section Famous Canadians and our Identity (pages 270–273). Choose one of the individuals examined there.
a) Follow the think-read-ask-jot-gather-write process (Step 1) to develop a thesis about that person's significance in helping to develop the Canadian identity. b) Create a paragraph of persuasive writing (Steps 2 to 4) to support your thesis.

Chapter Summary

In this chapter you learned that Canada was an interesting place in the 1960s and 1970s. As a middle power, Canada played a strong role in the international arena. Specifically, you learned that:

- Canada developed a greater sense of its distinctiveness in these years.
- Canada made important military contributions in the Cold War era.
- Many Canadians' accomplishments drew attention to Canada.
- Canada played a significant role in United Nations and aid programs.

The next chapter examines how technology and free trade have affected Canada since the 1980s.

1960 –1980

OAS

CPP

the Canadian flag

CIDA

Wrap It Up

Understand It

1. This chapter has examined some of the things that help make Canada distinctive. See the examples in the chart below. Use an organizer like this to fill in six things about Canada today. Did Canada have greater or lesser distinctiveness in the 1960s and 1970s than it does today? Explain.

Symbols	People	Roles
maple leaf flag	Rosemary Brown	supervise ceasefire, Korea

Think About It

2. Individual Canadians can make a difference in the world by playing any number of different roles. Choose one of the following: (1) a politician dealing with international affairs, (2) a soldier serving with the United Nations in a war-torn country, (3) a general involved in a operating a defence organization such as NATO, (4) an international aid project manager in a developing nation, (5) a famous individual Canadian spreading ideas throughout the world.
   a) What qualities do you think you have that would suit you to the role you chose?
   b) Identify the main goal you'd set for yourself as you played this role.

Communicate It

3. Choose one of the famous Canadians examined in this chapter. Or, with your teacher's permission, choose another person who was famous during this period.
   a) Do some further research into the person's life and achievements.
   b) Make a brief presentation to a group of classmates about your subject.
   c) As a class, list how and why these people were so successful.
   d) Make a word wall, a collage, or some other representation that shows why Canada should be proud of these people.

Apply It

4. As a class, do some research into an international aid organization that's active in Canada, such as Oxfam Canada, Canadian Red Cross, UNICEF, Médecins Sans Frontières (Doctors Without Borders).

   Why do people make donations to these groups? On what types of projects do they spend their aid? What differences have their projects made to those receiving the aid?

Performance Task

Review Your Predictions

At the beginning of this unit you made predictions based on three photos. Refer back to your predictions. How accurate were they? List three key things that you learned about each of the main topics in the unit.

Organize a "Sit-In"

The 1960s and 70s were a period of rebellion and controversy. Youth would often protest by holding sit-ins in which activists would occupy a location, such as an administrative office or government building, and refuse to move. In this activity you'll use some of the same tools that activists in the 1960s and 70s used to get across a protest message.

Step 1

Review the History Skills from this unit:

- Chapter 12: Recognizing Fact, Opinion, and Inference (page 244)
- Chapter 13: Identifying Point of View and Detecting Bias (pages 260–261)
- Chapter 14: Writing a Thesis Statement and Opinion Piece (page 280)

You'll be using these skills in the following activity.

Step 2

Review the Inquiry Method on page xii. Use these steps to guide your research for the activities in Step 3.

Step 3

Work in groups to research one of the controversial issues discussed in this unit, and prepare the following:

- a speech explaining the facts about the issue and expressing what action or attitude you're promoting

Hint

Remember that your arguments should make sense coming from someone living in the 1960s or 70s. For example, don't refer to events that have happened since that period.

- a protest song about the issue
- a button with an appropriate slogan (make enough for everyone in your group to wear)
- a poster or picket sign

Here's how to go about writing a protest song:

- Choose a song from the 1960s or 70s that you like. If possible, get a recording of the song.
- Write your own lyrics to fit the topic of your protest.
- Make sure these lyrics are "singable"—that they fit the metre or rhythm of the original song.

Step 4

Hold a class sit-in—and take turns presenting your issue and opinions to others in the class.

Step 5

Exchange materials with another group. Look for examples in their materials of each of the following:

- bias
- fact
- opinion
- inference

Write a brief summary of what you found.

Possible issues for your sit-in include the following:

- Quebec sovereignty
- Aboriginal rights (e.g., James Bay, or reaction to the 1969 White Paper)
- women's liberation (e.g., daycare, equal rights, equal pay)
- Trudeau's use of the War Measures Act during the FLQ crisis
- Francophone rights
- workers' rights (e.g., maternity leave, civil servants' right to strike)
- cruise missile tests in Canadian airspace

To make your sit-in realistic . . .

- hang your posters on the wall or hold up your picket signs
- wear your buttons
- present your speech to the class
- record or perform your protest song (if possible), or post the lyrics on the wall and play the song you used as the basis for your lyrics (or hand out copies of the lyrics and get everyone to sing along!)
- dress in 60s or 70s-style clothing

Reaching Maturity, 1980-Present

Your Predictions Please # 5

Study the three photographs, which show some features of Canadians' lives between 1980 and today. Consider the clues for each one. Then make some predictions about what you think you'll discover in this unit.

Clue 1 How would you describe the living conditions on Mir?

Clue 2 What three flags do you see on the wall? (These are the nations that supplied crew members on the Mir mission.)

Clue 3 What does this photograph tell you about international cooperation in space?

▲ Canadian astronaut Chris Hadfield plays a special collapsible guitar on board the Mir space station. Hadfield gave the guitar to Mir's Russian crew during his stay there in 1995.

Prediction 1

In this unit, what do you think you'll learn about technology and international cooperation since the 1980s?

Clue 4 What appears to be the mood of the local residents?

Clue 5 What appears to be their reaction to the Canadian troops?

Clue 6 Why might Canada become involved in such aid missions?

▲ Canadian forces on an aid mission to Southeast Asia in early 2005, in the aftermath of the tsunami.

Prediction 2

Based on the clues, what do you think you'll learn about Canadians and international aid missions?

▲ Quebeckers demonstrating in support of sovereignty, 1995.

Clue 7 What is the mood of this scene?

Clue 8 What flags do you see flying?

Clue 9 Why do people participate in demonstrations like this one, in your opinion?

clue

Prediction 3

Based on the clues, what do you think you'll learn about Canada's relationship with Quebec since 1980?

Experience History

History isn't always about extraordinary individuals acting alone. We can all make history happen when we act together for a common purpose. In your own life, you know that a group working toward a common goal can often achieve a lot more than one person acting on his or her own.

Look at the photographs shown here, and decide how each image reflects this theme of working with others. Create a mind map to show your ideas.

In this unit you will explore . . .

- how technology and globalization have influenced Canada
- some forces and events that have influenced Canada's policies and identity
- how Canada has contributed to peacekeeping and security
- changes in Canada's role in the world
- some constitutional changes and their effect on French–English relations
- how the lives of Canadians have changed since 1914
- communicating the results of your research

Unit 5 Performance Task

At the end of this unit you'll use what you've learned to **create a current events show.**

Chapter 15

Technology, Globalization, and Free Trade

Words to Know

microchip
Internet
dot-com companies
satellite
biotechnology
genetically modified foods
globalization
free trade
North American Free Trade Agreement (NAFTA)
World Trade Organization (WTO)

Did You Know?

In 2003, some 3.2 million Canadian households spent $3 billion shopping on the Internet. In other words, each of these households spent an average of about $940 online during 2003.

Can you imagine a world without personal computers, photocopiers, or cell phones? Because you've probably grown up in the Computer Age, you may not realize how much technology has changed in just a few short decades. The following timeline shows when some familiar devices and services were introduced.

TIMELINE: Technological Advances in the Last 50 Years

1969	First message sent over ARPAnet (the predecessor of the Internet)
1971	First e-mail system
1974	First fax machine First build-it-yourself home computer kits available
1981	First IBM PC
1982	The term "Internet" is coined
1983	First cell phone
1991	WWW created
1992	First audio and video broadcasts on the Internet
1998	First MP3 player
2003	First high-definition TV broadcast in Canada

Key Learnings

In this chapter, you will explore

- how new technologies have changed the lives of Canadians
- how globalization and free trade have affected different sectors of the Canadian economy and society

The Technological Revolution

You may not be aware of it, but you're growing up in the middle of a technological revolution. And it all started with a tiny piece of electronics.

The Microchip

In the earliest days of computer technology, companies used what were called "mainframe" computers. These were room-sized computers that connected to all the other computers within the company. All the data from individual computers were stored on the mainframe.

Then, in 1961, scientists invented the **microchip**—a tiny silicon chip that replaced several parts of the conventional electrical circuit. That made it possible to develop smaller and smaller computers. By 1974, the first home desktop computers came on the market.

Over the course of the next 30 years, personal computers became a practical necessity. Today, about 70 percent of Canadian homes and virtually all schools and offices have personal computers. They've changed the way we shop, work, learn, and play.

Literacy Hint

Before you read this section, make a point-form list of all the ways you use computers in your daily life. What do you use them for most?

Did You Know?

Spacewar, the very first computer game, was created in 1962 by a group of computer scientists at Digital Equipment Corporation.

◀ **Figure 15-1** The large machine in the background is part of ENIAC (electronic numerical integrator and computer). This first general-use computer, was built in 1946—and the whole machine is ten times this big! The tiny black dot on the card in the foreground contains a modern microprocessor. Twenty of these tiny chips provide the same computing power as the entire ENIAC computer.

The use of "icon" to mean an image on a computer screen entered dictionaries in 1982. The word originally referred to small religious paintings or mosaics.

The Internet

The **Internet** started out as a way for the U.S. military to communicate safely during the Cold War. At that time, it was known as the ARPAnet, after the agency that created it (the Advanced Research Project Agency). Gradually, its use spread to include universities and research institutes.

In the 1980s new software was developed to make it easier for different types of computers to access the network. Computer companies started including this software in personal computers. Within just a few years, the number of users worldwide had reached 50 million. Today, about 840 million people are using the Internet.

Canadians were quick to adapt to this new technology, and we remain one of the most wired nations on earth. The following figures give some idea of the recent impact of computers on Canadians' lives.

Figure 15-2 Computer ▶ Use in Canada, 1999–2003 (Percentage of All Households).

	1999	2000	2001	2002	2003
Home	28.7	40.1	48.7	51.4	54.5
Work	21.9	27.5	32.6	34.2	36.5
School	14.9	19.2	22.2	22.9	23.1
Library	4.5	6.5	7.9	8.2	8.7
Other	3.9	3.2	9.6	10.4	10.4
Any Location	41.8	51.3	60.2	61.6	64.2

Source: Adapted from Statistics Canada, Household Internet Use, by Location of Access, 2005.

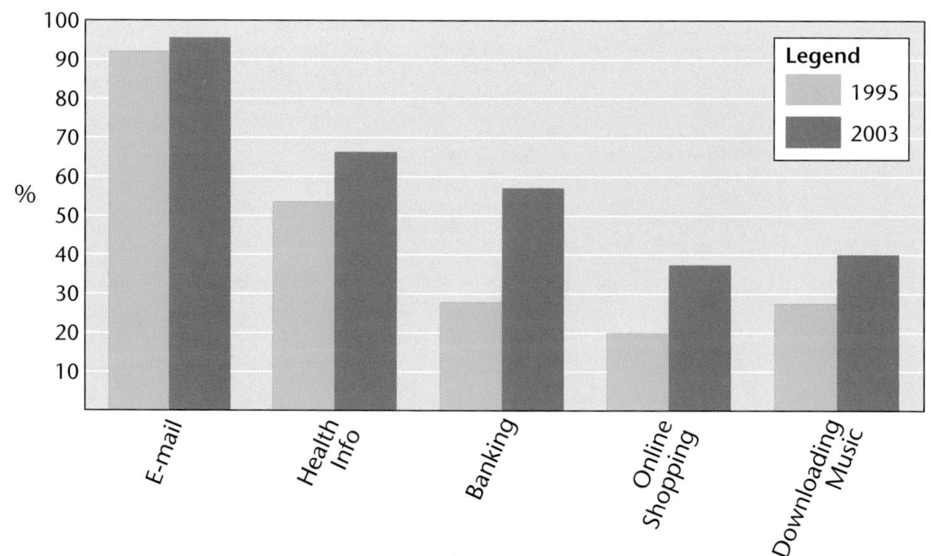

Figure 15-3 Percentage ▶ of Online Households That Used Home Internet Access for Selected Tasks, Canada, 1999–2003. Which uses are growing the fastest?

Source: Statistics Canada, Household Internet Use at Home by Internet Activity, Cat. No. 56F0003X.

The Dot-Com Bubble

The boom in personal computers and the popularity of the Internet led to the creation in the 1990s of thousands of **dot-com companies**—start-up firms offering goods or services online. All sorts of new services were offered—from online grocery shopping to instant messaging.

By the late 1990s there were countless dot-com companies. Although it was well known that most Web-based companies were losing money, investors saw them as stars of the future and poured money into them. The price of their shares rose fantastically, and many people became instant millionaires—at least on paper.

But many of the dot-coms were poorly organized, badly managed, and had no clear business plan. In 2000 the dot-com bubble burst. Their shares plummeted in value. Many companies went bankrupt, and lots of investors were ruined.

LIVING LANGUAGE

"Cybercafé" became a recognized word in 1994. Customers can drink coffee and log on to the Internet, making it easier to stay in touch when travelling. Postcard sales have dropped as a result.

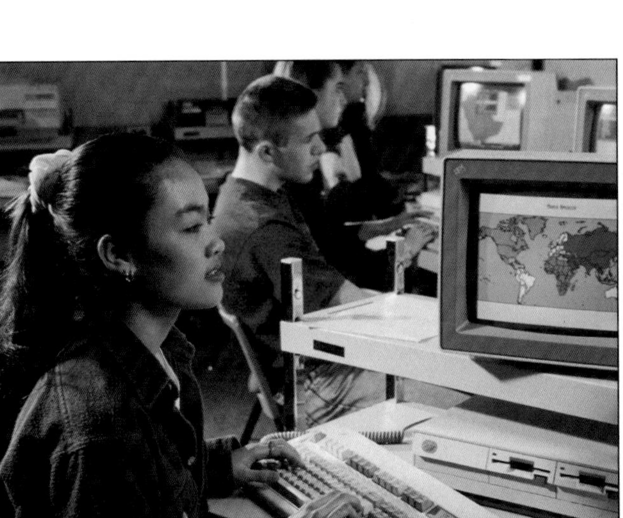

◀ **Figure 15-4** Some dot-com companies survived the bubble and have gone on to become successful, well-established businesses. Among these are eBay, Yahoo!, Google, and Amazon.com.

Checkpoint ✓

1. Why do you think investors were so anxious to invest in the dot-com companies, despite the fact that many of them didn't even have a business plan?
2. What are the advantages and disadvantages of online businesses compared with traditional businesses? Work with a partner to make a pro and con chart.
3. Explain how three figures from this section show how computer Internet use is changing the lives of Canadians.

Satellite Technology

A **satellite** is an object that orbits the Earth. As part of their space programs, the United States and the Soviet Union first launched human-built satellites in the 1950s to send information to Earth about conditions in space.

In 1962 Canada became the third country in space. But instead of sending astronauts up to explore, Canada launched an unmanned satellite—the *Alouette 1*. It was the first satellite in the world whose purpose was to study the atmosphere.

Anik

Then, in 1967, Canada launched the *Anik 1*, a communications satellite. It allowed all of Canada to receive live broadcasts and provided television signals to remote areas in the North for the first time. Receiving dishes for individual consumers weren't available yet, but television companies could transmit and receive signals through *Anik*.

In the years that followed, the Canadian space program focused on satellite technology designed to improve communications here on Earth. New uses for the technology are being found all the time, including

- cellular phone transmissions
- Internet connections
- satellite television services
- global positioning systems, which can be used with a portable transmitter to find a location anywhere on earth
- telemedicine, which allows doctors to diagnose and even perform operations remotely via satellite
- distance education, which allows schools, colleges, and universities to offer courses by satellite to smaller communities

Did You Know?

When the first cell phones appeared on the market in the early 1980s, they cost about $3500 and weighed about 450 grams. Today, cell phones are much less costly, and often weigh just a few grams.

For links to sites about satellite technology

◀ **Figure 15-5** Canada's RADARSAT satellite, launched in 1995. RADARSAT is a remote sensing satellite, used to monitor the environment and take pictures of Earth. What uses can you think of for this satellite?

Biotechnology

Biotechnology—adapting biological processes—is another area of research in which Canada has taken a leading role. In fact, Canada has the third largest number of biotech companies in the world.

Scientists have been cross-breeding plants for centuries as a way of improving their characteristics as foods, medicines, and for other uses. However, recent advances in the field of genetics (the study of genes) have opened up new possibilities. Here are some examples.

- Aquaculture—farming fish and aquatic plants in tanks or cages—has grown from a $100 million industry in the early 1980s to over $600 million in 2005.
- Crops have been genetically modified to reduce the use of pesticides, herbicides, and fertilizers; increase crop yields; and produce more nutritious foods.
- Biotechnology firms are working to produce biodegradable plastics made from renewable plant sources.
- Scientists have created transgenic organisms—plants and animals that have been injected with a gene from another organism. This method has been used to grow plants for use in medicines, as well as to "grow" organs in animals for human transplant.

◀ **Figure 15-6** The University of Guelph in Ontario has done research into modifying plants and animals to increase their yields. It is also raising genetically modified pigs that may be able to supply valves and hearts for transplant into humans who have suffered heart damage.

Literacy Hint

Try breaking unfamiliar scientific words into parts. Then think of other words that are similar. For example, "biotechnology" contains *bio*, which also occurs in words like *biology* (the study of life forms) and *biography* (a written account of someone's life). So "biotechnology" might be about applying technology to life forms. How could you use this method to guess the meaning of "transgenic" or "aquaculture"?

Did You Know?

Canada produces over 50 genetically modified crops, including insect-resistant corn and rice that isn't affected by herbicides.

- Plants can be used to produce sources of renewable energy, such as ethanol and biodiesel, that reduce our reliance on oil and gas.
- Natural products are being developed that can monitor poisons in air, soil, and water—for example, a plant has been developed that changes colour when it grows near hidden land mines.

Genetically Modified (GM) Foods

Not everyone supports these uses of biotechnology, especially in our food sources. Critics point out that the long-term effects of eating these foods are unknown. They feel that **genetically modified foods** should be labelled in stores so that consumers can decide for themselves whether to buy them. The European Union, Japan, and several other countries already require foods to be labelled in this way.

Did You Know

It is estimated that about 70 percent of the foods sold in grocery stores in Canada and the United States have been genetically modified in some way. This percentage is much lower in countries that require GM foods to be labelled.

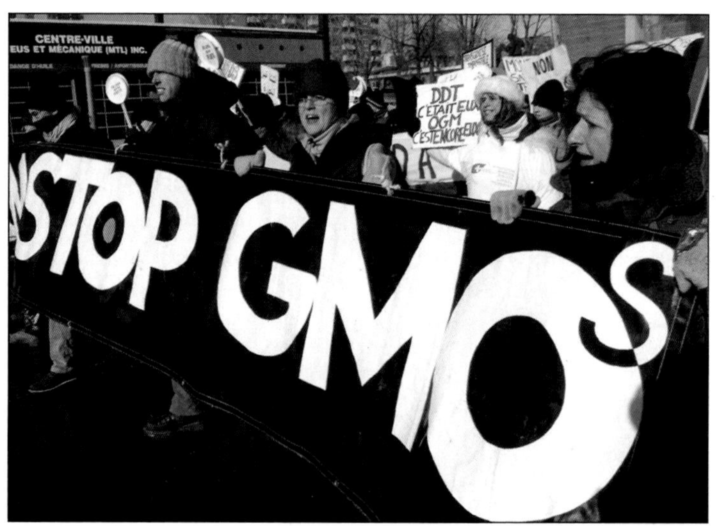

Figure 15-7 These Montreal protestors are demonstrating against the use of genetically modified organisms (GMOs). How do you feel about eating GM foods?

For links to sites about GMOs

Checkpoint ✓

4. What are the three most important things that satellites can be used for, in your opinion? Explain your choices to a partner.
5. In your own words, explain what biotechnology is. From what you've read, do you think the use of genetically modified food products is a good thing? Explain.
6. How has the development of the Internet and biotechnology made Canada increasingly subject to international influences?

Globalization and Free Trade

One of the most profound effects of technological advance is a rapid trend toward **globalization**—the tendency for economies and even cultures to become more closely connected. Consider the following examples of globalization in action.

- As late as the early 1980s, Canada had many companies that manufactured such things as televisions and clothes. Today, most of these items are made offshore and imported.
- In the 1960s, oil tankers could carry around 50 000 tonnes of crude oil across the sea from oil well to refinery. Today's monster tankers can carry around 250 000 tonnes. And whereas oil was once shipped fairly short distances to market, today it's shipped vast distances across the oceans.
- It's not unusual to see teenagers in Nigeria or Thailand listening to the same music as teenagers in Canada or the U.S. do. At the same time, "world music" has become popular in North America and elsewhere. It showcases traditional music from cultures around the globe.

As a result of globalization, there are no guaranteed markets for products any more. Canadian companies must look to export their goods wherever they can.

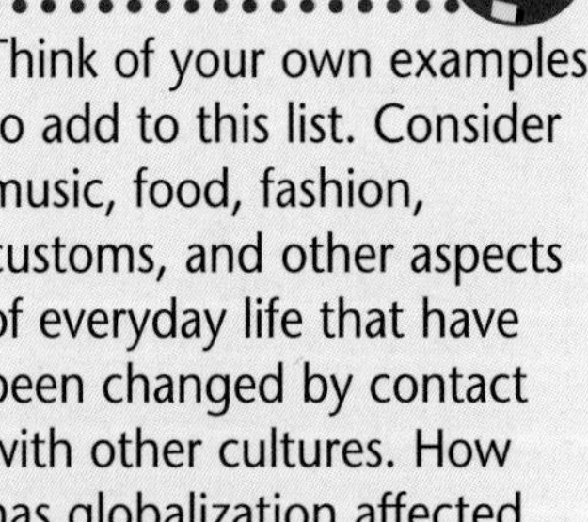

Literacy Hint

Think of your own examples to add to this list. Consider music, food, fashion, customs, and other aspects of everyday life that have been changed by contact with other cultures. How has globalization affected your life?

▲**Figure 15-8** A garment factory in Cambodia. Under free trade manufacturers tend to move to regions where labour is cheap and regulations less strict, such as Asia or South America. What moral issues does this raise for North American consumers?

The FTA and NAFTA

Globalization has affected all aspects of modern life, but none more so than trade. No nation exports a larger percentage of its goods and services than Canada does. (Just over 40 percent of all the goods and services produced in Canada are exported.) So international trade agreements are particularly important to Canadians.

In 1985 Prime Minister Brian Mulroney announced that he would begin negotiations with the United States government to sign a free trade agreement. **Free trade** between two countries means that tariffs (import duties) and other trade barriers are eliminated. Mulroney pointed out that other regions in the world were already signing trade agreements, and if Canada didn't follow, it would fall behind.

Mulroney's announcement started a huge debate in Canadian society. Would Canada be better or worse off if economic barriers were eliminated? Would access to the huge American market lead to an economic boom? Or would smaller Canadian industries, such as manufacturers of medical drugs or household goods, be overwhelmed by the sheer size of American companies? Even worse, would Canada lose its culture and its sovereignty and become part of the United States? Everybody had their own ideas.

Agreeing on the terms of the deal was tricky, too. Negotiations with the Americans went on for years, and a deal was arrived at only in January 1988. It was finally passed into law the following year.

Five years after the original deal was signed, Mexico joined the FTA and it was renamed the **North American Free Trade Agreement (NAFTA)**.

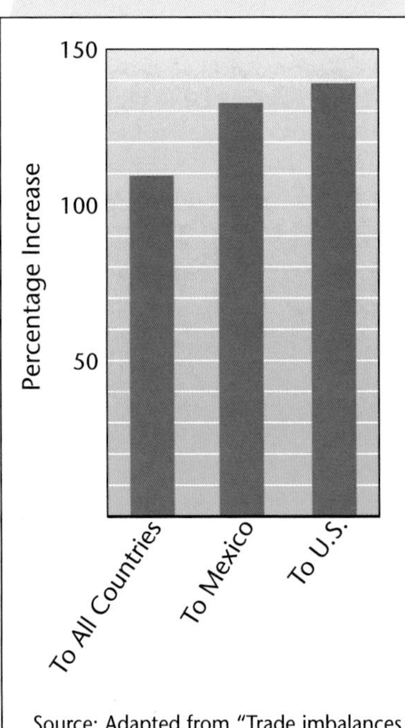

Source: Adapted from "Trade imbalances growing within NAFTA," accessed 26 March 2005, p. 1.

▲**Figure 15-9** Percentage Increase in Value of Canadian Exports, 1990–1998.

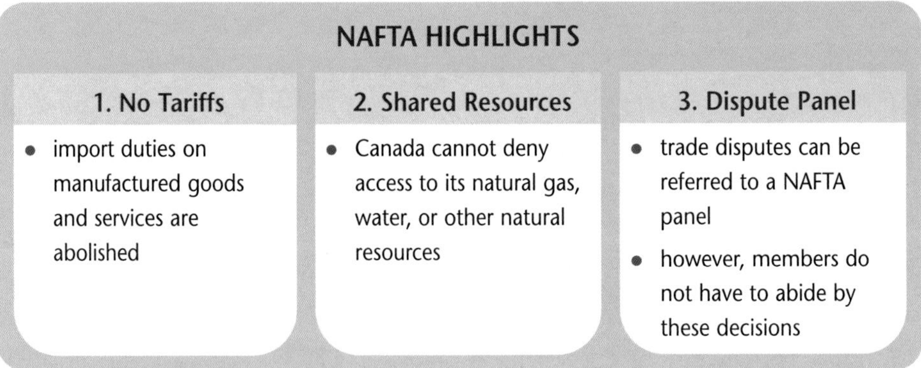

NAFTA HIGHLIGHTS

1. No Tariffs	2. Shared Resources	3. Dispute Panel
• import duties on manufactured goods and services are abolished	• Canada cannot deny access to its natural gas, water, or other natural resources	• trade disputes can be referred to a NAFTA panel • however, members do not have to abide by these decisions

▲**Figure 15-10** Some highlights of NAFTA. What advantages and disadvantages do you see with each of these terms?

Trade Disputes Since NAFTA

Because international trade is so aggressive, it's important to ensure that countries compete with each other fairly. The **World Trade Organization (WTO)** provides a panel to help settle trade disputes when they arise. However, the WTO rulings, like those of the NAFTA panel, are not binding, and disagreements still occur. In the following sections, you'll read about two important disputes involving Canada and the United States.

The Softwood Lumber Dispute

In the late 1990s the U.S. government charged that some Canadian provinces were allowing logging companies to harvest trees on Crown land at low prices. This meant Canadian companies could produce lumber at lower prices than U.S. companies because American companies had to pay higher cutting fees. Americans claimed that Canadians were unfairly subsidizing lumber exports and that American loggers were being harmed by Canadian producers. As a result, the U.S. government imposed a special tariff on Canadian softwood lumber.

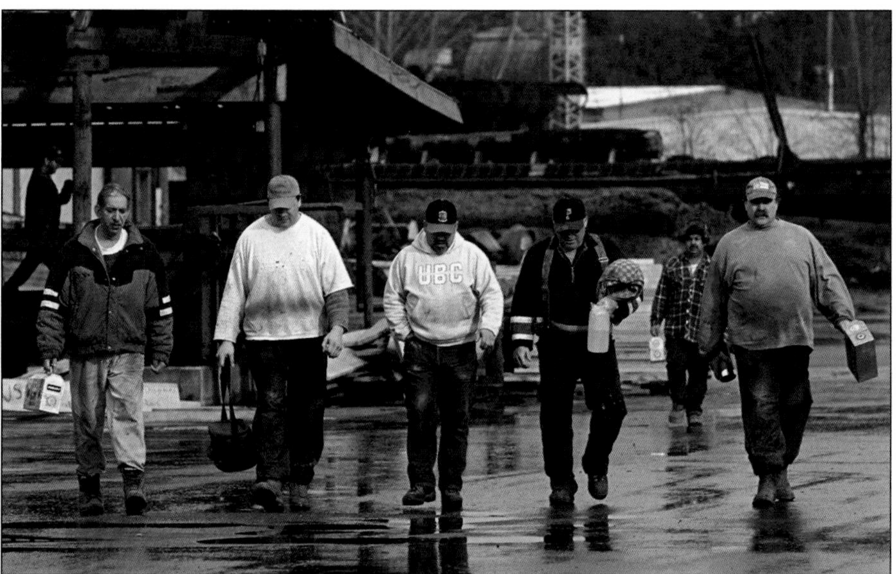

▲**Figure 15-11** Workers at a sawmill in B.C. leave their shift. Many sawmill workers have lost their jobs due to the softwood lumber dispute with the United States. Who benefits from the high U.S. tariffs on Canadian softwood?

NAFTA isn't the last word on the subject. Its members want to extend the trade area to include all nations in North and South America by 2020. The Free Trade Area of the Americas (FTAA), as it would be known, would be the largest free trade area in the world.

Did You Know

The WTO was formed in 1995 as a means of encouraging international trade. It has 146 member nations, including all three NAFTA nations.

Both the WTO and a NAFTA panel have ruled that Canadian lumber is not unfairly subsidized and that prices are fair. They have also ordered the U.S. to refund the billions of dollars in tariffs it has charged Canadian lumber producers. The U.S. has so far refused.

Mad Cow Disease

In May 2003 a single cow on an Alberta farm contracted mad cow disease. Humans eating infected meat can get a similar disease, for which there is no cure. The U.S. government and several other countries immediately banned all Canadian cattle exports. In December of the same year, another infected cow was found in Washington state. DNA evidence showed that it had originated in Canada.

The U.S. border remained closed for about two years, until July 2005. Despite strong sales of Canadian beef within Canada, cattle farmers were hit hard.

The issue strained relations between the two nations. Canada felt that, given the small number of cases, the U.S. was being overly cautious. Some suggested that the ban was payback for Canada's decision not to send troops to Iraq (more on this in Chapter 16). The U.S., however, pointed out that it had to protect its own market interests. Japan had threatened to ban imports of American beef unless it could be assured that no infected meat would be sent.

Did You Know?

Exports to the United States made up 40 percent of Canadian cattle exports before the ban. After the border closed, cattle prices dropped from about $1300 a head to just $15.

Figure 15-12 A cattle ranch near Medicine Hat, Alberta. Cattle ranchers usually sell off their herds in the fall to avoid the cost of keeping animals over the winter. What do you think would be the main expense of keeping a large herd over the winter?

Checkpoint ✓

7. Look at Figure 15-9. Write down one conclusion that you can draw from this figure about how much Canada's exports increased between 1990 and 1998.
8. Why do you think disagreements among NAFTA and WTO members still occur even when a decision has been made by a panel? Discuss with a partner and prepare a mind map of your ideas.
9. Explain how the mad cow disease dispute affected Canada's relationship with the U.S. Do you think the dispute could have been settled in another way? Explain.

For links to sites about NAFTA and Canada–U.S. relations

How Has NAFTA Affected Canadians?

So who was right—the critics or the supporters of free trade? The answer is not clear cut. The government of Canada believes that over time NAFTA has been good for Canada. Today, 86.6 percent of all our exports go to our NAFTA partners, and 2.3 million jobs have been created here by the agreement. However, the transition to free trade hasn't been easy. The diagram on the next page summarizes how NAFTA has affected different groups in Canadian society.

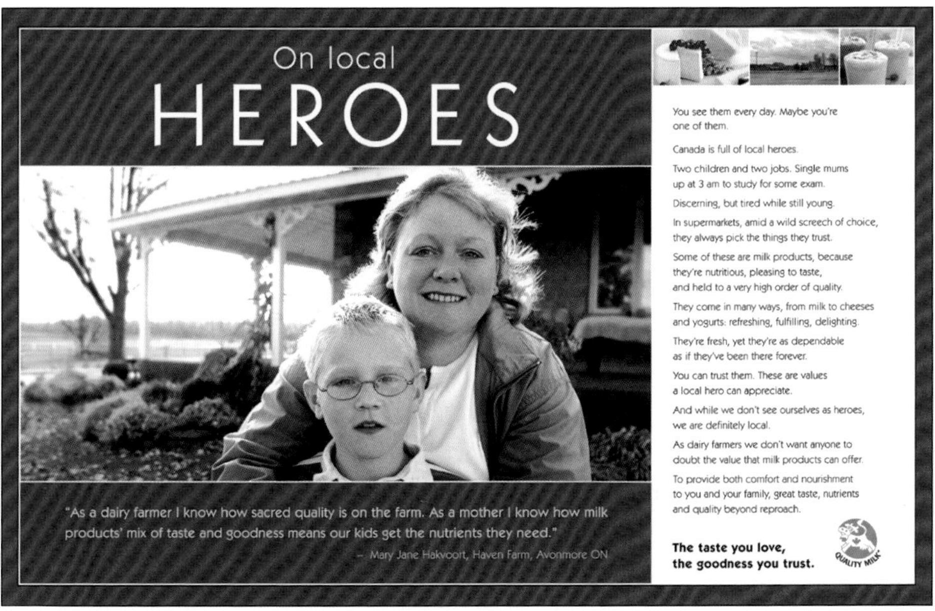

◀ **Figure 15-13** Marketing boards once controlled agricultural markets. Since NAFTA, their role has changed. This ad was sponsored by the Canadian Milk Marketing Board. What does it tell you about the role of marketing boards today?

Did You Know?

The Council of Canadians is a citizens' organization that was formed in 1985 to fight the free trade deal. It proposes five reasons why NAFTA is bad for Canada:

- It gives foreign corporations too much power to challenge our laws.
- It reduces Canada's sovereignty over its resources.
- It makes water a commodity—something that can be bought or sold.
- It poses a threat to our health care and other public services.
- It could lead to even deeper ties to the U.S.

EFFECTS OF FREE TRADE

FARMERS

Before NAFTA, Canadian marketing boards set quotas for many farm products—they told farmers how much they could produce in a given year. This allowed them to regulate prices and guarantee farmers a good return. NAFTA reduced the role of marketing boards, and Canadian farmers now have to compete directly with Mexican and U.S. producers. Many small, family-owned farms have disappeared as a result.

BUSINESS OWNERS

The transition has been difficult, especially for small, low-tech industries such as furniture, clothing, and shoe factories, which simply could not compete without tariff protection. Those that survived have been forced to find ways to produce things more quickly and cheaply.

WORKERS

Many factory workers lost their jobs when companies closed or moved elsewhere to find cheaper labour. Some have retrained and found work in other industries, while others have had to take a pay cut or give up some benefits.

CONSUMERS

Consumers have been the big winners under free trade. TVs, household appliances, and many other goods and services have come down in price now that they're made overseas where production costs are lower.

▲ **Figure 15-14** Free trade under NAFTA has been a mixed blessing for Canadians. Which of these groups has benefited the most? The least?

Checkpoint ✓

10. When you consider all these people, do you think your family has been helped or hurt by globalization?
11. Should Canada focus on ensuring that NAFTA works to our advantage? Or should we try to expand our trade to non-NAFTA nations so that we don't have "all our eggs in one basket"? State your own opinion on these matters, giving your reasons.

History Skill: Preparing a Research Report

A report is a summary of the most important information about a topic, either orally or in writing. These steps will help you prepare for both kinds of reports.

Step 1

Get an overview of your topic. Read through history texts, encyclopedia entries, and short, online summaries of the time or subject you've been assigned to get a general idea of the topic.

Step 2

Based on your overview, choose two to four specific subtopics to focus on in your report. For example, if you were writing about Canada's contributions to the technological revolution, you might choose the following subheads: Computer Technology, Satellite Technology, and Biotechnology, just as we have in the first section of this chapter.

Step 3

Write a draft. As you write, bear in mind how long your report is supposed to be. If you're writing a three-page report and have three subheadings, you need to summarize the most important information about each subtopic in about a page. If the whole report is only a page, you'll need even less information in each section. Include an introduction that describes what your report will be about. Also include a short conclusion that summarizes what you've found out.

When preparing a report . . .

- ✓ get an overview of the topic
- ✓ choose two to four subheads for further research
- ✓ write a draft
- ✓ revise your draft by adding, cutting, and rearranging the text
- ✓ for an oral report, try to make eye contact with your audience
- ✓ for a written report, check the language is suitable and proofread for spelling and grammar

Step 4

Revise your draft. Revising means cutting unnecessary information and/or adding information that's missing, and changing the order of the sections or of sentences within each section. As you revise, ask yourself: Does each sentence relate to the topic? Have I backed up my information with facts or examples? Do my facts and ideas flow in a logical order? As a final check, go back to your original assignment and ask yourself: Does my report meet all the requirements set out in the assignment?

Step 5

Present your report. Reports can be presented either orally or in writing. If you're doing an oral presentation, practise a few times until you can look up from the text every so often and address your audience directly. If you're handing in a written report, check that the language you've used is suitable and that there are no spelling or grammatical mistakes.

Practise It!

1. List two or three subtopics you could cover in a report on each of the following. You may need to do some research to get an overview of the topic.
   a) Free Trade in Canada
   b) How Globalization Affects Various Groups in Canadian Society
   c) Canada's Space Program

Chapter Summary

In the past few decades, technology has made the world smaller and globalization has expanded Canada's trade horizons. In this chapter, you learned about the following developments that have affected Canada's trade with other countries:

- Technology has transformed the way we live, work, and play.
- Every nation, including Canada, has been affected by globalization.
- The creation in 1994 of NAFTA, a free trade zone covering Canada, the U.S., and Mexico has had profound effects on manufacturers, workers, farmers, and consumers in different ways.
- Several major trade disputes have erupted among NAFTA members.

In the next chapter, you'll learn about Canada's developing role as a global citizen.

1980–
Present
technology transforms lives
NAFTA created
consumers benefit
trade disputes

Wrap It Up

Understand It

1. Create a diagram or chart to show how changes in technology, globalization, and free trade are connected.

Think About it

2. Survey your classmates to find out which of the following functions he or she performs online, and how often (e.g., frequently, sometimes, occasionally, never):

a) e-mail
b) look up information
c) shop online
d) online banking
e) download music

Then have each student ask an adult the same question. Create a bar graph to illustrate your findings. What conclusions can you draw?

3. Read about a recent trade dispute between Canada and the U.S. If you had to solve the dispute, how would you go about it?

Communicate It

4. Ask people from a previous generation about what changes they have noticed in their lives that result from increasing globalization. Do they see these changes as positive or negative? Summarize your findings in an oral report or an illustrated bulletin board display.

Apply It

5. a) What other time in the 20th century involved a massive rise and sudden fall on the stock market, similar to the one that occurred during the dot-com bubble of 2000?

b) Which situation had the greater effect on the general population? Explain.

Chapter 16

Canadians: Citizens of the World

In September 2005 a hurricane devastated the city of New Orleans, Louisiana. Canadians responded quickly. The government sent ships with supplies and military personnel. Non-governmental organizations (**NGOs**), such as the Canadian Red Cross, also sent volunteers and supplies. Young people pitched in through fundraising and collecting toys and clothes. Contributing to the world has become the Canadian way.

Figure 16-1 These young Canadians donated toys for New Orleans children forced from their homes after Hurricane Katrina. What other actions could young people take to help disaster victims?

American writer Pico Iyer identifies Canadians as "Can-globalists," meaning that we have a dual identity. Along with our sense of pride in our own nation, we view ourselves as world citizens. This can be seen in our participation in international organizations. It can also be seen through the work Canadians have done as disaster relief donors, peacekeepers, and human rights activists. This chapter is full of examples of how Canadians contribute to the world.

Checkpoint ✓

1. Think of some other examples you might know of where students helped disaster victims in Canada or in other countries.
2. Brainstorm five reasons to explain why Canadians can be considered "global citizens." Which one do you think is most important? Explain why.

Key Learnings

In this chapter, you will explore
- how Canada's participation in world events and organizations contributes to national identity
- Canadian responses to some major tragedies in recent years
- the roles and functions of the Canadian Armed Forces since 1980
- Canada's changing relationship with the United States
- Canada's role as a world leader in defending human rights

Words to Know

NGO
la Francophonie
G8
tied aid
civil war
genocide
collateral damage
weapons of mass destruction
land mines

International Organizations

One way Canadians have become world citizens is through participating in several international organizations. Canada is a member of many international organizations as well, including the Commonwealth, la Francophonie, and the G8.

The Commonwealth

The Commonwealth of Nations was formalized in the 1931 Statute of Westminster. It is currently made up of 53 members, all independent nations that were once British colonies. More than 1.5 billion people live in the Commonwealth member states, which include Britain, India, Pakistan, and New Zealand. As a Commonwealth nation, Canada supports economic development and human rights for developing nations in the group. Every four years the Commonwealth Games also bring together the best amateur athletes in the organization, an important preparation for the Summer Olympics.

Did You Know?

The Commonwealth Games are the only Games where the athletes and officials share a common language. Because participants find it so easy to talk with one another in English, the Commonwealth Games have become known as the "friendly games."

La Francophonie

La Francophonie means "French-speaking people." This organization brings together countries that feel a connection with the French language and with other French-speaking cultures around the world. It was founded in 1970 and includes 63 member countries and states. Canada, Quebec, and New Brunswick each have separate membership in la Francophonie. Nearly half of the members are countries in Africa

and the Middle East. The organization holds a world summit conference every two years to sign agreements on economic assistance and cultural exchanges.

The G8

Canada has been a member of the **G8** (Group of Eight) countries since 1976, one year after the organization began. The G8 are the United States, Britain, France, Germany, Italy, Russia, and Japan—all major industrialized democracies. It meets once a year to discuss economic issues and foreign policies. Members take turns hosting the group's annual summit meeting. Canada has hosted four times, most recently in 2002.

Critics believe that the G8 countries want to force their economic and foreign policies upon the rest of the world through their wealth and power. As a result, some Canadian citizens have participated in protests at G8 meetings. G8 supporters, however, believe that it's in Canada's best interest to be included in the G8. They point out that past summits have addressed such important issues as terrorism, international crime, and the AIDS crisis (see pages 318–320).

Checkpoint ✓

3. Complete a four-column chart comparing information about the Commonwealth, la Francophonie, and the G8. Compare the date of origin, number of members, reason for joining, and two other points of your choosing.
4. Brainstorm a list of three important world issues or problems that you'd like to see the G8 take action on. Explain each choice briefly.

Did You Know?

The people put in charge of planning and organizing the next year's G8 Summit are called sherpas. This term also refers to mountain guides in Asia who lead climbers up to the summit, that is, the peak of the mountain.

Literacy Hint

When you finish reading a section of text, read it again to make sure you understand the main idea and the facts that support it. Think about how this information adds to or changes what you already know about the topic.

Disaster Relief and Foreign Aid

Canadians have a reputation for contributing to the world. As private citizens we donate our own money to such causes as disaster relief. Our government, meanwhile, provides foreign aid. This combination was clearly illustrated in Canada's response to the tsunami crisis in 2004–2005.

Tsunami Relief

On December 26, 2004, disaster struck Southeast Asia. A very strong undersea earthquake triggered a wall of water—a tsunami—which killed more than 250 000 people. Millions more lost their homes and possessions. Within weeks, the Canadian government announced a

◀ **Figure 16-2** The aftermath of the December 2004 tsunami. Why did so many Canadians respond to this crisis?

$425 million aid package for immediate relief and long-term rebuilding in the region. This included $150 million to match public and corporate contributions. Including later donations, Canadians contributed more than $600 million to tsunami relief, an average of about $20 for every person. Canada was among the world's most generous nations during this disaster.

For links to sites about foreign aid

Canada's Foreign Aid Record

Soon after the tsunami occurred, wealthy nations were reminded of their past foreign aid performance. Oxfam, a major world aid agency, urged donor countries to help Southeast Asia with outright grants (gifts), not loans. Oxfam also said that donations should not be tied to the interests of donor countries. (Sometimes foreign aid can be used only to purchase supplies from the donor country, like a gift certificate. This is called **tied aid.**) Canada's tsunami relief pledges met both of Oxfam's donor requirements.

Oxfam also suggested that wealthy countries provide debt relief, either freezing or cancelling the $300 billion owed by the countries struck by the tsunami. World leaders are now considering how to handle the debt problem in the disaster region.

The process of debt relief began in earnest in the late 1990s, mostly in the poorest African countries, where repayment of old loans cripples their economies. In July 2005 Prime Minister Paul Martin met

Figure 16-3 In the summer of 2005, big-name performers donated their talents in a series of Live 8 concerts held at the same time in each of the G8 countries and South Africa. They aimed to focus world attention on the G8 Summit and pressure the leaders to take action on poverty in Africa. More than 35 000 people attended Canada's concert in Barrie, Ontario. Do you think celebrities should become involved in politics?

with G8 leaders to discuss poverty and debt in Africa. At the meeting, they announced a $25 billion increase in foreign aid to Africa and the cancellation of the debts of 18 impoverished nations.

Despite Canada's participation in the G8 Summit, foreign aid spending through the Canadian International Development Agency (CIDA) accounts for only about 0.3 percent of its Gross Domestic Product. This amounts to three cents out of every $10, an amount lower than that contributed by several European nations. Canadian foreign aid peaked at .5 percent of GDP in 1987, then gradually dropped to the current level.

Did You Know?

During the 1960s, Prime Minister Lester Pearson headed a UN Commission urging wealthy nations to pledge 0.7 percent of their Gross Domestic Product to foreign aid. GDP is the total value of all the goods and services produced in one year. In 2004, Canada's GDP was over one trillion dollars!

Checkpoint ✓

5. Use your own examples to show the difference between the terms *foreign aid, tied aid,* and *debt relief.*
6. Should Canada increase its foreign aid contribution or is it already doing enough to help other countries? What do you think?

Canada's Military at Home and Abroad

Canada's Armed Forces have served both the nation and the world. Besides helping Canadians in times of need, they have served around the world both independently and as part of the United Nations.

In fact, Canadians have participated in more United Nations peacekeeping assignments than any other country. Master Corporal Frank Misztal is proud of his job in the Armed Forces.

I am Canadian . . .

- . . . I don't just speak English or French, nor am I bilingual. I can speak many languages.
- Although I am trained to fight in a war, I don't cause them.
- When I am not deployed on a mission of peace, I travel all over my country; fighting forest fires, battling floods, rescuing lost souls or repairing damages caused by an ice storm.
- I try not to take sides and believe in treating all humanity equally.
- In my off-duty hours while deployed, I occupy myself by rebuilding schools or playgrounds, and I teach children in a war-torn country about peace and harmony.
- I am my country's best ambassador, and I am respected the world over for what I do best.
- I carry my country's flag shamelessly and hold my head up high wherever I go.
- My name is Frank, and I am . . . a proud Canadian peacekeeper.

Master Corporal Frank Misztal, www.peacekeeper.ca/stories3.html

Did You Know?

More than 100 000 Canadians have served on United Nations peacekeeping missions, and 100 have died "in the service of peace." Although people from every province have joined the military, 5 percent of Canada's Armed Forces come from Newfoundland and Labrador, which has less than 2 percent of Canada's total population.

Serving in Canada

Master Corporal Misztal points out the military's value within Canada. When the military is battling natural disasters, for example, it is giving aid to the civil power. For example, in 1999 troops cleaned up after a severe January ice storm paralyzed eastern Ontario and southern Quebec. Then, in the hot, dry summer of 2003, they fought raging forest fires in British Columbia.

The military's aid to the civil power also includes keeping the peace during political disputes. In Chapter 12 you learned that Prime Minister Trudeau sent troops into Quebec during the October Crisis of 1970. Twenty years later they were ordered into Quebec again, but this time at the insistence of the Quebec premier.

A land dispute had flared up between the town of Oka and the Kanesatake Mohawk First Nation near Montreal. The town wanted to

For links to sites about Canada's military

build a golf course on ancient burial grounds and a sacred pine tree grove. After an officer was killed, tensions ran high between the Quebec police and the Mohawks. About 4400 armed Canadian troops replaced the police until a peaceful settlement was successfully worked out. Later, the Canadian government purchased the disputed grounds and turned them over to the Kanesatake reserve.

Serving the World

Besides serving in Canada, the armed forces bring their services to the world. In December 2004 the Disaster Assistance Response Team (DART) of the Canadian Armed Forces was sent to help in the tsunami region. One military unit went to Sri Lanka, a Commonwealth member country, where 10 000 had died and 180 000 were left homeless.

Nurse practitioner Captain Karen Trainor was a DART member. She helped treat between 30 and 70 people daily in mobile health clinics throughout the area. "Most of the hospitals were destroyed, and many doctors and nurses were killed," she explained. "DART made a big difference in the eyes of the Sri Lankan people." During its two-month posting, Trainor's team treated 5500 people and supplied millions of litres of fresh drinking water. They also repaired schools, built emergency shelters, and cleared away rubble.

▲ **Figure 16-4** Captain Karen Trainor treating a girl in a health clinic in Sri Lanka. Why was the DART team's help so important to the people in Southeast Asia?

Checkpoint ✓

7. a) Choose two phrases from the "I am Canadian" quotation that you find most admirable. Explain why you chose each one.
   b) Identify phrases from the quotation that seem to fit closely with the events of the Oka land dispute.
8. Using the information that you've read so far, write a want ad describing the ideal candidate for a job in the Canadian military.

Career Profile

Frank Misztal, The Canadian Military

The Canadian Armed Forces offers a wide range of training programs for young people with an interest in a career with the military. One of these programs is communications training, in which recruits learn to operate different types of equipment for sending and receiving messages during field operations.

This was Frank Misztal's specialty during his years in cadets—an organization for students interested in the military—and the Armed Forces. Born in Belgium to Polish parents after World War II, he emigrated to Toronto with his family in 1956. He became a Canadian citizen in 1967. In high school, Misztal studied electronics and joined the school's cadets. He then joined the Canadian Forces reserves (part-time soldiers).

By 1989 Misztal was a member of the Canadian Armed Forces regulars. "I did a six-month tour of duty in the Golan Heights (Israel/Syria) in 1991, starting the day after the first Gulf War," he says. "My second tour in 1994/95 was in Bosnia and Croatia. Both were UN peacekeeping missions." Upon his return to Canada, he was posted to the National Defence Headquarters in Ottawa to solve problems with computer communications systems. He retired from the Canadian military in 2002, and continues to apply his computer talents as webmaster for four different Canadian military websites.

Misztal notes that "I'm often asked: 'How can I become a Canadian peacekeeper?' Peacekeeping is only one task of many that a Canadian soldier would perform. . . I think that the cadets would be a good stepping stone toward a career in the Canadian Forces. The Canadian Forces reserves would provide a person a better insight into a future military career."

Name: Frank Misztal

Job Title: Communications Specialist, Canadian Armed Forces

What I liked about my work:

"I enjoyed the challenges of everyday military life, as well as the travel and adventure, where I met people of varied cultures. Adventure, friendship, and the opportunity to serve my adopted country were key factors for my military career."

1. Make a list of character traits that you think would be required to serve in the Canadian Armed Forces.
2. a) How is a military career different from other jobs?

   b) Use Frank Misztal's example to show how a military career can also prepare people for civilian life.

The Military: Peacekeepers and Peacemakers

Ever since Lester Pearson created the role of international peacekeeper in 1957, the light blue UN helmet or beret has been a part of our global identity. But the role of international peacekeeper has changed with world politics.

Before 1990, most UN missions could easily be identified as peacekeeping activities. Troops from different countries were sent in to keep the peace after a truce or ceasefire had been agreed to. Their job was to keep the two opposing sides apart until a final peace treaty was worked out by diplomats. UN peacekeepers were often accompanied by foreign civilians, and organized refugee camps and other activities to help rebuild the country. One peacekeeping mission lasted for 30 years. From 1964 to 1994 Canadian peacekeepers helped supervise a truce between Greek and Turkish forces on the Mediterranean island of Cyprus. It was a tough mission.

> There were many threats. . . . These included the possibility of being shot by either Greek or Turkish soldiers during patrols, Cannon or Artillery fire, stepping on or driving over [land]mines and setting off unexploded bombs. . . . During some foot patrols both the Greek Cypriot National Guard and Turkish soldiers tried to intimidate us by pointing their weapons at us and even on occasion threatened to kill us.

Sgt. John Campbell, "Glad to Be Canadian," www.peacekeeper.ca/stories2.html

intimidate: to try to frighten a person either by using threats or actual violence

◀ **Figure 16-5** Canadians are proud to wear the light blue helmet or beret that identifies the peacekeepers of all nations. How does their participation in peacekeeping forces earn them respect from the world community?

In the 1990s Canada's military became increasingly involved in armed combat. When necessary, aggression was met by force and peace was kept by military action. The United States took a much more active role in directing key UN missions and using its own allies outside the UN for peacemaking operations. Canada was involved in some of these missions.

America's increased focus on peacemaking resulted primarily from changes in world power. In Chapters 9 and 14, you learned that two superpowers—the U.S. and the Soviet Union—dominated world politics. But in 1990 communism collapsed in the Soviet Union, and the country divided into 15 nations, including Russia. This left the United States unchallenged as the world's only superpower—what President George Bush called "a new world order."

In 2002 the United States spent US$340 billion on its military, more than the rest of the world combined. By 2005, the U.S.-led operations in Iraq alone were costing America about US$200 billion per year.

Checkpoint ✓

9. What dangers did peacekeeper John Campbell experience in Cyprus? Why do you think both sides in the dispute threatened Canadian peacekeepers?
10. Should patient UN negotiations always be attempted before resorting to forceful peacemaking? Discuss the question in small groups, making a list of examples to support each side.

Peacekeeping Challenges in the 1990s

The United Nations has been involved in dozens of peacekeeping missions since 1980. Canadian peacekeepers were especially active during the latter years of the 20th century. For example, Canada supervised the withdrawal of Soviet troops from Afghanistan between 1988 and 1990. However, three difficult missions in the 1990s showed the shortcomings of international peacekeeping.

Did You Know?

Rebellious members of Canada's Fifth Airborne Regiment serving in Somalia killed four suspected thieves. They also photographed a 16-year-old Somalia teenager they had beaten. As a result of public anger in Canada, this regiment was permanently disbanded.

Civil War in Somalia

In 1992 the East African nation of Somalia was torn by a **civil war**. This is a war between opposing groups within the country—in this case, rival warlords—not an invasion from outside the country. A ceasefire was agreed to and United Nations peacekeepers entered Somalia in March 1992. Canada's Armed Forces participated as peacekeepers, mainly by distributing humanitarian aid. But the ceasefire agreement was repeatedly broken, and many relief supplies were stolen by rival gangs. The mission fell apart and UN forces withdrew in 1995.

Genocide in Rwanda

Soon after the disappointing Somalian campaign ended, an even greater challenge arose in central Africa. Extremist ethnic Hutus in Rwanda began a **genocide** to eliminate the Tutsi ethnic minority. Genocide is the planned extermination of an entire national, religious, racial, or ethnic population. Between 500 000 and 800 000 Tutsis—as well as moderate Hutus and Europeans (both often defending Tutsis from attack)—were slaughtered. Thousands more were permanently maimed and disfigured. Some call this a peacemaking mission because no truce or ceasefire was in place before the small United Nations force arrived.

Figure 16-6 Genocide in Rwanda. After the failure of the U.S.-led United Nations mission to Somalia, the UN Security Council was very slow to take action on Roméo D'Allaire's urgent call for a massive force for Rwanda. Why do you think the UN peace efforts were ineffective?

Hutu Ethnic Majority

- made up about 90 percent of Rwanda's population
- extremists resented the power of the Tutsi minority
- extremists plotted genocide to exterminate the Tutsi

Tutsi Minority

- made up only about 5 percent of Rwanda's population
- many were well-educated and worked in urban communities
- very powerful in Rwandan government and business

Roméo Dallaire

- Canadian Major General in charge of all UN forces in Rwanda
- urgently appealed for large UN and U.S. military peacemaking forces
- his requests were not heeded and the genocide reached a peak

UN Peacekeepers

- a small detachment of UN peacekeepers entered Rwanda in 1994
- Canada distributed relief supplies and flew medical services
- UN forces were greatly outnumbered and also came under attack

France and Belgium

- former colonial powers in central Africa
- sent troops to keep the peace as Hutu extremists attacked Tutsis
- unable to control the situation as genocide spread

"Ethnic Cleansing" in Yugoslavia

Background: The country of Yugoslavia was created after World War II and combined several religious and ethnic rivals. In 1991 the northern states of Slovenia and Croatia declared independence. Another state, Serbia, had dominated the country and fought to keep their power. The Muslim minority in the state of Bosnia was caught in the middle. Extremist Serbs used genocide (they called it "ethnic cleansing") to try to eliminate Muslims from Bosnia and later from the Kosovo region of Serbia itself.

Peacekeeping: In 1991 the United Nations sent a large peacekeeping force, including many Canadians, into the region to monitor a short-lived ceasefire. Canada's Major General Lewis Mackenzie led the UN forces in Yugoslavia. But warfare soon resumed, and the peacekeepers were given little respect. For example, thousands of Muslims were attacked and killed by Serbia in areas designated by the UN as safe havens. The cartoon summarizes Major General Mackenzie's criticism of the impossible situation in which the UN had put peacekeeping forces.

Peacemaking: By 1995 it was clear that the UN had failed to control the situation. So NATO allies decided to force a ceasefire by launching air attacks on Serbian offensive positions. By 1996 the warring parties had signed the Dayton Accord. Then, two years later, the largely Muslim state of Kosovo declared its independence from Yugoslavia. The Serb leader, Slobodan Milošević, ordered more "ethnic cleansing," and this in turn sparked a new NATO bombing campaign. Canadian pilots flew many missions before the conflict ended.

The term "ethnic cleansing" was first used by Serbian nationals in 1991. It described their efforts to eliminate the Muslim population in Bosnia (and later Kosovo) by terror and mass murder. Former Serb president Slobodan Milošević is on trial at the UN International Court of Justice for genocide.

▲**Figure 16-7** Why was it so difficult for the UN to keep the peace in Bosnia?

Checkpoint ✓

11. Make a three-column chart of the three UN missions in this section. List the name of each mission, the causes of the conflict, and the problems faced by the peacekeepers.
12. Look again at the political cartoon in Figure 16-7.
    a) What is the artist's opinion of UN peacekeeping in Bosnia?
    b) As a class, discuss how the cartoonist gets his message across.

Collateral damage is a military term for unintended civilian injury and death and the destruction of private property in war. Critics ask why military planners would not expect high civilian casualty rates when heavily populated areas are attacked or bombed.

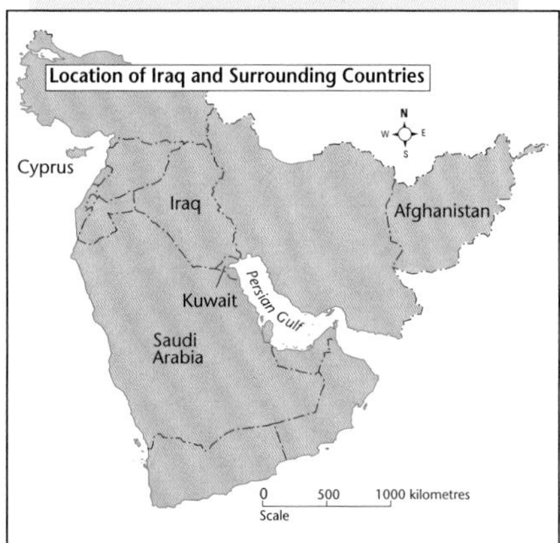

▲**Figure 16-8** Iraq, Kuwait, and the Persian Gulf. Why do you think the United States led a peacemaking force to this area?

Peacemaking in the "New World Order"

The Gulf War and "Operation Desert Storm"

This peacemaking operation led to the deaths of one hundred and fifty peacemakers and 125 000 Iraqis. Among the dead and injured were large numbers of civilians—"collateral damage" in massive bombing raids carried out over Iraq's capital. Critics claim that the Gulf War was little more than "blood for oil."

President Saddam Hussein was considered a ruthless dictator who violated human rights by imprisoning and torturing his opponents.

The United States demanded military action, and early in 1991, UN forces led by American troops invaded Iraq.

In 1990 Iraqi forces invaded neighbouring Kuwait, a small oil-rich nation that blocked Iraq's strategic access to the Persian Gulf.

Land forces launched "Operation Desert Storm" from Saudi Arabia. This high-speed assault completely overwhelmed Iraqi forces.

Several UN resolutions and threats of economic sanctions urged Hussein to withdraw from Kuwait, but this approach didn't work.

About 4 500 Canadian Armed Forces personnel served in the Gulf War, both on ships and in the air. There were no Canadian casualties.

Though Iraq was driven out of Kuwait in 1991, Saddam Hussein remained in power. The UN continued economic sanctions against Iraq and demanded that Hussein get rid of chemical weapons.

Afghanistan: The Hunt for bin Laden

On September 11, 2001, terrorists crashed two hijacked airliners into New York's World Trade Center, and another into United States military headquarters at the Pentagon in Washington, D.C. A fourth plane crashed in a field as passengers overcame the terrorists on board. The 9/11 attacks killed more than 2500 civilians and caused at least US$150 billion damage to the American economy. Al-Qaeda, considered by many to be an extremist Islamic global terrorist network led by Osama bin Laden, carried out these acts. Bin Laden, a wealthy Saudi Arabian, founded the group after the Gulf War to oppose the power of the United States and its military allies.

Shortly after these attacks, the Canadian government passed an Anti-Terrorism Act. It seeks to protect Canadians from terrorist activities at home and abroad. It also includes safeguards to protect basic rights and freedoms.

Osama bin Laden operated al-Qaeda out of Afghanistan. This isolated Asian nation was ruled by a strict religious Islamic dictatorship called the Taliban. It made Afghanistan a friendly environment for al-Qaeda terrorists to set up global training and operations.

After 9/11, American President George W. Bush decided to invade Afghanistan in order to destroy al-Qaeda. He already had all the allies he needed, because according to the NATO agreement, any attack on one member is considered an attack on the others.

Soon, Canada and other NATO members, led by the United States, were at war in Afghanistan. By early 2005, 13 500 members of Canada's military had served in the campaign. This included ground forces in Afghanistan, sailors on 20 naval warships, and air force crews flying from a Canadian base along the Persian Gulf. To date, Osama bin Laden has eluded capture, and Afghanistan has held democratic elections. NATO troops, including about 750 Canadians, remain on duty there.

Did You Know?

In April 2002, a serious incident in Afghanistan angered Canadian officials and the general public. An American pilot bombed Canadian troops, mistaking their practice gunfire for enemy aggression. His "friendly fire" killed four soldiers and injured eight others. Later, a U.S. military court did not discharge the pilot.

For links to sites about 9/11 and the 2001 invasion of Afghanistan

◀ **Figure 16-9** Canadian troops continue to risk their lives peacemaking in Afghanistan. Would you be willing to risk your life in order to help people in other countries?

Operation Iraqi Freedom

After 9/11 the United States government became even more vigilant about protecting its own interests. One country that America viewed as a threat was Iraq. In 2003 President George W. Bush made two claims against Iraq:

- Saddam Hussein was deceiving UN weapons inspectors and hiding deadly **weapons of mass destruction** (WMDs). These include chemical nerve gases, biological weapons, and nuclear bombs.
- Saddam Hussein and Iraq were working with and providing funds to al-Qaeda terrorists.

President Bush was determined to invade Iraq and drive Saddam Hussein out of power. However, many other nations were not convinced that invading Iraq was the best tactic. France, Germany, and Canada were among the countries that refused to participate in another invasion of Iraq. They wanted to support patient UN negotiations with Iraq regarding weapons inspection. They were not willing to automatically be drawn into every U.S.-led military operation.

The situation didn't fall within the NATO agreement either. Instead, the United States assembled its own "coalition of the willing"—Britain, Australia, Spain, and a group of other nations, each of which sent a small number of troops. Saddam Hussein was captured in 2004, and democratic elections were held early in 2005. However, terrorist attacks on troops and civilians occur almost daily. England and Spain, members of the coalition, have also endured terrorist bombings.

By late 2005 many Americans thought their government had made a mistake by invading Iraq, particularly because President Bush had admitted that no weapons of mass destruction had been found there. He also admitted that no proof existed of Saddam Hussein's support of al-Qaeda.

Literacy Hint

Bulleted lists are often used in this text. These lists help break up information so that the key points stand out and are easier to understand. Use bulleted lists in your notes to help you summarize and remember what you've read.

Checkpoint ✓

13. a) Identify three important differences between the war with Iraq in 1991 and 2003.
b) Explain why Canada joined one campaign but not the other.

14. Discuss the following questions in small groups:
a) Should Canada be supporting the U.S. and Britain with troops in Iraq?
b) Do you think Canada faces a threat from al-Qaeda?

History Skill: Documenting your Sources

Whenever you present information from another source, you must let your reader know exactly where your information came from. A bibliography is a record of your sources.

Step 1

Whenever you take notes from a source, write down all the details for a bibliography. Almost all social science writing uses the guidelines developed by the American Psychological Association (APA) to document sources. The APA format uses the following order:

1. The authors' names are arranged by last name followed by the first name, in alphabetical order of last name
2. Publication date
3. The full title in italics
4. The place the book was published
5. The name of the publisher

The proper APA bibliographical entry for this book looks like this:

Bain, C., & DesRivieres, D. (2006). Experience history. Don Mills, ON: Oxford.

Step 2

Article entries contain a) the full article title in quotation marks; b) the title of newspaper or magazine in italics; and c) page numbers. In every other way, they are the same as book entries. Here is an example:

Contenta, S. (2005). G-8 set to forgive billions. (2005, June 2). *Toronto Star*, pp. A1, A12.

Step 3

Website entries contain the full Internet address and the date you accessed the site. Here is an example:

Freeman, M. (2005). *The road to Kandahar*. Retrieved November 2, 2005 from http://www.forces.gc.ca/site/Feature_Story/2005/06/22_f_e.asp

When creating a bibliography . . .

- ✓ create a rough-note entry for each book you use
- ✓ create a rough-note entry for each article you use
- ✓ create a rough-note entry for each Internet source
- ✓ create your finished bibliography

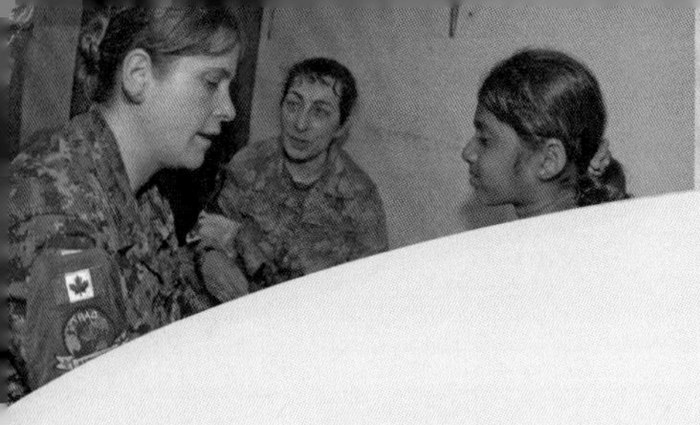

Step 4

To create a completed bibliography, arrange your rough-copy bibliographical notes in alphabetical order by the last name of the authors.

Practise It!

1. Record a full bibliographical entry for each of the following: a) a book, b) a magazine or newspaper article, c) an Internet page.
2. List each source from question 1 in alphabetical order by author on a page headed "Bibliography."

Did You Know?

The War Crimes Tribunal has trials for the following types of crimes:

- **War crimes:** the murder, torture, rape, and hostage-taking of civilians, and/or large-scale destruction of their property
- **Crimes against humanity:** the murder, torture, rape, enslavement, and deporting of innocent civilians
- **Genocide:** the deliberate mass murder of any national, ethnic, racial, or religious group

Canadians Working for a Better World

Peacekeeping and peacemaking, as well as the efforts of concerned individuals, show Canada's international commitment. From war crimes to land mines to HIV/AIDS, concerned Canadians are working hard to find solutions to global issues.

War Crimes

In 1996 almost a hundred countries, including Canada, agreed to set up the UN War Crimes Tribunal. This UN court investigates and prosecutes people accused of serious violations of human rights during an international or civil war.

Canadian judge Louise Arbour served as chief prosecutor at the new War Crimes Tribunal from 1996 to 1999. She built cases against those accused of genocide and war crimes in Rwanda and the former Yugoslavia by visiting massacre sites and mass graves to gather evidence and interviewing witnesses and survivors. Arbour was successful in achieving the new court's first "guilty" verdicts. In 2004 Louise Arbour became the United Nations High Commissioner for Human Rights.

◀ **Figure 16-10** Louise Arbour investigating a war crimes scene in Bosnia. What personal characteristics do you think she would require to do this work?

Canadians and Land Mines

Land mines are a serious problem in many war-torn countries. These inexpensive weapons are set just below ground surface to slow down an advancing enemy. About 100 million mines have been buried in the past half century. When a land mine is stepped on, its explosion can cause serious injury or death. During this time at least 250 000 civilians (mostly children) are estimated to have been killed or injured by land mines.

Many people are active in working to ban and clear land mines. Daryl Toews and Meredith Daun started the Manitoba Campaign to Ban Landmines after seeing the problem first-hand in Bosnia and Cambodia in Southeast Asia. This is just one of the over 1400 non-government organizations (NGOs) in 90 countries that make up the International Campaign to Ban Landmines. Toews says: "We . . . are removed from the situation. But we can play an important part in helping solve the problem with other countries."

The International Campaign to Ban Landmines started the process that led to the Ottawa Treaty. At a 1997 meeting in Ottawa, Canada's Foreign Minister Lloyd Axworthy challenged governments to agree to ban anti-personnel land mines. The Ottawa Treaty was signed by 123 countries that pledged to stop making, selling, and using land mines. However, there have been problems. Some major producers and users of land mines, including the United States and several countries in the Middle East, have not yet signed.

AIDS in Africa

During the past two decades, AIDS has become a serious international problem. About one Canadian adult in 1000 either has AIDS or has tested HIV positive, meaning they carry the virus that may eventually develop

Did You Know?

Lloyd Axworthy was the first Canadian since Lester Pearson to be nominated for a Nobel Peace Prize. Although he was not selected, Axworthy's nomination recognized his leadership in the 1997 Ottawa Treaty. The International Campaign to Ban Landmines and its coordinator Jody Williams received the award that year.

AIDS stands for Acquired Immune Deficiency Syndrome, a disease first named in 1982. It weakens the body's immune system and opens it to many infections, eventually causing death. AIDS is spread both through sexual activity and the sharing of needles that inject intravenous drugs.

into AIDS. Almost three-quarters of all cases are in Africa. In one African country, Botswana, more than a third of the adult population suffers from HIV/AIDS.

Any disease that affects this many people in an area is called a **pandemic**, a widespread epidemic. Large numbers of African children are either orphaned by AIDS or die from it themselves. Drugs are available that can treat HIV/AIDS. Although they won't save a person with the disease, they can extend life by many years. However, these drugs are much too expensive for most people in Africa to afford.

One of the strongest voices spreading awareness about the AIDS issue is Canadian humanitarian Stephen Lewis. In 2001, Lewis became the United Nations Special Envoy (spokesperson) on AIDS in Africa. He challenges drug companies to produce more affordable HIV/AIDS medicines. Lewis claims that the cost of these medicines could be reduced by up to 90 percent and still bring in a reasonable profit.

Did You Know?

Moved by his many experiences with people suffering from this deadly disease, Lewis created the Stephen Lewis Foundation in 2003. It raises funds for three different purposes:

- to provide care for women who are dying of AIDS
- to help orphans and AIDS-affected children
- to support AIDS groups in sharing information

Figure 16-11 Stephen Lewis's work has helped countless people like these Zambians at an African girls' home. How could you become involved in helping people around the world?

For links to sites about war crimes, land mines, and AIDS issues

Checkpoint ✓

15. Why did the UN believe The War Crimes Tribunal was necessary?

16. List three different ways in which Canadians have been active in solving the land mines problem.

17. What can be done to help HIV/AIDS patients in Africa?

18. Consider the issues of land mines, war crimes, and AIDS. Write a persuasive letter to the editor urging the Canadian government to become more actively involved in the issue that you consider the most important.

Chapter Summary

Canadians are becoming known as "Can-globalists"—people who are proud of their own nation, but who also see themselves as citizens of the world. In this chapter, you have learned about:

- Canada's participation in international organizations such as the Commonwealth, la Francophonie, and the G8.
- How Canada provides both monetary and non-monetary humanitarian aid to countries in need or experiencing natural disaster.
- The role of the Canadian Armed Forces, in Canada and the world, including peacekeeping and peacemaking.
- How individuals such as Louise Arbour and Stephen Lewis contribute to the world as "global citizens."

The final chapter of the book will show how the basic rights of all Canadians have changed since the 1980s and how the lives of several different groups within Canada's population have changed since 1914.

disaster relief

foreign aid

war crimes

land mines

AIDS

Wrap It Up

Understand It

1. Identify the differences between peacekeeping and peacemaking. Then, classify each of the following Canadian Armed Forces missions as either peacekeeping or peacemaking missions: a) The Gulf War (1991) b) Somalia c) Afghanistan d) Yugoslavia
2. Make an information chart to summarize the "world citizen" role of Canada or individual Canadians in each of the following: a) debt forgiveness b) tsunami relief c) banning land mines d) UN War Crimes Tribunal

Think About It

3. What is your opinion of "Can-globalism"? Is it possible for people to see themselves as world citizens and as proud Canadians at the same time? Write an opinion piece using information and examples to support your view.

Communicate It

4. Use the Internet to research and prepare a poster to support the International Campaign to Ban Landmines.

Apply It

5. Work with a small group to develop a plan for an awareness-raising event in support of the world campaign to fight AIDS. First brainstorm ideas, then make each group member responsible for a different part of the planning. Remember, the AIDS awareness theme must be clear to all who attend your event.

Chapter 17

Politics and the Canadian People: 1980 to the Present

In this chapter you'll read about the Canadian Charter of Rights and Freedoms, and the protections that it gives us. How does it affect you in your daily life? Consider the list below.

Section	Right or Freedom	Example
2	Everyone has the right of freedom of association	I can join organizations that protest peacefully against government policies
3	Citizens may vote in federal elections and elections in their own province or territory	I'll be eligible to vote in two years
15(1)	Citizens have the right to equal protection under the law, regardless of race, national or ethnic origin, colour, religion, sex, age, or mental or physical disability	Our community provides bus services for people with physical disabilities
6(1)	Citizens may enter, remain in, and leave Canada	My friend's family just returned from visiting relatives in China
20(1)	Citizens may communicate with the federal government in either English or French	I can talk to my MP in French, even though I live in an area that's mostly English-speaking
27	The Charter protects the multicultural heritage of Canadians	Our school offers heritage language courses; my Sikh friend can wear his turban to school
28	The Charter guarantees the equality of males and females	My father's employer has a policy to encourage more women to apply for management jobs

Did You Know?

Most of these rights listed in the Charter also apply not only to citizens, but to landed immigrants—permanent residents who aren't citizens. Even people visiting Canada on vacation are protected by some parts of the Charter.

Checkpoint ✓

1. Choose three of the rights and freedoms in the chart and give an example from your own life to illustrate it.
2. Why do you think it's important that these rights be written down formally as laws?

Key Learnings

In this chapter, you will explore

- how the patriation of the Constitution affected Canadians
- how Canadians and their leaders responded to the 1995 referendum in Quebec
- how Aboriginal people have worked to achieve recognition of their right to self-government
- two political parties that emerged in the 1980s
- how the lives of Canadians have changed since 1914

Words to Know

Constitution
patriate (patriation)
Charter of Rights and Freedoms
Meech Lake Accord
distinct society
Charlottetown Accord
Calgary Declaration
Clarity Act
Reform party
Bloc Québécois
self-government

The Canadian Constitution

During the referendum of 1980 Prime Minister Trudeau promised Quebeckers that he would reform the **Constitution** and find a new place for Quebec in Canada. To do so, he needed the support of the provinces. In November 1981, Trudeau and the provincial premiers met in Ottawa to discuss Trudeau's proposals:

- He wanted to **patriate**, or bring home, the Constitution from Britain.
- He wanted to add a **Charter of Rights and Freedoms** to the Constitution. This document would be the highest law in Canada, and no other law would be allowed to disagree with it.
- He wanted to create a system for making amendments (changes) to the Constitution without needing Britain's approval.

Did You Know?

Before Trudeau patriated the Constitution, it was still a document of the British Parliament. Any changes to the document had to be approved by Britain. The British didn't want this responsibility, and were happy to hand it over to Canada.

Figure 17-1 The Constitutional Conference, 5 November 1981. Which of Trudeau's three goals in your opinion might be hardest for the provinces and federal government to agree on?

Reaching a deal proved difficult. Quebec Premier René Lévesque feared that the proposed Charter would take power from Quebec and give it to the federal government. He also felt that it didn't do enough to protect the French language and Quebec's right to govern itself. Frustration grew. Finally, on November 4, 1981, Trudeau and the other premiers reached an agreement without Lévesque and announced it to him in the morning. Lévesque left the conference. He later wrote:

> **We had been betrayed in secret, [by dishonest men]. . . . Tricked by Trudeau, dropped by the others, all we could do was tell them briefly our way of looking at things before returning to Quebec.**

René Lévesque, *Memoirs* (Toronto: McClelland & Stewart, 1986), pp. 332–333

The federal government and the other nine provinces went ahead with the patriation without Quebec. On April 17, 1982, Queen Elizabeth II signed into law the new Canadian Constitution, including a brand-new Charter of Rights and Freedoms and an amending formula. Pierre Trudeau had achieved all three of his goals—but at what cost?

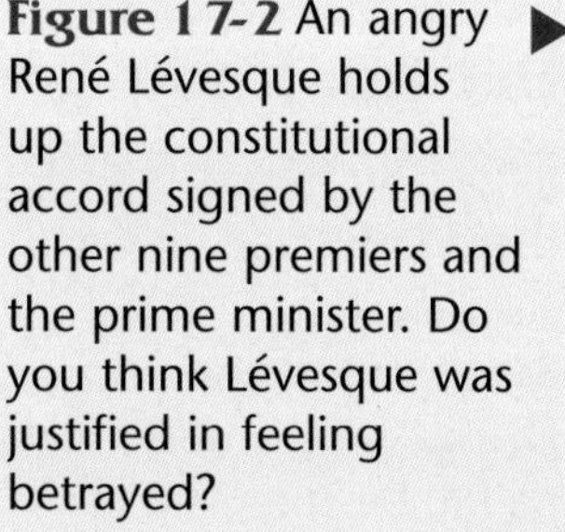

Figure 17-2 An angry René Lévesque holds up the constitutional accord signed by the other nine premiers and the prime minister. Do you think Lévesque was justified in feeling betrayed?

Profile: Doris Anderson, born 1921

Doris Anderson was born in Calgary in 1921. She had a happy childhood, but was confused about what her role in life should be. Her mother scolded her for being "unladylike" whenever she was loud and outgoing. But her female teachers showed that women could have other roles besides being mothers and raising families. Anderson became a teacher herself, and earned a degree from the University of Alberta in 1945.

After graduation Anderson moved to Toronto, where she became a journalist. In 1950 she began to work for *Chatelaine*, a magazine for women. She eventually became its editor, and began to include articles about topics that had never been covered in the magazine before: birth control, divorce law reform, racism, and Aboriginal women's problems, for example. Circulation rose from 480 000 to 1.6 million during her years as editor.

In 1978 Anderson left *Chatelaine* and became chair of the Canadian Advisory Council on the Status of Women (CACSW). In this position, she pushed for guarantees for women in the new Charter of Rights. But it wasn't easy to convince the prime minister. Trudeau believed in individual rights. He felt that if the Charter said that all individuals were equal, there would be no need for a clause saying women and men were equal. But Anderson wanted to include a clause protecting group rights (the rights of women as a group), and so she quit her role as chair of CACSW and organized a women's conference on the Charter.

Eventually, Trudeau was persuaded by Anderson's arguments. The federal government accepted the conference's recommendations, and the following clause was placed in the Charter.

28. Not withstanding anything in this Charter, the rights and freedoms referred to in it are guaranteed equally to male and female persons.

It was Doris Anderson's finest moment.

Anderson went on to other jobs. She was president of the National Action Committee on the Status of Women (NAC) from 1982 to 1984. Up until 1992 she also wrote a column for the *Toronto Star*. Anderson received honorary degrees and awards across the nation. But she'll be best remembered for her determination to secure equality for women in the Charter.

Checkpoint ✓

3. Why do you think it was important for Pierre Trudeau to bring the Constitution home?
4. In a small group, discuss which of the following you think would be the most appropriate amending formula for the Constitution. Try to agree on one solution and be prepared to defend it.
   - the federal government can make any changes it wants
   - a majority of provinces must agree with the suggested changes
   - all provinces must agree with the suggested changes
   - all Canadians must vote on the suggested changes in a referendum
5. Doris Anderson supported group rights. Pierre Trudeau believed individual rights were more important. In your own words, explain the difference.

Brian Mulroney and the Meech Lake Accord

In 1984 Brian Mulroney became the first Progressive Conservative prime minister in 21 years. Mulroney hoped he could succeed where Trudeau had failed in getting Quebec to accept the Constitution.

So in 1987 Mulroney met with all the premiers at Meech Lake, outside of Ottawa. The new Liberal premier of Quebec, Robert Bourassa, also agreed to take part in the discussions. The result was a proposed constitutional amendment that became known as the **Meech Lake Accord**. Here are the main changes proposed in the Accord:

- recognition of Quebec as a **distinct society** within Canada
- a renewed commitment to official bilingualism
- more provincial power over immigration
- restoration of Quebec's traditional power to veto—overrule—changes to the Constitution
- more provincial power in the appointment of Supreme Court justices and members of the Senate and a guarantee that Quebec would never have fewer than three Supreme Court justices

Did You Know?

The Accord would have given all the provinces more powers. For example, they could choose not to participate in federal social programs and get compensation instead. They would be allowed to nominate candidates for the Senate and the Supreme Court. The Accord also proposed greater provincial control over immigration.

Figure 17-3 Prime Minister Mulroney reading the agreement reached at Meech Lake in April 1987. Behind him are the premiers of all 10 provinces. Why did Mulroney feel it was so important to amend the Constitution to include Quebec?

To become law, the Accord had to be approved by the House of Commons and every provincial legislature within three years. As the deadline approached, the two holdouts were Newfoundland and Labrador and Manitoba.

Clyde Wells became premier of Newfoundland and Labrador in 1989. He felt that giving Quebec special status and powers would weaken the country. He spoke out against the Accord, but agreed to allow debate on the issue in the legislature. In the end, events in Manitoba made the Newfoundland and Labrador vote unnecessary.

Aboriginal groups were told their concerns would be addressed in future constitutional talks. That wasn't good enough for Elijah Harper, an Aboriginal MLA. He blocked the Manitoba legislature from debating the issue, and in doing so defeated the Accord. Harper later explained that he wasn't against giving Quebec distinct society status—he just wanted the special status of Aboriginal peoples to be recognized as well.

▲ **Figure 17-4** Elijah Harper held an eagle feather for spiritual strength as he blocked debate on the Meech Lake Accord in the Manitoba legislature.

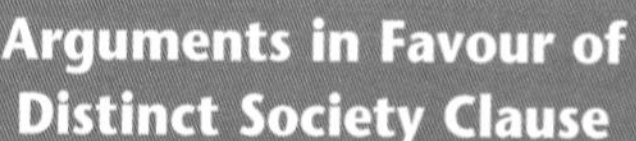

Arguments in Favour of Distinct Society Clause	Arguments Against Distinct Society Clause
• Quebec is the only province with a French-speaking majority • Quebec has a different justice system • Quebec requires special powers to deal with its unique situation • Giving special powers to Quebec will allow it to remain in Canada	• Canada is founded on the idea that all people and provinces are equal • Other provinces may also demand special powers like Quebec • Sovereigntists may use the distinct society clause to promote separation • Giving special powers to Quebec will weaken Canadian unity

Did You Know?

After the Accord was defeated, Mulroney wrote in his private journal: "The experience has been like a death in the family and I have not been able to shake fully the feeling of loss. To have come so close . . . and to have it snatched away needlessly . . . is like a throbbing pain that refuses to go away."

Checkpoint ✓

6. In your own words, summarize the position of
   a) those who support giving special powers to Quebec
   b) those who oppose giving special powers to Quebec
   Which position comes closer to your own views? Explain.

The Charlottetown Accord

Mulroney reached another agreement with the provinces in 1992. It was called the **Charlottetown Accord**. Quebec would get the same powers as in the Meech Lake Accord, but this time the politicians tried to avoid some of the pitfalls that had defeated Meech. Aboriginal representatives were included in the talks, and the agreement included a promise to work toward Aboriginal self-government. The Accord also included plans for Senate reform, which the western provinces were asking for. A referendum would be held to approve the deal.

While politicians praised the Accord, the Canadian people had other ideas. Some still felt that it gave Quebec special status. Others, especially in the larger provinces of Ontario and Quebec, disagreed with giving each province the same number of seats in the Senate. Still others were angry that the Accord was presented as an "all or nothing" deal made by politicians in private meetings.

In October 1992, voters rejected the Charlottetown Accord. Constitutional reform had failed for the second time in five years.

Province	Yes (%)	No (%)
Newfoundland and Labrador	62.9	36.5
P.E.I.	73.6	25.9
Nova Scotia	48.5	51.1
New Brunswick	61.3	38.0
Quebec	42.4	55.4
Ontario	49.8	49.6
Manitoba	37.8	61.6
Saskatchewan	44.5	55.2
Alberta	39.7	60.1
British Columbia	31.7	68.0
Yukon	43.4	56.1
N. W. T.	60.6	38.7
Total Canada	44.6	54.4

Source: *Canadian Annual Review*, 1992, p. 27.

◀ **Figure 17-5** Results of the Charlottetown Accord referendum, 1992. In which province were the yes and no sides closest?

Checkpoint ✓

7. Brainstorm ideas for a radio or print ad persuading voters to vote either for or against the Charlottetown Accord. Make sure to include reasons why they should accept or reject the Accord.
8. Work in small groups or as a class to role-play a radio talk show, with one person acting as the host and others as people calling in to give their opinion of the Charlottetown Accord.

The Second Sovereignty Referendum

Brian Mulroney resigned in 1993, and was replaced by Kim Campbell. However, Campbell's reign was short-lived. Just four months after taking office, she and the rest of the Conservative party were routed in a general election. They lost all but two of their seats. One of Canada's oldest and most established political parties was practically destroyed.

The new Liberal prime minister, Jean Chrétien, was strongly opposed to special powers for Quebec, and announced that the country needed a break from constitutional talks. While most Canadians seemed to agree, many in Quebec felt angry and rejected. They saw the failure of the Meech and Charlottetown accords as proof that the rest of Canada wasn't interested in them. Quebec premier Jacques Parizeau decided that the time was right for another sovereignty referendum.

The date for the referendum was set for October 30, 1995. At first, the federal government thought the "no" side would win an easy victory. But in the final weeks, support for the "yes" side grew as popular politician Lucien Bouchard campaigned for sovereignty. When the support for the "no" side began to slide, Chrétien and other federal politicians went on a whirlwind tour of Quebec. A huge unity rally was held in Montreal, with people travelling from all over the nation to take part. The whole country seemed to hold its breath.

Did You Know?

Kim Campbell was Canada's first female prime minister.

Figure 17-6 The massive unity rally held in Montreal three days before the referendum. Over 100 000 people from all over Canada asked Quebeckers to vote "no." How do you think it would feel to be part of a rally this big?

Results and Aftermath of the Referendum

In the end, the "no" side won with 50.6 percent of the vote. Sovereigntists were crushed at their close defeat, and the day after the referendum, an embittered Premier Jacques Parizeau resigned. But the results had been too close to make anyone on the "yes" side feel comfortable in victory.

Did You Know

This is the question posed during the 1995 referendum:

"Do you agree that Quebec should become sovereign after having made a formal offer to Canada for a new economic and political partnership within the scope of the bill respecting the future of Quebec and of the agreement signed on June 12, 1995, Yes or No?"

Many people, including Jean Chrétien, felt that this wording was much too complicated to provide a clear answer.

▲ **Figure 17-7** Supporters of the "yes" (left) and "no" (right) campaigns react to the results of the Quebec referendum.

For links to sites about the Quebec referendum

The Calgary Declaration

In 1997 nine provincial premiers met in Calgary. Although he was invited, Quebec premier Lucien Bouchard refused to attend. The goal of the meeting was to find common principles on which future constitutional talks could be based. These principles became known as the **Calgary Declaration**. They included the following points:

- Provinces have many differences but are equal in status.
- If a province receives new powers in the future through constitutional amendment, these powers must be available to all provinces.

- Quebec has a "unique character" because of its language, culture, and legal system, and this uniqueness should be protected and developed by the government of Quebec within Canada.
- All provinces should commit to work with the federal government to deliver good programs to Canadians.

In other words, Quebec was unique, but so was every other province. Bouchard dismissed the statement as "meaningless."

The Clarity Act

The federal government took a different approach. The same year that the Calgary Declaration was signed, it passed a law popularly called the **Clarity Act**. This law lays out clear rules that must be followed for any future referendum on sovereignty. Here are the most important rules:

- The question in any referendum must be short and clear, so that people know what they're voting on.
- Before a referendum takes place, the federal government may decide what percentage of voter support is necessary for the results to be considered binding.

Did You Know?

The Clarity Act states that any question asked in a referendum on sovereignty must be clear, and that the federal government has the right to decide this. Even after a vote, the government could decide that a referendum is invalid if it feels the question was in any way misleading.

Checkpoint ✓

9. a) Look at Figure 17-6. What effect do you think the unity rally in Montreal might have had on undecided voters in Quebec? Do you think they'd be swayed by this kind of action, or do you think they'd see it as too little too late?

b) If you had had the opportunity to go to the rally, would you have gone? Why or why not?

10. Make a timeline to show the major political events mentioned in this chapter, starting with the patriation of the Constitution and ending with the Clarity Act.

Literacy Hint

When reading textbooks, it can be helpful to skip ahead to the questions, then go back and read the text to find the answers. This technique allows you to focus on the most important information in a section.

Two New Parties

The 1993 election revealed a very divided country. Not only did the Progressive Conservative party lose all but two of its seats, but two relatively new parties—Reform and the Bloc Québécois—made significant gains. Both parties won over 50 seats in the election, but their support came from two very specific regions of the country.

▲ **Figure 17-8** Preston Manning, the founder of the Reform Party. The woman in the background is Deborah Grey, the first elected Reform MP. Why do you think new political parties are formed?

The Reform Party

Alberta politician Preston Manning started the **Reform Party** in 1987. Its slogan, "The West wants in," expressed the concerns of some westerners that the federal government ignored their needs. Reform opposed any special powers for Quebec, and supported changes to give smaller provinces more power, including a so-called "Triple E" Senate that was:

- equal (it would have the same number of seats for each province, instead of more for Ontario and Quebec)
- elected (currently, the prime minister appoints members)
- effective (its power would be expanded to give all regions a powerful voice in Ottawa)

Profile: Rahim Jaffer, born 1972

When Rahim Jaffer was first elected as a Reform MP in 1997, he was just 25 years old—one of the youngest members of the House of Commons. "The media and others . . . wanted to find out if it was a fluke that I got elected, or if I actually had credibility and substance," he recalls.

In 2001, as the only Muslim MP in Parliament, Jaffer played a key role in urging the prime minister to show public support for Muslim communities after the September 11 terrorist attacks.

Jaffer's family is Pakistani, but they were living in Uganda in the 1970s when Ugandan dictator Idi Amin forced them to leave the country. His parents lost everything they had, including their business and their home. They arrived in Canada with nothing.

Today, in addition to representing his riding of Edmonton-Strathcona, Jaffer owns a restaurant franchise in Edmonton. His experiences as an entrepreneur are part of what drew him to politics. He's held several important posts as Opposition critic, including Intergovernmental Affairs, Foreign Affairs, and Industry and Environment. He also served as interim deputy leader for the Canadian Alliance. Jaffer frequently visits schools to encourage young people to get involved in politics.

Reform party members also favoured allowing business to compete with government (for example, in health care). As well, they supported spending cuts to social programs, and a smaller government role in providing services.

In 1993 the Reform party won 52 seats, becoming the third largest party in the House of Commons. It was unable to gain much support in Ontario and Quebec, however. So in 2000 the Reform party joined with other small groups to form the Canadian Alliance. Two years later the Alliance and the Progressive Conservatives merged to create the Conservative party.

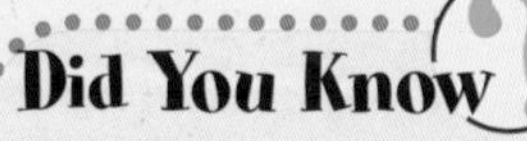

Did You Know?

The BQ lost support in the elections of 1997 and 2000, but bounced back in the election of 2004, again with 54 seats.

The Bloc Québécois

In the 1980s, Lucien Bouchard was a Progressive Conservative MP. But after the failure of the Meech Lake Accord in 1990, he left and formed a new federal party called the **Bloc Québécois** (BQ). Its goal was to defend Quebec's interests in Ottawa until sovereignty could be achieved. In the 1993 election, the BQ won 54 of Quebec's 75 seats in Parliament.

The BQ worked with the Parti Québécois to organize the 1995 referendum. When the "yes" side lost, the party decided that it didn't want another referendum until conditions were right for victory. In the meantime, the Bloc works to make sure that Quebec's voice is heard in Ottawa. It doesn't take positions on issues that don't concern Quebec.

▲ **Figure 17-9** Bloc Québécois leader Lucien Bouchard was an inspiring speaker for the "yes" side in the 1995 referendum. How much difference do you think a popular leader like Bouchard can make in promoting the message of a political party or cause?

Checkpoint ✓

11. Name three ways that a Triple-E Senate would benefit smaller provinces such as Alberta.
12. Why do you think Lucien Bouchard and the BQ thought it was important after Meech Lake failed to have a voice for Quebec at the federal level?
13. a) Based on what you've read, has the federal government dealt effectively with the issue of Quebec's relationship with Canada? Explain.
    b) What would you do about this issue if you were prime minister?

The Charter Today

For links to sites about the Charter of Rights and Freedoms

You've seen in this chapter that attempts to patriate and amend the Constitution have left many issues unresolved. Nevertheless, the Charter has been the highest law of the land for over 20 years now, and it has had a profound effect on Canadian society. In some cases, the Supreme Court has ruled that existing laws are unconstitutional. The government must then change, remove, or replace the law. Some critics feel that this gives the courts too much power. But surveys show that the Charter is usually near the top of the list when Canadians are asked what makes them proud of their country.

Profile: Sandra Lovelace Nicholas, born 1948

What would you do if someone decided you no longer belonged to the nation into which you were born? If your name was Sandra Lovelace Nicholas, you would fight back.

Lovelace Nicholas is a member of the Maliseet First Nation in Tobique, New Brunswick. In the 1970s she married a non-Aboriginal man and moved away from the reserve. She returned several years later, newly divorced, to discover that she was no longer considered a member of her own community.

Under the Indian Act, a First Nations woman who married a non-Aboriginal man lost her Indian status—forever. That meant she and her children had no right to housing or education on the reserve, or membership in the band. (The same rules did not apply to First Nations men.) Lovelace Nicholas was shocked—and angry. She set out to fight for her rights.

After trying unsuccessfully for years to convince the government the law was unfair, she took her case to the UN. It was a bold move, and it paid off. In 1981 the UN's Human Rights Committee ruled that the government's policy violated First Nations women's civil and political rights. Four years later the law was changed, and the rights of all First Nations women who had lost their status through marriage were reinstated.

Sandra Lovelace Nicholas lived on the Tobique reserve in a house she built herself until 2005, when she was appointed to a seat in the Senate by Prime Minister Paul Martin.

Checkpoint ✓

14. Write a list of 10 things that make you proud to be a Canadian. Compare your list with a partner's. Is the Charter on your lists? Why or why not?

15. a) The Charter of Rights hadn't yet been introduced when Sandra Lovelace Nicholas first took her case to the United Nations. If it had been, how could it have helped her?

b) Which of the Charter sections listed in the chart at the beginning of this chapter do you think might have been used to challenge the Indian Act's treatment of Aboriginal women? Explain.

The Face of Canada: Yesterday and Today

History isn't just about events that happened in the past. It's also about understanding the present more fully. With that in mind, let's look at how much Canada has changed since 1914.

How Has Work Changed?

In 1914, just over half of Canadians lived in rural areas, mostly on farms. Today the rural population has shrunk to 20 percent, and only about 2 percent are farmers. This major shift is the result of both urbanization and immigration. Most new immigrants to Canada since World War II have settled in urban areas.

This switch from rural to urban life has brought changes in the workplace. In 1914, most Canadians worked on farms or in lumber camps, mines, or other resource-based industries. Today, three-quarters of all Canadians work in services, from selling ice cream to researching genes.

Did You Know?

Canada has about 50 percent more farmland today than in 1914. Immigration in the 1920s pushed the farming frontier right to its northern limits. Meanwhile, there are only about one-third as many farms, so the average Canadian farm is much larger than in 1914.

Year	Percentage Rural *	Percentage Urban
1901	62	38
1921	51	49
1941	46	54
1961	30	70
1981	24	76
2001	20	80

* Includes both farm and non-farm.

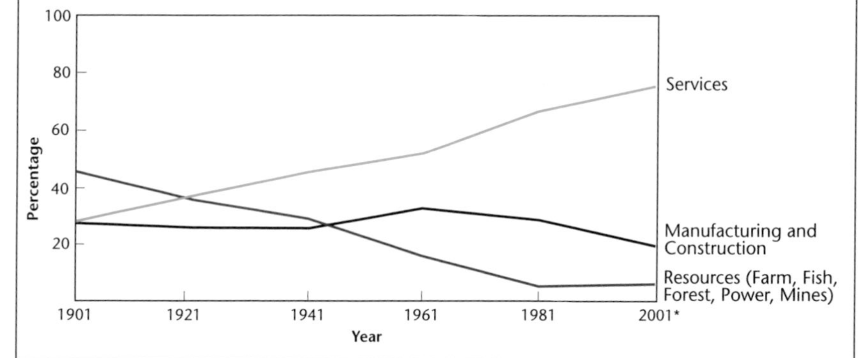

Source: Ministry of Supply and Services, *Canada Year Book*, 1994, and Statistics Canada, "Employment 2004."

▲ **Figure 17-10** Canada's Rural and Urban Population, 1901–2001. When were Canada's rural and urban populations almost equal?

▲ **Figure 17-11** Types of Employment, 1901–2001. Which of the three sectors has changed the most since the turn of the century?

Checkpoint ✓

16. Look at Figure 17-10. When did the biggest change in Canada's population occur? Suggest two good reasons why the urban population increased rapidly during this time. (Check Chapter 10 if you're unsure.)

17. Make a cartoon, drawing, poster, or collage to contrast working in a Canadian community in 1914 and today.

How Has Canada's Population Changed?

Literacy Hint

The stories and photographs on this and following pages profile individual Canadians. As you read them, notice how the information in the stories relate to the information in the main text. How is each individual representative of a particular group of Canadians?

In 1914 Canada's population was mostly made up of people with European and Aboriginal backgrounds. Since then, Canada has become one of the most multicultural nations in the world, with about one in seven people belonging to a visible minority.

The resulting population changes are most noticeable in Canadian cities. Urban areas with a half million people or more attract the largest numbers of immigrants. Several factors draw newcomers to Canada's population centres. Family and sponsors, jobs, and a familiar cultural community all help make the tough transition to a new life a little easier.

Wais Dost arrived in Winnipeg with his family on Canada Day, July 1, 2004. They had been forced to leave their native Afghanistan when Wais's father, Azim, was thrown in prison by a Panjshiri warlord. In order to get him released, the family had to pay a large sum of money. That meant selling everything they had, then quickly slipping into Pakistan, where they applied for immigration. A relative in Winnipeg agreed to sponsor the family, and gave Wais a job in his pizza shop. Wais explains, "I don't feel like a refugee. I feel like a new Canadian. Working in this pizza place is just the beginning. I would like to study computer technology or become a businessman." (Marina Jimenez, "From Pakistan to the Prairies," *The Globe and Mail*, September 24, 2004, p. F4)

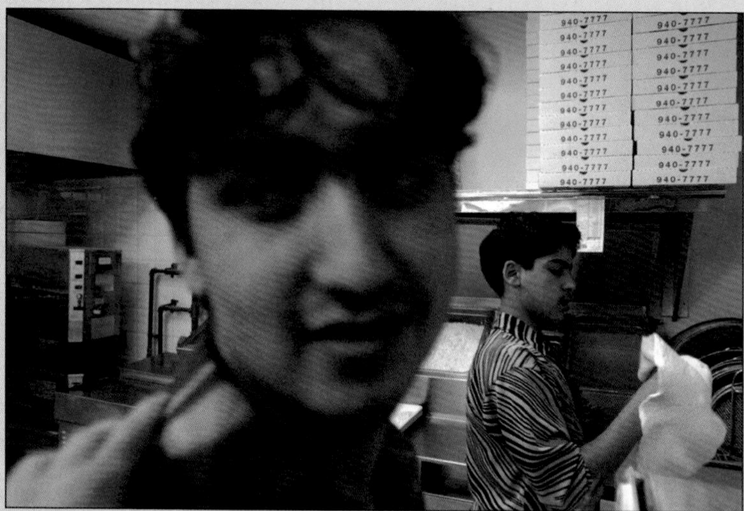

▲ **Figure 17-12** Wais Dost (foreground)

Checkpoint ✓

18. a) Identify the push and pull factors for the Dost family. Why did they leave Afghanistan? Why did they choose Canada?

b) In 1914, most immigrants were settling in rural areas, not in big cities as they do today. Work with a partner to outline three reasons for this change.

19. How well does Wais Dost seem to be adjusting to life in Canada? Use evidence from the text.

How Have the Lives of Youth Changed?

You would find life hard back in 1914. After Grade 8, you would probably be expected to either help provide family income or to work on the farm. You would have had little choice in your career, since most young people followed in their parents' footsteps to become farmers and mechanics, wives and mothers. With the start of World War I in 1914, boys of 18 (and sometimes younger) went to face the horrors of battle.

Today, Canada has one of the best-educated workforces in the world. About half of all Canadian workers are graduates of community colleges, universities, or some other post-secondary training. And with education comes choice—you're much freer to choose a career than you would have been back in 1914.

LIVING LANGUAGE

The term *spam* to refer to unwanted e-mail first appeared in 1994. SPAM (short for *sp*iced h*am*) was originally the name of a precooked canned meat product made by Hormel Foods Corp. It was a popular food ration for Allied troops during World War II.

Education	Employment
Less than Grade 9	22.5%
Some high school	44.9%
High school grad	66.1%
Some post-secondary	64.3%
College or Trades certificate	73.0%
Bachelor's degree	76.9%
Above Bachelor's degree	77.6%
Total Employed	62.7%

Source: Statistics Canada, People Employed by Education Completed, 2004.

◀ **Figure 17-13** People Employed by Education Completed, 2004. How much better will your chances of being employed be when you finish high school than they are now?

▲ **Figure 17-14** Sabrina Lue

Like you, Sabrina Lue belongs to a techno-literate generation, surrounded by cell phones, MP3 players, video games, computers, and satellite TV. She sees that technology "allows us to cut ourselves off from others, avoiding personal contact. We can use music to block out our surroundings or the Internet to ignore those around us so that we can talk online with people we aren't even with." Sabrina has her eye on a career in sciences, perhaps in medicine. But with all the homework, deadlines, and exams, Sabrina finds that school can be stressful. So she cautions students about working too many part-time hours: "If you spend too much time at a job, your grades may drop too low to even qualify you for post-secondary education."

How Have Seniors' Lives Changed?

In 1914 many people didn't have the chance to retire as they do today. There were no government or company pension plans to pay the bills. Instead, people usually just worked until they were no longer able to. After that, they either lived on their own savings or relied on their grown children for support. Today, Canadian life expectancy is much longer than it was in 1914. On average, men and women can expect to live to the age of 80. Most Canadians retire when they're between 55 and 65 years old, supported by their own savings and by government and/or company pensions.

Fred Concisom was a young teacher in Malaysia before he immigrated to Canada in 1970. He retired in 1995 after 23 more years in the teaching profession. And he's an active retiree, coaching his favourite sport, field hockey, at the local and university levels. (He was inducted into the community Sports Hall of Fame in 2003.) Fred claims that, between the Teachers' Pension Fund and other government pensions, he earns more than he did while teaching! He's an optimist about the country's diversity: "The future is bright for Canada. In 50 years, because of our multicultural mix we will all be called Canadians, and not hyphenated either. This will be our unique Canadian experiment for the future, a far cry from the past."

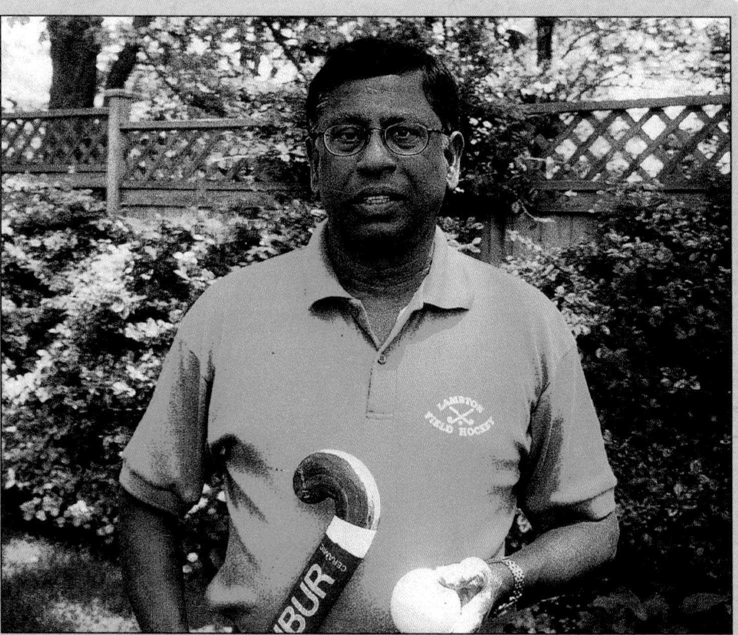

▲ **Figure 17-15** Fred Concisom

Checkpoint ✓

20. Do you think the pressures you face now are greater or less than those you would have faced if you were young in 1914? Discuss with a partner.

21. Using Fred Concisom as an example, list five ways retirees can have a positive influence on young Canadians.

22. Use the number table in Figure 17-12 to draw and label a bar graph. Draw a line across the graph at 62.7% to show the total number actually employed. What trend do you see when employment and education are compared?

How Has Life Changed for Women?

In 1914 women had limited rights in Canada. They couldn't vote, and weren't even considered "persons" under the law. Most stayed home and looked after their family (and the farm, if they lived on one). Although there was only one woman in the workforce for every six to seven men, this did change temporarily during the Great War of 1914–1918. But when the war ended, women were expected to give up these jobs to returning soldiers—and many did.

Of course, life now is very different for Canadian women. For example, today about 47 percent of the Canadian workforce is female, three times higher than in 1914. And women are no longer expected to fill traditional female careers like nurses, teachers, or seamstresses. Now they work at all types of jobs in every part of the economy. Barriers to full participation have steadily fallen since the Charter of Rights and Freedoms became law in 1982.

One Supreme Court decision that helped open doors for women was the Meiorin case. Tawny Meiorin was a firefighter who lost her job when she failed a running test. She sued, claiming the test unfairly excluded women. The Supreme Court agreed. They ruled that the employer had not proved that the test was necessary to do the job.

▲**Figure 17-16**
Brenda Brennan Felton

Brenda Brennan Felton is a successful real estate agent. As well, she and her husband lead a busy life with two teenagers. "It is hard to juggle a fast-paced career and all the demands at home. To have both parents working full-time means a lot of team effort for everyone in the family." Communications technology helps her balance career and family. "I have an office at [work] and another one at home, where I can look after all my listings, set up showings, and type offers. I carry a pager and a cell phone, so when the kids get home from school, they page me." Brenda's clients are often people she knew in high school. "Treat people well," she advises, "because you never know when you'll face them again."

How Has Life Changed for Aboriginal Peoples?

In 1914, the Canadian government was determined to assimilate Aboriginal peoples into "mainstream" culture. Starting in the 1920s, young First Nations were forced to leave their families and attend residential schools. They were denied the basic right to speak their language and live in their own communities.

Today, the residential schools are gone, and Aboriginal peoples are finding ways to heal the wounds the schools have caused. In many Aboriginal communities, young people are rediscovering the traditions, culture, and languages of their peoples.

Aboriginal groups are working to negotiate **self-government**. Exactly what this new relationship will look like is still being determined, but two important examples are already in place.

- In 1998, the federal government, the government of B.C., and the Nisga'a First Nation signed a treaty that recognizes the right of the Nisga'a to self-government on over 2000 square kilometres of land in northwestern B.C.
- On April 1, 1999, a huge area in northern Canada was renamed Nunavut. The Inuit are equal partners with the government of Canada in managing this new territory.

Did You Know

Achieving self-government does not mean that Aboriginal lands will become separate countries. The new governments will fit in with existing levels of government, while giving communities more control over such things as health care, child and family matters, education, and housing.

For links to sites about Nunavut

Luane Lentz grew up in Kenora, Ontario, and is registered at the Sandy Lake First Nation. Recently she completed the Native Child and Family Worker Program at Confederation College. Now at the University of Waterloo, Luane belongs to the campus Aboriginal Student Association. She hopes to help change the negative views some people still hold about Aboriginal people. "I believe that cultural revival is very important, especially for young people. In some aspects Aboriginal heritage has become lost, due to such things as residential schools. I think that media such as APTN (Aboriginal Peoples Television Network) and magazines like *Spirit* and *Say* are great because they're distributed to a wide audience. Self-government is another good way to regain what was lost."

▲ **Figure 17-17** Luane Lentz

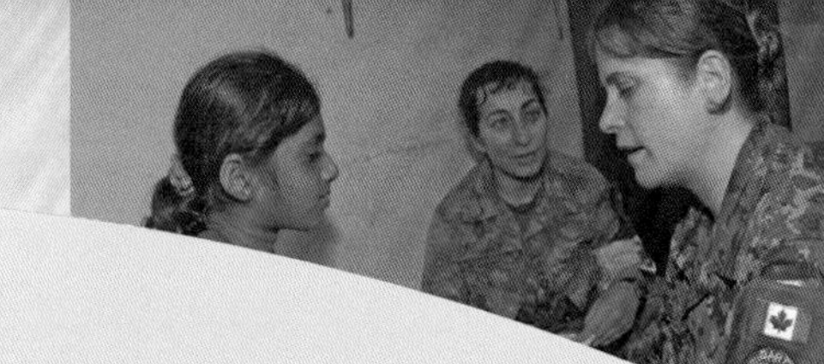

History Game:

START | START

- Ran for cancer research (11)
- Father of Canadian medicare (10)
- English-Canadian labour leader (13)
- Founders of Canadian Tire Corp. (4)
- Wrote about the Japanese-Canadian internment (8)
- Famous Inuit graphic artist (14)
- Inspired the Group of Seven (3)
- Actor, writer, Aboriginal spokesperson (14)
- Prosecutor on the War Crimes Tribunal (16)
- Lobbied for gender equality in the Charter (17)
- Baked many famous food brands (13)
- Actor, Vision TV host, program creator (13)
- Employed 8 percent of New Brunswickers (13)
- Fought discrimination against Blacks (7)
- World-famous jazz musician (14)
- MP first elected at age 25 (17)
- Fought for Aboriginal women's rights (17)
- First woman president of the Canadian Labour Congress (13)
- First Black woman elected in Canada (14)
- Quebec painter blending Japanese and Canadian cultures (14)
- Coined the phrase "global village" (14)
- One of the Famous Five (2)

People Make History

START | START

Required to Play:
- game board
- one die
- score sheet and pencil
- a playing piece for each player

Purpose:
- To review some of the people featured in this book.

Objective: To be the player with the most points after all the people have been identified.

How to Play:
1. Players start on the corners of the game board. On your turn, roll the die and move your playing piece clockwise. Read the description on the space where you land (the numbers indicate what chapter the person was featured in).
2. You get only one guess per turn. Check your answer using the textbook. If you were right, score one point.
3. Continue to play until all 22 people have been correctly identified.

Follow-Up:
1. Which of the people featured in this game do you find most admirable? Why?

Conclusion: Identity and Story

Everyone has a story to tell—that's what makes history interesting. Your own history, as well as the time and place in which you live, has shaped who you are. The history you've read about in this book will help you understand the continuing story of your country as it unfolds in the years to come.

Checkpoint ✓

23. Which group—women or Aboriginal peoples—do you think has experienced the greatest changes since 1914? Why? Discuss your ideas in a small group and see if you can agree on an answer.

24. Write a caption that could accompany a photograph of yourself if one were included in this section. Use the captions for Figures 17-11 and 17-14 to 17-16 as models. In the caption, explain how you're representative of some aspect of Canadian society. Conclude your caption with your own quotation about the importance of knowing about Canada's history.

▲ **Figure 17-18** Canada's future. How does your own personal history reflect the history of your country?

Chapter Summary

Throughout the 1980s and 1990s Canadians struggled to find common ground on which to build their society, both politically and socially. In this chapter you read about the following events and themes in Canada's recent history:

- The Constitution was patriated in 1982, but without Quebec's support.
- Two attempts to amend the Constitution to include Quebec failed.
- After the failure of the Meech Lake and Charlottetown accords, Quebeckers narrowly rejected sovereignty in another referendum.
- Two new parties were founded—the Bloc Québécois and Reform.
- The lives of youth, seniors, women, and Aboriginal peoples have changed dramatically since 1914.

Charter of Rights and Freedoms

Wrap It Up

Understand It

1. Make a summary chart to compare the lives of five Canadian population groups in 1914 and today.

Population Group	1914	Today
New Immigrants		
Youth		
Seniors		
Women		
Aboriginal peoples		

Think About It

2. In your opinion, has Trudeau's dream of patriating the Constitution been positive or negative for Canada overall? Create a pro and con chart to organize your ideas, then write a short opinion piece to express your view.

Communicate It

3. Imagine that it's 1995, just a week or so before the second Quebec referendum. Write a letter to a francophone friend in Quebec, and explain whether you think he or she should vote to stay in Canada or separate. Draw on your knowledge of French–English relations and Canadian history in general.

Apply It

4. Arrange to interview another student from your school or neighbourhood who comes from a different cultural background. Prepare by creating eight good questions that will help you learn more about his or her personal history. Present your findings as an oral report or multimedia presentation.
5. Find out who leads the Bloc Québécois and the Conservative party today, and how many seats each party holds in the House of Commons. Compare this information to each party's status in 1993. Which party has been more successful since then? Identify reasons for this success.

Performance Task

Review Your Predictions

At the beginning of this unit you made predictions based on three photos. Refer back to your predictions. How accurate were they? List three key things that you learned about each of the main topics in the unit.

Videotape a Current Events Show

One problem with writing about contemporary history is that it's hard to keep up to date. To conclude your exploration of Canadian history, your challenge will be to research current news reports on some of the issues covered in this unit and create your own current events television show or website.

Step 1

Review the History Skills from this unit:

- Chapter 15: Preparing a Research Report (pages 299–300)
- Chapter 16: Documenting Your Sources (pages 317–318)

You'll be using these skills in the following activity.

Step 2

Review the Inquiry Method on page xii. Use these steps to guide your research for the activities in Step 3.

Step 3

Work in groups to research, create, and videotape a current events TV show. Each group of two to four students will be responsible for submitting a report on a topic that's been covered in this unit.

Step 4

Videotape or perform your news show in front of the class.

You should include the following in your report:

- a summary of the historical background of the issue
- an explanation of recent developments
- a bibliography listing all the sources you consulted (to be handed in separately)

Here are some possible topics from Unit 5:

- an update on trade disputes between Canada and the United States or Mexico (e.g., softwood lumber)
- reports on Canada's peacemaking, peacekeeping, or military involvement
- recent disaster relief operations that Canada has contributed to
- Canada's recent contribution to the G8, Commonwealth, or la Francophonie
- recent news about technological advances or research in Canada (e.g., biotechnology, satellites or space exploration, computer technology)
- constitutional reform
- Aboriginal self-government
- recent Supreme Court cases that made the news
- Quebec–Canada relations
- another topic assigned by your teacher

Consider the following suggestions to make your current events show more interesting:

- do person-on-the-street interviews to get opinions about the issue
- role-play an interview with an "expert" who gives his or her opinion on the issue
- if possible, videotape your report at an appropriate location—the local courthouse for a story about the Charter, for example
- see if you can arrange an interview with an official or expert who knows about the issue you're reporting on
- choose one student to act as the anchor for the show, introducing each story in turn

Hint

Watch some television news shows to get ideas about how to present your report.

Glossary

Key Term	Definition	Example/Explanation
Aboriginal land claims	claims to land that Aboriginal people make because they were the original inhabitants	The Supreme Court has ruled that governments must recognize Aboriginal land claims and negotiate agreements on them.
alliance systems	groups of countries who supported each other in war	In World War I, there were two alliance systems—the Triple Entente (Britain, France, and Russia) and the Triple Alliance (Germany, Austria–Hungary, and Italy).
anti-Semitism	hatred towards Jews	Graffiti and vandalism expressing hatred towards Jews are examples of anti-Semitism.
appeasement	the British and French policy of giving Adolph Hitler what he wanted (usually more territory) in order to avoid war	Appeasement failed and Britain and France declared war on Germany, after the invasion of Poland, in September 1939.
armistice	an agreement to end fighting (also known as a "cease-fire")	The armistice to end World War I became effective on November 11, 1918.
arms race	the race between the U.S. and the Soviet Union after World War II to have the most effective weapons of mass destruction	The arms race threatened the peace of the world and many people were convinced there would be a nuclear war.
Auto Pact	the agreement between Canada and the U.S. in 1965 concerning the automobile trade	Under the Auto Pact, companies could ship many products across the Canada–U.S. border duty free.
baby boom	the high birth rate in many countries between 1946 and 1965	The baby boom was partly caused by people marrying young and wanting large families; they were eager for the security of home and family after six years of uncertainty between 1939 and 1945 (World War II).

Key Term	Definition	Example/Explanation
Balfour Report	the report submitted in 1926 by former British prime minister, Lord Balfour, recommending that Britain recognize Canada, Newfoundland, and some other former colonies as independent nations	It was considered pay back for the contributions these former colonies had made to helping Britain win World War I.
ballistic missiles	long-range rockets that deliver bombs to their targets	Ballistic missiles are much more difficult to defend against than bombs dropped from planes.
Battle of the Atlantic	the struggle between the German submarines and the convoys shipping goods across the ocean in World War II	The defeat of the German submarines in the Battle of the Atlantic had a great effect on the outcome of the war.
Bill 101	the Quebec law that made French the only official language there, and limited the use of English in many ways	Under Bill 101, outside advertising signs must be in French only.
biotechnology	adapting biological processes to commercial goals	Using pig hearts for transplantation into humans is an example of biotechnology.
birth rate	the number of births, in one year, for every thousand people in the population	Between 1946 and 1965, Canada had an unusually high birth rate.
Black Tuesday	October 29, 1929, the day the stock market crashed; shares nose-dived and many investors were financially ruined	On "Black Tuesday", the money many people owed on their shares was more than the shares were worth, forcing them to sell things like their house or car.
Bloc Québécois	the political party founded in 1990 that seeks to represent and defend Quebec's interests in Ottawa	The Bloc Québécois worked in support of the "yes" side in Quebec's sovereignty referendum in 1995.

Key Term	Definition	Example/Explanation
Bolsheviks	people who supported the Communist revolution in Russia in 1917	Canadian Bolsheviks were blamed for the rash of strikes for higher pay after World War I.
branch plants	factories or businesses operating in Canada, owned by companies in another country	Many automobile companies (like General Motors and Toyota) have branch plants in Canada.
British Commonwealth Air Training Plan (BCATP)	An agreement signed by Canada, Britain, Australia, and New Zealand; it made Canada a base for training of Allied air personnel for war planes during World War I	The BCATP trained over 130 000 people, most of them from Commonwealth nations, for the Allied air force.
business cycle	the normal rising (high sales) and falling (low sales) pattern or cycle that most economies experience	Today, governments try to regulate the business cycle so that sales never get too high or too low.
buy on margin	to borrow money to buy shares, hoping to pay off the loan by selling the shares for more money	In the 1920s, you could buy shares on a margin of only 10% cash. Today, you need about 60% cash to buy on margin.
Calgary Declaration	the 1997 statement by nine provincial premiers about future constitutional talks	The Calgary Declaration said Quebec has a "unique character" but that all provinces must be treated equally.
Camp X	a special facility set up in Canada for intelligence training—that is, secretly gathering information about the enemy	Camp X was established near Whitby, Ontario, in December 1941.
Can-con	the minimum amount of radio and TV programming that must be Canadian content	Prime-time Can-con (i.e., Canadian content) is 30% for radio stations and 60% for TV stations located in Canada.

Key Term	Definition	Example/Explanation
cash economy	the situation, mainly in cities and towns, when people rely on cash to buy the things they need to survive	During the Great Depression, unemployed people had virtually no money, making it difficult to survive in a cash economy.
Charlottetown Accord	the unsuccessful 1992 attempt to get Quebec to sign the Canadian Constitution and make other reforms to it	The Charlottetown Accord failed when voters in six provinces and one territory rejected it in a referendum.
Charter of Rights and Freedoms	the document that lays out the rights and freedoms that Canadians enjoy under the law	The Charter is the highest law in Canada, and no other law may disagree with its terms.
civil servants	people who work for governments (also "public employees")	Until 1967, it was illegal for Canadian civil servants to go on strike.
civil war	a war between two opposing groups in the same country	In 1992, Canadian troops helped to restore peace in Somalia after a vicious civil war.
Clarity Act	the 1997 federal government act laying out the rules for any future referendums on a province separating from Canada	The Clarity Act says that the question to voters must be clear, and that the federal government can decide beforehand how much voter support is necessary for the referendum to be binding.
coalition government	a government in which opposing parties agree to work together for the nation's interest	In 1917, Sir Robert Borden (Conservative) tried unsuccessfully to form a coalition with the Liberals.
Cold War	tension and threats of war between the U.S. and the Soviet Union without actual fighting	The Cold War dominated the period from 1945 to the early 1990s.

Key Term	Definition	Example/Explanation
collateral damage	the unintended killing or injury of civilians when forces try to destroy enemy positions	In the Gulf War of 1991, over 125 thousand Iraqi civilians were killed in collateral damage.
collectivist society	a society in which the government has a role in citizens' personal welfare	In collectivist societies (e.g. Canada) governments provide lots of services and taxes are higher.
concentration camps	special camps built by the Nazis to imprison and kill Jews and other "undesirables"	There were concentration camps in Germany, Austria, and Poland during World War II.
conscientious objectors	people who refuse to fight in war time because their conscience does not allow it	Many religious groups—like Mennonites, Hutterites, Quakers, and Doukhobors—were conscientious objectors in Canada in World Wars I and II.
conscription	drafting people into the armed forces to fight for their country (i.e., military service was required by law)	Conscription of Canadian men ages 20–45, was used as a last resort in World Wars I and II when the number of volunteers began to decline.
Constitution	the document that sets out the basic rules and laws in a country	In 1980, Prime Minister Trudeau promised to reform the constitution and find a new place for Quebec in Canada.
consumerism	the purchase of products not out of need but out of want and because they make one feel good	In Canada, consumerism began in the 1920s, with the invention of many household gadgets.
convoy	a group of supply ships, protected by navy escorts, taking supplies to the war zone	Halifax, Nova Scotia, was a favourite place for assembling convoys to Britain.

Key Term	Definition	Example/Explanation
Cooperative Commonwealth Federation (CCF)	the political party, founded in Manitoba by J.S. Woodsworth in 1933, that favoured government ownership of key industries	The CCF has formed the provincial government in British Columbia, Saskatchewan, Manitoba, and Ontario—it is known today as the New Democratic Party (NDP).
corvette	a fast naval ship used to escort and protect convoys	There were no cabins or sleeping quarters in a corvette.
counterculture	a large group of people who have a different outlook on society, with a strong focus on personal freedom	In the 1960s, counterculture people wore long hair, peace symbols, and colourful clothes.
credible	something that is believable	It is important to do research only from sources that you believe are credible.
D-Day	June 6, 1944—the successful Allied invasion of France which led to the German surrender in 1945	D-Day, the Allied invasion force numbered 150 000 troops, of which 30 000 were Canadian.
death rate	the number of deaths, in one year, for every thousand people in the population	Canada's death rate declined after World War II because of better health care.
depression	an unusually low point in the business cycle when there are severe production cuts and extremely high unemployment	The depression of the 1930s is known as the Great Depression; life everywhere—on farms, in towns, and cities—was extremely difficult.
development aid	giving money, advice, and assistance to help developing nations	The Canadian International Development Agency (CIDA) gives development aid to countries that need it.

Key Term	Definition	Example/Explanation
distinct society	the idea that Quebec is different from other provinces because of its Francophone majority and French civil law	Some provinces feel that if Quebec were recognized as a distinct society, it might get powers that other provinces did not have.
distinctiveness	the ways in which a nation differs from other nations	One way a nation shows its distinctiveness is through its symbols (e.g., its flag).
dot-com companies	small start-up firms that sell goods or services online	In 2000, many dot-com companies went bankrupt as the stock market fell.
Dust Bowl	the phenomenon that occurred in the 1930s when much of the top soil blew away from farmland on Canada's prairies	The Dust Bowl was caused by unusually dry summers that led to drought, and inefficient farming methods.
embargo	deliberately shipping less of a product, such as oil, to force prices up	During the oil embargo of 1973–74, Canadians were asked to cut down on their driving.
enemy aliens	people born in countries that were Canada's enemies during war	In World War I, enemy aliens were those people born in Germany, Austria–Hungary, or Turkey.
entrepreneurs	individuals who start and run their own businesses	Some entrepreneurs start out small and end up owning huge companies.
equalization payments	transfers of money by the federal government to lower-income provinces	Equalization payments are a way of making incomes in Canada more equal.
Fascist	a person who supports dictatorship and an economy dominated by large corporations	Fascists were enemies of the Communists (who also favoured dictatorship but wanted government control of the economy).

Key Term	Definition	Example/Explanation
federalism	the belief that Canada should stay together under a single federal government	One of federalism's key ideas is that there should be a strong central government in Ottawa to hold the country together.
Final Solution	the plan, approved by Hitler in 1942, to exterminate all Jews in Nazi-controlled Europe	In all, some 6 000 000 Jews were exterminated by the Nazis.
flapper	a young woman in the 1920s who dressed and acted unconventionally	Flappers liked to dance the "Charleston," drive cars, and smoke cigarettes.
foreign investment	money invested in a country from foreign countries	Britain was the largest foreign investor in Canada until the 1920s, when the U.S. took over.
Foreign Investment Review Agency (FIRA)	a body established to approve or reject foreign takeovers of existing Canadian companies	FIRA had many critics who said that it scared off investors from Canada, resulting in fewer jobs.
free trade	trade between two countries on which no import duties (tariffs) are charged	Canada first started to negotiate with the U.S. about free trade in 1985.
Führer	the title Adolph Hitler took after abolishing the German parliament in 1933	Führer means "leader" or "driver" of the German state.
general strike	a strike in which all labour unions urge their members to walk off the job	In the Winnipeg General Strike of 1919, 30 000 workers walked off the job.
genetically-modified foods	foods in which the genes have been altered by scientists, usually to get higher yields	Scientists have produced a genetically-modified wheat that will not be destroyed by pesticides.

Key Term	Definition	Example/Explanation
genocide	the deliberate act of trying to kill off an entire ethnic, racial, or religious group	In Rwanda, close to 800 000 Tutsis were murdered in an act of genocide by the Hutu majority.
ghettoes	specially barricaded areas in cities where the Nazis forced Jews to live and not leave during World War II	The largest ghetto was in Warsaw, Poland, where about 400 000 Jews from across Europe were crammed and barricaded in.
global village	the idea that people in most countries tend to dress, think, and act more alike than they did a hundred years ago	The global village has largely been caused by improvements in transportation and communications.
globalization	the tendency for economies and cultures around the world to become more closely connected	An example of globalization is the tendency for young people in dozens of countries to dress in a similar manner.
Group of 8 (G8)	the eight-member group of wealthy nations that meets each year to discuss common problems	The G8 countries are: Canada, U.S., Britain, France, Germany, Italy, Russia, and Japan—all major industrialized democracies.
Holocaust	the systematic destruction, by the Nazis, of about 6 million Jews and an additional 1 million people in other "undesirable" categories	Holocaust survivors included those who managed to get out of Germany and Austria in 1938 and 1939.
home front	refers to civilians in Canada and their efforts to support the war in a number of ways (e.g., by producing war goods)	Many women and children worked or volunteered on the home front to help win the war.
hyperinflation	a situation when prices rise out of control	Hyperinflation occurred in Germany after World War I. People eventually lit fires with banknotes as they had so little value left.

Key Term	Definition	Example/Explanation
imperialism	the policy of extending a country's rule over other countries or territories	In the nineteenth century, most powerful countries practiced imperialism.
individualistic society	a society that considers people responsible for their own personal welfare	In individualistic societies (e.g. the U.S.), governments provide fewer services and taxes are lower.
inflation	the rate at which prices rise	In the early 2000s, inflation is low, but in the 1970s, inflation rates were high.
Internet	the electronic links that allow computers to "talk" to each other	By 2004, the Internet allowed 840 million people to get information online.
internment camps	special camps, guarded by the army, where people judged to be an enemy of Canada were imprisoned during wartime	In World War I, 8600 men, plus about 200 wives and children, were sent to internment camps for suspicion of being allied with the enemy because of their place of birth—Germany, Austria–Hungary, or Turkey.
Iron Curtain	the dividing line between the democratic and communist countries of Europe	The term "Iron Curtain" became common after it was used by Sir Winston Churchill in 1946.
Just Society	a society that is fair to all its members	To help create a Just Society, Pierre Trudeau made divorce laws more liberal.
King-Byng Crisis	the dispute between Prime Minister King and Governor-General Byng, in 1926, about who should form the next government	Byng wanted Arthur Meighen to have a chance to form the government before an election was held. Meighen's government lasted only days.

Key Term	Definition	Example/Explanation
Kristallnacht	the night in November 1938 when Nazi mobs attacked Jewish businesses and homes	The name "Kristallnacht" comes from the broken window glass that shone like crystal in the streetlights.
La Francophonie	the international organization of French-speaking countries	Canada is a member of La Francophonie because French is one of our official languages.
land mines	small devices buried in the ground that explode when someone drives or walks across them	In the Ottawa Treaty, signed in 1997, 123 countries agreed to ban the manufacture, sale, or possession of land mines.
League of Indians	an organization of First Nations representatives formed in 1919, to address their common issues	Two issues addressed by the League of Indians included government refusal to recognize some First Nations land claims, and poor economic and health conditions on many reserves.
lobby group	people who try to convince politicians to take a particular view on issues	NAC—a women's lobby group—persuaded the government to guarantee women's equality in Canada's new Charter of Rights and Freedoms.
Meech Lake Accord	the unsuccessful attempt (1987–1990) to get Quebec to sign the Canadian constitution	The Meech Lake Accord would have recognized Quebec as a "distinct society" within Canada.
merchant marine	the civilian ships that carried food supplies and war materials to the war zone	Merchant marine ships suffered high losses in World Wars I and II as Germany tried to sink them to prevent supplies getting through.
microchip	a tiny silicon chip that is the heart of modern computers	Because of the microchip, home computers became available in 1974.

Key Term	Definition	Example/Explanation
middle power	a country that does not have the military power to invade nations but has influence in international affairs	Canada is a middle power. It has a small military but is still influential in the United Nations and NATO.
multiculturalism	the policy that all cultures and ethnic groups should be promoted	Since 1971, multiculturalism has become a key feature of Canadian identity—the customs and traditions of all cultures are supported in Canada.
munitions	military equipment, weapons, and, ammunition	Women played an important role in the production of munitions during World Wars I and II.
nationalism	a feeling of pride in one's country or nation	A century ago, citizens were expected to show nationalism.
naval blockade	an attempt to prevent trading ships from entering an enemy port	During World War I, Britain established a naval blockade on German ports, which soon resulted in food shortages in Germany.
Nazi	the German fascist political party led by Adolph Hitler	"Nazi" comes from its German title, meaning "National Socialist."
New Deal	Prime Minister Bennett's plan to assist people during the Depression	The New Deal included an unemployment insurance program—the first in Canada's history.
no man's land	in trench warfare, the area between the opposing trench lines	No man's land was often filled with the dead bodies of soldiers who could not be rescued.
Non-governmental organization (NGO)	international aid organizations that are not directly controlled by a government	Most well known international charities, like the Red Cross, are NGOs.

Key Term	Definition	Example/Explanation
North American Air Defence (NORAD)	the 1957 agreement between Canada and the U.S. to have a central defense system for the whole of North America	NORAD was created out of fear that the Soviet Union might launch rockets over Canada at the United States.
North American Free Trade Agreement (NAFTA)	the free trade agreement among Canada, Mexico, and the U.S., which went into effect in 1994	Under NAFTA, goods manufactured in one member nation can enter the other two nations duty-free.
Nuremberg Laws	the German laws passed in 1935 that restricted the rights of Jews	Jews were not allowed to go to university, hold a government job, marry a non-Jew, etc.
official languages	languages chosen by the Canadian government to be used by Canadian citizens	In Canada there are two official languages—English and French.
oil crisis	the rapid increase in oil prices in the 1970s	During the oil crisis, prices rose from US$2.50 to US$15.00 in seven years.
On-to-Ottawa Trek	the famous 1935 Union protest—a march by unemployed workers, from British Columbia to Ottawa	The march was broken up by police after a riot in Regina.
pacifists	people opposed to war who believe that nations should settle differences through negotiation	Pacifists often paid a heavy price for their beliefs, for instance losing their jobs for taking this position.
Parti Québécois	a Quebec party seeking independence through peaceful means	René Lévesque formed the Parti Québécois in 1968.
patriate (patriation)	to bring something home from another country	In 1982, the federal government patriated the constitution from Britain, where it had been since 1867.

Key Term	Definition	Example/Explanation
patronage	privileges and positions that politicians give to favourites (i.e., selected people)	The Union Nationale party ruled Quebec for most of the time between 1936 and 1959; it operated through corruption and patronage.
peacekeepers	countries that use their troops to enforce a peace already made (often by the United Nations) between enemies, sometimes by using armed force to keep the sides apart	Canada has contributed troops to be peacekeepers, as part of the United Nations effort in Cyprus since the 1970s.
peacemakers	countries that use their troops to stop a war in progress by forcing the sides to agree to a peace. If a peace is successfully established, the operation may become a peacekeeping one.	Canada contributed troops to the NATO effort to make peace in the civil war in Yugoslavia in the 1990s.
Persons Case	a high-profile legal battle that resulted in the decision of the British Privy Council, in 1929, that women could be considered persons eligible for appointment to the Senate	Canadian law had previously been interpreted to mean that women were not "persons" for the purpose of being eligible "to hold public office in the Senate."
plebiscite	a vote by the people on a "yes or no question," but whose result is not binding on the government (i.e., the government may choose to ignore the result)	In a plebiscite in 1943, a majority of Canadians favoured conscription (i.e., the compulsory enlistment of citizens into the armed forces).
points system	a system used to score applicants from around the world to decide who would be allowed to immigrate into Canada	Canada's refugee points system awards points for language skills, education, job experience, and a number of other factors.

Key Term	Definition	Example/Explanation
primary source	an original document that historians use to find out about the past	Primary sources include letters, speeches, maps, and other records that were created at the time the events took place.
private companies	companies whose owners are members of an individual family or private group	Private companies do not have to reveal their profits to the public.
prohibition	the law banning the sale or possession of alcohol except for religious or medical purposes	Every province in Canada, except Quebec, passed prohibition laws between 1915 and 1917; the last province removed it in 1930.
public companies	companies in which anyone can buy a share of the ownership	Public companies are required to reveal their profits to the public.
public employees	people who work for governments (also "civil servants")	Public employees are the largest occupational group in Canada.
public works	projects paid for by governments to create jobs	Hitler used such programs in Germany in the 1930s to create loyalty to his government.
pull factors	conditions that made countries like Canada attractive for immigrants (i.e., pulled them in)	Such conditions included the availability of work and housing, and the safety of living there.
push factors	conditions that forced (i.e., pushed) people to emigrate to other countries	Such conditions included unemployment, poverty, and civil war.
Quiet Revolution	the period 1960–1966 in which great change came to Quebec	During the Quiet Revolution, Quebec's education system was completely reformed.

Key Term	Definition	Example/Explanation
radar	a device for detecting objects like enemy aircraft through radio waves	Radar allowed the Allies to know how many enemy planes there were in an attack before they could be seen.
recession	when the business cycle is at a low point, businesses are closing rather than expanding, and unemployment rises	A recession is usually accompanied by layoffs and declining sales of products.
Red Ensign	the red flag with the Canadian coat of arms that was the official flag from 1924 to 1965	It replaced the British Union Jack as Canada's official flag.
referendum	a vote by the people on a question whose result is binding on the government	Quebec held two referendums on sovereignty (1980 and 1995). In both, the majority of voters said "no."
Reform party	the political party founded in 1987 that sought to give a more equal balance to the political regions of the country	The Reform Party has merged with other parties and is now known as the Conservative Party.
refugee status	recognizing peoples' right to live in another country because they are afraid to return to their homeland	About 25 000 people are annually granted refugee status to live in Canada because they face cruel or unfair treatment in their homeland.
refugees	people left homeless as a result of war in their homeland	Between 1947 and 1952, 186 000 refugees moved to Canada.
relief	the government program begun in the 1930s, that provided some money to unemployed people to help them survive	Government relief programs in the 1930s were not generous—the average weekly food allowance was $4.22 per person.

Key Term	Definition	Example/Explanation
reparations	money Germany was forced to pay to its enemies after World War I for the damage it had caused	Reparations to the Allies, by Germany, were set at about $30 billion (over $250 billion in today's money).
residential schools	schools where all First Nations children aged 7 to 15 were forced to attend and live during the school year	These schools were an attempt to remove the children from their traditional culture and absorb them into Canadian society.
Satellite	an object that orbits the earth	*Anik 1*, launched in 1967, was Canada's first communications satellite.
secondary source	a document about the past that was created after the event being studied took place	Secondary sources include textbooks, biographies and other similar items.
self-government	the power that people have to make laws that affect them	Aboriginal-self government would give Aboriginal people greater power to run their own affairs.
separatists	people who want an independent Quebec	In 1967, separatists were overjoyed when France's President seemed to support them.
Social Credit party	the political party, founded by William Aberhart and elected in 1935 as the provincial	The Prosperity Certificates were never paid, but Social Credit formed the provincial government in Alberta from 1935 to 1971.
social welfare programs	government of Alberta; it proposed "Prosperity Certificates" for all citizens government programs to help those in need	Social welfare programs, like unemployment insurance benefits and free medical care, were first developed in Canada in the 1920s.

Key Term	Definition	Example/Explanation
sovereignty-association	the idea that Quebec should be independent but with economic ties to Canada	Under sovereignty-association, Quebec would have its own prime minister but would use Canadian currency.
status Indian	a person registered under the Indian Act and so eligible to live on a reserve	Until 1985, status Indian women who married non-Indians lost their Indian status and could not live on reserves.
Statute of Westminster	the British law that established legal equality between the parliament of Britain and those of its former colonies, such as Canada and Newfoundland	Australia, New Zealand, and South Africa were also affected by this law.
stereotype	a generalized mental image of a place, time, or social group that doesn't always match reality	TV shows in the 1950s often showed the stereotype of the happy family life.
stock market	places where investors can buy and sell shares in companies that make products or provide services	Investing in the stock market allows ordinary people—shareholders—to vote for company managers and share in the profits of the company.
Storm troops	troops making sudden attacks on heavily defended enemy positions	Storm troops suffered high casualty rates because they usually attacked dangerous places.
tariffs	taxes on goods imported from other countries	Tariffs are designed to protect Canadian jobs by making it possible for Canadian producers to sell more of their own goods within Canada.

Key Term	Definition	Example/Explanation
temperance movement	the movement led by women's groups that worked to have alcohol banned or strictly controlled during World War I and for a number of years thereafter	Temperance was led by Nellie McClung; Canadians were persuaded that it was wrong to drink alcohol when the troops were sacrificing so much.
theatres of war	areas or sites where military action takes place	There were theatres of war in both Europe and Asia during World Wars I and II.
tied aid	international aid money that can only be spent to purchase supplies in the country giving the aid	Tied aid limits the choices that receiving countries can make in spending international aid donations.
U-Boat	a submarine maintained by the German navy in World Wars I and II	U-Boats were used to torpedo and sink enemy ships.
unemployment insurance	a government program to pay money to people while they look for work	Unemployment helps to provide income to people who have jobs that are seasonal or lose them when their company lays them off.
unification of the armed forces	the 1968 joining of the army, navy, and air force into the Canadian Armed Forces	No other country has created a unification of its armed forces the way Canada has.
Union Nationale	the political party, founded by Maurice Duplessis in 1935, that believed Quebec was being hurt by American and English Canadian business owners	The Union Nationale formed the provincial government in Quebec, between 1936 and 1970, in three separate periods, for a total of 22 years.
Universal Declaration of Human Rights	the 1948 statement by the United Nations that all people are entitled to equal rights	The Declaration recognized that all people had the right to freedom and security, among other things.

Key Term	Definition	Example/Explanation
unrestricted submarine warfare	Germany's policy in 1917 of attacking all ships approaching Britain, even civilian ones as they might be carrying war supplies or food imports	The U.S. entered World War I in 1917 in opposition to unrestricted submarine warfare.
urbanization	the growing concentration of a nation's population in cities and towns	In Canada, urbanization began to take hold in the 1920s.
War Measures Act	a law that gives the Canadian government special powers in a state of emergency (e.g., war)	During World War I, The War Measures Act meant that: 1) new laws could be passed without being debated in Parliament; 2) officials could arrest and imprison civilians without charging them with an offence; and 3) people born in enemy countries could be deported without trial.
Wartime Elections Act	the Canadian law that gave women connected to the military the right to vote in the election of 1917 in an attempt to ensure a Conservative victory	Only women who had a relative in the armed forces received the vote, and they were likely to vote Conservative.
weapons of mass destruction (WMD)	biological, chemical, and nuclear weapons that cause death on a huge scale	In 2003, the U.S. invaded Iraq, wrongly believing that its government and forces possessed WMD.
World Trade Organization (WTO)	an international organization, founded in 1995, which tries to ensure fairness in trade among most of the world's nations	The WTO has been unable to solve some disagreements between Canada and the U.S.—the softwood lumber dispute is one example.
youthquake	a large group of young people eager to change the world	In the 1960s, the youthquake questioned everything the older generation believed in.

Index

C

U

V

W

Y

Photo Credits

t = top; **c** = centre; **b** = bottom; **l** = left; **r** = right
AO = Archives of Ontario
CTA = City of Toronto
CWM = Canadian War Museum
Glenbow = Glenbow Archives, Calgary, Alberta, Canada
Granger = The Granger Collection, New York
LAC = Library and Archives of Canada
PANL = Provincial Archives of Newfoundland and Labrador

2 t AO/S14443, **b** PANL/B-5-173; **3** LAC/C-000242; **4** CWM/*Gunners in the Mud* by A.T.J. Bastien/CN#8095; **8** Naval Historical Center/NH 61014; **9** Granger; **10** LAC/C-022740; **11 t** LAC/C-002468, **bl** LAC/C-147822, **bc** AO/I0016181, **br** AO/I0016177; **12** Windsor's Community Museum/P6110; **14** LAC/C-014145; **15** PANL/VA-37-23; **16** Imperial War Museum/Q5574; **17** LAC/PA-183630; **19** Courtesy Elizabeth Anderson; **20** LAC/PA-003747; **21** Granger; **23** CWM/*Canada's Answer* by Norman Wilkinson/#19710261-0791; **31** LAC/PA-D61; **32 l** McGill University Libraries/Rare Books and Special Collections/War Poster Collections, r AO/I0016138; **33** McGill University Libraries/Rare Books and Special Collections/War Poster Collections; **35** *The Canadian Liberal Monthly*, Ottawa, December 1917; **36** Coloured Women's Club of Montreal; **37** CWM/*Women Making Shells* by Henrietta Mabel May/#197110261-0389; **38** Glenbow/NA-273-2; **39** McGill University Libraries/Rare Books and Special Collections/War Poster Collections; **41** Glenbow/NA-1870-6; **42** Glenbow/PA-3487-17; **46** LAC/C-019945; **47** CWM/*Armistice Day* by George Reid/#197110261-0550; **48** PANL VA-33-59; **50** Newfoundland Studies Archives (Coll-137, 22.03.001), Memorial University of Newfoundland Library, St. John's, Newfoundland; **51** Provincial Archives of Manitoba, Still Images Section, Winnipeg Strike Collection, Item Number 4, Negative 12295; **55** Canadian Press Picture Archive (Richard Lam); **52** Courtesy Dan McCaffery; **56 t** Bettmann/Corbis, **b** Glenbow/ND-3-6742; **57** USHMM/11291; **59** LAC/C-019586; **60** Canadian Heritage; **61 t** LAC/PA-121719, **b** *The West Wind* by Tom Thomson, (1917)/Gift of the Canadian Club of Toronto, 1926/Art Gallery of Ontario/Photo: Carlo Catenazzi; **66** Glenbow/ND-3-939; **67** Glenbow/NA-3876-26; **68** Granger; **69** Provincial Archives of Alberta/A11419; **70** LAC/PA-12795; **71** Courtesy Famous Five Foundation; **72** Granger; **73** Granger; **74** all The Thomas Fisher Rare Book Library/University of Toronto; **75** J. Armand Bombardier Museum/www.museebombardier.com; **78** Courtesy Janet Forjan; **79** Glenbow/NA-463-49; **82: l,r** Copyright © Canadian Tire/Reprinted with permission; **83** Courtesy Roger and Pauline Williams; **84** *Miners' Houses, Glace Bay* by Lawren S. Harris, (c. 1925)/Art Gallery of Ontario/Bequest of Charles S. Band, Toronto, 1970/Photo: Carlo Catenazzi; **85** Glenbow/ND-3-4095a; **86** Canadian Pacific Railway Archives/A.21396; **87** Woodland Cultural Centre; **88 t,b** Saskatchewan Archives Board, R-A8223-1 and R-A8223-2; **93** Granger; **96** uperstock/maXximages.com; **99** Glenbow/NA-2256-1; **100** Glenbow/NA-2685-85; **102** Vancouver City Archives/N10.09; **103** LAC/C-029399; **105** Glenbow/NB-16-199; **109** City of St. John's Archives; **110** CP Picture Archive (Adrian Wyld); **112** LAC/PA-130023; **113** Bettmann/Corbis; **115** USHMM/08094; **116** Granger; **117** USHMM/01620; **119** USHMM/86838; **120** USHMM/73193; **121** CP Picture Archive/(Press Association); **122** LAC/PA-119013; **123** USHMM/61127; **126** LAC/C-38723; **131** BBC/Corbis; **132 t** LAC/PA-14215, **b** Bettmann/Corbis; **133** Genevieve Naylor/Corbis; **134** LAC/C-38723; **135 t** CWM/detail from *Dieppe Raid* by Charles Comfort/#12276, **c** LAC/Harold G. Aikman/Canada. Dept. of National Defence/PA-133244, **b** LAC/PA-114617; **137** LAC/Canada. Dept. of National Defence/PA-112993; **138** LAC/PA-108181; **140** CWM/*Dieppe Raid* by Charles Comfort/#12276; **142** LAC/PA-151738; **146** CP Picture Archive (Ryan Remiorz); **147** Bettmann/Corbis; **149** LAC/PA-125929; **151** CP Picture Archive; **153** LAC/PA-114617; LAC/PA-125929; **154 l** NFB/LAC/e000761869; **c** AO/I0002726; **r** CTA/Fonds 1266/Item 7587; **157** Glenbow/PD-324-210; **158** NFB/LAC/C-085214; **160** LAC/PA-148464; **161 l** NFB/LAC/PA-116147; **r** FB/LAC/e000761165; **163** CTA/GM/98887; **164 l** CTA/Fonds 1266/Item 83771, **r** CTA/Series 340, Subseries 8, File 56, Sheet 7; **165** Courtesy Carol Radford-Grant; **166** LAC/C-057365; **167** The Gazette (Montréal)/LAC/PA-107910; **169** NFB/LAC/C-024452; **170** Copyright © Linda Ohama/Reprinted with permission; **172** Bob Krist/Corbis; **174** UN/DPI photo; **176** Courtesy Canada Post; **177** Corbis; **179** LAC/PA-129625; **181** CWM/*Welcome Party* by Edward F. Zuber/#19890328-004; **183** LAC/C-94168; **184** UN/DPI/NICA-85665; **187** LAC/PA-209888; **188** CP Picture Archive; **190 tl** CP Picture Archive/Everett Collection, **tr** CP Picture Archive/Everett Collection, **bl** CP Picture Archive/Everett Collection, br Granger; **193** CP Picture Archive/Everett Collection; **197** Bettmann/Corbis; **199** Bettmann/CORBIS; **201** Genevieve Naylor/Corbis; **203** CP Picture Archive/(Globe and Mail/ Boris Spremo); **204** CP Picture Archive; **207** Ivy Images; **208 t** CP Picture Archive, b AO/C193-5027 24; **209** CP Picture Archive/(Toronto Star/Colin McConnell); **210** CP Picture Archive; **212** LAC/e000990880; **213** The University of Manitoba Archives & Special Collections, Winnipeg Tribune Collection/PC 18, Box 68, Folder 6924-6925, Item 18-6472-159; **214 t** Glenbow/NA-2864-244668, **b** CP Picture Archive; **217 l** CP Picture Archive, **r** CP Picture Archive; **219** CP Picture Archive (Chuck Mitchell); **223** Bryan & Cherry Alexander; **226** Maritime History Archive, Memorial University/PF-317.072; **228** CP Picture Archive (Montreal La Presse); **230 l** Peter Quine/search4stock, **r** Roger Ressmeyer/Corbis; **231** CP Picture Archive; **232** Courtesy Collège Boréal; **233** CP Picture Archive; **234** CP Picture Archive (Drew Gragg); **235** CP Picture Archive (Montreal Star); **236 t** CP Picture Archive (Montreal Gazette), **b** LAC/PA-111213; **237** Roy Peterson/Artizans; **238** CP Picture Archive (Journal de Québec); **240** Jacques Pavlovsky/Sygma/Corbis; **241** Nora Penhale/The Sarnia Observer; **243** Courtesy Canadian Auto Workers; **248** Bettmann/Corbis; **253** CP Picture Archive (Marcos Townsend); **254** Vince Pietropaolo; **255** CP Picture Archive (Chronicle Herald/Pete Parsons); **256 t** Courtesy Canadian Labour Congress, **b** CP Picture Archive; **258 t** CP Picture Archive (St. John Telegraph-Journal), **b** Courtesy Rita Deverall; **259** Courtesy George Weston Limited; **262** Courtesy Shannon Prince; **266** LAC/Vic Roschkov Collection/Toronto Star/1990-110-45; **267** LAC/Duncan Cameron/PA-136153; **268** Richard Comely; **270** CP Picture Archive (Fred Chartrand); **271 t** CP Picture Archive (John Goddard), **b** LAC/Harry Palmer /PA-182399; **272 t** Bettmann/Corbis, **b** John Reeves; **273** University of Toronto; **274** LAC/Edwin McNally© Estate of Edwin McNally/Montreal Star/C-141136; **276** CP Picture Archive(Paul Chiasson); **279** Pierre St-Jacques/CIDA; **283** Canadian

Press Picture Archive; **284 t** NASA, **b** MCpl Paul MacGregor/Combat Forces Camera; **285** CP Picture Archive (Tom Hanson); **287** CP Picture Archive (AP Photo/George Widman); **289** Richard T. Nowitz/Corbis; **290** Canadian Space Agency; **291** CP Picture Archive (Globe and Mail/Fred Lum); **292** CP Picture Archive (Paul Chiasson); **293** CP Picture Archive (AP Photo/Isabelle Lesser); **295** CP Picture Archive (Victoria Times Colonist/Debra Brash); **296** CP Picture Archive (J.P. Moczulski); **297** Courtesy Dairy Farmers of Canada; **302** Nora Penhale/The Sarnia Observer; **305** CP Picture Archive (Scanpix/Foto César Gretser); **306** CP Picture Archive (Tobin Grimshaw); **308** MCpl Paul MacGregor/ CanadianForces Combat Canada; **309** Courtesy Frank Misztal; **310** CP Picture Archive (Tom Hanson); **313** Nease/Oakville Beaver; **315** CP Picture Archive (AP Photo/Apichart Weerawong); **319** CP Picture Archive (Amel Emric); **320** Stephanie Nolan/The Globe and Mail; **323** CP Picture Archive (Ron Poling); **324** CP Picture Archive (Ron Poling); **325** Keith Beaty/Toronto Star; **326** CP Picture Archive (Charles Mitchell); **327** CP Picture Archive (Winnipeg Free Press/Wayne Glowacki); **329** CP Picture Archive (Ryan Remiorz); **330 l** CP Picture Archive (Tom Hanson), **r** CP Picture Archive (Fred Chartrand); **332 t** CP Picture Archive (Ray Giguere), **b** CP Picture Archive (John Ulan); **333** CP Picture Archive (Jacques Boissinot); **334** CP Picture Archive (New Brunswick Telegraph-Journal/Noel Chenier); **336** Reprinted with permission of *The Globe and Mail*; **337** Courtesy Sabrina Lue; **338** Courtesy Fred Concisom; **339** Courtesy Brenda Brennan Felton; **340** Courtesy Luane Lentz; **342** Ivy Images; **345** Jeff Greenberg/Photo Edit

Text Credits

Statistics Canada information is used with the permission of Statistics Canada. Users are forbidden to copy the data and redisseminate them, in an original or modified form, for commercial purposes, without the expressed permission of Statistics Canada. Information on the availability of the wide range of data from Statistics Canada can be obtained from Statistics Canada's Regional Offices, its World Wide Web site at http://www.statcan.ca, and its toll-free access number 1-800-263-1136.

All extracts from *Voices of a War Remembered* by Bill McNeil are copyright © 1991 by Bill McNeil and reprinted with permission of Doubleday Canada. **36** "Work force by occupation and sex, census years 1891–1961" based on data from the Statistics Canada publication "Historical statistics of Canada," 1983, Catalogue 11-516, July 29, 1999; **43** From *Canada: Our Century, Our Story: Student Text* by Fielding/Evans, page 69. © 2001/ Reprinted with permission of Nelson, a division of Thomson Learning: www.thomsonrights.com. Fax 800-730-2215; **62** "Immigration to Canada, 1920 to 1929" based on data from the Statistics Canada publication "Historical statistics of Canada," 1983, Catalogue 11-516, July 29, 1999; **65** "Canada, Rural and Urban Population, 1871–1931," based on data from the Statistics Canada publication "Historical statistics of Canada," 1983, Catalogue 11-516, July 29, 1999, Series A67-69; **80 b** "Foreign investment in Canada, 1918-1926," based on data from the Statistics Canada publication "Historical statistics of Canada," 1983, Catalogue 11-516, July 29, 1999; **99 l** "Exports of Selected Agricultural Goods, Canada, 1920–1935," based on data from the Statistics Canada publication "Historical statistics of Canada," 1983, Catalogue 11-516, July 29, 1999; **99 r** "Wholesale Prices of Selected Farm Products, 1928–38" based on data from the Statistics Canada publication "Historical statistics of Canada," 1983, Catalogue 11-516, July 29, 1999; **101** "Hourly rates for men in selected building trades, Toronto, 1928–1938," based on data the Statistics Canada publication "Historical statistics of Canada," 1983, Catalogue 11-516, July 29, 1999; **158** "Employment figures in key sectors, Canada, 1933, 1935, and 1939-1945," based on data from Statistics Canada publication "Historical statistics of Canada," 1983, Catalogue 11-516, July 29, 1999; **160** "Persons with jobs and persons seeking work, by gender, Canada, 1936–1946," based on data from the Statistics Canada publication "Historical statistics of Canada," 1983, Catalogue 11-516, July 29, 1999; **161** Table based on data from the Statistics Canada publication "Historical statistics of Canada," 1983, Catalogue 11-516, July 29, 1999; **188** Belleville, Canadian Press/Belleville Intelligencer, "Search to Begin For Avro Arrow Models," Windsor Star, August 10, 1998/ Reprinted with permission of CP Press News Limited; **192** "Immigrant arrivals to Canada, 1945–1960," based on data from the Statistics Canada publication "Historical statistics of Canada," 1983, Catalogue 11-516, July 29, 1999, Series A350; **194** "Changes in population through natural increase," based on data from the Statistics Canada website http://www40.statcan.ca/101/cst01/demo03.htm; **195** "Mineral production line graph" based on data from the Statistics Canada publication "Historical statistics of Canada," 1983, Catalogue 11-516, July 29, 1999, Series P1-26 and Q19-25; **211** "Canada" Words and music by Bobby Gimby © 1967 (Renewed) Gordon V. Thompson Music/Exclusive Worldwide Print Rights administered by Alfred Publishing Co., Inc./All rights reserved/Used by permission; **215** "Average weekly earnings, Toronto, 1967," based on data from the Statistics Canada publication "Historical statistics of Canada," 1983, Catalogue 11-516, July 29, 1999, Series E60-68 and E326-375; **224** Copyright © 1999 by *The New York Times Co*/Reprinted with permission; **214** Adapted from the *Sarnia Observer*, "Remembering freedom's flight: Sarnia Man Searches for Those Who Shared His Escape From Saigon" by Shawn Jeffords, Tues. April 19, 2005, page A1 and "Replies pour in to Kilner's quest" by Jack Poirier, and it appeared on Tues. April 26, 2005, page A1; **288 t** "Computer use in Canada, 1999–2003," based on data from the Statistics Canada website http://www40.statcan.ca/101/cs01/cst01/comm12a.htm; **288 b** "Computer use in Canada, 1999–2003," based on data from the Statistics Canada website http://www40.statcan.ca/101/ cs01/cst01/comm09b.htm; **335 l** "Population urban and rural, by province and territory (Canada) [1851–2001]," based on data from the Statistics Canada website http://www40.statcan.ca/101/cs01/ cst01/demo62a.htm; **335 r** "Types of employment: Population involved in resources, manufacturing, and services, 1901–2001," based on data from the Statistics Canada publication "Canada Year Book," 1994, Catalogue 11-402, November 12, 1993, and from the Statistics Canada CANSIM database http://cansim2.statcan.ca, Table 282-0008; **336** Marina Jimenez, "From Pakistan to the Prairies," *The Globe and Mail*, September 24, p. F4/Reprinted with permission from *The Globe and Mail*; **337** "People employed by education completed, 2004," based on data from the Statistics Canada website http://www40.statcan.ca/101/cst01/labor62.htm